Topography of Trauma: Fissures, Disruptions and Transfigurations

At the Interface/Probing the Boundaries

VOLUME 126

The titles published in this series are listed at *brill.com/aipb*

Topography of Trauma: Fissures, Disruptions and Transfigurations

Edited by

Danielle Schaub, Jacqueline Linder, Kori D. Novak, Stephanie Tam and Claudio Vescia Zanini

TUTA SUB AEGIDE PALLAS · 1683 ·

BRILL
RODOPI

LEIDEN | BOSTON

Cover illustration by Danielle Schaub. Used with permission.

Library of Congress Cataloging-in-Publication Data

Names: Linder, Jacqueline, editor. | Schaub, Danielle, editor. | Novak, Kori D., editor. |
Tam, Stephanie, editor| Zanini, Claudio Vescia, editor.
Title: Topography of trauma : fissures, disruptions and transfigurations /
edited by Jacqueline Linder, Danielle Schaub, Kori D. Novak, Stephanie Tam,
Claudio Vescia Zanini.
Description: Leiden ; Boston : Brill, [2019]
Identifiers: LCCN 2019021485 | ISBN 9789004405431 (paperback ; alk paper)
Subjects: LCSH: Psychic trauma. | Psychic trauma in art. | Psychic trauma in literature.
Classification: LCC BF175.5.P75 T67 2019 | DDC 616.85/21–dc23
LC record available at https://lccn.loc.gov/2019021485

Typeface for the Latin, Greek, and Cyrillic scripts: "Brill". See and download: brill.com/brill-typeface.

ISSN 1570-7113
ISBN 978-90-04-40543-1 (paperback)
ISBN 978-90-04-40794-7 (e-book)

This book is printed on acid-free paper and produced in a sustainable manner.

Contents

Illustrations

Notes on Contributors

Peter Bray
is a senior lecturer and programme leader for counselling in the Faculty of Education and Social Work at the University of Auckland in New Zealand. He has recently edited a number of interdisciplinary volumes which reflect his developing interest in the relational characteristics of client work and the transformational aspects of loss and trauma. Currently, his work focuses on the role that emergent spiritual experiences play in posttraumatic growth and how self-actualisation might positively intersect with concepts of heroic identity.

Francesca Brencio
is Researcher in Philosophy and Human Sciences at the HERAF – Consolidate Research Group in Hermeneutics, Anthropology and Phenomenology at the University of Zaragoza (Spain) and member of The Oxford Research Centre in the Humanities.

Mark Callaghan
a former Art History Lecturer for the Highgate Institution and Associate Tutor at Birkbeck College, University of London – completed PhD thesis on *Trauma, Memory and Aesthetics: The Berlin Holocaust Memorial Competition and the Representation of Negative History*. He graduated from Oxford University and the University of Manchester, and served as General Editor and Art History Editor of the academic journal *Dandelion*. His research interests include Holocaust memorialisation, cultural memory and trauma studies.

M. Candace Christensen
is an Assistant Professor of Social Work at the University of Texas San Antonio. Her research centres on the use of feminist and arts-based methodologies to address gender-based violence. She was granted the Feminist Manuscript Scholarship Award for 2013 from the Council on Social Work Education and the UTSA Presidential Achievement Award for Excellence in Teaching in 2018.

Diedra L. Clay
is a licensed clinical psychologist and a licensed chemical dependency professional, with positions in a wide variety of clinical settings since 1989. Originally

educated as a musician and philosopher, she was a former Associate Professor and Chair of multiple university Psychology Departments. She now runs SeaGate Psychological Services, PLLC, a thriving group psychotherapy practice in the Madison Park area in Seattle, WA, USA.

Leanne Dodd
is a lecturer in Literary and Cultural Studies and PhD candidate at Central Queensland University. She has published three independent crime thrillers with themes of trauma. This research is supported by an Australian Government Research Training Program (RTP) Scholarship.

Marie France Forcier
is a Canadian dance artist whose work has been seen internationally. On faculty at the University of Calgary's School of Creative and Performing Arts, she engages in practice-based research investigating the post-traumatic landscape as a choreographic aesthetic.

Gen'ichiro Itakura
is Professor at the Faculty of Letters, Kansai University, Japan. He has published several books, and his articles have appeared in journals including *ARIEL*.

Jacqueline Linder
is Director of Canadian Master of Counselling Programs at City University of Seattle and a trauma psychologist in Edmonton, AB, Canada. She is the Program Director of City University's Counselling Program in Edmonton, CEO of the Spiral Phoenix Trauma Institute, Executive Director of the Chrysalis Anti-Human Trafficking Network and former Clinical Director of a treatment centre for sexually abused children.

Kori D. Novak
specialises in degenerative neuro-cognitive disease, end-of-life care and aging in the United States corrections system. She was a post-doctoral fellow in palliative and end-of-life care at The Stanford School of Medicine, is a Researcher with The Oxford Research Centre in the Humanities and a visiting scholar at Suffolk University (England).

Cassie Pedersen
is an early career researcher who has recently completed her doctoral studies at Federation University Australia. Her thesis, titled *The Immanence of*

Traumatic Rupture: From the Extra/Ordinary to the Originary, maps a set of significant theoretical impasses which dominate the interdisciplinary space of trauma theory and facilities an innovative approach to re-theorising trauma and re-thinking trauma studies.

Nicholas Quin Serenati
is the Director of Television and Professor of Digital Media Production and Media Studies in the Department of Communication at Flagler College in Saint Augustine, Florida. With a vast background in the research and practice of medical humanities, film/video art and media studies, Serenati's scholarly-art practice explores interdisciplinary approaches to critical inquiry involving preoccupations with illness, metaphor, spirituality and art.

Danielle Schaub
an Associate Professor at Oranim Academic College of Education in Israel and an Adjunct Professor at the University of Alberta in Canada, as well as a poet, short-story writer, photographer and bibliotherapist – has published a monograph on Mavis Gallant (1998), a prized collection of photographs and texts entitled *Reading Writers Reading: Canadian Authors' Reflections* (2006) and *Interior Views: Photopoetry* (2009). She has (co)edited several collections of essays on cultural space, ethnicity and identities, community and nation, and mixed heritage in Canadian literature. With Elspeth McInnes, she co-edited both *Trauma and Meaning Making* (2016) and *What Happened? Re-presenting Traumas, Uncovering Recoveries: Processing Individual and Collective Traumas* (2018). Her research currently focuses on literary representations of trauma and psychoanalytic interpretations of cinematographic works.

Elwin Susan John
holds a doctorate from the University of Hyderabad, India, and teaches English Literature at Sophia College in Mumbai, India. Her research interests include Body Studies and Travel Literature.

Aslı Tekinay
is Professor of English, Coordinator of the American Studies Program and Chair of the Department of Western Languages at Bogazici University, Istanbul, Turkey. She holds a BA in English from Bogazici University (1985), an MA from South Illinois University (1987), and a PhD from Bogazici University (1992). Her research areas include Modern British and American Drama as well as African American Literature.

Tony M. Vinci
is an Associate Professor of English at Ohio University-Chillicothe, where he teaches literature, creative writing, and composition. His research areas include twentieth-century American literature and culture, trauma studies, critical animality studies, posthumanism, ethics, and speculative fiction.

Claudio Vescia Zanini
is an adjunct professor of literatures in English at the Federal University of Rio Grande do Sul, Brazil. He is a member of the International Gothic Association (IGA), as well as a founding member of *Estudos do Gótico*, the first research group on Gothic Literature in Brazil. Besides articles and book chapters, he is the author of *The Orgy is Over: Phantasies, Fake Realities and the Loss of Boundaries in Chuck Palahniuk's Haunted* (2013), as well as a co-editor of *This Thing of Darkness: Shedding Light on Evil* (2016), *VERTIGO – Vertentes do Gótico no Cinema* (*Approaches to the Gothic in Cinema*, 2017) and *O Insólito nas Literaturas de Língua Inglesa* (*The Uncommon in Literatures in English*, 2015). His main areas of interest are horror literature, horror cinema, the Gothic, dramatic literature, and the interfaces between cinema, literature and psychoanalysis.

Introduction: Mapping the Topography of Trauma

Danielle Schaub

In *L'espace Humain*, Georges Matoré contends that to ward off chaos, human beings strive to control their spatial environment.[1] Reflecting their existential desire for safety and for shunning precarious situations, they need to delimit the place they inhabit, the realm they move into, in a manner akin to the nomads' custom of laying down a carpet to demarcate the territory that grounds their home. Those who live in built dwellings, do so metaphorically through the spatial arrangement of both furniture and decoration that come to signal home for them. Feeling secure, therefore, emanates from the circumscription of the space inhabited and the knowledge that it does not involve any danger, that it has become a place whose parameters grant safety. To put it differently, contrary to uncircumscribed space, place in its bounded and graspable dimensions satisfies human needs; as Yi-Fu Tuan contends in *Space and Place: The Perspective of Experience*, place affords security and nurture because 'it acquires definition and meaning'.[2] To further their intrinsic need for preservation and ascendency over the surroundings in which they evolve, humans also 'secure an anchor for themselves' 'by exploiting spatial language'.[3] Such language involves words – whether nouns, adjectives, verbs, deictics, or particles – that define the position, length, width, height, movement, quantity, colour and even temperature of that which it describes. Consider giving directions without spatial markers to arrive at a given place and soon the impossibility of such an endeavour looms up. Spatial metaphors and polarities[4] allow humans to ground their experiences and apprehend

1 Georges Matoré, *L'espace humain: L'expression de l'espace dans la vie, la pensée et l'art contemporains* (Paris: La Colombe [Sciences et techniques humaines, 2], 1962), 13–28.

2 Minneapolis: University of Minnesota Press, 1977, 3–4, 136.

3 Danielle Schaub, ' "a separate world, a small and enclosed universe": Phobic De/Construction of Space in Joan Barfoot's *Dancing in the Dark* to Circumscribe Trauma', *Text* 42 (October 2017; Special Issue on 'Writing and Trauma'), Edited by Bridget Haylock & Suzanne Hermanoczki, 2. Viewed 15 April 2018. http://www.textjournal.com.au/speciss/issue42/content.htm. Yi-Fu Tuan (op. cit. 37–50) discusses the values attributed to the vocabulary of 'spatial organization', remarking that humans choose themselves as the reference point.

4 For a discussion of the use of spatial metaphors and polarities, see Jean Weisgerber's *L'espace romanesque* (Lausanne: L'Age d'homme, 1978), 15–20, and his thought-provoking chapter on 'Romanruimte' [space of the novel] in *Proefvlucht in de romanruimte* (Amsterdam: Athenaeum – Polak & Van Gennep, 1972), 148–189.

 | DOI:10.1163/9789004407947_002

their reality better; by spatialising the perceptions of their world, they increase the feeling of vigorous command. While positive spatially-laden polarities translate the stability afforded by mastering the physical and social environment, negative polarities transpose the insecurity resulting from the inability to do so.[5]

Given the protective assurance granted by place and the devastatingly threatening potential of space, spatial perception allows to reconsider the frame adopted so far to explore the subject of trauma. For '[w]hen faced with traumatic experiences, human beings tend to lose their bearings'[6] and to perceive the world as space fraught with danger, no longer a secure place. The decision to discuss the topography of trauma therefore stems from the loss of a realm affording immunity after having faced a life-threatening event or series of events. *Topography of Trauma: Fissures, Disruptions and Transfigurations* therefore graphs the spatial character of traumatic events shattering one's feeling of safety. Even when concerned with temporal issues related to trauma, the chapters tend to delineate the spatiality of trauma, be it through its ruptures, intrusiveness, locus, mapped regions, non-habitual or confining spaces, paralysing effect, progression or retroaction, the external and internal worlds of the traumatised.

This international and interdisciplinary collection of articles comprises three sections focusing on dissimilar perspectives: the first conceptualises different outlooks on trauma, the second explores transfigurations through writing and painting, and the last considers various therapeutic approaches to trauma, such as scriptotherapy, dharma art, sound art, photovoice and choreography. The collection presents theoretical as well as illustrative and therapeutic discussions of trauma. The examinations, however, do not remain restricted to one field, for the perspectives adopted open up to intermingling.

5 I wish to acknowledge my indebtedness to the late Jean Weisgerber, whose enlightening lectures on space in fiction during my B.A. alerted me to the diverging values ascribed to spatial polarities and gave me a tool to approach fiction that matched my own territorial awareness on account of my disruptive itinerant life in childhood. For a discussion of the traumatic impact afforded by multiple unannounced, and unprepared-for, relocation and the concomitant translation of the self, see Danielle Schaub's 'Reading Myself and Worlds: Coping Strategies in the Face of Cumulative Trauma' in Eds. Elspeth McInnes and Danielle Schaub's *What Happened? Re-Presenting Traumas, Uncovering Recoveries: Processing Individual and Collective Trauma* (Leiden: Brill, 2018), 158–186.

6 Danielle Schaub, ' "a separate world, a small and enclosed universe": Phobic De/Construction of Space in Joan Barfoot's *Dancing in the Dark* to Circumscribe Trauma', *Text* 42 (October 2017; Special Issue on 'Writing and Trauma'), Edited by Bridget Haylock & Suzanne Hermanoczki, 2. Viewed 15 April 2018. http://www.textjournal.com.au/speciss/issue42/content.htm.

At times the theoretical borders on the therapeutic and the illustrative, as happens with Jacqui Linder's and Peter Bray's respective chapters or with Toni M. Vinci's; at others the illustrative borders on the theoretical as manifested by Gen'ichiro Itakura's analysis and Leanne Dodd's discussion or on the therapeutic/psychoanalytic as occurs with Danielle Schaub's chapter, to mention but a few examples. The interconnection of the papers highlights the common grounds in the researchers' standpoints and theoretical approaches as well as their desire to reconsider the frame adopted so far to look into the multidimensional subject of trauma.

The first section, which conceptualises trauma, starts with the phenomenological investigation on which Francesca Brencio and Kori Novak embark in their chapter on 'The Continuum of Trauma'. It examines the deep chasms that appear in the colourless worlds of the traumatised and the high percentage of incarceration after undergoing trauma, a form of spatial limitation encouraging further traumatisation. They conclude that even in the face of healing, a continuum characterises trauma. Cassie Pedersen's chapter on 'Encountering Trauma "One Moment too Late"' yields insights into the complex, though most meaningful, Freudian concept of *Nachträglichkeit*. With the help of observations garnered from the theories of Cathy Caruth and Jean Laplanche on the dual temporality of trauma, Pedersen concludes that trauma weighs as much on the past as on the present and the future, the former bearing on the latter that modifies the former, giving it different dimensions. Tony M. Vinci's chapter on 'Auschwitz, Androids, and the Ethical Demands of Reading Trauma and the Fantastic in *Willing Unbelief*' examines how trauma literature maps the unreal by instilling 'homeopathic' dosage of traumatising ruptures not only through narrative techniques but also through the rhetoric of the fantastic. By scrutinising the testimonies of Primo Levi, Jean Améry and Charlotte Delbo in comparison with Paolo Bacigalupi's science fiction novel *The Windup Girl*, Vinci demonstrates how by entering the ordinary 'unreal' worlds of survivors in '*unbelief*' owing to the rhetoric of the fantastic, readers of trauma narratives suffer from the rupture of stability and dismantled concepts taken for granted. He concludes with 'coding homeopathic trauma as a mode of ontological transformation, social revision, and ethical action'. Equally calling for a modified approach of the traumatised, Jacqueline Linder also clarifies her point by turning to fiction in her chapter on 'Through the Looking-Glass: Child Sexual Abuse from the Inside-Out'. She poignantly juxtaposes factual snippets of her personal CSA with subversive interpretation of extracts from Lewis Carroll's *Through the Looking-Glass* to highlight the darker and disruptive reality of what may seem innocuous from the outside. As she does so, she intimates that to understand survivors' realities non-survivors must abandon an external distancing perspective and favour instead stepping into the world of survivors. The same holds for Peter Bray's findings in his chapter on 'Working with Addiction and Trauma : Mental Health Professionals Reflect on Their Use of Spirituality'. In it he formulates the essence of the discussions mental health professionals held over a period of twelve months on their own practice, spirituality and clients' addictions in relation to trauma. In the end, even against institutional expectations, the group agreed that since their clients call upon their spiritual beliefs, their own spirituality may yield benefits to the healing process if allowed to enter the clinic.

The second section devoted to the contemplation of trauma involves discussions of traumas represented in plays, novels, crime fiction and murals. Aslı Tekinay's chapter addresses the impact of wars as represented in two plays, namely David Rabe's *Sticks and Bones* and Sam Shepard's *States of Shock*. Upon returning home, both lead actors – the one a veteran of the Vietnam War, the other a veteran of the Gulf War – cannot readjust to the narcissistic values of the United States. Transformed by trauma, both emerge as voices of dissent, denouncing middle-class superficial patriotism as well as narcissistic, hypocritical, and racist values. Concerned with the traumatic impact of captivity and torture on a human being, Danielle Schaub turns to the psychoanalytical theories of Michael Balint, Wilfred R. Bion, Frances Tustin and Judith Mitrani to fathom the depth of annihilation endured in Alan Cumyn's novel *Man of Bone*. Hooded for most of the narration, the protagonist gives way to a wide range of responses, his narrative evoking the terror of uncertainty and life threat in its disjunctive presentation, hallucination, dream realm, stylistic fragmentation and spatial language aptly adequate for a novel staying at ground zero. As such it offers bibliotherapeutic benefits for survivors of trauma and empathetic knowledge for non-survivors. Considering another form of confinement, Claudio Vescia Zanini discusses Chuck Palahniuk's novel *Haunted* set on a retreat with wannabe writers whose interactions and short stories intertwine as their confinement allows them to revisit, or invent, debilitating past traumas. To increase their potential readership, the wannabe writers magnify the traumatic content of their narratives through self-inflicted mutilation of their bodies to bend age or gender, or through deformation resulting from cancer, terrorism or transvestite longing. If Zanini's chapter treats postmodern approaches, Gen'ichiro Itakura's chapter focuses on modernist tactics. He explores literary representation of trauma in the context of post-9/11 Afghanistan through analysis of Nadeem Aslam's *The Wasted Vigil* and Atiq Rahimi's *The Patience Stone* (*Syngué sabour*), novels that represent the protagonists' trauma and its locality or time-specific nature paradoxically by appropriating European modernists' textual strategies. By updating these, the writers extend the scope of post-9/11 literature and the possibility of literary representation of trauma and suffering. Elwin Susan John's chapter addresses the chaos as well as visible scars emerging after the Bhopal Gas Tragedy and the Endosulfan Tragedy in Kerala. Considering the victims' bodily and mental transformations and their position outside society, she studies the survival tactics portrayed in three novels, namely Indra Sinha's *Animal's People* and Anjali Deshpande's *Impeachment,* both set in Bhopal, and Ambika Sudhan Mangadu's *Enmagaje,* set in Kerala's title village. John concludes that, within the local context, victims of the chemical tragedies can only 'move on with their limited options in their specific cultural locations'. Also set in post-traumatic time, the Northern Irish murals that Mark Callaghan studies engage in dialogue among groups estranged by contention while spatially signalling heritage and identity. The replacement of aggressive details or scenes with milder ones has further divided the population, for some favour visual reminders of past traumas as affirming their right to existence and others welcome the glossed-over past upheavals to lighten the weight of the past. In addition, the division questions whether sanitised versions mark a post-conflictual transition or enhance the past conflicts. Furthering the concern over the erasure of traumatic scenes and its non-healing power, Leanne Dodd's chapter on crime fiction as a subset of trauma literature highlights its healing benefits for readers. Basing her considerations on its comparable pace and narrative strategies, she embarks on a discussion of the valid reassessment that crime fiction should undergo, raising its position to the level of literary text with a true therapeutic gain. In particular, she contends that authentic re-presentation of past traumas in crime fiction benefits readers and most specifically those affected by similar experiences. Like Schaub, Dodd points to bibliotherapy, 'a therapeutic approach using texts as a basis for discussion of emotional and/or social problems', consisting in 'the interaction with fictional and/or poetic texts reflecting emotions, situations and relational issues of patients'; the bibliotherapeutic interaction 'engages the latter's emotions in the safe distance of other bodies, other places, other times and frees them, allowing productive unconscious work on the self at a remove'.[7]

After its consideration of the beneficial impact afforded by literary texts, *Topography of Trauma* addresses not only the theoretical and the practical, but also the survivor as narrator, meaning maker, and presenter. The third section indeed engages trauma from that angle, dealing with various therapeutic approaches to trauma, mostly from the presenter's experiential perspective.

7 Danielle Schaub, 'Michel Deville's *La Lectrice*: Honouring or Deriding Freud's Theories Through Bibliotherapy?' *International Journal of Psycho-Analysis* 89 (2008): 1238.

A case in point, Nicholas Quin Serenati manages to recontextualise leukaemia through dharma art and relocate it spatially. In doing so, he adopts Susan Sontag's challenge of debilitating illness metaphors likely to demoralise, stifle or debase patients and he assigns a new locus to illness. By combining meditation and creation in his consideration of the various stages involved in handling illness, he embarks on a journey that spatialises and aestheticises the experience so as to alter its perception spatially from *here* to *there*, signalling that illness opens up a window to look through for spatial healing. His consciousness that situating illness in a place such as a window clarifies and demystifies it, encouraging understanding that eventually fosters healing. To fathom the process that led to his 'liberation', he examines the practice of fellow artist Bill Viola, deepening his own position. In a different fashion, yet with similar results, Candace Christensen turns to photovoice and an autoethnographic lens to engage trauma she experienced from sexual violence. Using herself as both subject and researcher, she voices the various phases of her individual trauma in a totally unemotional report that enables her to witness and process the trauma. By engaging in the process, she learns both to voice rather than silencing the trauma and to live with it rather than trying to negate it. In so doing she manages to rebound and find creative inspiration, turning the experience into a place where hope and creative energy exist. Marie France Forcier uses her own knowledge of complex sexual and abusive trauma to choreograph post-traumatic realities through the performance of her work *Scar Is All the Rage*. Her description and analysis of the creative process, the intervention of the company sponsoring the performance and the response from the audiences evidence the need to render post-traumatic realities physically visible to survivors and non-survivors alike so as to engender better support of victims and to spur re-assessment of the sentences pronounced against perpetrators. In the last chapter of this section, Diedra Clay reviews historical, cultural, religious, traumatic and therapeutic contexts for eating disorders, most specifically anorexia nervosa and bulimia nervosa, with a view to improving therapeutic interventions. To increase chances of successful treatment, she recommends not only focusing on triggers, such as pejorative corporeal perceptions that affect self-esteem detrimentally, and encouraging more positive self-evaluation but also combining therapeutic approaches. Her prompting for combined perspectives calls to mind the previous successful blend of therapeutic approaches to traumatic contexts that reposition traumatic experiences by giving them a place to be in and/or from where to move on.

The interconnection of the chapters and the sections in the collection highlights the common grounds in the researchers' theoretical approach as well as their desire to reconsider the frame adopted to explore the subject of trauma so far. From the dialogue that emerges it appears that the common understanding of trauma needs rethinking and re-examining, as classical treatments of the problem involved – moving away from, recovering from, healing, amputating the harrowing experience – do not recognise the potential for transfiguration inherent in the trauma itself. Investigating the fissures, disruptions and shifts that occur after punctual traumatic events or prolonged exposure to verbal and physical abuse, illness, war, captivity, incarceration amongst others may lead to alternative approaches that yield a firmer ground from which to examine trauma and a deeper understanding of its locus, inner and outer reality, intrusiveness, evasive spaces and disruptive fractures. Among the options for post-traumatic transformation, moving towards, embracing, immersing in and transfiguring trauma allow survivors to arrive at a new understanding of the transformed self. By engaging in a debate about whether one can overcome, heal, evade, or capture trauma through the theoretical discussion, the presentation of artistic performances or the analysis of cultural artefacts, and the analysis of case studies, the texts presented here speak the unspeakable and ground that which cannot be delimited. In so doing they give a more secure place to the marooned, eliciting a way out of isolation and utter despair. Through the combination of theory, representation and practice, the collection signals and illustrates empowering post-traumatic developments that confirm Boris Cyrulnik's claim for resilient outcomes to the most traumatic experiences.[8] In other words, the collection lays ground for a reconsideration of the transformation survivors of trauma can effect.

Bibliography

Cyrulnik, Boris. *Un Merveilleux malheur*. Paris: Odile Jacob, 1999.

Matoré, Georges. *L'Espace humain: L'Expression de l'espace dans la vie, la pensée et l'art contemporains*. Paris: La Colombe (Sciences et techniques humaines, 2), 1962.

Schaub, Danielle. 'Michel Deville's *La Lectrice*: Honouring or Deriding Freud's Theories Through Bibliotherapy?' *International Journal of Psycho-Analysis* 89 (2008): 1237–1250.

Schaub, Danielle. '"a separate world, a small and enclosed universe": Phobic De/Construction of Space in Joan Barfoot's *Dancing in the Dark* to Circumscribe Trauma'.

8 For ample examples of resilience in the face of countless harrowing experiences see Boris Cyrulnik's *Un Merveilleux malheur* (Paris: Odile Jacob, 1999), whose oxymoronic title translates the paradoxical ability of transforming adversity, indeed dehumanising affliction and wretchedness, into an experience from which to learn and to grow.

Eds. Bridget Haylock & Suzanne Hermanoczki. *Text* 42 (October 2017; Special Issue on 'Writing and Trauma'): 1–11. Viewed 15 April 2018. http://www.textjournal.com.au/speciss/issue42/content.htm.

Schaub, Danielle. 'Reading Myself and Worlds: Coping Strategies in the Face of Cumulative Trauma'. *What Happened? Re-Presenting Traumas, Uncovering Recoveries: Processing Individual and Collective Trauma*. Eds. Elspeth McInnes and Danielle Schaub, Leiden: Brill, 2018. 158–186.

Tuan, Yi-Fu. *Space and Place: The Perspective of Experience.* Minneapolis: University of Minnesota Press, 1977.

Weisgerber, Jean. 'Romanruimte' [the space of the novel] in *Proefvlucht in de romanruimte.* Amsterdam: Athenaeum – Polak & Van Gennep, 1972. 148–189.

Weisgerber, Jean. *L'Espace romanesque*. Lausanne: L'Âge d'homme, 1978.

PART 1

Conceptualising Trauma

CHAPTER 1

The Continuum of Trauma

Francesca Brencio and Kori D. Novak

Abstract

The word 'trauma', used in everyday language, means a highly stressful event that provokes an interruption of ordinary life and time, such as when one receives a diagnosis of a serious or life limiting illness, or when one is incarcerated. A traumatic event or situation creates psychological trauma when it overwhelms the individual's ability to cope, and leaves that person fearing death, annihilation, mutilation, or psychosis. The individual may feel emotionally, cognitively, and physically overwhelmed. Trauma comes in many forms, and there are vast differences among people who experience trauma. Using some tools coming from phenomenology, we can say that trauma disturbs the *ek-static* unity of temporality: it is an 'event' that irrupts in the life of a human being, devastating his or her existence. When this kind of 'event' enters into a life, everything changes. This chapter focuses initially on a personal journey of trauma, then follows the experience through an empirical research lens of this type of trauma as experienced by the incarcerated. Our analysis will proceed using a phenomenological approach, showing the peculiarity of a phenomenological psychopathology and hermeneutic phenomenology. We focus on trauma as a catalyst for healing. By examining the philosophical aspects of trauma, we can understand the foundations of the traumatic experience. From there we will move forward to show how the theoretical morphs into the psychological by analysing how trauma affects personality. Sociological applications will be addressed, particularly how trauma often leads to incarceration. Finally, the exploration will transverse the journey that several individuals have taken through their diagnoses of life-altering diseases, abuse and neglect that ultimately led to the loss of freedom and the trauma surrounding being incarcerated. Through their eyes, we will follow the journey that trauma takes to healing.

Keywords

phenomenology – psychology – trauma – inmates – prison – temporality

 | DOI:10.1163/9789004407947_003

1 Introduction: Aims and Goals

This chapter focuses on trauma as a foundational element that extends through the lifespan. By examining the philosophical aspects of trauma through a phenomenological and hermeneutic approach, we will underline how a traumatic event gets into the ontological constitution of a human being, modifying the perception of temporality and spatiality, the meaning if his or her life and the attitude to project his or her existence. One of the main features of this experience is to confront anxiety as a pervasive emotion experienced by human beings. In our experience of anxiety, we are interrogated by life itself in terms of understanding how we conceive our world and the meaning we give it. Perhaps this is the most unusual and difficult part of the story: confronting anxiety directly in order to discover *how* we can understand ourselves, our relationships and the meaning that life can still have after a traumatic event.

From there we will move forward to how the theoretical morphs into the psychological by analysing how trauma affects personality. Then we will provide sociological applications on how trauma affects sociological and criminal behaviours resulting in incarceration. Finally, we will follow the journey of trauma as a potential catalyst for the 'healing process'.

2 Phenomenology of Trauma: Foundational Aspects

The word 'trauma', used in everyday language, means a highly stressful event that provokes an interruption of ordinary life and time, such as when one receives a diagnosis of a serious or life-threatening illness, or when one commits a crime and is subsequently incarcerated. We could say that the first feature of trauma is the interruption of our existence: something unpredictable happens that definitively modifies our life, our ability to give meanings, to perceive, and to live temporality. In her discussion of contemporary traumatic theory, Judith Herman notes that 'unlike commonplace misfortunes traumatic events generally involve threats to life or bodily integrity, or a close personal encounter with violence and death'.

Martin Heidegger's philosophy may offer some useful tools to understand the original constitution of human beings, since his analysis illuminates the relationship between temporality and existence. In doing so, his work may contain some suggestions on how to cope with trauma. According to Heidegger, the ontological feature of human beings is the *Dasein*, a German word designating the way a human being 'has to be' (*zu-sein*).[1] *Dasein* doesn't mean

1 Martin Heidegger, *Being and Time* (Oxford: Blackwell, 1962), 67–69.

simply 'existence'. *Dasein* means the potential ways human beings can be, some of which they pursue through their projects. *Dasein* is not to be understood in terms of everyday human existence or embodied agency, but as an unfolding historical horizon or space of meaning already 'there' (*Da*), prior to the emergence of the human body and its various capacities. For Heidegger, the fundamental state of *Dasein* is its being-in-the-world. *Dasein* and world are not separated but must be grasped together, avoiding Cartesian dualism between subject and object and overcoming the subjectivism on which all western philosophy is based. Being-in-the-world is a unitary phenomenon that characterises every relationship, not a kind of 'property' of human being, but rather the fundamental assumption of our existence. In other words, a human being's primordial being-in-the-world is not an abstraction but always a concrete occurrence. Its being-in-the-world occurs and fulfils itself only in and as the manifold particular modes of human behaviour; this kind of being presupposes a unique openness of existence. *Dasein* stresses the transcendental and constitutive openness of human beings towards life, towards events, and towards projects – trauma included.

The openness that Heidegger calls disclosedness consists in the unique openness of humanity's existence, an openness into which the particular beings encountered can disclose themselves as they are, with all the context of their meaningful references.[2] According to Heidegger, hermeneutics is to make the *Dasein* understand itself. This understanding is not comportment toward something, but rather how *Dasein* itself gives its own self-interpretation,[3] the main question of our life: we face every experience with the will to meaning, as Viktor Frankl says, not just the mere attempt to give an explanation to facts but also to give meanings to people, affects, and so on.[4] Our innate meaning-making capacity makes us uniquely able to explore the question: *what does it mean for me?* As *homo symbolicus* (as Cassirer used to define man), human beings tend to interpret and develop their lives on the basis of these meanings.[5] Some of them will be appropriated in understanding, others will remain relegated to non-understanding. Using Heideggerian jargon and simplifying some aspects of his meditation, we face the dialectical movement between concealment and unconcealment in which the human being is called to *ek-sist*. The meaning we are searching for is not present-at-hand, and for this reason

2 Martin Heidegger, *Zollikon Seminars* (Evanston: Northwestern University Press, 2001), 120.

3 Martin Heidegger, *The Basic Problems of Phenomenology* (Bloomington: Indiana University Press, 1982), 2.

4 Viktor Frankl, *Man's Search for Meaning* (New York: Washington Square Press, 1984), 8–15.

5 Ernst Cassirer, *An Essay on Man* (New Haven: Yale University Press, 1944), 26.

we must deal with the unconcealment.[6] For some aspects, this movement also characterises the eruption of trauma into our lives as it modifies human existence, its historicity and its relationship with temporality and spatiality potentially developing into crisis.[7] As such, the appropriation and expropriation of the authenticity of life depends on the human's ability to signify trauma.

In their attempt to signify every event they experience, human beings face anxiety in its rich and complex phenomenology.[8] Besides its association with a range of psychiatric conditions (such as psychosis, personality disorders, and mood disorders), anxiety also expresses *who we are,* in that it reveals the fragmentation of the self as well as the finitude and vulnerability of being human. We constantly deal with our original vulnerability in our bodies, in our affectivity, in our social dimension, in our desire for recognition, and so on. In this respect, the experience of vulnerability connects to the broader issue of anxiety, in terms of existential features and clinical conditions, because it recalls our original constitution as human beings. When we discuss anxiety, we should also distinguish between existential anxiety, neurotic anxiety and normal anxiety. The differences in meaning denote various aspects of the subject focussed on by scholars who follow a range of models.[9]

If we go carefully through Heidegger's analysis of anxiety, we can see how he assigns to anxiety a pivotal role in the understanding of the authenticity of human life and of our choices. Both in *Being and Time* (1927) and *What Is Metaphysics?* (1929), he defines anxiety as a mode of being of *Dasein*, together with fear (*Furcht*), both ontological features of our existence.[10] Unlike fear, always defined by objects, anxiety has no objects. Rather, it hinders any possibility of openness to others and to situations. Anxiety breaks the transparency of self-constitution so that human beings lose their capacity to recognise themselves in relation to others. By this anxiety, Heidegger does not mean common anxiousness, ultimately reducible to fearfulness. Rather, he means the fundamental characteristic that shows us who we really are, what our lives are really

---

6 Francesca Brencio, 'Heidegger and Binswanger: Just a Misunderstanding?' *The Humanistic Psychologist* 43.3 (2015): 278–296.

7 Francesca Brencio, 'World, Time and Anxiety: Heidegger's Existential Analytic and Psychiatry', *Folia Medica, Special Issue on the XVIth International Conference on Philosophy, Psychiatry and Psychology* 56.4 (2015): 297–304.

8 See Rollo May, *The Meaning of Anxiety* (New York: The Ronald Press Co, 1950), 13–26.

9 See Susan Iacovou, 'The sine qua non of true vitality'. An examination of the difference between existential anxiety and neurotic anxiety, in '*Existential Analysis: Journal of the Society for Existential Analysis*' 22.2 (2011): 357.

10 Martin Heidegger, *Being and Time*, 179–182 and Martin Heidegger, *What Is Metaphysics?*, in *Pathmarks* (Cambridge University Press, Cambridge, 1998), 82–96.

about, thereby highlighting our ability to choose what really matters in our existence, which Heidegger defines in *Being and Time as* the choice between authentic (*Eigentliche*) existence and inauthentic (*Uneigentliche*) existence. In anxiety, we lose the experience of our ordinary identity: frozen, we cannot feel 'at home' in the world. In this situation, we are faced with our own 'uncanny' presence, the mode of not-at-home (*Unheimlich*).[11] Such an experience amounts to some disconnection from reality that can provoke anxiety disorders.

Anxiety seems to mean a breakdown of all ordinary understanding and activity in the space of a moment, perhaps because the total withdrawal from the activities of the world only lasts for a moment. The alienation that comes from this hiatus – being in the world but not-at-home in the world – shows us that the world, in this particular moment, has nothing to offer us. The possibility of the future loses its meaning and the world suddenly falls down. Anxiety does not see any definite 'here' or 'there' from which it comes. Rather, feeling anxiety characterises the location nowhere of what threatens even as it signifies nothing.

3 Psychological Aspects: Trauma, Personality, Mental Illness

A traumatic event or situation creates psychological trauma when it overwhelms the individual's ability to cope, and leaves that person fearing death, annihilation, mutilation, or psychosis. The individual may feel emotionally, cognitively, and physically overwhelmed. Trauma comes in many forms with vast differences among people who experience trauma. This includes responses to powerful one-time incidents like accidents, natural disasters, crimes, surgeries, deaths, and other violent events. Trauma also includes responses to chronic or repetitive experiences such as child abuse, neglect, combat, urban violence, concentration camps, battering relationships, and enduring deprivation.

In other words, trauma disturbs the *ek-static* unity of temporality: it consists of an 'event' that erupts in the life of human beings, devastating their existence and resulting in depression, anxiety disorders, panic attacks and so on.[12] When this kind of 'event' intrudes on one's life, nothing is as before. This experience becomes freeze-framed into an eternal present in which one remains

11 Martin Heidegger, *What Is Metaphysics?*, 88–89.

12 Thomas Fuchs, 'Melancholia as a Desynchronization: Towards a Psychopathology of Interpersonal Time', *Psychopathology* 34 (2001): 179–186.

forever trapped, or to which one is condemned to be perpetually returned. In the region of trauma, all temporal duration or stretching along collapses; past becomes present, and future loses all meaning other than endless repetition. In this sense, trauma is timeless rather than the unconscious – as Freud claimed.[13] Both in trauma and in psychopathological phenomena (i. e. depression, anxiety) the sense of life is altered. This alteration is not only related to the content of what has happened however, as a formal alteration also exists in that the experience of determination by the past and its resolution undergoes a profound change. This bears on everything in the past, consolidating memory falsifications and fabrications, for trauma exposes 'the unbearable embeddedness of being'.[14] The worlds of traumatised persons are fundamentally incommensurable with those of others; they experience deep chasms in which an anguished sense of estrangement and solitude takes form.

Trauma reflects the feeling of 'being stuck', not able to move forward. The world around appears colourless; days endlessly repeat sameness, sometimes agony, sometimes dull emptiness; the world becomes almost a monothematic one of loss. The precipitating event has wiped out a horizon of possibilities in which the one and only thing that matters, the one and only thing cared for is not there anymore.[15] This 'there', devoid of contents that matter, often gives rise to questions of 'what if', where personal responsibility and feelings of guilt prevail. Noteworthy, however, events are not necessarily the only catalyst of this type of trauma.

The spectre of mental illness can have a dramatic effect on the experience of trauma, potentially an actual root cause for the feelings of being stuck or empty. In addition, feelings may also incite conduct which leads to additional traumatic events. Specifically, this correlates with the phenomenon of incarceration, both in the paradigm of internal confinement by mental illness as well as actually physical confinement. The physical aspects of incarceration – confinement and restraint – demonstrate how the traumatic distress of mental illness often significantly affects personality and can alter the temperament of an individual permanently.

This way of questioning deepens the spiral of deprivation, including its almost obsessive attempt to redefine the context of life as something over which we have absolute control. This pre-existing ontological claim that we, as

13 Robert Stolorow, *Trauma and Existence* (New York: Francis &Taylor, 2007), 20.

14 Stolorow, *Trauma and Existence*, 16.

15 Matthew Broome and Matthew Ratcliffe, 'Existential Phenomenology, Psychiatric Illness and the Death of Possibilities', *Cambridge Companion to Existentialism*, ed. S. Crowell (Cambridge: Cambridge University Press, 2012), 361–382.

human beings, can have control over life events – manifestations of being – often makes the experience of trauma unbearable. These traumatic events eradicate the 'familiar', one to which we were already predisposed, one that contributes to the formation of what cannot be anymore.[16] The familiar here does not signify something strictly negative from a moral standpoint: the bond with the child, mother, loving wife, parents, siblings, professional identity are all forms of familiarity. So are social norms that promote certain forms of being-in-the world as the acceptable. Linguistic paradigms such as the scientific one or the one for evidence-based medicine are all forms that conceal the uncanny that comes to light at the manifestation of a traumatic event. By losing 'our' 'familiar', we are cut away from the rest of society.[17]

In a more neurological and mental illness focused sense, the existence of an altering experience creates stress, which produces excess stimuli and excitation in the brain. When overstimulated, the brain has difficulty processing the external environment or additional stimuli. As this transpires, we find that the brain begins to shut down typical emotional responses as a defence mechanism. This psychological numbing may serve as a precursor to different levels of dissociation, which could ultimately lead to a Dissociative Identity Disorder (DID) diagnosis (formally known as Multiple Personality Disorder). Clinicians tend to agree that the diagnosis of DID often indicates an earlier trauma, which the patient may or may not recall.

Examining the narrative of internationally acclaimed neonatologist Dr. SP allows to illustrate the embodiment of trauma and its effect on personality.[18] Socially and culturally Dr. SP's personality was one of a successful physician and family man. He had reached the heights of his profession and was honoured by his peers, until the discovery of financial discrepancies in his practice that led to his incarceration. It transpired that significant traumas inflicted on Dr. SP at an early age manifested their impact in his adult life. Ultimately Dr. SP was diagnosed as suffering from Dissociative Identity Disorder. His mental illness/ personality disorder directly correlated with the trauma he experienced earlier in his life. While incarcerated in the United States prison system on account

16 Scott D. Churchill, 'Heideggerian Pathways through Trauma and Recovery: A "Hermeneutics of Facticity"', *The Humanistic Psychologist* 41.3 (2013): 219–230.

17 Francesca Brencio, 'La Analítica Existencial de Martin Heidegger y Sus Implicaciones sobre la Relación entre Trauma y Temporalidad', *La Filosofía como Terapia en la Sociedad Actual*, eds. J. J. Garrido Periñán, C. De Bravo Delorme, J. Ordóñez García, 183–205 (Sevilla: Fenix Editora, 2016).

18 Permission was granted to the authors to use the physician's initials and story for this chapter.

of the crimes committed due to his affliction, Dr. SP received appropriate therapeutic treatment for the disorder so as to reintegrate his multiple identities into one functional mentally stable individual, ultimately re-establishing himself back into mainstream society (S. P., personal communication, June 1, 2016). His story illustrates the correlation between trauma, personality, mental illness and, in many cases, criminality.

4 Sociological Aspects: Trauma, Crime, Incarceration

In 91% of incarcerated individuals in the United States, criminal pathology has been traced back to significant trauma.[19] The life-altering experience of prison is not only overwhelming, but can also be a harbinger for severe mental illness. Conversely, mental illness is often the forerunner for aberrant behaviours or, at the very least, conduct that does not meet acceptable social standards. In the United States, 76% of women incarcerated have had trauma in the form of abuse (mental, emotional, physical or sexual) prior to committing their crime.[20] Research has indicated that the crimes committed by a majority of women in prison are related to, or in some cases re-enact, their previous traumas. Sociologists and psychologists can often trace the continuum of trauma for incarcerated individuals from the initial traumatic event through to later traumas experienced or perpetrated that resulted in incarceration.[21] While exploration into the correlation between early childhood trauma/attachment disorders and the subsequent commission of legal violations is incomplete, early evidence suggests that significant traumas underpin attachment and behavioural disorders that manifest in later criminal activity. Further, there are few illustrations of the criminal archetype with only a single traumatic event present. As experiences of trauma multiply, the manifestation of aberrant behaviours increases and the perpetration of crime not only surges but also intensifies. Often, the seriousness of the crime mimics the austerity of the perceived or inflicted foundational trauma.

19 Vivenne Heins, 'Speaking Out to Improve the Health of Inmates', *American Journal of Public Health* 95.10 (2005): 1685–1688.

20 Leonard Snipes, *Statistics on Woman Offenders* (Washington, D.C.: U.S. Department of Justice, 2015), Viewed 15 January 2016, http://www.corrections.com/news/article/30166-statistics-on-women-offenders.

21 Andrew P. Wilper, et al., 'The Health and Health Care of U.S. Prisoners: Results of a Nationwide Survey', *American Journal of Public Health* 99 (2009): 4.

One inmate, whom we will call Lisa, explained she had little contact with her mother as a child. Early in her life, she exhibited signs of reactive attachment disorder but no neurological or physiological ailment. However, she could not handle her emotions or create a secure attachment with a parental figure. Her first trauma, namely her early lack of secure attachment, goes back to both her mother emotionally abusing her in her childhood and several of the men in her mother's life sexually abusing her. These multiple traumatic events compounded and began to manifest as rage, self-mutilation, and sexual promiscuity. This type of early childhood sexual and physical abuse can lead to various manifestations of trauma, as discussed in Jacqueline Linder's chapter 'Through the Looking-Glass: Child Sexual Abuse from the Inside-Out', in this volume. Such soul loss does not just impose an internalised solitude on those experiencing it, but can often perpetuate external manifestations such as socially unacceptable behaviours and engagement in criminal activity.

After several petty crimes such as shoplifting and prostitution, teenage Lisa turned to drugs as an escape. This trauma led to an addiction, multiple rapes, and ultimately a charge of murder when, at age 19, Lisa killed a man in a fit of rage. Her short life prior to incarceration abounded in the traumas that built upon each other, as well as the escalation of her inappropriate behaviour. While the continuum of trauma may not manifest itself as obviously in all case studies, it is not a difficult path to trace. External signs, such as body mutilation (whether inflicted upon oneself or by another person) often evidence prior trauma. Such type of mutilation itself causes additional emotional trauma, as discussed in Zanini's 'Body and Trauma in Chuck Palahniuk's *Haunted*' in this volume. Principally, the supposition of body trauma influenced or directly caused by pressure or fear among peers is uniquely relative in prison systems as the constant exposure to traumatised individuals in prison has significantly increased. It becomes undeniable, then, that for many individuals, trauma functions as a significant component of the narrative that leads to incarceration.

A growing movement of behaviourists and forensic psychologists examine how institutionalisation promotes an extended perpetration of trauma against inmates.[22] Stripping convicted offenders of basic rights and freedoms, lack of healthy neurological stimulation or human relations, and continuing loss or diminishment of dignity and humanism compounds traumas already

22 Ann Frodi, et. al., 'Current Attachment Representations of Incarcerated Offenders Varying in Degree of Psychopathy', *Attachment and Human Development* 3 (2001): 3.

experienced before by the incarcerated. The concepts of solitary confinement and of death penalty, both still widely used in the United States, also cause both impending and realised trauma for individuals who become wards of the state. However, there is little or no recourse or adjustment considered in current prison reform recommendations. Further, reform alone would not change the condition of the facilities or the treatment of offenders to the point of ameliorating persistent trauma. Meaningful change would require the examination of core assumptions about incarceration as opposed to reforms of the status quo. Any attempts to modify the existing system would be tantamount to short term stopgap solutions when the greater obstacle is continuous exposure to and accumulation of traumatic encounters.

In a correctional system, where the vernacular used (i.e. 'penal system') promotes punishment, the question of rehabilitation can often be diminished or completely ignored. However, factions of US society continue to perpetuate the notion of rehabilitation as an option providing offenders a venue for absolution, both towards the greater society as well as a personal method of repentance. Scholars and practitioners often disagree as to the methods or efficacy of current rehabilitative models. Offenders are often stigmatised according to the severity of their crime and sent to facilities deemed 'minimum', 'medium' and 'maximum' security levels. Some offenders are even classified as individuals who can never be rehabilitated to a point of safety for society. They are sent to even stricter facilities where their schedules are further controlled and solitude is the norm. Thus, the culture relegates these offenders to a life of perpetual trauma and punishment without societal adjudication, which eradicates the basic mammalian need for connection and compounds the trauma deemed to persists. The longer this occurs, the more likely it will manifest in compelling, problematic ways as the individual ages.

During incarceration, offenders are typically encouraged to attend individual and group therapies as a means of 'rehabilitation' or, at least, relief from trauma. Unlike Dr. SP, for some inmates, these therapeutic encounters do not suffice to overcome their foundational traumas, let alone the continued trauma of incarceration. In fact, the mere act of confinement can exacerbate early traumas and hinder healing. The conundrum faced by scholars and practitioners alike is to create a methodology by which to gauge the depth of trauma. From a purely utilitarian aspect, we know this is not possible, given the vicissitude of trauma, its internalisation by human beings, and the complexity with which it displays within individuals. Nonetheless, once the depth of the trauma discovered thanks to a skilled therapist, the trauma itself can become a catalyst for healing.

5 Trauma as a 'Healing' Mechanism

This inquiry challenges the notion that 'psychological healing' does not resemble physical 'healing' without claiming that one returns to a precise point and time of 'wellness' or status quo. One may question the possibility of 'returning' to a baseline mental status where one can be deemed 'healed'. For many individuals who have experienced multiple or continual trauma, the concept of 'baseline' or 'normal' is non-existent or itself aberrant or dysfunctional. The notion of 'normal' begets a trauma in and of itself as it infers the covering up of the past in order to heal or erase it, thus bringing the individual into the social norms of present society. Much as in the chapter 'Painting Over the Past' in this volume, where Callaghan explores the issues of covering or repainting revolutionary murals in Ireland, covering an individual's past does not create a new normal. Rather, it represents an additional trauma to the already traumatised and a new trauma for those experiencing 'normal' for the first time. Research has revealed that, in some ways, offenders work to discover a new belonging by using shared traumas in an effort to find normalcy in their incarcerated world rather than ignoring past transgressions in the 'free' world. In fact, for some such solution helps establish a sense of 'rightness' where shared traumatic experiences create a historical 'normal' they can return to and in that sense 'heal'. For others, the simple acknowledgement of a traumatic theme, or the sense that 'I'm not the only one' suffices to perpetuate healthy grief and the ability to progress emotionally.

Understanding that trauma is a foundational personality aspect for many individuals, deterring or terminating the cycle of trauma in exchange for the promotion healing is regularly challenged. The overall construct of 'healing' in this context is a complex concept. Prison psychologists have found that traumatic events can be healed in various manners. One of the most widespread hypotheses considered is to ameliorate the initial or foundational trauma to achieve any significant reconciliation of subsequent traumas. Thus, in theory, with the acknowledgement of each trauma that allows recognition or acceptance to occur, individuals would experience rehabilitation.[23] As with any type of therapy, however, the concept of 'healing' is as individualised as the trauma itself.

As research has begun to show, the foundational traumas experienced by individuals continue throughout their lives, regardless of the age or stage

23 Stephen Smallbone, and Mark R. Dadds, 'Childhood Attachment and Adult Attachment in Incarcerated Adult Male Sex Offenders', *Journal of Interpersonal Violence* 5 (1998): 555–573.

in life the trauma occurs. From the point of trauma, the linear progression of manifestation begins. This does not suggest that all expressions of trauma are unacceptable. Contrary to the prevailing social belief that external emotional or physical upheaval is improper or unprincipled, the display of trauma in either a physical or emotional way can assist in the healing of the trauma at any age, as supported by Marie France Forcier's work reported in 'Creating and Contextualising Trauma-Related Contemporary Choreography' in this volume. Marie France Forcier examines in detail how choreographed movement can both tell the story of trauma as well as heal those who experienced it, including the choreographer, the performers and the audience.

Addressing traumas as they have transpired and then manifested themselves is critical in progressing through traumatic emotional processing. Ultimately, how trauma manifests itself and how we choose to address these manifestation dictates the narrative of a life well-lived or a more difficult life fraught with emotional turmoil, crime and a looming potential of incarceration.

6 Conclusion

Mounting evidence exists that if foundational traumas are not addressed appropriately, they will continue to manifest themselves in various ways throughout the life of an individual. Further, as these traumas manifest, they beget additional traumatisation, which often results in self-harm, pernicious decisions, and/or choices leading to incarceration. Disregarded trauma can lead to personality or behavioural afflictions and mental illness. Trauma follows a continuum, even when properly addressed. Both society and the individual must work not only to become cognizant of this continuum but also to aid in breaking the cycle of trauma.

As you continue to read throughout this book, you will see that trauma appears in various forums, manifesting itself in various ways, including sound, dance, literature, spectacle as well as the recurrence of intimate and personal abuses. It progresses from an early foundational setting, manifests itself throughout the traumatised person's lifespan, and continues through to the final stages of death. Even when addressed, traumas linger, and without correct treatment they will continue to produce incongruous manifestations over one's lifetime. The following pages address the continuum of trauma – how it is exposed, acknowledged and ultimately reckoned with, evidencing the complex ways of perceiving and living with trauma, as well as those of undergoing the impact of trauma and possibly healing from it.

Bibliography

Brencio, Francesca. 'Heidegger and Binswanger: Just a Misunderstanding?' *The Humanistic Psychologist* 43.3 (2015): 278–296.

Brencio, Francesca. 'World, Time and Anxiety: Heidegger's Existential Analytic and Psychiatry'. *Folia Medica, Special Issue on the 16th International Conference on Philosophy, Psychiatry and Psychology* 56.4 (2015): 297–304.

Brencio, Francesca. 'La analítica existencial de Martin Heidegger y sus implicaciones sobre la relación entre trauma y temporalidad'. *La filosofía como terapia en la sociedad actual*, edited by J. J. Garrido Periñán, C. De Bravo Delorme, J. Ordóñez García, 183–205. Sevilla: Fenix Editora, 2016.

Broome, Matthew, and Matthew Ratcliffe. 'Existential Phenomenology, Psychiatric Illness and the Death of Possibilities'. *Cambridge Companion to Existentialism*, edited by in S. Crowell, 361–382. Cambridge: Cambridge University Press, 2012.

Cassirer, Ernst. *An Essay on Man.* New Haven: Yale University Press, 1944.

Churchill, Scott. D. 'Heideggerian Pathways through Trauma and Recovery: A 'Hermeneutics of Facticity''. *The Humanistic Psychologist* 41.3 (2013): 219–230.

Frankl, Viktor. *Man's Search for Meaning*. New York: Washington Square Press, 1984.

Frodi, Ann, Mats Dernevik, Anneli Sepa, Johanna Philipson and Maria Bragesjö. 'Current Attachment Representations of Incarcerated Offenders Varying in Degree of Psychopathy'. *Attachment and Human Development* 3.3 (2001): 269–283.

Fuchs, Thomas. 'Melancholia as a Desynchronization: Towards a Psychopathology of Interpersonal Time'. *Psychopathology* 34 (2001): 179–186.

Heidegger, Martin. *The Basic Problems of Phenomenology*. Bloomington: Indiana University Press, 1982.

Heidegger, Martin. *Being and Time*. Oxford: Blackwell, 1962.

Heidegger, Martin. *What Is Metaphysics?*, in *Pathmarks.* Cambridge: Cambridge University Press, 1998.

Heidegger, Martin. *Zollikon Seminars.* Evanston: Northwestern University Press, 2001.

Heins, Vivenne. 'Speaking Out to Improve the Health of Inmates'. *American Journal of Public Health* 95.10 (2005): 1685–1688.

Iacovou, Susan. ' "The sine qua non of true vitality". An Examination of the Difference Between Existential Anxiety and Neurotic Anxiety'. *Existential Analysis: Journal of the Society for Existential Analysis* 22.2 (2011): 338–357.

May, Rollo. *The Meaning of Anxiety*. New York: The Ronald Press Co, 1950.

Smallbone, Stephen, and Mark R. Dadds. 'Childhood Attachment and Adult Attachment in Incarcerated Adult Male Sex Offenders'. *Journal of Interpersonal Violence* 5 (1998): 555–573.

Snipes, Leonard. *Statistics on Woman Offenders.* Washington, D.C.: U.S. Department of Justice, 2015. Viewed 15 January 2016. http://www.corrections.com/news/article/30166-statistics-on-women-offenders.

Stolorow, Robert. *Trauma and Existence.* New York: Francis & Taylor, 2007.

Wilper, Andrew P., Steffie Woolhandler, J. W. Boyd, Karen E. Lasser, Danny McCormick, David H. Bor and David U. Himmlestein. 'The Health and Health Care of U.S. Prisoners: Results of a Nationwide Survey'. *American Journal of Public Health* 99.4 (2009): 666–672.

CHAPTER 2

Encountering Trauma 'Too Soon' and 'Too Late': Caruth, Laplanche, and the Freudian *Nachträglichkeit*

Cassie Pedersen

Abstract

While the term 'trauma' was originally used in medicine to denote a wound to the tissues of the body, it has more recently come to refer to the wounding impact of a shocking and overwhelming event on the mind or psyche. Trauma is a phenomenon that ruptures – rather than enters – consciousness; it is a failed experience that cannot be cognitively assimilated at the time of its arrival. Instead, the impact of trauma manifests belatedly in intrusive symptoms such as nightmares, flashbacks and other repetitive phenomena that have been classified under the rubric of Post-Traumatic Stress Disorder (PTSD).

This chapter draws on the theoretical insights of Sigmund Freud, Cathy Caruth, and Jean Laplanche to explicate the dual temporal structure of trauma. I contend that the locus of trauma can neither be posited in the event that brought on the traumatic symptoms, nor can it be situated in the traumatic symptoms that follow. Drawing on the Freudian concept of *Nachträglichkeit*, I argue that the complex temporality of trauma is a missed encounter that manifests belatedly – so that which occurs too soon paradoxically occurs too late. Instead of privileging the past at the expense of the present (or future), or the present (or future) at the expense of the past, I argue that these extremes are caught up in a reciprocal and dialogic exchange. Accordingly, the past assumes a belated impact on the present and the present retroactively modifies the event of the past. Consequently, trauma bears just as much weight on the present and the future as it does on the past.

Keywords

trauma – *Nachträglichkeit* – double wound – afterwardsness – progression – retroaction – hermeneutics – determinism

 | DOI:10.1163/9789004407947_004

1 Introduction

> The story of trauma [...] as the narrative of a belated experience, far from telling of an escape from reality – the escape from a death, or from its referential force – rather attests to its endless impact on life.[1]

The term 'trauma' etymologically derives from the Greek term that refers to a 'wound' and was originally used in medicine to denote a wound to the tissues of the body.[2] More recently, however, trauma has come to refer to the wounding impact of a sudden, overwhelming shock to the mind or psyche.[3] Rather than simply referring to a specific violent event, trauma cuts across two scenes, consisting of an event too overwhelming to be experienced at the time of its arrival, followed by the delayed onslaught of repetitive symptoms that return the survivor to the initial traumatic event. Given this, trauma is irreducible to one event alone – it bypasses conscious awareness at the time that it occurs only to manifest itself belatedly. While trauma is often understood to reside in an event having occurred in the past, it is not until after this event has passed that the impact of trauma is felt. It is thus difficult, if not impossible, to identify the precise origins of trauma. Trauma, as Francesca Brencio and Kori Novak explain in this volume, exists on a continuum.

Attempts to discover the origins of trauma have the tendency of privileging either the disruptive event of the past at the expense of the present or vice versa. As this chapter will show, *Nachträglichkeit* is often misconstrued as involving a temporal trajectory that moves from either the past to the present or the present to the past. The former interpretation, to which I will hereafter refer to as the progressive reading, posits the initial event as the cause of the belated onset of symptoms. The latter reading, to which I will hereafter refer as retroactive, posits the act of interpreting the traumatic symptoms in the present as the retroactive cause of the event of the past. Instead of favouring either one of these readings at the expense of the other, I argue that trauma places both the past and the present into a reciprocal

1 Cathy Caruth, *Unclaimed Experience: Trauma, Narrative, and History* (Baltimore and London: John Hopkins University Press, 1996), 7.

2 Ibid., 3.

3 Ibid.; Ruth Leys, *Trauma: A Genealogy* (Chicago and London: University of Chicago Press, 2000), 4.

and dialogic exchange. I will therefore demonstrate the means through which trauma disrupts linear notions of temporality and causality, so that the past assumes a belated impact on the present and the present retroactively modifies the past.

The chapter begins by providing a detailed overview of the difficulties that the bidirectional structure of *Nachträglichkeit* poses for interpretation and translation. Where the progressive interpretation grounds trauma in a factual and dateable event to have occurred in an individual's past, the retroactive version rejects the factuality of the past and suggests that it is all but an internal construct of the present. The first section of the chapter sets up the central problematic that this chapter responds to and stresses the necessity of accounting for both temporal trajectories of *Nachträglichkeit*.

The second section considers the dual temporality of trauma through the literary trauma theory of Cathy Caruth, who characterises trauma as a 'double wound' that strikes consciousness 'one moment too late'. Through Caruth's discussion of latency, a simplified translation of *Nachträglichkeit*, this section reveals that the precipitating event of trauma serves as a failed experience of the past that assumes a belated impact on the present.

Thereafter, the third section of the chapter turns to Freud's remarks on trauma and repetition compulsion in *Beyond the Pleasure Principle* ([1920] 1961) to consider what it means for an event that could not be experienced in the past to manifest itself belatedly in the present. I will show that the repetitive symptoms of trauma constitute an attempt to retroactively master an event too overwhelming to be experienced at the time of its arrival. The third section of this chapter considers Caruth's commentary on the compulsion to repeat, where she posits the moment of awakening from traumatic dreams as echoing the missed encounter with trauma.

The fourth section draws on Freud's case study of Emma in the 'Project for a Scientific Psychology' ([1895] 1950), one of his first attempts to examine the dual temporality of *Nachträglichkeit*. This section reveals that the hermeneutical process of interpreting trauma is a necessary aspect of its bidirectionality. Through the case of Emma, I consider the means through which trauma defies historical chronologisation and causality, by revealing that the symptoms experienced by the traumatised individual paradoxically precede the event of the past and that the so-called past succeeds the present.

The fifth section of this chapter turns to Jean Laplanche's reconceptualisation of *Nachträglichkeit* – which he translates as *après-coup* in French and afterwardsness in English – to amalgamate the bidirectional temporalities of trauma. Laplanche's notion of afterwardsness synthesises the progressive and the retroactive temporalities of *Nachträglichkeit*. In so doing, he accounts for both the external event of the past and the internal moment of reconstruction from the present and neither one of these extremes at the expense of the other.

2 The Freudian *Nachträglichkeit*: between Progression and Retroaction

Freud's theoretical insights play an essential role in the conceptualisation of trauma; however, his writings on the topic are intermittent and constitute far from a coherent trauma theory. Trauma functions as a key focus in Freud's earlier work on hysteria, but he eventually discontinues this line of inquiry to develop his famous theories of psychoanalysis. Nonetheless, Freud repeatedly returns to the problem of trauma in his writings, with trauma emerging as a disruption to his psychoanalytic insights.

Theorisations of dual temporalities of trauma – where that which occurs too soon paradoxically arrives too late – owes much to Freud's concept of *Nachträglichkeit*, which he first developed in his early studies of hysteria. *Nachträglichkeit* has a variety of English translations, including 'latency', 'belatedness', 'deferred action', 'retroactive temporarily', 'retroactive modification', 'double wound', 'double blow', and 'retrospective attribution', to name only a few. Translating *Nachträglichkeit* from German into English proves problematic insofar as the term lends itself to two seemingly conflicting views of temporality: a progressive one and a retroactive one. Where the progressive version abides by a forward temporality that precedes from the past to the present or future, the retroactive model encompasses a backwards temporal movement that travels from the present or future to the past.

Interpreters of Freud have struggled to reconcile the bidirectional connotations of *Nachträglichkeit*. This is exacerbated by the lack of words in English to capture both meanings of the term and by Freud's neologism not included in any German dictionary.[4] Translators of Freud tend to privilege either the progressive or retroactive version of the term at the expense of the other. Where translations such as 'deferred action' and 'latency' privilege the former, 'retrospective modification' and 'retroactive attribution' favour the latter.[5] As already mentioned, the progressive interpretation of *Nachträglichkeit* posits the past

---

4 Friedrich-Wilhelm Eickhoff, 'Nachträglichkeit from the Perspective of the Phylogenetic Factor in Freud's *Moses and Monotheism*', *The Scandinavian Psychoanalytic Review* 29 (2006): 54.

5 Jonathan House and Julie Slotnick, 'Après-Coup in French Psychoanalysis: The Long Afterlife of Nachträglichkeit: The First Hundred Years, 1893 to 1993', *Psychoanalytic Review* 102.5 (2015): 685.

event as the cause of the belated onset of traumatic symptoms. Conversely, the retroactive interpretation lends itself to a backwards model of temporality, implying that the later moment of interpretation retroactively causes the past event. With its focus on interpretation, the latter reading of *Nachträglichkeit* has hermeneutic, as well as retroactive, connotations. The progressive and retroactive interpretations overlook the bidirectional structure of *Nachträglichkeit*, which consists of a dialogic exchange between the past and the present, in which the past belatedly manifests itself in the present and the present retroactively reconstructs the past.

In the *Standard Edition*, James Strachey adheres to the progressive interpretation, translating the adjective/adverb, *nachträglich*, to 'deferred', 'subsequently', 'in arrears', 'later', etc., and the noun, *Nachträglichkeit*, to 'deferred action'.[6] This translation overlooks the hermeneutic connotations of the term and gives rise to determinism.[7] Deferred action implies a forward linear movement in which the past determines what follows. Laplanche illustrates this temporal trajectory through the analogy of the time-bomb: the assemblage of a bomb at an earlier moment in time causes its explosion at a later moment in time.[8] However, relying on a purely retroactive interpretation of *Nachträglichkeit* also gives rise to determinism, only one that proceeds in the opposite direction. The retroactive position reverses the arrow of time and no longer moves from the past to the present or future, but from the present or future to the past.[9] In this context, the past event is determined by its retroactive construction from a future perspective.

These oversimplified versions of *Nachträglichkeit* reduce trauma to either a factual event of the past or to an internal construct of the present, with one of these extremes automatically foreclosing the possibility of the other. Moreover, the former reading posits trauma in a factual, dateable event that exists independently of any interpretative efforts. This suggests that an objective, external reality is awaiting its belated discovery, as though uncovering this past will both explain and cure the intrusive traumatic symptoms of which the past event is the supposed cause. This inevitably leads in the direction of

6 Ibid.; Jean Laplanche, *Essays on Otherness* (London and New York: Routledge, 2005), 267; Helmut Thomä and Neil Cheshire, 'Freud's Nachträglichkeit and Strachey's "Deferred Action": Trauma, Constructions and the Direction of Causality', *The International Review of Psycho-Analysis* 18.3 (1991): 407.

7 John Fletcher, *Freud and the Scene of Trauma* (New York: Fordham University Press, 2013), 71; House and Slotnick, 'Après-Coup in French Psychoanalysis', 685; Laplanche, *Essays on Otherness*, 265–266.

8 Laplanche, *Essays on Otherness*, 265.

9 House and Slotnick, 'Après-Coup in French Psychoanalysis', 686.

naïve realism and historical positivism.[10] Conversely, the retroactive interpretation posits the past as both inaccessible and irrelevant, with the past being perceived as an internal construct of the present. This leads to a relativistic dismissal of the external factuality of the past event.

I contend that the progressive and retroactive interpretations of *Nachträglichkeit* are symptomatic of a false dichotomy which overlook the fact that the term necessarily implicates both the external and the internal, the past and the present. In this chapter, I plan to move beyond the two conflicting views and to demonstrate their intricate entanglement. Trauma, I argue, necessitates both an external event of the past and an internal moment of reconstruction from the vantage-point of the present. Only when these factors are taken together does trauma assume its traumatic quality.

3 Encountering Trauma 'One Moment Too Late'

While Caruth invokes the concept of *Nachträglichkeit*, she does not explicitly refer to the term in her work. Nonetheless, her characterisation of trauma as a 'double wound', and her remarks on the inherent latency of trauma, clearly resonate with this Freudian concept. Caruth maintains that as an event, trauma arrives both too soon and too late: it 'occurs too soon, too unexpectedly, to be fully known and is therefore not available to consciousness until it imposes itself again, repeatedly, in the nightmares and repetitive actions of the survivor'.[11] Trauma bypasses conscious awareness at the time that it occurs only to manifest belatedly in intrusive and repetitive symptoms. Accordingly, the 'overwhelming immediacy' of trauma gives rise to its 'belated uncertainty'.[12]

In theorising the peculiar temporality of trauma, Caruth draws on Freud's *Moses and Monotheism* (1939) to configure trauma as 'the story of an accident':[13]

> It may happen that someone gets away, apparently unharmed, from the spot where he [*sic*] has suffered a shocking accident, for instance a train collision. In the course of the following weeks, however, he develops a series of grave psychical and motor symptoms, which can be ascribed only

---

10 Laplanche, *Essays on Otherness*, 42.

11 Caruth, *Unclaimed Experience*, 4.

12 Cathy Caruth, *Introduction to Trauma: Exploration in Memory* (Baltimore and London: John Hopkins University Press, 1995), 6.

13 Ibid., 7.

> to his shock or whatever else happened at the time of the accident. He has developed a 'traumatic neurosis'. This appears quite incomprehensible and is therefore a novel fact. The time that elapsed between the accident and the first appearance of the symptoms is called the 'incubation period', a transparent allusion to the pathology of infectious disease [...]. It is the feature one might term *latency*.[14]

In her reading of this passage, Caruth draws attention to the gap between the traumatic event and the belated onset of symptoms. While the person in Freud's example could very well be seen as repressing the traumatic accident only to remember what happened later, Caruth insists that what occurred could not have been forgotten or repressed. Instead, she argues that the traumatised individual did not actually experience the event as it occurred. Freud's example does not reveal a movement from the event to its repression to its return but, rather, demonstrates the feature of latency. Trauma, according to Caruth, is not an event simply forgotten; instead, an inherent feature of trauma is the 'latency within the experience itself'.[15] The traumatic event, in other words, was not actually experienced at the time that it occurred and not until after the event is its reality realised for the first time.

For Caruth, the central aporia of trauma lies in the impossibility of voluntarily accessing one's own traumatic past; this past belatedly imposes itself on the individual against their conscious will. She argues that a defining feature of trauma is 'the way it was precisely *not known* in the first instance – then returns to haunt the survivor later on'.[16] The impact of the traumatic event manifests after the fact of its occurrence in symptoms such as flashbacks, nightmares, intrusive thoughts, and other traumatic affects that have since been classified under the banner of Post-Traumatic Stress Disorder (PTSD).[17] As an event too overwhelming to be experienced at the time of its arrival, trauma continually re-emerges long after the initial traumatic scene.

Given its inherent latency, trauma cannot be reduced to either the precipitating event or the repetitive symptoms that follow. Instead, Caruth famously argues that trauma resides in the '*structure of its experience* or reception: the event is not assimilated or experienced fully at the time, but only belatedly'.[18]

14 Sigmund Freud, *Moses and Monotheism*, trans. Katherine Jones (Hertfordshire: Hogarth Press, 1939), 109–110, emphasis in original.
15 Caruth, 'Introduction', 8.
16 Ibid., emphasis in original.
17 Ibid.
18 Caruth, 'Introduction', 4, emphasis in original.

Trauma breaches the psyche and cannot be registered through ordinary mechanisms of experience and cognition. The traumatic event defies conscious awareness and experiential frameworks as it occurs; it bypasses consciousness as the initial event unfolds. Caruth thus refers to trauma as an *unclaimed experience*, a phrase which she also uses as the title of her 1996 monograph. Caruth's remarks raise the following question: if the traumatic event was not actually experienced in the past, what does it mean for trauma to manifest itself in the present through the repetitive symptoms of trauma?

4 Traumatic Awakening as Repetition Compulsion

In her conceptualisation of trauma as an event that strikes consciousness '*one moment too late*',[19] Caruth turns to Freud's *Beyond the Pleasure Principle*, where he considers the compulsion to repeat traumatising events. Written in the immediate aftermath of the First World War, *Beyond the Pleasure Principle* considers the repetitive symptoms suffered by soldiers returning from battle. These symptoms include recurring dreams, flashbacks and re-enactments of the situations in which the individual fell ill. What strikes Freud as peculiar is that the repetitive symptoms of trauma return the survivor to the initial traumatic scene against their conscious will.

Before extrapolating the compulsion to repeat traumatic events, it is worth reflecting on Freud's definition of trauma as a breach in the protective shield of consciousness. This, in turn, requires considering his notion of consciousness. While traditionally conceived through its ability to receive stimuli emanating from the external world, consciousness according to Freud fulfils its most important function through its ability to keep stimuli out.[20] Consciousness, Freud contends, is equipped with a protective layer that filters the powerful energies of the external world in a diminished quantity. If not for this protective layer, these overpowering energies would be too overwhelming for consciousness to assimilate. Having speculated on the nature of consciousness, Freud argues that trauma occurs when 'excitations from outside which are powerful enough [...] break through the protective shield'.[21] Trauma, in other words, is 'a consequence of an extensive breach being made in the protective shield against

19 Caruth, *Unclaimed Experience*, 62, emphasis in original.

20 Sigmund Freud, *Beyond the Pleasure Principle*, trans. James Strachey (New York and London: W.W. Norton & Company, [1920] 1961), 21.

21 Ibid., 23.

stimuli'.[22] Where the protective shield would ordinarily protect consciousness from the violent energies of the external world, trauma results from an atypical breach in the protective shield, in which the psychical apparatus is flooded with excessive quantities of stimuli.

Freud attributes what he terms 'traumatic neurosis' to the quality of 'fright', which denotes the state of psychical unpreparedness to encounter danger. He differentiates 'fright' from 'fear' and 'anxiety'.[23] Where fear is directed towards 'a definitive object of which to be afraid', and anxiety 'describes a particular state of expecting danger or preparing for it, even though it may be an unknown one', fright refers 'to the state a person gets into when he [*sic*] has run into danger without being prepared for it; it emphasizes the factor of surprise'.[24] Neither fear nor anxiety give rise to trauma; in fact, Freud believes that anxiety actually protects the individual from trauma, since it prepares them for impending danger (regardless of whether or not this danger is known to them). Freud posits fright as conducive to the onset of trauma, which is caused 'by *a lack of preparedness* for anxiety'.[25]

Fright plays an important role in the repetitive dreams experienced by traumatised individuals: 'dreams occurring in traumatic neuroses have the characteristic of repeatedly bringing the patient back to the situation of his [*sic*] accident, a situation from which he wakes up in another fright'.[26] Traumatised individuals are not consciously aware of their trauma while awake, but are repeatedly and involuntarily returned to the original scene of the trauma in their dreams. 'These dreams', continues Freud, 'are endeavouring to master the stimulus retrospectively, by developing the anxiety whose omission was the cause of the traumatic neurosis'.[27] Thus repetitive dreams – and other repetitive symptoms for that matter – arise 'in obedience to the compulsion to repeat',[28] an attempt to master an experience that could not cognised at the time that it occurred.

In her commentary on *Beyond the Pleasure Principle*, Caruth argues that the lack of preparedness to respond to an external threat results in a missed encounter with this threat.[29] The shock to the mind's relation to the external

22 Ibid., 25.
23 Ibid., 6.
24 Ibid.
25 Ibid., 25, my emphasis.
26 Ibid., 7.
27 Ibid., 26.
28 Ibid.
29 Cathy Caruth, *Literature in the Ashes of History* (Baltimore and London: John Hopkins University Press, 2013), 6.

threat, in other words, interrupts the possibility of directly experiencing it. Given this, the locus of trauma does not simply reside in a threat to one's bodily existence, 'but in the fact that the threat is recognised by the mind *one moment too late*'.[30] Trauma is a breach in the psyche that interrupts – rather than enters – consciousness. This disruption forms the basis of repetition in dreams, which attempt to master an event that bypassed consciousness at the time that it occurred.[31] The repetitive symptoms of trauma return the survivor to not only 'the reality of a violent event but also the reality of the way that its violence has not yet been fully known'.[32] The dreams suffered by traumatised individuals constitute an attempt to relive the original event that led to the trauma; however, such attempts inevitably fail and instead wake the person up in another fright.[33]

Having defined trauma as a missed encounter with a threat to the psyche, Caruth goes on to consider the act of waking up in fright as a repetitive symptom of trauma. She argues that repetitiveness characterises not only the experience *within* the dream that repeats the trauma, but also the experience of *waking* from the dream.[34] As well as bringing the survivor back to the reality of the precipitating event, traumatic nightmares re-enact the psyche's unpreparedness to encounter this reality.[35] 'It is the surprise of waking', Caruth explains, 'that repeats the unexpectedness of trauma'.[36] Hence, it is the moment of awakening as well as the manifest content in the dream that repeats the missed encounter with trauma.[37]

While Caruth examines the dual temporal structure of trauma in Freud's *Moses and Monotheism* and *Beyond the Pleasure Principle*, she does not consider Freud's earlier work on hysteria, which offers a richer understanding of not only the temporal, but also the hermeneutic, aspects of trauma. The role of interpretation forms a crucial relation to the retroactive temporality of trauma, in which an event of the past not assimilated at the time that it occurred is only realised after its occurrence. As Brencio and Novak remark, trauma disrupts not only the human being's historicity and relationship to time, but also one's ability to prescribe lived experiences with meaning.[38] Indeed, our capacity to

30 Ibid., 62, emphasis in original.
31 Ibid., 6.
32 Caruth, *Unclaimed Experience*, 6.
33 Ibid., 139.
34 Caruth, *Literature in the Ashes of History*, 6.
35 Ibid., 3–4.
36 Ibid., 6.
37 Ibid.
38 Francesca Brencio and Kori Novak, 'The Continuum of Trauma' in this volume.

assimilate phenomenon into frameworks of meaning is what makes us uniquely human.

In order to enrich the notion of trauma developed by Caruth, the following section of this chapter will consider Freud's 'Project for a Scientific Psychology', one of his earliest discussions of *Nachträglichkeit*. In his famous case study of Emma, Freud elaborates on the bidirectional structure of trauma as involving a belated moment of interpretation that retroactively modifies the unassimilable event of the past through hitherto unavailable interpretative frameworks. Rather than characterising the initial event of trauma as traumatic in and of itself, Freud gestures towards the dynamic interplay between two scenes, traumatic only when taken together.

5 Freud and Emma

In this section, I will examine the Freudian *Nachträglichkeit* through the case study of Emma to explicate the complex temporality of trauma. In so doing, I stress that trauma cannot be reduced to one scene alone but, rather, involves a circular interplay between two scenes. Where this chapter has thus far examined the *temporality* of trauma, this section will consider the element of *interpretation* as a crucial factor of the traumatic event. Having examined the double wound of trauma as involving an initial shock to the psyche followed by the incursion of intrusive repetitive symptoms, I will discuss the subsequent reconstruction of the meaning ascribed to an event of the past from the perspective of the present.

In the 'Project for a Scientific Psychology', Freud presents Emma as suffering from a phobia that prevents her from entering shops alone. Emma traces the onset of this phobia to an incident that occurred when she was twelve years old. She had gone into a store to buy something, had noticed that the two shop-assistants working there were laughing, and had fled from the store in a state of fright. Emma thought that the shop-assistants were laughing at her clothing and confessed to Freud that she had found one of them sexually pleasing. Ever since this incident, labelled by Freud as 'Scene I', Emma could not enter shops by herself.

It strikes Freud as strange, however, that the account provided by Emma 'explain[s] neither the compulsion nor the determination of symptom'.[39] It

39 Sigmund Freud, 'Project for a Scientific Psychology', *The Standard Edition of the Complete Psychological Works of Sigmund Freud* (1886–1899), trans. James Stratchey (London: Hogarth Press, [1895] 1950) 1: 353.

presents a discrepancy between the event described by Emma and her extreme reaction to it. If Emma was embarrassed by her clothes as a child, she could have fixed this issue long ago – she is now an adult who can choose her own clothing. Freud moreover observes that 'it makes no difference to her clothes whether she goes to a shop alone or in company'.[40] Finally, the phobia of entering shops alone does not appear in any way related to Emma finding one of the shop-assistants sexually pleasing.

On further investigation, Emma relates to Freud another memory hitherto unavailable to her. When Emma was eight years old, she had gone into a store to buy some sweets and was molested by a grinning shop-keeper who had grabbed her genitals through her clothing. Freud refers to this earlier event as 'Scene II'. Emma admits that she went back into the store a second time and that she feels reproachful towards her childhood self – it was as if 'she had wanted in that way to provoke the assault. In fact, one can trace a state of 'oppressive bad back to this experience'.[41]

Although Emma denies having in mind the memory of Scene II at the time of Scene I, associative links between the incidents, when compounded, explain her traumatic symptoms. There exists a link between the laughter of the two shop-assistants in Scene I and the grin of the man who molested her in Scene II. Another association between the incidents emerges as Emma was on both occasions in a shop alone. Furthermore, clothes appear in both scenes: in Scene I, Emma thought that the two shop-assistants were laughing at her clothing and in Scene II, the shop-keeper had grabbed her genitals through her clothing. Freud explains that the residual element of clothing is the only thing that entered Emma's consciousness at the time of Scene II. Given this, Emma arrived at what Freud regards as a false observation concerning the laughter of the shop-assistants in Scene I, supposedly directed at her clothes.[42]

Having identified the associative links between the two events described by Emma, Freud highlights a fundamental difference between them. Emma had not yet reached puberty in Scene II and lacked the discourse of sexuality to make sense of the occurrence. Scene I, on the other hand, took place after Emma had gone through puberty and had acquired the relevant 'physiological powers and understandings' to process the event that occurred earlier.[43] Freud explains:

40 Ibid., 353.
41 Ibid., 354.
42 Ibid., 355.
43 Fletcher, *Freud and the Scene of Trauma*, 73.

> Here we have the case of a memory arousing an affect which it did not arouse as an experience, because in the meantime the change [brought about] in puberty had made possible a different understanding of what was remembered.
>
> Now this case is typical of repression in hysteria. We invariably find that a memory is repressed which has only become a trauma by *deferred action* [*Nachträglichkeit*]. The cause of this is the retardation of puberty as compared with the rest of the individual's development.[44]

Freud refers to the impression that Scene II left on Emma's psyche as a 'memory', but it cannot be thought of as a memory in the proper sense of the term. Scene II could not have formed a memory because it was not psychically processed until the time of Scene I. This aside, Freud explains that the 'memory' of Scene II was belatedly awoken at the time of Scene I, giving rise to an affect that Emma could not experience when molested in the past. The reactivated 'memory' of Scene II released a sexual excitation which Emma directed at the shop-assistant she found sexually pleasing. Having for the first time realised what had occurred in Scene II, Emma fled from the store in a state of fright. Emma's extreme response to Scene I was therefore a delayed reaction to Scene II. It was not until Scene I that the 'memory' of Scene II entered into Emma's unconscious because, prior to Scene I, Emma was unable to cognitively process Scene II.

The case of Emma aptly demonstrates the peculiar temporal structure of *Nachträglichkeit* evinced in Freud's work on hysteria. Here, an event that occurred at an 'earlier' moment in time is reactivated at a 'later' moment in time. More importantly, the case of Emma also reveals a hermeneutic aspect to trauma, whereby an event that occurred 'later' retroactively modifies an event that occurred 'earlier'. The catalyst of Emma's trauma cannot be situated in either event alone: it is not until the 'later' scene that the impact of the 'earlier' scene becomes apparent, with the 'earlier' scene taking on new meaning through the advent of puberty, which 'ma[kes] possible a different understanding of what [is] remembered'.[45] I have placed the terms 'earlier' and 'later' in inverted commas because the structure of *Nachträglichkeit* problematises chronological temporalisation – indeed, the event that historically occurred earlier was not psychically registered until the event that historically occurred later. Interestingly Freud himself does not number the scenes chronologically, but in the

44 Freud, 'Project for a Scientific Psychology', 356, emphasis in original.

45 Ibid.

order that these scenes occur to Emma in her treatment. I contend that neither of the scenes are traumatic in and of themselves; trauma arises through a dialogic exchange between (at least)[46] two scenes, in which the past assumes a belated impact on the present and the present retroactively interprets the past.

However, the problem remains concerning how to overcome the conflict between the progressive and retroactive connotations of *Nachträglichkeit*. Freud's commentary on Emma illuminates the dual temporalities of *Nachträglichkeit*, as well as the hermeneutic dimension of trauma. Freud does not, however, consider the tension that arises between these terms, nor does he suggest a means to overcome this tension.

6 Laplanche's Afterwardsness: Synthesising the Bidirectional Trajectories of *Nachträglichkeit*

To move beyond the mutual exclusivity between the external event of the past and the internal moment of construction from the present, I will move on to consider Laplanche's reformulation of the Freudian *Nachträglichkeit*. As mentioned in the introduction to this chapter, Laplanche translates *Nachträglichkeit* into *après-coup* in French, thereafter translated as 'afterwardsness' in English. When discussing Laplanche's work, I will use the English translation of his neologism, afterwardsness, unless otherwise made obvious. Laplanche both illuminates and synthesises the dual structure of afterwardsness by turning to a famous anecdote provided by Freud in his *Interpretation of Dreams* ([1899] 2010):

> A young man who was a great admirer of feminine beauty was talking once – so the story went – of the good-looking wet-nurse who had suckled him when he was a baby: 'I'm sorry', he remarked, 'that I didn't make better use of my opportunity'. I was in the habit of quoting this anecdote to explain the factor of deferred action [*Nachträglichkeit*] in the mechanism of the psychoneuroses.[47]

Laplanche highlights the progressive and retroactive temporalities of afterwardsness at play in this anecdote. On the one hand, the infant's encounter

46 Freud situates Emma's trauma as occurring across two moments in time, but more scenes can be introduced into the equation. There is also the scene in which Emma returned to the store after she had been molested by the shop-keeper as well as the scene in which she receives treatment from Freud.

47 Cited in Laplanche, *Essays on Otherness*, 268.

with the wet-nurse reads as abiding by a progressive temporal movement from the past to the present, in which the infant's sexuality is later reawakened in the sexuality of the adult via deferred action.[48] On the other hand, the anecdote provided by Freud can be read as illustrating a retroactive temporal trajectory from the present to the past, in which 'the adult man, who sees the child at the wet-nurse's breast retrospectively imagines all that he could have drawn erotically from that situation if only he had known'.[49]

Laplanche argues that although Freud's anecdote exemplifies the dual temporalities of afterwardsness, Freud himself does not reconcile the conflict between the progressive and retroactive meanings of the term. In moving towards a resolution, Laplanche identifies an oversight in Freud's commentary – namely, that he only considers 'the two interlocutors equally centred on the subject: that is, the infantile subject, and the adult subject; the one sucks the breast, the other experiences erotic pleasure'.[50] Laplanche draws attention to the fact that Freud's remarks reduce the wet-nurse to a breast – 'an *object* for the infant' – whilst failing to perceive the breast as an erogenous zone of the woman.[51] In overcoming the mutual exclusivity between progression and retroaction, Laplanche introduces a third figure into the equation – the wet-nurse and the unconscious message she passes on to the infant.[52]

In considering the enigmatic message of the wet-nurse, Laplanche argues that it 'is no longer possible to consider afterwardsness as a combination of two opposed terms'.[53] He explains that

> right at the start, there is something that goes in the direction of the past to the future, from the other to the individual in question, that is in the direction from the adult to the baby, which I call the implantation of the enigmatic message. This message is then retranslated, following a temporal direction which is, in an alternating fashion, by turns retrogressive and progressive.[54]

In Laplanche's formulation, the first instance of afterwardsness marks the implantation of the enigmatic message in the undeveloped psyche of the infant.

48 Ibid., 106.
49 Ibid., 268.
50 Ibid.
51 Ibid., 269, emphasis in original.
52 Ibid.
53 Ibid.
54 Ibid.

The initial depositing of the message abides by a progressive temporal movement from the past to the future. However, the infant is ill-equipped to decipher the message at the time that it is received, which gives rise to a second instance, in which the infant – now an adult – belatedly attempts to translate the message. The later moment adheres to a retroactive temporal trajectory that moves from the present to the past. Here, the adult retroactively modifies the event of the past from the vantage-point of the present.

Like Freud, Laplanche identifies the structure of *Nachträglichkeit* as constitutive of Emma's trauma; however, Laplanche has a different interpretation of the case study, which he formulates in accordance with his theory of afterwardsness. Where the scene in which Emma is molested by the shop-keeper indicates the moment at which an alien message is deposited in her underdeveloped psyche (at that stage, her psyche is underdeveloped because she lacks the ideas necessary to make sense of her sexual abuse); the scene in which she is confronted with the laughing shop-assistants signifies the moment at which she can for the first time translate the message. Unlike Freud, Laplanche numbers the scenes chronologically. The first scene has sexual content, but Emma cannot make sense of this content; he sees 'sexual content in the explicit behaviour of the adult protagonist [...] it is a sexual content, as it were, *in itself* and not *for the subject*'.[55] On the contrary, the second scene occurs at a time when Emma has the capacity to understand the nature of a sexual assault even though she is not sexually assaulted in the scene (ibid.).

Laplanche explains that during the interval between the first and second scene, the 'memory' of the earlier scene exists in neither a conscious nor an unconscious repressed state.[56] The unprocessed fragment of the first scene does not reside in Emma's consciousness because it was not registered as an experience at the time it occurred. It cannot reside in Emma's unconscious either, for it was not repressed until the later scene. Laplanche suggests that during the interval between the two scenes, the uncognitised trace of the earlier scene was 'waiting in a kind of limbo, in a corner of the "preconscious"; the crucial point is that it is not linked to the rest of psychical life'.[57] At the time of the second scene, the unbound residue of the first scene attacked Emma's psyche from within, acting as 'a veritable 'internal alien entity''.[58]

55 Jean Laplanche, *Life and Death in Psychoanalysis*, trans. Jeffrey Mehlman (Baltimore and London: John Hopkins University Press [1970] 1985), 40, emphasis in original.

56 Ibid., 42.

57 Ibid.

58 Ibid.

In accordance with the complex structure of afterwardsness, Laplanche emphasises the necessary relation between the two scenes in the production of Emma's trauma. Scene II – to use Freud's terminology – was not traumatic; it produced 'neither excitation or reaction, nor symbolization or psychical elaboration'.[59] But if Scene II was not traumatic, Scene I was even less so – it was a non-sexual, everyday visit to a shop. Nonetheless, Scene II released the unprocessed residue of Scene I and, along with it, the excitation which had remained dormant and unactualised in that scene. The decisive point lies in the impossibility of grounding the traumatic event in a precise moment: 'in situating the trauma, one cannot appreciate its traumatic impact, and vice versa'.[60] Neither scene is traumatic in and of itself – only when the scenes are taken together does the trauma emerge. Laplanche thus situates the trauma 'in the play of "deceit" producing a kind of seesaw effect between the two events'.[61]

7 Situating Trauma: between the Past and the Present, the External and the Internal

> [I]t is simply taken for granted that time and causality move *from* the traumatic event *to* the other criterial features [of trauma] and that the event inscribes itself on the symptoms. Because the traumatic event is the cause of the syndromal feelings and behaviours, it is logical to say that it precedes them. If this were not true, if it were acceptable for syndromal features to occur before the traumatic event, then the term 'reexperience' would lose its accepted meaning.[62]

Trauma is often reduced to a causal linear axis, in which an event of the past is construed as determining the belated onset of symptoms. In accordance with this logic, the past event is belatedly reexperienced in the present via the process of deferred action. In this chapter, I have evoked this temporal trajectory through the progressive version of *Nachträglichkeit*. However, I have also considered another, less common, characterisation of trauma, which posits the later moment of interpretation as retroactively constructing the event of the past.

---

59 Ibid.

60 Ibid., 41, emphasis in original.

61 Ibid.

62 Allan Young, *The Harmony of Illusions: Inventing* Precipitating event (New Jersey: Princeton University Press, 1995), 115–116, emphasis in original.

The retroactive reading of trauma is more sophisticated than the progressive version in that it considers not only time, but also hermeneutics. Yet both versions give rise to a deterministic view of trauma where either the past assumes a belated impact on the present or the present retroactively constitutes the past. Where the progressive version reduces trauma to a factual and dateable event to have occurred in the past, the retroactive version reduces the past to a mere construct of the present. Rather than favouring either of these interpretations at the expense of the other, this chapter has demonstrated the means through which trauma implicates a factual event of the past and an internal moment of reconstruction in the present in a circular and dialogic exchange.

Trauma is at odds with chronological temporality insofar as not until after the original traumatic scene does the trauma first make its presence felt. The initial traumatic event does not present itself to consciousness at the time that it unfolds. Hence, it cannot be thought of as an event experienced in the past. The traumatic symptoms which manifest themselves in the present are not the re-experiencing of the past because the past event was not actually experienced to begin with. Instead, the symptoms retroactively attempt to experience an event that could not be experienced on its arrival.

Locating the precise origins of trauma is a thwarted process because trauma implicates at least two events constructively fractured across time. The bidirectional structure of *Nachträglichkeit* problematises the view that trauma can be situated in either an external event of the past or in the internal reconstruction of the past projected backwards in time from the present. Irreducible to either the external or the internal, the past or the present, trauma necessitates a dynamic interplay between both of these extremes. Trauma occurs 'too soon' insofar as it strikes consciousness in a state of unpreparedness. Trauma occurs 'too late' because not until after the precipitating event of trauma is its impact felt. The dual temporality of trauma – where that which occurs too soon paradoxically arrives too late – means that trauma bears just as much weight on the present and the future as it does on the past.

Bibliography

Barnaby, Andrew. 'Coming Too Late: Freud, Belatedness, and Existential Trauma'. *SubStance* 41.2 (2012): 119–138.

Caruth, Cathy. Preface to *Trauma: Explorations in Memory*, edited by Cathy Caruth, vii–ix. Baltimore and London: John Hopkins University Press, 1995.

Caruth, Cathy. Introduction to *Trauma: Explorations in Memory*, edited by Cathy Caruth, 3–12; 151–157. Baltimore and London: John Hopkins University Press, 1995.

Caruth, Cathy. *Unclaimed Experience: Trauma, Narrative, and History*. Baltimore and London: John Hopkins University Press, 1996.

Caruth, Cathy. *Literature in the Ashes of History*. Baltimore and London: John Hopkins University Press, 2013.

Erikson, Kai. 'Notes on Trauma and Community'. In *Trauma: Explorations in Memory*, edited by Cathy Caruth, 183–199. Baltimore and London: John Hopkins University Press, 1995.

Eickoff, Friedrich-Wilhelm. 'Nachträglichkeit from the Perspective of the Phylogenetic Factor in Freud's *Moses and Monotheism*'. *The Scandinavian Psychoanalytic Review* 29 (2006): 53–59.

Eickoff, Friedrich-Wilhelm. 'On *Nachträglichkeit*: The Modernity of an Old Concept'. *International Journal of Psychoanalysis* 87 (2006): 1453–1469.

Faimberg, Haydée. 'A Plea for a Broader Concept of *Nachträglichkeit*'. *Psychoanalytic Quarterly* 76 (2007): 1221–1240.

Fletcher, John. 'Introduction: Psychoanalysis and the Question of the Other'. *Essays on Otherness* by Jean Laplanche, 1–52. London and New York: Routledge, 2005.

Fletcher, John. *Freud and the Scene of Trauma*. New York: Fordham University Press, 2013.

Forter, Greg. 'Freud Faulkner, Caruth: Trauma and the Politics of Literary Form'. *Narrative* 15.3 (2007): 259–285.

Freud, Sigmund, and Josef Breuer. *Studies on Hysteria*. Translated and edited by James Strachey. New York: Basic Books, (1895) 1955.

Freud, Sigmund. 'Project for a Scientific Psychology'. In *The Standard Edition of the Complete Psychological Works of Sigmund Freud (1886–1899)*, translated and edited by James Stratchey, 1: 281–391. London: Hogarth Press, (1895) 1950.

Freud, Sigmund. *The Interpretation of Dreams*. Translated and edited by James Strachey. New York: Basic Books, (1899) 2010.

Freud, Sigmund. 'Remembering, Repeating and Working-Through'. In *The Standard Edition of the Complete Psychological Works of Sigmund Freud (1937–39)*, translated and edited by James Stratchey, 12: 145–156. London: Hogarth Press, (1914) 1958.

Freud, Sigmund. 'From the History of an Infantile Neurosis'. In *The Standard Edition of the Complete Psychological Works of Sigmund Freud (1917–9)*, translated and edited by James Stratchey. 17: 1–124. London: Hogarth Press, (1918) 1955.

Freud, Sigmund. *Beyond the Pleasure Principle*. Translated by James Strachey. New York and London: W.W. Norton & Company, (1920) 1961.

Freud, Sigmund. *Moses and Monotheism*. Translated by Katherine Jones. Hertfordshire: Hogarth Press, 1939.

Eaglestone, Robert. 'Knowledge, "Afterwardsness" and the Future of Trauma Theory'. In *The Future of Trauma Theory: Contemporary Literary and Cultural Criticism*. Edited by Gert Buelens, Sam Durrant and Robert Eaglestone, 11–21. London and New York: Routledge, 2014.

House, Jonathan, and Julie Slotnick. '*Après-Coup* in French Psychoanalysis: The Long Afterlife of *Nachträglichkeit*: The First Hundred Years, 1893 to 1993'. *Psychoanalytic Review* 102.5 (2015): 683–708.

Laplanche, Jean, and Jean-Bertrand Pontalis. *The Language of Psychoanalysis*. Translated by Donald Nicholson-Smith. London: Karnac Books, (1970) 1985.

Laplanche, Jean. *Life and Death in Psychoanalysis*. Translated by Jeffrey Mehlman. Baltimore and London: John Hopkins University Press, (1970) 1985.

Laplanche, Jean. *New Foundations for Psychoanalysis*. Translated by David Macey. Oxford: Basil Blackwell, 1989.

Laplanche, Jean. *Essays on Otherness*. London and New York: Routledge, 2005.

Laplanche, Jean. 'Traumatic Temporality: An Interview with Jean Laplanche'. In *Listening to Trauma: Conversations with Leaders in the Theory and Treatment of Catastrophic Experience*, edited and interviewed by Cathy Caruth, 25–45. Baltimore: John Hopkins University Press, 2014.

Laub, Dori, and Nanette C. Auerhahn. 'Knowing and not Knowing Massive Psychic Trauma: Forms of Traumatic Memory'. *International Journal of Psycho-Analysis* 74 (1993): 287–302.

Laub, Dori, and Susanna Lee. 'Thanatos and Massive Psychic Trauma: The Impact of the Death Instinct on Knowing, Remembering, and Forgetting'. *Journal of the American Psychoanalytic Association* 51.2 (2002): 433–464.

Luckhurst, Roger. *The Trauma Question*. London and New York: Routledge, 2008.

Leys, Ruth. *Trauma: A Genealogy*. Chicago and London: University of Chicago Press, 2000.

Malpas, Simon. ' "History Balancing the Scales": Time and Trauma in Psychoanalysis'. *Time & Society* 5.3 (1996): 301–317.

Thomä, Helmut, and Neil Cheshire. 'Freud's *Nachträglichkeit* and Strachey's "Deferred Action": Trauma, Constructions and the Direction of Causality'. *The International Review of Psycho-Analysis* 18.3 (1991): 407–427.

Van der Kolk, Bessel A., and Onno Van der Hart. 'The Intrusive Past: The Flexibility of Memory and the Engraving of Trauma'. In *Trauma: Explorations in Memory*, edited by Cathy Caruth, 158–82. Baltimore: John Hopkins University Press, 1995.

Van der Kolk, Bessel A., and Rita Fisler. 'Dissociation and the Fragmentary Nature of Traumatic Memories: Overview'. *British Journal of Psychotherapy* 12.3 (1996): 352–61.

Young, Allan. *The Harmony of Illusions: Inventing Post-Traumatic Stress Disorder*. New Jersey: Princeton University Press, 1995.

CHAPTER 3

'A World of Death and Phantoms': Auschwitz, Androids, and the Ethical Demands of Reading Trauma and the Fantastic in *Willing Unbelief*

Tony M. Vinci

Abstract

Despite the central role the rhetoric of the fantastic plays in holocaust literature specifically and trauma literature more generally, critics have yet to address it in any depth. This paper takes seriously the aesthetic demands the literatures of trauma make upon us to translate the fantastic from a literary conceit to an ethical exigency. I suggest that the rhetorical strategies of the fantastic, as employed in both holocaust survivor testimony and popular literature and film of the fantastic, may instigate what Eric Santner defines as 'homeopathic traumas' – 'lesser' traumas instigated via literary texts that rupture the hegemony of the normal and generate spaces in which readers become distanced from the extraordinarily habitualising power of the everyday. Instead of inviting readers to consider the fantastic through a willing suspension of disbelief, trauma literature employs textual cues that encourage readers to enter the text in what might be termed *willing unbelief*: a mode of reading that allows readers to recognise the limits of their understanding regarding pain and loss while attempting to enter the world of the traumatic (rather than fragmenting and filtering portions of the traumatic into the quotidian). Such texts wound readers not primarily through the narrativisation of painful experiences, as one might expect; rather, they employ a rhetoric of the fantastic in tandem with textual traces of historical wounds to dismantle and work beyond such stabilising concepts as world, person, history, event, etc. By reading that which appears to be fantastic in *unbelief*, we become vulnerable to a radical ethics of confrontation, experimentation, and speculation, coding homeopathic trauma as a mode of ontological transformation, social revision, and ethical action.

Keywords

trauma – posthumanism – fantastic – ethics – holocaust – testimony – science fiction

 | DOI:10.1163/9789004407947_005

Trauma literature returns, again and again, to a lexical imaginary of the fantastic: *ghost, walking dead, zombie, living dead, spectre, phantom, apparition, presence*. Alone, each of these signifiers stumbles toward a denotation of *present absence*; together, they denote a zone of *un-* and *de-* and *in-* wherein unmaking, deconstructing, and inverting become the primary modes of being for the traumatised subject. As Lawrence L. Langer notes, the literatures of trauma are marked by their reliance upon a language of 'inconceivable reality', mapping a region of experience that does not fit easily within the confines of realistic narrative.[1] Interrogating the nature of this elusive realm, Langer quotes an anonymous holocaust survivor who insists that to narrate one's trauma is to describe a world that 'seems like a fantasy'; thus, 'what might seem like a fantasy' to the reader is merely a sign of 'ordinary reality' for the survivor.[2] In order to engage such narratives, Langer contends that the reader slips into an 'involuntary suspension of disbelief'.[3] I argue that the involuntary nature of this reading practice involves potential danger and possible unethicality in that, by allowing the suspension of our disbelief, we invite ourselves to believe that we can indeed fold the unimaginable pain of the other into the normal and comfortable quotidian boundaries. By doing so, we enclose these stories within a space that necessitates a filtering, a blunting, a trimming of these narratives for us to be able to *believe* them. Such an approach to trauma sidesteps the fantastic nature of the experience and normalises traumatic encounters, labels and contains them in such a way as to limit definitions of the human, police social boundaries, and lend authority to textual control mechanisms that code written testimony and realistic fiction alike as trans-rhetorical, not linguistic constructs but direct representations of ostensible reality.

Rather than enabling an involuntary suspension of disbelief, I suggest that trauma literature employs textual cues that encourage readers to engage the text in what might be termed *willing unbelief*: a mode of reading that compels readers to recognise the limits of their understanding regarding pain and loss while attempting to inhabit the world of the traumatic rather than fragmenting and filtering portions of the traumatic into the quotidian. If we enter the fantastic trauma narrative and accept its rules and impossibilities as both an analogue of, and an alternative to, our reality, we may be able to bring back to our lives traces of the inexplicable, the unknowable, the 'inconceivable'.[4]

---

1 Lawrence Langer, Introduction to *Auschwitz and After*, by Charlotte Delbo, ed. Lawrence Langer (New Haven: Yale UP, 1995), xvii–xviii.

2 Lawrence Langer, *Holocaust Testimonies: The Ruins of Memory* (New Haven: Yale UP, 1991), 358.

3 Langer, Introduction, 357.

4 Jacqueline Linder's 'Through the Looking-Glass: Child Sexual Abuse from the Inside-Out', included in this book, experiments with similar narrative terrain. By interweaving her personal

By willing ourselves to read the literatures of trauma in *unbelief*, readers may become vulnerable to a radical ethics of confrontation, experimentation, and speculation, enlarging our social sphere to become more hospitable to the inconceivable realities that haunt survivors.

I test this theory here through two dissimilar experimentations with the traumatic fantastic: holocaust testimony by Primo Levi, Jean Améry, and Charlotte Delbo as well as Paolo Bacigalupi's 2009 science fiction novel *The Windup Girl*. The former constructs a seemingly unreal universe in an effort to reset the coordinates of reality, making the fantastic central and relegating the reader's reality to the margins. The aftereffects of trauma are explored here through a series of fantastic experiences: a displacement of the traumatised subject from consensus reality to a disorienting and fantastic geography, a conscious ghosting of the subject into registers both present and absent, and an experimentation with a mode of subjectivity that transcends temporal and spatial limits by inhabiting multiple bodies. These traumatised voices establish an arena that positions the cruelty of the camps as secondary to the normalised cruelty of the everyday, which relegates the pain of the traumatised subject as *unreal* and prohibits its inclusion in the reality matrix of post-holocaust culture.

Bacigalupi's *The Windup Girl* also addresses traumatic experiences that resonate outside the boundaries of ostensible reality. Like Levi, Améry, and Delbo, Bacigalupi utilises fantastic rhetoric as a means to highlight the distance between the reader of the trauma narrative and the historical and imaginative traumas portrayed therein. While the novel foregrounds a post-apocalyptic future on the verge of economic, political, and ecological transformation, its plot hinges on the personal predicaments of a sexually-abused android. Through the eponymous windup girl, Emiko, Bacigalupi dismantles human subjectivity and replaces it with a subjective movement between human, animal, and android registers. Setting all of these modes of being at play within Emiko, the novel outlines the limits of knowledge regarding the traumatised subject, marking the fantastic portrayal of trauma as a desubjectifying experience that can wound the reader into new empathetic possibilities.

In *The Fantastic: A Structural Approach to a Literary Genre*, Tzvetan Todorov asserts a theory of the fantastic that engages the 'hesitation experienced by a person who knows only the laws of nature, confronting an apparently

---

narrative of abuse with scenes from Carroll's *Through the Looking-Glass* and key notions from trauma studies, Linder creates an unsettling dialogue between realistic portrayals of trauma, the fantastic, and the theoretical. These braided discourses invite readers to encounter and reckon with the frustratingly nebulous valences of trauma typically relegated to the margins of the real and the accepted.

supernatural event.[5] For Todorov, the fantastic is positioned between the uncanny (an event that initially seems supernatural but can be explained rationally) and the marvellous (an authentically extra-natural occurrence that necessitates a widening of the subject's worldview). While Todorov does not risk a theory for how this hesitation might function ideologically, I argue that it enables an intellectual space in which we may reconsider and potentially alter our conceptions of reality, especially in relation to narratives that engage trauma.

The 'inconceivable realities' described in trauma narratives invite readers into the borderland of Todorovian hesitation where the *seeming* unreality of events is positioned against the possibility that accepted definitions of the human and the real are horribly insufficient and in need of revision.[6] As Primo Levi argues of the German death camps' inhabitants, prisoners 'could barely acquire an overall vision of their universe'.[7] The edges of this reality blur even for its participants, and they cannot ascertain an understanding of the world inhabited, 'a world of death and phantoms',[8] in which Levi too is 'transformed into [one of] the phantoms' and exists as a form of absence.[9] While reading the trauma narrative, one can easily interpret this rhetoric of negation as a literary conceit constructed to express the intense effects of the brutal desubjectification experienced by victims. Such a reading positions the events that cause trauma to be uncanny, historical instances so far removed from the comforts of dominant Western culture that they seem distanced and unreal. For some trauma survivors, readings that privilege the reality of the everyday over the possibility of the marvellous becomes cause for frustration, provoking a severe but insightful critique of Post-Auschwitz culture's treatment of trauma.

Jean Améry haunts a post-holocaust world in which the holocaust 'has never ceased to take place'.[10] Through his memory-experiences of torture, he survives in a realm in between the present moment and a part of his life ejected by

---

5 Tzvetan Todorov, *The Fantastic: A Structural Approach to a Literary Genre*, Trans. Richard Howard (London: U of Case of Werstern Reserve P, 1973), 25.

6 In 'The Continuum of Trauma', included in this volume, Francesca Brencio and Kori Novak clarify the identity-rupturing influence of trauma, arguing that phenomenological psycopathology allows for an ontological openness that is crucial when considering how trauma impacts the ostensible human subject.

7 Primo Levi, *The Drowned and the Saved* (New York: Vintage, 1989), 17.

8 Primo Levi. *If This Is a Man and The Truce* (New York: Abacus, 1988), 177.

9 Levi, *If*, 32.

10 Giorgio Agamben, *Remnants of Auschwitz: The Witness and the Archive*, Trans. Daniel Heller-Roazen (New York: Zone Books, 2002), 101.

the social, namely his experience as victim. The slippage between the tortured-subject and his location in post-Auschwitz society results in an 'extreme *loneliness*' that refuses to accept a social reality that does not include negation and impossibility.[11] Responding to the psychological reading of the traumatised subject as 'warped', Améry suggests that this type of damaged or 'warped' subjectivity may offer insight into how dominant culture marginalises those in pain. For Améry, according to psychologists and moralists:

> The character traits that make up our personality are distorted. ... It is said that we are 'warped'. That causes me to recall fleetingly the way my arms were twisted high behind my back when they tortured me. But it also sets me the task of defining anew our warped state, namely as a form of the human condition that morally as well as historically is of a higher order than that of healthy straightness.[12]

Améry subverts the pejorative judgment of his subjectivity as 'warped' and appropriates the term (perhaps even valorises it) by conflating it with the narrative of his warped, tortured body. The rhetorical move may lack 'tact'[13] and may upset the 'extreme politeness'[14] of those who live in peace, untouched by the terrors of torture, but for Améry, the simple politeness, the cleanliness of the social creates an arena in which the victim's experience is coded as uncanny. In this realm, marvellous unreality is rejected and reformulated to defer that which threatens the tenets of polite Western sociality: 'The social body is occupied merely with safeguarding itself and could not care less about a life that has been damaged'.[15] Améry argues that the social, even its well-meaning components, needs to become disordered, for living within a social world where touching absence (and reminding others that this absence, this negation, this unreality does indeed exist as a necessary part of the real) is considered unhealthy or sick does not amount to living at all. The traumatic real, the torture Améry experienced and experiences 'revolt[s] against reality'[16] in an effort to allow trauma to be read as marvellous.

---

11 Jean Améry, *At the Mind's Limits: Contemplations by a Survivor on Auschwitz and Its Realities*, Trans. Sidney Rosenfeld and Stella P. Rosenfeld (Bloomington: Indiana UP, 1980), 70.

12 Améry, 68.

13 Ibid., 63.

14 Ibid., 62.

15 Ibid., 70.

16 Ibid., 72.

Like Améry, Charlotte Delbo writes herself as a ghost in a post-holocaust world, haunting both private and public spheres in an effort to puncture the normal and create a cultural space for her traumatised existence and memory. In his introduction to Delbo's trilogy *Auschwitz and After*, Langer situates Delbo as a writer who reveals the 'disfigured form' of the human image as well as the 'horror that [has] defaced it'.[17] By constructing 'a genre of discourse to pierce the skin of memory, to expose a naked self divested of its heroic garments, a self cold, filthy, gaunt, the victim of unbearable pain',[18] she allows us to 'gain access to this inconceivable reality'.[19] Her work establishes the negation of Levi and provides textual cues that intimate the mental operations necessary to reconceptualise the human and the real in such a way as to open a cultural space for Améry's warped subjectivity.

Upon her arrival at Auschwitz, Delbo remarks upon the unambiguous demarcation point between her old reality and the unreality of her new world: 'Ferried over to another world, we are subject to drawing breath in another life, we the living dead caught in ice, light, silence'.[20] She denotes this other world as fantastic and admits that she has forgotten 'the reflexes of the normal human being face-to-face with the preposterous'.[21] In a fantastic tableau, she observes 'mannequins' in the snow as 'Naked. Stacked side by side. White, a bluish whiteness against the snow. Heads shaved, pubic hair straight and stiff. The corpses are frozen'.[22] I insist that the images of the corpses within these moments should not be taken primarily as metaphor, as uncanny reminders of the moonlit dead freezing in snow or how unreal such images may *seem*. Certainly, the term 'dummy' or 'mannequin' functions as a metaphor to describe the state of the bodies; however, from Delbo's point of view, now encased within the marvellous realm of Auschwitz, she perceives or imagines she perceives movement in the dolls: 'Look. I'm sure she moved. That one, next to the last. Her hand ... her fingers are opening'.[23] From a comfortable home, reading descriptions of corpses that seem to move would clearly and understandably be coded as figurative images, conceits used to create the impression of a seemingly unreal atmosphere. However, this is not the type of world in which Delbo lived. After witnessing and experiencing the impossible-but-actual events

17 Langer, Introduction to *Auschwitz and After*, xvi.
18 Ibid., xiii.
19 Ibid., xvii.
20 Delbo, *Auschwitz and After*, 32.
21 Ibid., 37.
22 Ibid., 17.
23 Ibid., 19.

and effects of being stripped from one's universe and displaced in a hell of estranging language, casual violence, bios absent of culture, torture, thirst and hunger, and a sea of dead and emaciated bodies, the potential movement of the mannequin does not function as metaphor but as an empirical possibility.

Perhaps even more disorienting and potentially traumatic as the (un)life of the camps, the dislocation of herself back into the normal, social sphere deserves focusing on. Once the unreal nature of the camps becomes part of her subjectivity, it does not leave; in fact, the journey 'home' exacerbates it. She has been 'blurred spectral [...] become ghostly by the journey home'[24] where she discovers 'an abyss between the world and [her]self'[25] that remains a present and insistent part of her survival. She finds herself 'floating in a present devoid of reality',[26] and she makes 'no effort to return to the surface of reality'.[27] Like Améry, who resists becoming subsumed into the social, Delbo nurtures her spectral self by exploring the porous relationship between the worlds she lived in before Auschwitz, within Auschwitz, and afterwards:

> I've come back from another world/to this world/I have not left/and I know not/which one is real/tell me did I really come back/from the other world?/As far as I'm concerned/I'm still there/dying there/a little more each day/dying over again/the death of those who died.[28]

The mental geography of Auschwitz intermingles with both her memory and experience of the social, constructing a universe of multivalent time and space, corpses and ghosts, that enables her spectral subjectivity to inhabit the subjective positions of her old comrades. She comingles traces of herself with others in an effort to reset the coordinates of reality, making the marvellous central and relegating the reality of the social to the margins. Here, Delbo displays the disruptive and traumatic intrusion of social reality into the marvellous unreal. In the voice of her comrade Mado, she claims: 'I'm not alive. I'm imprisoned in memories and repetitions';[29] 'I'm not alive. I died in Auschwitz but no one knows it'.[30] And in the voice of her comrade Ida, she states: 'There was a ghost inside me wanting to adhere to its double yet unable to do so'.[31] Both instances

24 Ibid., 235.
25 Ibid., 181.
26 Ibid., 237.
27 Ibid., 238.
28 Ibid., 224.
29 Ibid., 261.
30 Ibid., 267.
31 Ibid., 299.

point toward twin inabilities: an inability to leave the unreal of the camps and an inability to become part of the reality of the social. Delbo's subjectivity becomes a possessing spectre hungry to be rendered real and whole but capable only of an incessant splitting. Instead of offering fruitful opportunities to find a site from which to emerge into a socially-recognised person, these hauntings offer only more pathways back to the traces of herself that died in the camps. This would not be so damaging if Auschwitz itself were not confined within the contemporary imagination as an uncanny site of past terrors, terrible but understood. Without a marvellous space in which to breathe, Delbo's ghosts remain trapped, not just within her own past but within the fantasy of the past that the contemporary has dreamt for her.

Unlike such testimony, which readers assume takes place in the same flesh-and-blood reality in which they reside, fantastic literature that privileges the marvellous offers entrance into a realm which *is not* but *is*. The reader venturing into this space knows that the events described in the narrative point to a multivalent universe, the levels of which are interpreted simultaneously. First, the narrative illustrates the experientially impossible, positioning the narrative in an anti-realm, one that does not in any way purport to be anything other than fictional but nonetheless is bound by the internal reality of narrative logic and laws. Once the anti-realm is entered, its marvellous elements take on not only literal but metaphoric (not necessarily allegorical) power. The metaphoric authority resonates both within the narrative as well as within the semiotic matrix of experiential history, thus charging the narrative with a negative trace of the historical trauma that allows us to interact with the unreality of the event through alternative means. While fantastic literature is frequently criticised as unliterary and escapist, it explores realities of pain and loss with an engagement open to what eludes knowing, giving readers access to fears that refuse to be simply aestheticised or compartmentalised. I argue that this literature performs the complicated task of taking seriously alternate points of view in which the feelings of the traumatised subject are no longer distant but unavoidably present. It positions its readers within fictional spaces in which fear and anxiety are dominant emotions but which can also be controlled, either temporarily (the page can always be turned) or more effectively, by learning to endure the unknowable. By fostering intimate interaction with radical otherness and dramatising events at the very edge of understanding, these texts demonstrate the possibility of surviving within trauma, even if fear is perpetual. Rather than dismissing such works as escapist, they should be valued for facilitating imaginative movements that open us to the mental and social operations necessary to overcome isolation and compensate for loss.

Winner of both the Hugo and Nebula awards for 'Best Novel', Paolo Bacigalupi's *The Windup Girl* (2009) imagines a post-apocalyptic future on the verge of economic, political, and ecological transformation. While the novel foregrounds the military and political manoeuvrings responsible for both the world's fall and eminent renewal, its plot hinges on the personal predicaments and decisions of a sexually-abused android. The eponymous windup girl, Emiko, provides the opportunity for the reader to consider the novel's political and ecological concerns through the ethical and social possibilities that become available once larger systems of influence and control become destabilised. These systems are founded upon unquestioned anthropocentric assumptions regarding the natural and the human. As Andrew Hageman explains, central to the novel 'is belief in a transcendental concept of "Nature" as an identifiable thing that must be preserved and revered. And folded into this idea of "Nature" is the belief in a stable definition of the "human being" and its place atop the hierarchy of "Nature" '.[32] To destabilise these assumptions, Bacigalupi employs the well-known generic tropes of genetic engineering and posthuman subjectivities to construct a narrative platform from which to assert a mode of ethics that reconsiders the relations between society and the trauma survivor. Bacigalupi refers to Emiko as a being that not only resists ontological classification but national and species identification as well, marking her as an interstitial creature: often aligned with the cheshires (genetically modified cats), she is described as a dog as well as an insect under a magnifying glass; twice her heart becomes a hummingbird; called 'animal' by her abusers and rapists, she is neither Japanese nor Taiwanese. While trying to 'pass' for human in daylight she is almost killed for being ' "some other creature" '.[33]

Bacigalupi's depictions of Emiko's abuse and her relationship with Anderson Lake reveal the limits of empathy between the reader and the survivor of trauma. Instead of contextualising rape and sexual violence within the dominant narratives of abuse and healing that permeate our culture – narratives which often mythologise, reduce, medicalise, or expunge the idiosyncratic pain of victims – Emiko's narrative takes place in an imagined realm of experiential impossibilities. Laura E. Tanner argues in *Intimate Violence* that what the reader encounters in scenes of sexual violence becomes 'suspended between material and semiotic worlds' that play between the victim's material body and the cultural and semiotic systems that construct both subjectivity

32 Andrew Hageman, 'The Challenge of Imagining Ecological Futures: Paolo Bacigalupi's *The Windup Girl*', *Science Fiction Studies* 39 (2012): 283–303, 284.

33 Paolo Bacigalupi, *The Windup Girl* (San Francisco: Night Shade Books, 2009), 107.

and narrative.[34] With this in mind, Emiko is a literary depiction of an android in an imagined future, a being we can neither understand nor know. Since she is a part of a speculative narrative, we know that she is not *meant* to stand mimetically for an actual victim. Precisely this distance and displacement makes Emiko such a significant figure in engaging trauma. She exists as site of displacement wherein readers feel 'safely' removed from the 'realities' of trauma – a set of coordinates that allow us to escape our prefigured notions of pain, sex, rape, and identity.

Emiko certainly operates as metaphor, but she also brings the reader into a multivalent engagement with the pain of the other by foregrounding our utter inability to know this pain. The recognition of our empathetic limitation makes the fantastic depiction of an impossible and unknowable trauma so effective. It maps an analogue of the *actual* distance between the reader and the traumatised subject – we do not pretend to understand an actuality, but we place ourselves in a position wherein we must imagine it. By doing so, we experience a traumatic intrusion into our lives, one that does not stand for the trauma of others but hurts us directly with our complicit consent. The pain, discomfort, disorientation we feel at Emiko's abuse is not a response to a metaphor for someone else's pain, nor is it a fantasy of empathic connection – it is the multivalent pain of experiencing our inability to empathise while experiencing the literary and imaginative realities of Emiko's trauma and her responses to it.

Emiko is introduced moments before her 'humiliation' – a time she uses to consider the disparate elements of her traumatised subjectivity. Emiko wonders if 'the part that struggles to maintain her illusion of self-respect is the part intent upon her destruction. If her body, this collection of cells and manipulated DNA – with its own stronger, more practical needs – is actually the survivor: the one with will'.[35] The dualism present in Emiko's thinking results from her indoctrination into dominant cultural attitudes regarding windups. According to prevailing wisdom, there are two parts to windup nature: 'The evil half, ruled by the animal hungers of their genes … and the civilised self, the side that knows the difference between niche and animal urge'.[36] Because she is a self-aware android, an 'artificial' creation, the notion that her consciousness, her 'I', is not necessarily 'hers' at all enables Emiko to explore beyond the limits of her subjectivity. If her consciousness results from cognitive programming as well as cultural indoctrination and her body from genetic programming, then

34 Laura E. Tanner, *Intimate Violence: Reading Rape and Torture in Twentieth-Century Fiction* (Bloomington: Indiana UP, 1994), 3.

35 Bacigalupi, *The Windup Girl*, 34.

36 Ibid., 154.

either half of this dualistic 'nature' is not necessarily 'her'. Bacigalupi introduces Emiko with this moment of her testing the boundaries of her subjectivity so that, throughout the novel, she, along with the reader via Anderson Lake, can experiment with other notions of identity and subjectivity that must necessarily include an affective speculation regarding the other. Emiko's crisis of subjectivity comes directly before her public rape and humiliation, coding the abuse as the instigating factor not only to her fragmentation but her awareness of it. Through pain, she comes to consider the 'nature' of her identity to try to understand her social coordinates.

The two scenes that depict Emiko's sexual trauma build from these ontological inquiries use them not only to critique a culture of belittling rhetoric and misogynistic attitudes, but also to explore the ways in which the post-traumatic subject operates beyond the boundaries of traditional notions of human subjectivity. As Tanner explains, 'Violence ... has the capacity to destroy not only the form of the victim's body but the familiar forms of understanding through which that victim constructs him- or herself as subject'.[37] She continues to clarify that victims of sexual assault often assert an essential humanity as a defence against violence – a call to the anthropocentric bonds that exist transcendentally between attacker and victim. Emiko has no such recourse. Even the attempt made by many victims to posit 'a distinction between body and mind'[38] becomes subverted by this android subject. Bacigalupi does not focus on the physical discomfort or pain Emiko is forced to go through. Rather, he stays centred on her cognitive manoeuvring regarding her internal and public identities. More than the acts of penetration, 'She can feel the crowd's eyes on her, a physical thing, molesting her. She is utterly exposed'.[39] This exposure to the desubjectifying gazes of the crowd is compounded with the restrictions placed on her body: 'men are holding her down, hands on her ankles and wrists'.[40] These physical, social, and psychological bonds each merge, constructing an ontological casing for Emiko rooted in degradation, pain, and shame. Moreover, this shame is an inbuilt aspect of Emiko's constructed being – her body is engineered to experience climax despite abuse (it is even intimated that she must have an orgasm as a physical response to rape and degradation):

> Kanninka's fingers join the jade between Emiko's legs, play at Emiko's core. Emiko's shame builds. [...] Emiko moans as her body betrays her.

37 Tanner, *Intimate Violence*, 4.

38 Ibid., 5.

39 Bacigalupi, *The Windup Girl*, 37.

40 Ibid., 38.

> [...] She cannot control it no matter how much she despises it. The scientists will not allow her even this small disobedience. She comes.[41]

The ontological exploration described before as a conscious deliberation is here performed as a public spectacle of forced desire and power. Emiko rebels against this programming but then feels shame at the very act of rebellion.

Emiko's crisis of subjectivity takes a turn when she begins a sexual/romantic relationship with Anderson Lake. Their relationship demonstrates the transformative power of allowing oneself to participate in a vulnerable being-with the other. Anderson sees Emiko as 'A hothouse flower, dropped into a world too harsh for her delicate heritage. ... Perhaps it was that vulnerability that moved him, her pretended strength when she had nothing at all'.[42] For Anderson, Emiko is always vulnerable, a creature not suitable to the cultural or ecological worlds she is forced to inhabit. While Anderson's vision of Emiko is tinged by a male fantasy of playing the saviour and thus legitimising a type of authority over his object of desire, it nonetheless results in breaking down his perspectives of social relationships and identity. When Emiko responds to his kindness with sexual advances, Anderson wonders, 'Does she wish this? Or only acquiesce? Is she even capable of refusing?'[43] These inquiries certainly comment on his ego and need to verify his sexual attractiveness and power, but, more importantly, as he engages with Emiko he recognises the cultural conditioning that he suffers from and considers alternatives. He attempts to understand how the other functions, which enables him to witness '[h]er soul, emerging from within the strangling strands of her engineered DNA'.[44]

For Emiko, her relationship with Anderson offers a means by which to individuate within a cultural framework. Crucially, for Bacigalupi's vision of traumatised subjectivity, this coming into being is not viewed as an ontological end but an unsatisfying limitation. While with Anderson, 'she feels entirely human'.[45] For a time, it enables her to rewrite the script of her social roles, talk to herself as if more than property. However, while this may seem to conclude a Bildungsroman – the windup girl finally made human via her 'loving' relationship with a human – this 'becoming human' functions as a limitation to Emiko. The second scene in which Emiko is shown raped and tortured becomes transformative in that Emiko now embodies a consciousness that transcends

41 Ibid., 38.
42 Ibid., 61.
43 Ibid., 115.
44 Ibid., 184.
45 Ibid., 221.

anthropocentric humanism and works to protect herself. The wounds inflicted are not to an indoctrinated android but to a burgeoning subjectivity at least partially 'humanised' via Anderson's kindness. When Kannika asks the audience if they'd like to 'Fuck the windup girl', Emiko verbalises her clear rebellion: 'No'.[46] This time, when her hands and ankles are bound by anonymous men and Kannika 'calls her a slut and a dog and a nasty windup toy',[47] Emiko is pained differently, and so is the reader.[48]

No longer witnessing the humiliation of an artificial consciousness, we witness the rape of a vulnerable being. Bacigalupi describes the internal ramifications of the abuse through animal metaphor: 'the falcon if there is any falcon in Emiko at all, if it ever existed, is a dead thing, dangling. Not meant to live or fly or escape. Meant to do nothing but submit'.[49] Emiko's desire for suicide, evinced in her request to the janitor to throw her away, becomes a prelude not to self-destruction or abdication but to a profound, if violent, agency – a rejection and rebellion against an entire system of normalcy.[50] When her boss reprimands her for harassing the janitor and pressing him to help her escape to the North where there may or may not be communities made entirely of windups, Emiko loses the last vestiges of 'human' hope. 'And she thinks that some things are worse than dying. Some things can never be borne'.[51] The thought that being unborn is worse than dying brings Emiko beyond the anthropocentric guidelines of her programming. By sinking beneath an ontology of the human subject and allowing herself to touch the coordinates of the unborn, Emiko empowers herself to violate her self. Bacigalupi marks this desubjectification by altering the narrative point of view, removing the reader from Emiko's perspective and describing the murderous aftermath in declarative, objective terms, suggesting that the consciousness we have come to know as

46 Ibid., 256.

47 Ibid., 256.

48 Cassie Pedersen's analysis of trauma's dual temporal structure included in this volume, 'One Moment Too Late', helps deepening our understanding of Emiko's traumatic experience. As Pedersen clarifies, one does not experience traces of the traumatic until some point in the future, when a new encounter provides a framework for an earlier encounter. Paradoxically, these events are not experienced chronologically; rather, they fall into an asynchronic dialogic circuit that both facilitates and obscures one's understanding of the traumatic experience.

49 Bacigalupi, op.cit., 257.

50 Brencio and Novak's 'The Continuum of Trauma', included in this volume, charts the ways in which trauma is often an impetus for criminal action. Emiko's trauma drives her to act out against a universe of pain and degredation as embodied by the individuals who abuse her.

51 Bacigalupi, op.cit., 259.

readers has been at least partially erased. In this way, Bacigalupi constructs an encounter between the reader and the deconstructed android cogito – a space of deep traumatic resonance that offers a sideshadow of the moment when traumatic rupture occurs.

Like the reader, Anderson understands the impossibility of empathising with Emiko, so he opens himself to an affective unsettlement. The next time we see Emiko after her murder of her abusers and the other state officials, she stands silent and bloodied outside of Anderson Lake's door. Anderson tries in kindness to remove her clothing but she stops him, slashing him violently while repeating her previous declaration of rejection: 'No!'[52] The rejection of what she perceives as a sexual advance, or at least an action that could have sexual consequences, becomes a profound moment of power for Emiko that affords her a social presence.[53] When Anderson hears that Emiko might be responsible for the murders at the sex club, he refuses to believe it until he remembers two images of her. The first: '*Emiko in bed, huddled. Sobbing. Her body torn and scratched*'.[54] The second: 'a wraith of movement and feral grace'.[55] In these two depictions, Bacigalupi allows Anderson, and thus the reader, to connect Emiko's vulnerable suffering at the ramifications of her public abuse and humiliation to her extra-human being as something both ghostly and animalistic. More importantly, Anderson comes to understand the ways in which Emiko's pain has become transformative for both of them. For her, it deconstructs her simulacral human status and impels a formulation of a posthuman identity as neither natural nor cultural. For him, it allows a space of openness, a way to be vulnerable to the unknown pain of the other.

Their final scene together involves strange compassion and reversals of power. Not until Anderson is moments from death does he speak to Emiko about her motivations for killing her abusers. She explains: 'I did not know. They hurt me. I was angry. I didn't know'.[56] She frames her experiences of hurt and anger with a lack of knowledge or understanding and, by doing so, evinces her ability to be traumatised as an act that transcends the human.

52 Ibid., 266.

53 In his chapter on 'Working with Addiction and Trauma: Mental Health Therapists Reflect on Their Use of Spirituality' included in this volume, Peter Bray argues that trauma can lead to a type of self actualisation, clarifying how struggling with the existential crises brought on by traumatic experiences can lead survivors to construct new beliefs and goals.

54 Bacigalupi, *op.cit.*, 271.

55 Ibid., 273.

56 Ibid., 239.

Not meant to belittle her reaction, but quite the reverse, such reading demonstrates Bacigalupi's ability to make the android a being that consistently resists anthropocentric thinking. Emiko's removed position from human drama establishes her power in the final scene, a fact made poignant by Bacigalupi with the entrance of cheshires: genetically modified cats that scavenge the wastes of Thailand for carrion while fading chameleon-like in and out of their environments. An animalistic analogue to Baudrillardian simulacra, the cheshires have replaced 'natural' domestic cats within twenty years of their introduction into the bioshphere and are now almost universally despised as unnatural pests. The cheshires were originally created as 'A party favor for' a gene-ripper's daughter 'when the little princess turned as old as Lewis Carroll's Alice'.[57] Aligning these creatures through both name and narrative history with Carroll's archetypal figure of literary fantasy (Dinah/the Cheshire Cat, and the real/fictional Alice Liddell), Bacigalupi positions the animal as a human construction, an appellation used to comingle the real, the literary, and the fantastical. Pointedly, Emiko finds sympathy with these little real/literary/fantastical beasts because, like her, 'They are too much improved for this world'.[58] They can not simply survive beyond their 'natural' counterparts; they exist successfully in multiple arenas that mark their specialised position for Emiko. The novel's treatment of the animal as a multivalent being removed from, but linked to, the 'real animals' known to the reader enables us to register multiple levels of reality – a manoeuvre that becomes essential to engage with Emiko's traumatised subjectivity. After attempting to shoo the scavenger away, Anderson tells her to let it stay. While possibly simply taken as an abdication of life and a sense of apathy for what happens afterward, I take it as an extraordinary act of vulnerability and care. The cheshire as metonym for Emiko will feed on Anderson's corpse – a tableau indicating Anderson's mindful acceptance of a new paradigm of subjectivity and power. After opening himself up to Emiko's pain, vulnerability, and transformation, Anderson turns himself into a sacrifice for the edification of a new world that allows space for the warped subjectivity of the survivor.

I conclude by suggesting that the rhetorical strategies of the fantastic, as employed in both holocaust survivor testimony and popular literature of the fantastic, may instigate what Eric Santner defines as 'homeopathic traumas' – 'lesser' traumas instigated via literary and cinematic texts that generate a space in which readers become distanced from the extraordinarily habitualising

57 Ibid., 26.
58 Ibid., 113.

power of the everyday.[59] By intruding upon and reconfiguring the reality of the reader, trauma literature itself can hurt, pain, wound, traumatise readers, employing a rhetoric of the fantastic in tandem with textual traces of historical wounds to dismantle and work beyond such stabilising concepts as world, person, history, event, etc. Because of many readers' readiness to accept the reality of witness testimony and realistic narrative *based on a true story* without considering narrative and linguistic mediation, well-intentioned realistic narratives may fall victim to fetishisation and political disempowerment by aligning the marvellous realities described in such work as simply uncanny. However, when read as fantastic, narratives may inscribe marvellous narratives into the present and create original homeopathic traumas that do not attempt to stand directly for historical events but enter into a negative arena. Here, traumatic moments, removed from the realms of realism and history, are re-contextualised within an explicitly fantastic universe. Adapted as a fantastic narrative, they penetrate the reader's consciousness through a psychological and ideological mimeticism of the marvellous. The wounds these texts write into the public consciousness have the authority to legitimise the traumatic marvellous as an occasion to rewrite the scripts of the human and the real, facilitating a tear away from the psychic comforts of normalcy and rescripting a more vulnerable relationship between self and other.

When read with an openness to the marvellous, narratives that engage trauma might be used in an effort to *avoid* making trauma real; instead, they might be read to make the human and the social *unreal*. Perhaps then we can breach our ontological and social borders and struggle to co-construct imaginary bridges between our lives as readers and those unknowable realms inhabited by survivors. Of course, such passages will not be for us to venture over – the gates to the other side of history and experience are immutable – but by remaining open to such connections, we knowingly and willingly invite ourselves to be haunted, not by the ghosts of the dead and the traces of the traumatised, but by their stories. If we accept this invitation, as I think we must, then we must also let go of our most cherished assumptions about what it means to be human. After all, our responsibility when we read the traumatic fantastic in willing unbelief lies in the creation of a world hospitable not to us or our imagined needs, but to the unknowable pain and confusion of phantoms.

59 Eric L. Santner, 'History Beyond the Pleasure Principle: Some Thoughts on the Representation of Trauma', *Probing the Limits of Representation: Nazism and the 'Final Solution',* ed. S. Friedlander (Cambridge: Harvard UP, 1992), 144.

Bibliography

Agamben, Giorgio. *Remnants of Auschwitz: The Witness and the Archive*. Trans. Daniel Heller-Roazen. New York: Zone Books, 2002.

Améry, Jean. *At the Mind's Limits: Contemplations by a Survivor on Auschwitz and Its Realities*. Trans. Sidney Rosenfeld and Stella P. Rosenfeld. Bloomington: Indiana UP, 1980.

Bacigalupi, Paolo. *The Windup Girl*. San Francisco: Night Shade Books, 2009.

Delbo, Charlotte. *Auschwitz and After*. New Haven: Yale UP, 1995.

Hageman, Andrew. 'The Challenge of Imagining Ecological Futures: Paolo Bacigalupi's *The Windup Girl*'. *Science Fiction Studies* 39 (2012): 283–303.

Langer, Lawrence. *Holocaust Testimonies: The Ruins of Memory*. New Haven: Yale UP, 1991.

Langer, Lawrence. 'Introduction'. *Auschwitz and After*, by Charlotte Delbo, edited by Lawrence Langer, ix–xviii. New Haven: Yale UP, 1995.

Levi, Primo. *The Drowned and the Saved*. New York: Vintage, 1989.

Levi, Primo. *If This Is a Man and The Truce*. New York: Abacus, 1988.

Santner, Eric, L. 'History Beyond the Pleasure Principle: Some Thoughts on the Representation of Trauma'. *Probing the Limits of Representation: Nazism and the 'Final Solution'*, edited by S. Friedlander, 143–54. Cambridge: Harvard UP, 1992.

Tanner, Laura E. *Intimate Violence: Reading Rape and Torture in Twentieth-Century Fiction*. Bloomington: Indiana UP, 1994.

CHAPTER 4

Through the Looking-Glass: Child Sexual Abuse from the Inside-Out

Jacqueline Linder

Abstract

Existing clinical literature on childhood sexual abuse (CSA) typically explores the topic from an etic or 'outside-in' perspective. This is done through the use of diagnostic labels and theories that seek to describe the outcomes of CSA from the clinician's, researcher's, or observer's point of view. While there is merit in understanding the problem from an objective lens, the experience of sexual abuse is an intimate and personal one. As such, explorations of the topic must include an emic, phenomenological, or 'inside-out' perspective. Failure to privilege survivors' voices within the scholarly discourse on CSA results in a sanitized conversation about a topic that is inherently dangerous. To better understand the problem of CSA, we have to be willing to write dangerously and read dangerously. This chapter explores the impact of sexual abuse from the dangerous lens of the survivor's lived experience. First-person vignettes from the author's own life are interwoven with excerpts from Lewis Carroll's novel *Through the Looking-Glass*.

Keywords

childhood – sexual abuse – CSA – trauma – soul loss – psychospiritual

1 A Sort of Mist

My very first memory of sexual violation is a fragmented one interspersed with shadow. I was approximately three years old. I remember a favourite aunt with long, beautiful hair that I loved to play with. I remember happiness when she took me by the hand during one of my parents' parties and led me down the dark hallway to their bedroom. I remember the feel of shoes pressing into my back as Aunt Lily laid me on the closet floor and harvested my innocence.

Judith Herman writes that 'certain violations of the social compact are too terrible to utter aloud; this is the meaning of the word *unspeakable*'.[1] Perhaps the most unspeakable aspect of my first sexual assault was not that it was painful but that it ruptured my access to everyday normalcy. As I lay in the dark staring up at my mother's clothing, I entered the world of the *upside down* and, quite possibly, have never returned.

As a trauma psychologist, researcher and CSA survivor, I see in clinical literature an unfortunate tendency to sanitize the horror of sexual abuse. Cold diagnostic labels such as posttraumatic stress disorder (PTSD), dissociation and depression in no way capture the magnitude of harm experienced by many survivors. If we wish to better understand and treat the impact of CSA, it becomes necessary to privilege survivors' voices within the scholarly discourse, because their lived experiences represent crucial streams of historical, retrospective data. In contrast, scholars without direct experience of CSA are limited to exploring the topic in much the same way that ethnographers describe the exotic cultures they visit. While the etic or outsider's perspective is valuable as it interprets cultures in ways that make them accessible to other outsiders, cultural insiders understand that considerable detail, nuance and texture are omitted from the outsider narrative.

In a field where the rights of the research subject or participant are an ongoing concern, it is also worth reflecting on the ethics of appropriation in relation to the CSA experience. Concerns about appropriation typically arise in relation to vulnerable cultural groups. CSA survivors clearly meet the test of vulnerability and can, therefore, be legitimately described as a marginalized population. In this context, it is necessary to consider whether scholars who are not survivors have the *moral right* to build careers focused on an experience they have not lived and whose most insidious implications they may never truly understand.

In *Decolonizing Methodologies*, Tuhiwai Smith explores the idea of insider knowledge as a commodity that was 'discovered, extracted, appropriated and distributed'[2] by cultural outsiders during the Age of Enlightenment. Such problematic approaches to the acquisition of knowledge should give us pause as they bear a striking resemblance to the way trauma researchers including myself currently advance our field. While I believe the acquisition of knowledge is necessary and inevitable, I am undecided as to whether such powerful,

1 Judith Herman, *Trauma and Recovery: The Aftermath of Violence from Domestic Abuse to Political Terror* (New York: Basic Books, 1992), 1.

2 Linda Tuhiwai Smith, *Decolonizing Methodologies: Research and Indigenous Peoples*, 2nd ed. (London: Zed Books, 2012), 61.

intimate, perhaps even sacred knowledge, should ever be accessed by the uninitiated.

Lewis Carroll's novel *Through the Looking-Glass* provides a useful metaphor for understanding the gap between the etic and emic perspectives.[3] The story of Alice, a little girl who steps through a mirror into a topsy-turvy world, parallels the experience of non-survivors who enter the secret domain of CSA to find that nothing is as it seems. In sharing vignettes of my own abuse, I intend to facilitate my reader's access to a more visceral understanding of the survivor experience. I will use *Through the Looking-Glass* as both a container and map as together we traverse this perilous kingdom.

2 Looking-Glass House

In their review of the existing literature on CSA, Martin and Silverstone found that more than 95% of survivors do not disclose their abuse to the authorities.[4] Such percentages seem incomprehensible in a culture with the protection of children embedded within the rule of law. Survivors of CSA understand better than anyone else, however, that the laws of the public domain and the laws of the private domain have very little in common.

Through the Looking-Glass opens with young Alice playing with her kittens. Gazing at the mirror hanging over the family fireplace, she wonders what the world on the other side is like. Climbing up on the mantel, Alice begins poking at the mirror and soon finds herself stepping through the glass into an inverted world.[5] Thus begin her adventures in a land filled with extraordinary people, places and things. The landscape is laid out like a chessboard. Her objective is to make her way to the eighth square and be made a queen. Before she steps through the mirror, Alice says to Kitty: 'there's the room you can see through the Looking-Glass – that's just the same as our drawing-room, only the things go the other way'.[6] In other words, the grounding assumptions of the Looking-Glass House are quite the opposite of the house Alice comes from. When she enters this alternate domain, she finds that the most basic conventions of the

3 Lewis Carroll, *Through the Looking-Glass and What Alice Found There* (Singapore: Pan Macmillan's Children's Books, 1992), 8.

4 Erin Martin and Peter Silverstone, 'How Much Child Sexual Abuse is "Below the Surface" and Can We Help Adults Identify It Early?', *Frontiers of Psychiatry* 4.58 (2013): 1, doi: 10.3389/fpsyt.2013.00058.

5 Carroll, 'Looking-Glass', 11.

6 Ibid., 8.

world she has known are suspended. Because she is prepared to abandon the idea of familiarity as a predictor of safety, she is able to relinquish her attachment to *that which should be* in favour of *that which is*.

Like Alice, children who live in families where abuse is common live in a world of inversion where the norms of everyday society are fundamentally irrelevant. That outsiders fail to notice this may have something to do with the banality of the family construct along with society's desire to retain the myth of families as inherently safe. To be fair, highly dysfunctional families quite often look normal from the outside. The archetypal, nuclear North American family unit of father, mother, siblings and pet is also, in many ways, the foundation of Western society. Embracing the reality that this prototype of goodness conceals all manner of evil could be destabilizing to the social fabric upon which we all depend.[7]

In his discussion on *Obedience to authority*, Philip Zimbardo notes:

> We are controlled not by the physical strength of adversaries but by the symbols, rules, and words manipulated by those of our own kind. The technology of behavior control begins with the subtle family processes involved in "civilizing" infants to be "good," "acceptable" children.[8]

It is important to notice here that nowhere in this civilizing process has society accounted for the reality that an undetermined portion of its membership consists of sexual predators who target children. In the attempt to stabilize the macro-structure of society then, we have inadvertently *groomed our own children into vulnerability through indiscriminate obedience to authority*. Stanley Milgram's work offers one of the best examples of this. He found that up to 65% of people can be manipulated into giving another person apparently lethal shocks when instructed to do so by someone in authority.[9] Imagine then the dilemma faced by a child, in whose eyes most adults possess absolute power. Survivors often sense that the adult controlling them is doing something bad, but realising it does not mean challenging the commands of someone with power.

Indiscriminate obedience to authority extends from the family hierarchy to society at large, where political, religious, and business leaders are blindly

7 Azubike Felix Uzoka, 'The Myth of the Nuclear Family: Historical Background and Clinical Implications', *American Psychologist* 34.11 (1979): 1095–1106.

8 Philip Zimbardo, 'Obedience to authority', *American Psychologist* 29.7 (1974): 566.

9 Jack Martin, 'Ernest Becker and Stanley Milgram: Twentieth-century Students of Evil', *History of Psychology* 19.1 (2016): 3–21, doi: 10.1037/hop0000016.

obeyed by millions of their constituents. With such a deeply ingrained obedience, any act of resistance against it must be viewed as heroic because, by virtue of its collusion, society is thoroughly implicated in the ongoing violation of its most vulnerable members.

In stark contrast to this guilty naivety, Toni Vinci invites a pose of 'willing unbelief'[10] that allows us to acknowledge the limits of our understanding in relation to pain and loss.[11] The Looking-Glass House of sexual abuse is riddled with guilt, shame, secrecy, violence and exploitation. *That* is the world we enter into when we dare to study CSA and we must be prepared to engage with that reality, should we *truly* wish to understand this type of trauma. Such dark voyages are not for the faint of heart, however, and they should probably be guided by those who know the way.

3 The Corkscrew Path

The whiskey-flavoured taste of betrayal as my Uncle Sammy forced his tongue down my throat broke something in me. I, who so carefully scrutinized all adults in my environment, had not seen this coming. The night it happened, my mother had been very angry for reasons none of us remember. Uncle Sammy offered to take my brother and me to his house so she could have an evening to herself. I was delighted, as Uncle Sammy was a trusted father figure. I had spent many evenings snuggled in his lap as the adults around us drank, cursed and chattered on about politics. Uncle Sammy never cursed and was always gentle and kind to me.

When we got to his house, it never once occurred to me that I was not safe. Then things took a decidedly unexpected turn. Uncle Sammy tucked my brother and me into his bed instead of in the guest room. I was annoyed because I got stuck in the middle. I always hated sleeping between my mother and brother because it was so hot! Grumpily settling in and contemplating the endless frustrations of my seven-year-old world, I froze when uncle Sammy pulled out his gun and started showing my brother how to use it. The shot he fired into the ceiling shocked me into stillness, but no more so than when he rolled over and pressed me into the mattress as my brother lay beside us in frozen, guilty silence. In that moment of quiet despair, I realized I did not know my Uncle

---

10 Tony Vinci, 'A World of Death and Phantoms': Auschwitz, Androids, and the Ethical Demands of Reading Trauma and the Fantastic in Willing Unbelief', in this volume.

11 Ibid.

Sammy at all. His avuncular persona had effectively cloaked his true identity as a stealthy hunter with a deeply disturbed mind.

When Alice tries to explore the Garden of Live Flowers in the Looking-Glass world, she finds herself wandering in circles and getting no closer to her destination.[12] Just so, child survivors of sexual abuse spend inordinate amounts of time seeking safe harbour in relationships with people who have not *yet* offended against them. The risk is their inability to discern, until far too late, the sleeping predators hidden behind benign masks. Like all prey in the natural kingdom, then, CSA survivors adopt a range of strategies to help them avoid danger. This includes the use of appeasement behaviours designed to induce compassion in the offender so as to reduce the frequency and intensity of the assaults.[13] It goes without saying that those strategies rarely succeed as the Uncle Sammys of the world invariably find our meagre hiding places and ruthlessly use our attempts to please against us. Along these lines, Cassie Pedersen describes trauma as a failed experience simply impossible to assimilate fully at the time it occurs.[14]

4 Getting Invisible

In my personal experience as a survivor of CSA, the essential aspect of self some might call the soul can die. When Alice first steps through the Looking-Glass, she comes across several chess pieces in the cinders of the drawing-room hearth. Among the pieces she finds the Red King and Queen and the White King and Queen. As she watches them walking about, she has a surprising realization: '… "I don't think they can hear me", she went on, as she put her head closer down, "and I'm nearly sure they ca'n't [sic] see me. I feel somehow as if I was getting invisible" '.[15] Like Alice, many CSA survivors in families with caregivers not available to support them experience some magical aspect of the self within fading away. Eyes of innocence that should sparkle like diamonds inevitably become dull, flat and empty.

12 Carroll, 'Looking-Glass', 22.

13 Chris Cantor and John Price, 'Traumatic Entrapment, Appeasement and Complex Post-traumatic Stress Disorder: Evolutionary Perspectives of Hostage Reactions, Domestic Abuse and the Stockholm Syndrome', *Australian & New Zealand Journal of Psychiatry* 41.5 (2007): 377–384, doi: 10.1080/00048670701261178.

14 Cassie Pedersen, 'Encountering Trauma 'Too Soon' and 'Too Late': Caruth, Laplanche, and the Freudian Nachträglichkeit', in this volume.

15 Cantor and Price, 'Traumatic Entrapment', 13.

In my dissertation, I define soul as the 'nucleus or structural hub in the architecture of the survivor's self'.[16] Soul loss is defined as the 'felt sense of psychological decompensation experienced at the deepest level of the survivor's identity'.[17] The anthropological literature has long been familiar with the concept of soul loss and contains extensive discussions on the subject. My dissertation presented an attempt to translate soul loss into Western clinical terms and elucidate a more nuanced understanding of the impact of CSA.

In 2014, I completed my qualitative research study on the psychospiritual injury of sexual abuse in 12 adult, female survivors. Thematic Content Analysis and a range of other techniques were used to analyse the transcripts of the semi-structured interviews. Thematic Content Analysis involves identifying and categorizing meaningful thematic patterns within the data set that help to answer one's research question. Despite the small sample size, the results identified a large spectrum of rarely acknowledged injury in this population, including soul wounding, soul withering, soul shattering, soul flight, soul theft and soul murder.[18] Soul Wounding involves 'a discrete injury to the most essential level of the survivor's being',[19] whereas Soul Withering feels as if 'one's soul has shrivelled slowly over time'.[20] Soul Shattering describes the feeling that 'a part of the self's core has been broken into pieces',[21] while Soul Theft feels like 'the perpetrator has stolen the survivor's soul from her very body'.[22] In Soul Flight, the survivor feels as if 'one's soul has voluntarily left one's body'.[23] Finally, Soul Murder involves the 'annihilation of the survivor's core sense of self. In this form of psychospiritual injury, the innermost level of identity is destroyed'.[24] Despite the evidence that CSA causes lasting harm to many survivors, however, one should note that some escape their circumstances, recover, and go on to fully embrace the whimsy of childhood.

---

16 Jacqueline Linder, 'The Psychospiritual Impact of Childhood Sexual Abuse (CSA) on Women who Experienced CSA as Soul Loss' (PhD diss., Institute of Transpersonal Psychology, 2014), 58.

17 Linder, 'Psychospiritual', iii.

18 Ibid.

19 Ibid., 273.

20 Ibid., 299.

21 Ibid., 301.

22 Ibid., 279.

23 Ibid., 304.

24 Ibid., 285.

5 Nothing to Cry About

I too wanted to be a ballerina, twirling across the stage in my sparkling tiara and gown. As I sat in the audience listening to the applause, I gazed with longing at the line of dancers that included my two playmates. *Their* mother had sent them to be trained in ballet. *Their* grandmother sewed costume after costume so they could curtsey to an adoring crowd in all their shimmering glory. I had no such beauty in my life, no such treasures, no such love … and I hungered.

Knocking on the door of my playmates' home, Grandpa Fred opened the door and invited me in. I had come to play with his granddaughters, Lisa and Megan, as I had done so many times before. We had been friends since early childhood and Grandpa Fred was a familiar presence always somewhere in the background. He told me to follow him into the house even though the girls were not home. When he led me down the hall to his bedroom, I was puzzled but not afraid. Then, in one fluid motion, he lifted me onto the bed, pushed me onto my back, and pulled down my panties. During the subsequent assault, I stared immobilized at the glittering ballerina dresses hanging on the wall behind him. Splayed out like a wax mannequin, cold, wet, and exposed, I fixated on the fairy-like costumes … and I hungered.

When Grandpa Fred was done with me, he pulled my panties on without a word. He stared at me and I stared at him. I knew he had done something very wrong; that he had taken something forbidden from me and a debt was owed. Unbidden, the words fell from my lips, 'I want to wear one of the dresses'. He barked 'No', led me out of the house, then closed the door in my face. I was devastated, humiliated, enraged. My first thought was, 'I've been robbed'. My next thought was, 'I'm a whore'.

When Alice meets Tweedledee and Tweedledum inside the looking glass, she discovers that the twins' every utterance is diametrically opposed. The sameness of their appearance combined with their radically different views is reminiscent of a split personality disorder. After Grandpa Fred's assault, I too felt split down the middle, my shock and outrage over what had happened warring with the horror of my collusion. Each time I thought about my failed attempt to bargain with him, I wanted to shrivel up and disappear. At one point, Tweedledee sagely advises Alice, 'You wo'n't [sic] make yourself a bit realer [sic] by crying … there's nothing to cry about'.[25] I never cried after what Grandpa Fred did to me, but the self-loathing I felt at what I had done was a fetid ball of shame at the core of my being.

---

25 Carroll, 'Looking-Glass', 75.

The root meaning of the word shame is associated with the idea of concealment and covering things up.[26] Herman describes shame as a 'chronic state of humiliation that distorts [survivors'] view[s] of self and others'.[27] Shame has both a public aspect associated with being socially dishonoured and a private aspect related to self and identity.[28] The shame I experienced after Grandpa Fred's assault and my failed attempt at justice, fundamentally altered my view of myself. By asking to wear one of the ballerina dresses, I believed I had given de-facto consent to the assault. Prepared to sell my silence for the price of a glittering gown, there was no question in my mind that I was complicit in the crime.

The Compass of Shame identifies four ways that individuals cope with shame experiences including: 1) the Attack Self pole, where shame messages are magnified and turned into self-contempt and anger; 2) the Withdrawal pole, where internalized shame manifests as anxiety and sadness; 3) the Avoidance pole, where shame is suppressed and masked by apparent happiness or excitement; 4) and the Attack Other pole, where shame is deflected and manifests as outward aggression.[29] A second model that explores how we deal with feelings of shame includes: 1) Prevention using fantasy or dependence; 2) Escape using withdrawal or misdirection; and 3) employing aggression or self-harm to manage shame.[30]

Nearly forty years after Grandpa Fred's assault, I now understand that I handled the trauma using both the Attack Self strategy of self-blame and the prevention strategy of fantasy creation. In response to that experience among others, I developed a private universe filled with magic and monsters, a psychic landscape of the seemingly impossible that remains with me to this day.

6 Six Impossible Things

One of the most psychologically dangerous experiences a CSA survivor can endure is to be victimized by two or more offenders within a single family or

26 Stephen Pattison, *Shame: Theory, Therapy, Theology* (Cambridge: Cambridge University Press, 2000).

27 Judith Herman, 'Shattered Shame States and Their Repair', *Shattered States: Disorganised Attachment and its Repair,* eds. Judy Yellin and Kate White (London; Karnac Books, 2012), 159.

28 David Konstan, 'Shame in Ancient Greece', *Social Research* 70.4 (2003): 1031–1060.

29 Donald Nathanson, *Shame and Pride: Affect, Sex, and the Birth of the Self* (New York: W. W. Norton & Company, 1992).

30 Michelle Schoenleber and Howard Berenbaum, 'Aversion and Proneness to Shame in Self- and Informant-Reported Personality Disorder Symptoms', *Personality Disorders* 3.3 (2012): 294–304, doi: 10.1037/a0025654.

group. While being targeted by one paedophile is always horrific, the secretive isolation within which such abuse occurs helps signal to the child the wrongness of the situation. When two or more paedophiles target the same child, however, the victim ends up feeling that something is wrong with *her.* To be fair, what are the odds that more than one sexual deviant could be produced by a single family? From this perspective, it seems reasonable for children to assume they are responsible for attracting multiple predators.

In the Looking Glass world, during a conversation with Alice, the White Queen remarks, 'Why, sometimes I've believed as many as six impossible things before breakfast ...!'[31] I suspect one would need such a casual acceptance of the impossible to believe that three of four sons of one of my mother's friends all offended against me. Trevor was the oldest brother of my babysitter Gregory and my mother sometimes dropped my brother and I off at their house on her way to work. One memorable day, even though I screamed and cried begging her not to leave me behind, she dashed away in a frenzy while I sobbed at the top of the stairs. Later that day, to my shock and confusion, Trevor dragged me into a closet and sexually assaulted me. I had been expecting an attack from Gregory not Trevor. Trapped in the dark and plundered in forbidden places, my only thought was, 'not you too!' Although I remember clearly being pulled into the closet, I have no recollection of coming out. The psychological dissociation I experienced that day was something I would continue to struggle with for many years.

Dissociation, arguably one of the least understood psychological conditions, involves a disruption of the functions of consciousness fostering a coherent sense of self.[32] Sexual violence is also the form of interpersonal violence most likely to induce dissociation.[33] In my personal view, it results from the body literally becoming the scene of the crime and the only way to escape is for the survivor to abandon the body itself. Brencio and Novak note that a defining feature of trauma is its disruption of temporality, which causes survivors to feel as if their suffering is frozen in an eternal present.[34]

As a trauma specialist, I routinely counsel clients experiencing depersonalization, a type of dissociation that results in a persistent sense of detachment from

---

31 Carroll, 'Looking-Glass', 92.

32 Daphne Simeon, 'Depersonalization disorder: A contemporary overview', *CNS Drugs* 18.6 (2004): 343–354, doi: 10.2165/00023210-200418060-00002.

33 John Briere and Natacha Godbout, 'Does Type of Trauma Predict Type of Dissociation? Is All Dissociation Posttraumatic?' (Paper presented at the American Psychological Association 2011 Convention, Washington, D.C., 4–7 August, 2011).

34 Francesca Brencio and Kori Novak, 'The Continuum of Trauma', in this volume.

one's body or mind.[35] Derealisation, involving chronic feelings of detachment from the outer world, is another type of dissociation commonly observed in survivors.[36] Although transient dissociation is a relatively normal occurrence,[37] a significant prevalence of traumatic dissociation exists in people with mental health issues.[38] In extreme cases of early abuse, some clients also present symptoms of structural dissociation, which can be thought of as a fragmentation of the survivors' personality architecture.[39] The diagnostic label most closely associated with this internal state is known as Dissociative Identity Disorder. In addition to CSA, disruptions in the nurturing bond between a caregiver and child can result in internalized shame and compromised identity development.[40]

Psychological dissociation has neurological underpinnings that result from ongoing exposure to interpersonal trauma.[41] Exploring these functional brain abnormalities represents some of the most exciting areas of modern trauma research. To those in the dissociative state, however, the most striking aspect of the disorder lies in the profound sense of isolation and separateness. Survivors experience the world around them as if the segregation induced by the sexual abuse is mirrored at the biological level. Because CSA typically occurs early in the life-span, alienation from self and the world is all that many survivors know. For them, dissociation is such an integral coping strategy that it is entwined in the personality, fusing trauma and identity.[42]

7 I Know My Name Now

My sexual abuse at the hands of Gregory, the middle son, went on for some years. He generously offered to babysit whenever my mother was working

35 American Psychiatric Association, *Diagnostic and Statistical Manual of Mental Disorders*, 5th ed. (Arlington: APA, 2013).

36 Ibid.

37 Simeon, 'Depersonalization disorder'.

38 Brad Foote, Yvette Smolin, Margaret Kaplan, Michael Legatt, and Deborah Lipschitz, 'Prevalence of dissociative disorders in psychiatric outpatients', *American Journal of Psychiatry* 163.4 (2006): 623–629.

39 Ellert Nijenhuis, Onno van der Hart and Kathy Steele, 'Trauma-related Structural Dissociation of the Personality', *Activitas Nervosa Superior* 52.1 (2010): 1–23, doi: 10.1007/BF03379560.

40 Allan Schore, *Affect regulation and the origin of the self: The neurobiology of emotional development* (New York: Psychology Press, 1994).

41 Paul Frewen and Ruth Lanius, 'Neurobiology of Dissociation: Unity and Disunity in Mind–Body–Brain', *Psychiatric Clinics of North America* 29.1 (2006):113–128, doi: 10.1016/j.psc.2005.10.016.

42 Nijenhuis et al., 'Trauma-related Structural Dissociation'.

late, which happened often. Whenever he came to our house, Gregory loved to play hide-and-seek. He had an uncanny knack for finding my hiding places and whenever he caught me alone, he made the most of the opportunity. He became my most prodigious and dedicated instructor of learned helplessness, a state of mind where individuals who repeatedly fail to escape aversive situations come to believe in the impossibility of escape.[43] Whenever Gregory walked in our front door with his cheerful laughter and smiling eyes, a grey wave of hollow resignation would sweep over me. I had nothing left within me with which to experience fear. Instead, I began to strategize about what I could do to get the inevitable assault over with as quickly as possible. One of my dear counselling clients once said to me during a session: 'When you've been raped as often as I have, it's just not that big a deal'. Despite the differences in our ages and genders, he and I gazed at one another in perfect understanding.

As Alice steadfastly makes her way towards the eighth square of the Looking-Glass chessboard, she stumbles upon a wood 'where things have no names'.[44] Entering the wood, she forgets who she is until a Fawn, having also lost its memory, wanders over. The Fawn coaxes Alice to leave the wood and together they make their way to a field where their memories are reclaimed. Like Alice and the Fawn, children trapped in a web of repeated sexual violation can also lose their identities. However, sometimes a moment of serendipity arises, and we find our liberation unexpectedly at hand.

I no longer remember exactly how I reached my breaking point. Within the context of chronic CSA, multiple assaults eventually bleed into one another, refracting backwards and forwards in the survivor's consciousness until the skeins of memory become a tangled ball. I do remember clearly the feeling of being truly and utterly *done* with my situation. I remember Gregory sitting in a chair to my brother's right in the very bedroom where I had so often been assaulted. I marched up to him and demanded aggressively: 'How old are you?' He was completely taken aback and replied in a surprised voice: 'I'm 18'. Leaning forward I met and held his eyes hissing: '*Well I'm eight. What do you see in me?*'

Peter Bray notes that, for mythic heroes, what is most worthy within them often emerges only as they traverse the perilous way.[45] He adds that spirituality

43 Martin Seligman and Steven Maier, 'Failure to Escape Traumatic Shock', *Journal of Experimental Psychology* 74.1 (1967): 1–9, doi: 10.1037/h0024514.

44 Carroll, 'Looking-Glass', 55.

45 Peter Bray, 'Campbell's Monomyth and the Journey to Post-traumatic Growth: Hamlet, the Hero and the Client' (Paper presented at Trauma 6 Conference, Inter-Disciplinary.Net, Budapest, Hungary, 11–13 March 2016).

presents an important resource in trauma recovery.[46] Characteristics traditionally associated with heroic figures include courage, integrity, altruism, honesty, selflessness, determination, helpfulness, protectiveness, conviction, being inspiring, and saving others.[47] In the case of CSA, however, I would argue that an equally important domain of heroism lies in Truth-speaking. This is because in the sticky web of familial and societal collusion that makes CSA possible, speaking the truth is both a dangerous and creative act. A new identity emerges when the survivor names the abuse, as she or he takes the step from being a nameless, helpless, invisible victim to someone embracing individual agency. That such dark truths frequently come to light in unplanned, even accidental moments of action, does not make them any less heroic. In the final analysis, heroes are who they are based on the *results* of their actions. Truth-speakers shatter the compact of silence surrounding the more sinister proclivities of the human condition and, by doing so, force society to see itself with ruthless clarity.

After our clash of wills, Gregory never touched me again. Neither did any of my other offenders for that matter. There is a moment in the lives of many survivors when we realize we can simply go no further down the path of suffering. One way or another we *shall* be free, even if we must pay for the attempt with our lives. During our moment of confrontation, Gregory understood that he had finally lost all power over me. In a gambit born of raw desperation, I had made my bid for freedom and won.

8 Having Seen Each Other

In Alice's adventures on the other side of the Looking-Glass, Lewis Carroll deftly introduces a world of whimsy, innocence, and magic that, once upon a time, many of us wanted to visit. For this reason, it may be uncomfortable to dwell too closely on what some believe was Carroll's own problematic relationship with children. Certainly, his close relationship with the Liddell sisters, the youngest of whom served as the inspiration for Alice, has been looked upon in recent years with a considerably more jaundiced eye.[48]

---

46 Peter Bray, 'Working with Addiction and Trauma: Mental Health Therapists Reflect on their use of Spirituality', in this volume.

47 Elaine Kinsella, Timothy Ritchie, and Eric Igou, 'Zeroing in on Heroes: A Prototype Analysis of Hero Features', *Journal of Personality and Social Psychology* 108.1 (2015): 114–127, doi: 10.1037/a0038463.

48 Terry Ramsey, 'The Secret World of Lewis Carroll, Review: "Excellent" ', *The Telegraph*, 16 April 2016, Viewed on 20 April 2016, http://www.telegraph.co.uk/culture/tvandradio/tv-and-radio-reviews/11380814/The-Secret-World-of-Lewis-Carroll-review.html.

This chapter adopts a subversive reading of Alice's story because the juxtaposition of magical innocence against the background of CSA presents an excellent metaphor for the contrast between those pleasant families we see in our communities every day and the reality of what may be going on behind their closed doors. Carroll's tale gives us the opportunity to enter into Alice's world and understand her experiences from an emic or 'inside-out' perspective. The ongoing discourse on CSA also presents an opportunity to privilege the insider narrative. If our goal is to fully understand survivors' experiences, we have to be willing to step through the Looking-Glass into their *real* world, one that bears little resemblance to any we would choose to live in.

When Alice stumbles across a Unicorn during her travels, both she and the Unicorn are completely astonished. They resist the reality confronting them because neither possesses a framework that allows for the other to exist. Just so, survivors and non-survivors often study one another in abject fascination from opposite sides of a chasm. On some occasions, survivors will risk inviting a non-survivor into their inner world. However, such attempts at rapprochement are not always met with success. Non-survivors are often prevented from stepping through the Looking-Glass by their lack of readiness to accept humanity's infinite capacity for darkness. If it were not so, however, there would not be millions of survivors in the world today. In order to enrich the existing discourse on CSA, what is needed is a mutual leap of faith. In the immortal words of Alice's Unicorn: 'If you'll believe in me, I'll believe in you. Is that a bargain?'[49]

Bibliography

American Psychiatric Association. *Diagnostic and Statistical Manual of Mental Disorders*, 5th ed. Arlington: APA, 2013.

Bray, Peter. 'Campbell's Monomyth and the Journey to Post-traumatic Growth: Hamlet, the Hero and the Client'. Paper presented at the Trauma 6 Conference, Inter-Disciplinary.Net, Budapest, Hungary, 11–13 March 2016.

Briere, John, and Natacha Godbout. 'Does Type of Trauma Predict Type of Dissociation? Is All Dissociation Posttraumatic? Paper presented at the American Psychological Association 2011 Convention, Washington, D.C., 4–7 August 2011.

Cantor, Chris, and John Price. 'Traumatic Entrapment, Appeasement and Complex Post-traumatic Stress Disorder: Evolutionary Perspectives of Hostage Reactions, Domestic Abuse and the Stockholm Syndrome'. *Australian & New Zealand Journal of Psychiatry* 41.5 (2007): 377–384. doi: 10.1080/00048670701261178.

49 Carroll, 'Looking-Glass', 137.

Carroll, Lewis. *Through the Looking-Glass and What Alice Found There*. Singapore: Pan Macmillan's Children's Books, 1992.

Foote, Brad, Yvette Smolin, Margaret Kaplan, Michael Legatt, and Deborah Lipschitz. 'Prevalence of dissociative disorders in psychiatric outpatients'. *American Journal of Psychiatry* 163.4 (2006): 623–629.

Frewen, Paul, and Ruth Lanius. 'Neurobiology of Dissociation: Unity and Disunity in Mind–Body–Brain'. *Psychiatric Clinics of North America* 29.1 (2006):113–128. doi: 10.1016/j.psc.2005.10.016.

Herman, Judith. 'Shattered Shame States and Their Repair'. *Shattered States: Disorganised Attachment and Its Repair,* eds. Judy Yellin and Kate White (London: Karnac Books, 2012), 157–170.

Herman, Judith. *Trauma and Recovery: The Aftermath of Violence from Domestic Abuse to Political Terror*. New York: Basic Books, 1992.

Kinsella, Elaine, Timothy Ritchie, and Eric Igou. 'Zeroing in on Heroes: A Prototype Analysis of Hero Features'. *Journal of Personality and Social Psychology* 108:1 (2015): 114–127. doi: 10.1037/a0038463.

Konstan, David. 'Shame in Ancient Greece'. *Social Research* 70.4 (2003): 1031–1060.

Linder, Jacqueline. 'The Psychospiritual Impact of Childhood Sexual Abuse (CSA) on Women who Experienced CSA as Soul Loss'. PhD diss., Institute of Transpersonal Psychology, 2014.

Martin, Erin, and Peter Silverstone. 'How Much Child Sexual Abuse is "Below the Surface" and Can We Help Adults Identify It Early?' *Frontiers of Psychiatry* 4.58 (2013): 1–10. doi: 10.3389/fpsyt.2013.00058.

Martin, Jack. 'Ernest Becker and Stanley Milgram: Twentieth-century Students of Evil'. *History of Psychology* 19.1 (2016): 3–21. doi: 10.1037/hop0000016.

Nathanson, Donald. *Shame and Pride: Affect, Sex, and the Birth of the Self*. New York: W. W. Norton & Company, 1992.

Nijenhuis, Ellert, Onno van der Hart and Kathy Steele. 'Trauma-related Structural Dissociation of the Personality'. *Activitas Nervosa Superior* 52.1 (2010): 1–23. doi: 10.1007/BF03379560.

Pattison, Stephen. *Shame: Theory, Therapy, Theology*. Cambridge: Cambridge University Press, 2000.

Ramsey, Terry. 'The Secret World of Lewis Carroll, Review: "Excellent."' *The Telegraph*, April 16, 2016. Viewed on 20 April 2016, http://www.telegraph.co.uk/culture/tvandradio/tv-and-radio-reviews/11380814/The-Secret-World-of-Lewis-Carroll-review.html.

Schoenleber, Michelle, and Howard Berenbaum. 'Aversion and Proneness to Shame in Self- and Informant-Reported Personality Disorder Symptoms'. *Personality Disorders* 3.3 (2012): 294–304. doi: 10.1037/a0025654.

Schore, Allan. *Affect Regulation and the Origin of the Self: The neurobiology of Emotional Development*. New York: Psychology Press, 1994.

Seligman, Martin, and Steven Maier. 'Failure to Escape Traumatic Shock'. *Journal of Experimental Psychology* 74.1 (1967): 1–9. doi: 10.1037/h0024514.

Simeon, Daphne. 'Depersonalization disorder: A contemporary overview'. *CNS Drugs* 18.6 (2004): 343–354. doi: 1172–7047/04/0006-0343/$31.00/0.

Tuhiwai Smith, Linda. *Decolonizing Methodologies: Research and Indigenous Peoples*. 2nd ed. London: Zed Books, 2012.

Uzoka, Azubike Felix. 'The Myth of the Nuclear Family: Historical Background and Clinical Implications'. *American Psychologist* 34.11 (1979): 1095–1106.

Zimbardo, Philip. 'Obedience to authority'. *American Psychologist* 29.7 (1974): 566–567.

CHAPTER 5

Working with Addiction and Trauma: Mental Health Professionals Reflect on Their Use of Spirituality

Peter Bray

Abstract

The following chapter reports on a series of discussions held over a twelve-month period with a group of New Zealand mental health professionals working with clients who have alcohol and substance addictions. Having a common understanding that addiction could be a form of survival behaviour activated by traumatic events, the group wanted to examine how spirituality as a developmental asset could be more fully utilised in the process of recovery. As most of the participating therapists work in a setting influenced by the medical model they also wanted to understand to what extent their spiritually-focussed professional practices might fit in with, or contradict, institutional expectations. As members of the group freely disclosed their own spirituality and their professional relationships with clients and the institution, they began to value the positive benefits of their own non-denominational spirit-led practices. In addition, by recognising self-actualisation as a potent component of this survival process, they perceived that addiction and recovery are likely to be catalysed by spirituality. Thus, by exploring the significance of spirituality in clients' presentations and identifying similar principles and beliefs that might underpin their own professional practices, the participants felt a stronger theme resonating deeply with them. It suggested that trauma, in forcing individuals down less effective pathways to the achievement or recovery of higher levels of consciousness, may significantly disrupt human beings' tendencies to actualise. Addiction, therefore, although conceived by the group as a false or unwelcome outcome of the struggle to meaning – a detour in the journey to actualisation – was simultaneously regarded as an adaptive process that might reconnect clients with their lost potentials.

Keywords

addiction – counselling – co-existing problems – competence – growth – mental health – New Zealand – recovery – self-actualisation – spirituality – trauma

1 Introduction

Trauma and addiction are uniquely linked.[1] It is estimated that the incidence of alcohol and substance addiction in individuals in the general population affected by stressful life events, such as physical and sexual traumas, is greater than those who have not.[2] Evidence also strongly suggests that individuals with co-existing problems (CEP) of mental health use drugs and alcohol to avoid and/or to suppress the distressing effects of trauma. Such substance abusing lifestyles making them increasingly vulnerable to further traumas.[3] Consequently, clients treated for substance addiction may also benefit from trauma services and *vice versa*. Traumatic events force people to question their existence and spiritual beliefs. Addressed sympathetically psychological and behavioural wellbeing are likely to improve.[4] In her chapter, Jaqueline Linder suggests that, as a wound, trauma is often felt deeply in the psycho-spiritual dimension.[5]

Spirituality is an important factor in predicting recovery and improving addiction treatment outcomes. In cases where recovery has been effectively

---

1 Center for Substance Abuse Treatment, 'Anxiety Disorders', in *Assessment and Treatment of Patients with Coexisting Mental Illness and Alcohol and Other Drug Abuse: Treatment Improvement Protocol (TIP) Series No. 9, DHHS Publication No. SMA 95–3061* (Rockville, MD: Substance Abuse and Mental Health Services Administration, 1994), viewed 19 August, 2018, https://www.ncbi.nlm.nih.gov/books/NBK64659; Office of Applied Studies, Substance Abuse and Mental Health Services Administration (SAMHSA), 'Mental Health Screenings and Trauma-Related Counseling in Substance Abuse Treatment Facilities', *The N-SSATS Report*, September 30, 2010; Center for Substance Abuse Treatment, *Trauma-Informed Care in Behavioral Health Service: Treatment Improvement Protocol (TIP) Series No. 57, DHHS Publication No. SMA 14–4816* (Rockville, MD: Substance Abuse and Mental Health Services Administration, 2014), 19 August, 2018, https://www.ncbi.nlm.nih.gov/books/NBK207201/.

2 Louise Langman and Man Cheung Chung suggest that the incidence falls within a range of 15–55% higher than the general population. Louise Langman and Man Cheung Chung, 'The Relationship Between Forgiveness, Spirituality, Traumatic Guilt and Posttraumatic Stress Disorder (PTSD) among People with Addiction', *The Psychiatric Quarterly* 84 (2013): 11–26; Lori Keyser-Marcus, et al., 'Trauma, Gender, and Mental Health Symptoms in Individuals with Substance Use Disorders', *Journal of Interpersonal Violence* 30.1 (2014), 3–24.

3 Martina Reynolds, et al., 'Co-Morbid Post-Traumatic Stress Disorder in a Substance Misusing Clinical Population', *Drug and Alcohol Dependence* 77 (2005): 251.

4 Alan N. Baroody, 'Spirituality and Trauma during a Time of War: A Systemic Approach to Pastoral Care and Counseling', in *Families Under Fire: Systemic Therapy With Military Families*, eds. R. Blaine Everson and Charles R. Figley (New York: Routledge, 2010), 165–190; Peter Bray, 'A Broader Framework for Exploring the Influence of Spiritual Experience in the Wake of Stressful Life Events: Examining Connections Between Posttraumatic Growth and Psycho-Spiritual Transformation', *Mental Health, Religion and Culture* 13 (2010): 293–308.

5 See Jaqueline Linder's contribution to this volume, 'Through the Looking-Glass: Child Sexual Abuse from the Inside-Out'.

maintained, increasing levels of spirituality have been recorded between the times of treatment entry and the individual's release.[6] Consequently, recovery from addiction, arguably a parallel to post-traumatic growth processes, depends on the management of behaviour change that successfully resolves struggles with existential meaning, and the construction of durable life narratives.[7] Thus interventions that utilise the individual's spiritual resources can provide support and strength in effectively assisting clients to resolve addiction, traumatic responses and other CEPs.[8] Despite the difficulty of evaluating interventions that involve spiritual, those that incorporate non-denominational approaches appear to be effective at reducing trauma symptoms.[9]

The chapter provides some background and the context of one group of health professionals in New Zealand and incorporates their personal and professional reflections on spirituality and its relevance to their practice. Here they discuss their experiences of trauma and spiritual work with clients affected by alcohol and substance addictions.

2 A Special Interest Discussion Group on Spirituality

2.1 *The Group*

A few years ago, I was invited to give a workshop at an addictions centre in New Zealand on spiritual emergence and emergency.[10] The audience of mental health professionals, therapists and their clients was small but highly engaged by the material, which linked trauma and spirituality together with the potential for post-traumatic growth. Subsequently, the centre invited me to lead a series of ten ninety-minute conversations with their clinical team aimed at 'freely examining the role of spirituality post-trauma with clients who had been traumatised by life events and had turned to alcohol and substance addictions'.[11] At the time, the group of nine professionals were employed by the local health board's mental health and addictions service to provide specialised therapeutic and assessment

6 Adrienne J. Heinz, et al., 'A Focus-Group Study on Spirituality and Substance-Abuse Treatment', *Substance Use Misuse* 45.1–2 (2010): 134–153.

7 Lawrence G. Calhoun and Richard G. Tedeschi, eds., *Handbook of Posttraumatic Growth: Research and Practice* (Mahwah, NJ: Lawrence Erlbaum Associates, 2006).

8 Langman and Chung, op. cit. 12.

9 Center for Substance Abuse Treatment, *Trauma-Informed Care*, 104–105.

10 Stanislav Grof and Christina Grof, eds., *Spiritual Emergency: When Personal Transformation Becomes a Crisis* (New York: G. P. Putnam's Sons, 1989).

11 These, and subsequent, unreferenced comments were recorded by group members who agreed to make them available for discussion and dissemination.

interventions. Although broadly experienced and trained, the group perceived that their practice in the centre was guided and informed by the simple assertion that 'addiction is a chronic relapsing brain disease characterised by compulsive behaviour'.[12] This then translates into psychological and physical harm in individuals, their families and communities. Significantly, as a group they wanted to understand how their knowledge of spirituality might penetrate their clients' complex psychological defences and assist in their processes of recovery.[13]

As registered health professionals and highly experienced addictions workers they confirmed that almost all of their clients were troubled by mental health CEPs, particularly PTSD and Axis II disorders.[14] As one member of the group explained, 'I have yet to meet a person who doesn't have a reason for addiction'. In short, clients have active mood, anxiety, personality, and eating disorders, as well as PTSD characterised by persistent trauma symptom including blunted emotional responses, hyper-arousal, and flashbacks.[15] These make their drug-free residents particularly vulnerable to stigmatising myths and prejudices about 'addicts'. They may also lead clients back to addictions, crime, violence, injury, and accidents and further traumatising events that, even in the absence of PTSD, can precipitate relapse in recovering addicts.[16] In their study of childhood trauma and dissociation in patients with alcohol and drug dependence, Ingo Schafer and her colleagues confirm that the patients had been exposed to high levels of early potentially traumatic experiences.[17] As one group member explained:

> Issues in early development like the trauma of abandonment are very important in our work. Traumas created by ruptures in attachment can

12 Benita Walton-Moss, Ellen M. Ray, and Kathleen Woodruff, 'Relationship of Spirituality or Religion to Recovery from Substance Abuse: A Systematic Review', *Journal of Addictions Nursing* 24.4 (2013): 224–225.

13 Harold E. Doweiko, 'Substance Use Disorders as a Symptom of a Spiritual Disease', in *Addiction and Spirituality: A Multidisciplinary Approach*, eds. Oliver J. Morgan and Merle Jordan (St. Louis: Chalice Press, 1999), 51.

14 Andrew McGarrol. '2014 Matua Raki Workforce Innovation Award', *Hawke's Bay District Health Board* (2014): 10.

15 Marian L. Logrip, Eric P. Zorrilla, and George F. Koob, 'Stress Modulation of Drug Self-Administration: Implications for Addiction Comorbidity with Post-Traumatic Stress Disorder', *Neuropharmacology* 62 (2012): 552–564.

16 Marc Galanter, 'Spirituality and Addiction: A Research and Clinical Perspective', *The American Journal on Addictions*, 15 (2006): 290; Logrip, Zorrilla, and Koob, 'Stress Modulation of Drug Self-Administration', 552–553; Reynolds, et al., 'Co-Morbid Post-Traumatic Stress Disorder', 251.

17 Ingo Schafer, et al., 'Childhood Trauma and Dissociation in Patients with Alcohol Dependence and Drug Dependence, or Both: A Multi-Centre Study', *Drug and Alcohol Dependence* 109 (2010): 87–88.

> present themselves in adulthood as addiction. One client was raised by heroin users in her first five years and the damage it caused is happening right now in our sessions as an adult … the whole family gets recreated here … she's lost the middle ground because there has been no bridging.

Over time as our conversations extended into spirituality, addictions, and trauma, a genuine need to examine the impact of the members' spiritual experiences on their professional practices became clear. It initiated a good deal of self-reflection and comment. From the outset, as group members seemed relatively receptive to spiritual ideas and comfortable with their own spirituality, they could recognise its value as a potential resource for their clients.[18] Surprisingly, the group was very excited about examining spirituality in practice. Studies of health professionals tend to show a reluctance to discuss or use spiritual interventions, considering them as belonging 'more to the private than to the public dimension of their own approach to the treatment of "addictions" '.[19]

Nevertheless, although engaged by the project, the group's clinicians were cautious about being identified as participants. They did not wish to offend their institution's clinical expectations by aligning themselves too much with their clients' psychological positions. As one of the group put it, 'How much of ourselves, the person and the clinician, are we to acknowledge and accommodate in our future discussions? I fear disclosing my spiritual side to the institution, to judgement'. Consequently, the group agreed to talk anonymously about their spirituality and its impact on their work in addictions and mental health, and trauma, and recovery. They confirmed that they used spiritual resources in their counselling, as an intervention whilst recognising that 'It is still an uncomfortable fit with the medical model' and was not a demonstrable part of their practice. Even after a century, it seems, what William James called 'medical materialism'[20] still influences therapeutic practice at a grass roots level.

18 Julie Savage and Sarah Armstrong, 'Developing Competence in Spiritual and Religious Aspects of Counseling', in *Handbook of Multicultural Counseling Competencies,* eds. Jennifer A. Erickson Cornish, et al. (Hoboken, NJ: John Wiley, 2010), 379–413.

19 Valeria Zavan and Patrizia Scuderi, 'Perception of the Role of Spirituality and Religiosity in the Addiction Treatment Program Among the Italian Health Professionals: A Pilot Study', *Substance Use & Misuse* 48 (2013): 1157–1160.

20 William James, *The Varieties of Religious Experience* (New York: Modern Library, 1929). Here James explains psychology's difficulties to fully explain or articulate noetic religious and spiritual experience.

2.2 *The Mental Health and Addictions Treatment Centre*

The centre manages clients from diverse socio-economic backgrounds and ethnicities who do not have healthy environments to grow up in, cannot make healthy choices, or are afflicted by external traumatic events which have disempowered them. The team work intensively with clients assessed by community services as meeting the Diagnostic and Statistical Manual of Mental Disorders (DSM IV) definition for substance dependence: 'a pattern of repeated self-administration that can result in tolerance, withdrawal, and compulsive drug-taking behaviour'.[21] The advantage of this screening is that team members 'have the privilege of working with substance-free clients' motivated toward recovery and 'get to know people really well'. Because of the relationship between substance use and trauma-related mental health problems, it is useful to determine whether or not a client is suffering from a trauma-related illness.[22] Residents are admitted with moderate to severe spectrum addiction and CEPs such as depression, anxiety, and PTSD that interfere with their day-to-day living. However, limited research shows the effectiveness of integrated treatment models at reducing substance abuse, PTSD symptoms, and other mental disorder symptoms.[23] As one of the group explained,

> What we are really trying to get to are the behaviours that guide clients' addictive behaviours. Looking at the cause as well as the effect ... We don't often talk about drugs and alcohol but we do talk about behaviour and the things that led to substance use – these are just as much a part of the addictive behaviours as using the substances.

The centre works with a number of Māori clients and explicitly incorporates bicultural approaches that respect cultural practices and beliefs, and the staff have regular cultural training. Individuals who access the centre receive wrap-around care and are connected to wider services in primary care, mental health, family and other community agencies. A partnership with local and regional Kaupapa Māori health services provides a supportive pathway into treatment for Māori and ensures access to Kaupapa services, kaumatua/elders and cultural interventions identified in the client's Recovery Action Plan (RAP)[24]

---

21 American Psychological Association, *Diagnostic and Statistical Manual of Mental Disorders*, 4th ed. (Washington: American Psychiatric Association, 2000), 192.

22 Center for Substance Abuse Treatment, 'Anxiety Disorders'.

23 Center for Substance Abuse Treatment, *Trauma-Informed Care*, 93.

24 Mental Health and Addictions Service, 'Recovery Action Plan'. (Unpublished document): 1–5.

and clinical monthly review. According to the centre's statistics, this approach has proved effective for Māori, who are more likely to complete the programme than non-Māori.

Clients are admitted into a stringent eight-week residential programme where they receive person-centred and cognitive behavioural therapy, contingency management, CEP case formulation and motivational interviewing training. Therapists work with clients to develop skills to manage addiction by the time they are discharged.[25] As the programme meets the clinical service and organisational requirements of its parent institution, the staff are keen to develop a pragmatic and integrative service that responds holistically to the fullest range of client experiences, which means including and attending to spirituality. Unfortunately, most of the team echoes the statement 'I don't have anyone I can trust that material [spirituality] within the medical model of practice'. Thus, the group provides an opportunity to focus on personal and clinical concerns and to examine the utility of spirituality as a positive resource in their future work with clients.

2.3 *Pathways to Recovery*

Clients work with the therapeutic team in their first week at the centre to acclimatise themselves to residential living. At this time, the team identifies potential risks or issues concerning social interactions and health, or limiting factors to positive participation in the programme. The staff employ eight 'essential recovery components … designed to encourage the client to move towards managing his or her own recovery through increasing self-awareness, improving self-care and strengthening supports', in addition to the RAP. Clients attend to the 'Spiritual and Cultural' area in their plan, and our group showed particular interest in how they might work with this in a more effective manner.[26] Previously, counsellors had interpreted this aspect of their work quite narrowly with clients but used our discussions as permission to step outside their clinical remit and reinterpret their clients' 'church and religious activities in broader spiritual terms'. Strongly influenced by the medical model of practice, our groups suggested that the only areas where it seemed acceptable to deal with a client's spirituality were those that covered formal 'Christian values and Māori culture'. Consequently, group members felt they needed to be covert about introducing

25 After discharge, clients are followed up at three- and six-monthly intervals to identify functional improvements in relationships, employment and any reduction in criminal activities. Progress is monitored by use of the Alcohol and Drug Outcome Measure – Version 2 (ADOM), collecting data on alcohol and other drug use, lifestyle and wellbeing.

26 Ibid., 3.

unconventional spiritual ideas 'with one eye watching [their] backs'. We agreed that in our discussions together we would provide 'nurturing and self-care to support one another to safely articulate spirituality within the medical model', to make the group 'a place where we can only go when we are feeling safe – with permission'.

The programme supports clients' self-assessed needs, strengths and pathways to recovery by encouraging self-awareness and reliance, prioritising goals and developing strategies for achieving them. A fundamental practice rule is that 'in addiction change must be allowed to happen – we have the space and time to discuss and negotiate, reflect and meet the client's unique needs'. Consequently, the RAP is guided by five areas of need: current situation; goals and hopes; actions; sharing responsibility; and, progress. The counsellors, particularly, work on a number of structured activities with their clients to maintain motivation, engagement and transformation using individual and group psycho-educational training and skills development as well as the exploration of family and culture of origin relationships. In addition, regular recovery reviews involve consultation with staff and referrers to discuss post-treatment goals, recovery maintenance and, if transitioning back into the community poses risks to recovery, emergency relapse action plans. Unfortunately, the centre does not have the resources to follow up with their clients effectively. There are also ethical, communications, and boundary issues for the clients and the different agencies that might need to get involved, which explains 'why we have to have faith in the referrer – some good, some bad – this is something we struggle with'. 'The 12-step programme is out there too to provide support along with more conventional social and family networks'.[27]

Alcoholics Anonymous' 12 Steps to sobriety, and other 12-step groups, have traditionally provided a rational link between substance misuse and spiritual experience, which in terms of recovery is essentially facilitated through an 'awareness of a Power greater than ourselves'.[28] Interestingly, Betsy Robin Spiegel suggests that as the programme was originally used to 'heal

27 In Narcotics Anonymous' adaption of Alcoholic Anonymous' original programme, 12 steps are meant to be explored sequentially but certain steps may be visited and revisited over time. Narcotics Anonymous 'About the Narcotics Anonymous (NA) 12-Step Recovery Program', viewed 19 August 2018, http://www.recovery.org/topics/about-the-narcotics-anonymous-na-12-step-recovery-program/.

28 Herbert Spencer, *Alcoholics Anonymous: The Story of How Many Thousands of Men and Women Have Recovered from Alcoholism*, 4th ed.(New York: A. A. World Services Inc., 2001), 568.

highly traumatised alcoholics' it could also be used to restore a shattered psyche caused by a traumatic event.[29]

In practice, however, the 12-step programme no longer has a strong influence on the centre's programme though they accept the inherent wisdom of using spirituality as a tool for recovery, even if the centre only minimally 'officially' refers to it by name in documentation.[30] As one counsellor put it, 'I promote 12-step because it's pretty much the only support out there'. Another felt that it could create disempowerment and dependence by either the client getting stuck in the same disabling narrative of recovery or establishing an alternative addiction. The group had reservations that the fellowship's rigid linearity of one-size-fits-all approach, although it works for many, did not completely fit the unique lifestyles of their clients.[31] Nevertheless, they do incorporate elements such as 'making amends' and 'surrendering' and being 'powerless to your addiction' successfully in their therapeutic approaches.[32]

3 Talking About Trauma and Spirituality

3.1 *Approaches to Spirituality*

Studies suggest that although individuals recovering from addictions frequently cite spirituality as a supportive influence, 'clinicians' perceptions of patients' spiritual needs have sometimes appeared alarmingly inaccurate.[33] And, as has

---

29 Betsy Robin Spiegel, 'The Use of the 12 Steps of the Anonymous Program to Heal Trauma', *Journal of Social Work Practice in the Addictions* 5.3 (2005): 103–105.

30 See also, Marc Galanter, et al., 'Spirituality-Based Recovery from Drug Addiction in the Twelve-Step Fellowship of Narcotics Anonymous', *Journal of Addiction Medicine* 7.3 (2013): 189–195; and, Robert Walker, Theodore M. Godlaski, and Michele Staton-Tindall, 'Spirituality, Drugs, and Alcohol: A Philosophical Analysis', *Substance Use & Misuse* 48 (2013): 1233–1245.

31 Walker and colleagues present four problems that require satisfactory resolution before spiritual practices in the 12-step method are readily accepted by the client.

32 American Psychological Association's summary of steps as a six-phase process:
"(a) admit that he or she cannot control his or her drinking;
(b) recognize a supreme spiritual power, which can give the member strength;
(c) examine past errors, a process that is carried out with another member who serves as sponsor;
(d) make amends for these errors;
(e) develop a new code and style of life; and
(f) help other alcoholics who are in need of support."
American Psychological Association 'Dictionary of Psychology', viewed 5 May 2109, https://dictionary.apa.org/twelve-step-program.

33 Adrienne J. Heinz, et al., 'A Focus-Group Study on Spirituality', 134–153.

been noted elsewhere, there are any numbers of reasons given to explain why counsellors and other health professionals find it difficult to consider integrating spirituality into their professional practices.[34] Counsellors may be constrained by their own life experiences, knowledge and values, or the particular theories that underpin their work, as well as the context and disposition of clients. For example, atheistic denial of sacred realities, and a defensiveness in their presence and usage, a determined rejection of all but one's own authentic spiritual path without recognising or appreciating the diversity of others, or an inability to accept that individuals may construct their own spiritual meanings, might all contribute to a view that spirituality is beyond the purview of the counselling professional.[35] Similarly in addictions work, clients and their counsellors, who bring spiritual, religious, or mystical experiences and beliefs, may not always be sympathetically received or understood – particularly when associated with symptoms of substance misuse. Nevertheless, the language of the 'transformation from addiction to recovery is best explained by recovering addicts themselves'.[36]

James Nelson suggests a pluralistic approach to spirituality and psychology that promotes a reflexive, respectful and symbiotic relationship, that more effectively accommodates the holistic nature of human beings in counselling, more in keeping with the views and approaches of the discussion group.[37] Nelson's model suggests that when spirituality and psychology are separated individuals can 'have a good spiritual life in the midst of poor psychological functioning or *vice versa*'.[38] But the inherent danger in allowing this separation is that it permits counsellors and other clinical professionals and institutions to avoid the use of spirituality in their work with clients. Thus 'counsellors can acknowledge spiritual experience as valid but still exclude it from the therapeutic space on the grounds that they are presently not sufficiently competent to deal with it'.[39]

34 Peter Bray, 'Naming Spirituality in Counsellor Education: A Modest Proposal', *New Zealand Journal of Counselling* special issue (2011): 76–97.

35 Brian J. Zinnbauer and Kenneth I. Pargament, 'Working with the Sacred: Four Approaches to Religious and Spiritual Issues in Counselling', *Journal of Counseling and Development* 78.2 (2000): 162–171.

36 Mary Hansen, Barbara Ganley, and Chris Carlucci, 'Journeys from Addiction to Recovery', *Research and Theory for Nursing Practice: An International Journal* 22.4 (2008): 256–272; Jacqueline Linder also discusses the importance of prioritising the insider or researcher/survivor perspective in her contribution to this volume.

37 James M. Nelson, *Psychology, Religion, and Spirituality* (New York: Springer, 2009), 475–506.

38 Ibid., 492.

39 Bray, 'A Broader Framework', 293–330.

3.2 *Discussion Group Process*

Nearly half of the group had successfully recovered from their experiences of addiction and were able to intelligently discriminate between psychotic and positively transformative spiritual outcomes. However, their histories did make made them feel nervous about revealing the extent of their personal knowledge and values concerning the spiritual dimensions of their lives, especially 'things that would be on the addictive continuum ... including forms of trauma'.[40] Certainly, experiences and even experiments in recovery were influencing how they regarded spirituality and they carried with them a feeling that, like their client group, they might be judged severely by their medical peers.

Three important assumptions guided our discussions together that: clients and counsellors will always bring some spirituality to their counselling together; spirituality can be used as a positive resource to support clients with the trauma of addiction; and, that counsellors working in addiction recovery may be covertly working with their client's and their own spirituality.[41] Also, the group confirmed that, in order to work effectively with their clients' spiritualties, they would benefit from developing an awareness of their own spiritual needs. Consequently, they aimed to explore how spirituality might be positively admitted into the clinical setting of addictions work, the therapeutic relationship, and their broader counselling practices.

The group began by identifying how spirituality influences their work in the institution and how to integrate their 'common-sense' practice approaches into a working model.[42] Our sessions initiated a journey of self-discovery with members taking spiritual inventories, seeking intra-psychic connections, and considering spirit-centred therapeutic interventions and models that placed trauma and spirituality at their centre. The generous sharing of experience and rich moving disclosures led to a high level of trust within the group. Group members examined the triggers and outcomes of addiction through a spiritual lens as processes of psychological development and personal growth.

---

40 See Jacqueline Linder's contribution to this volume.

41 William West, *Psychotherapy and Spirituality: Crossing the Line between Therapy and Religion* (London: SAGE Publications, 2001); Bray, 'Naming Spirituality', 76–97.

42 Developed from a model of post-traumatic growth proposed by Lawrence Calhoun and Richard Tedeschi and combined with Stanislav and Christina Grof's 'holotropic' framework of psycho-spiritual growth. Bray, 'A Broader Framework', 293–30.

4 Spirituality and Addictions Work

Group members were encouraged to 'share the richness of their positions on spirituality, without prejudice, to improve mutual understanding and create a safer environment'. Over the course of our discussions it was mutually understood that 'If we know what spirituality means to us we might be able to assist clients in theirs'. During our earlier sessions, five significant practice issues, or questions, emerged that began to drive the meetings.

4.1 *What Is Spirituality in Counselling and Addictions Work?*

In a recent meta-analysis of 29 studies evidence found supported for a beneficial relationship between spirituality or religion and recovery from substance use disorders.[43] Nevertheless, in practice it has become stunningly difficult to define the term or quantify 'spirituality' in counselling and addictions work as it has become embellished far beyond its original meaning and used interchangeably with the term 'religion' in the literature.[44] 'Religions may ring fence doctrines but they are all broadly constructed around a desire to admit to something greater than the individual or group'. Spirituality is also widely understood as a concept associated with and dominated by Christian inspired 12-step modalities and recovery from addiction.[45] However, one member of the group stated, 'When I talk about my faith it is about my relationship with the spiritual and it's grounded in a whole frame of reference'.

Acknowledging the difficulty, bias, and ambiguity generated by distinctions, and rather than seeking specific definitions, the group chose to surrender personal definitions and to work within those existing traditions already formed by professionals working in an addictions and mental health service roles. Arguably a limitation, however it reflects in some measure the participants' hesitancy in offering a hitherto private aspect of themselves for scrutiny within the potentially judgemental shadow of the medical institution. Illustrating this, one of the group revealed her awareness of the almost permanent presence of parallel dream-like thread of consciousness that accompanies and informs her

---

43 Walton-Moss, Ray, and Woodruff, 'Relationship of Spirituality', 224–225.

44 Christopher C. H. Cook, 'Addiction and Spirituality', *Addiction* 99 (2004): 539; Peter C. Hill, et al., 'Conceptualizing Religion and Spirituality: Points of Commonality, Points of Departure', *Journal for the Theory of Social Behavior* 30.1(2000): 51–77; Bray, 'Naming Spirituality', 76–97.

45 Cook, 'Addiction and Spirituality', 546–547; Annick Shaw, Stephen Joseph and P. Alex Linley, 'Religion, Spirituality, and Posttraumatic Growth: A Systematic Review', *Mental Health, Religion, & Culture* 8.1(2005): 1–11.

day-to-day living and her practice like a continuous sense of déjà vu: 'I am not mad, but I have these experiences'. Clearly reluctant to reveal this to her senior colleagues, she suggested that if counsellors' experiences remain unexplained and their beliefs unspoken then what distinguishes them from their clients? Another member of the group went on,

> How do we identify spirituality in the medical model? Name it as part of our practice ... normalise it amongst our peers? We've talked about our own spirituality and the client's and how that comes together in a collaborative therapeutic partnership. Now we are talking about what we do in addictions and how spirituality fits into that. How our spiritual journey has led us to this moment and how we can become a vehicle for our clients' spiritualties and raise their awareness.

In our discussions, therefore, the group sought to recognise each other's definitions of spirituality even before they understood how these might favourably contribute to their work with their clients' experiences of trauma and addiction. Such ways of seeing spirituality offered powerful insights into the counselling process and relationship, whilst simultaneously interrogating our potential as human-beings. It was also established that owing to the large indigenous population in the country, New Zealand's mental health sector has begun to more fully recognise Māori's customary worldview of wairua/spirituality as a tangible force that permeates life. As a recent Ministry of Health report remarks,

> ... non-dominant cultures frequently have broader definitions of ill health and well-being, which includes such things as spiritual connectedness, access to a secure cultural identity ... access to education, and whānau/family or family capacities as crucial measures of well-being.[46]

Mason Durie notes that a person's condition reflects her culture, social relationships, and physical connectedness. He suggests that Māori use their wide whānau/family networks to participate in the culture of Aotearoa/New Zealand whilst simultaneously maintaining engagement with their own society and culture.[47] Significantly, as 'the physical realm is immersed in the

46 Fraser C. Todd, *Te Ariari o te Oranga: The Assessment and Management of People with Co-existing Mental Health and Substance Use Problems* (Ministry of Health: Wellington, 2010), 23.

47 Mason Durie, 'Counselling Māori: Marae Encounters as a Basis for Understanding and Building Relationships', *New Zealand Journal of Counselling* 27.1 (2007): 1–8.

spiritual realm' in the Māori worldview, so wairua/spirituality fundamentally guides people's relationships with the living and connects them to the dead and the environment.[48] Group members, though non-Māori, valued this too through effective use of Te Whare Tapa Wha, a Māori model of wellness that demonstrates the important contribution of wairua/spirituality in balancing social relationships, body, mind, and emotions.[49] That being so, the group felt challenged that, as counsellors and agents of change who 'walk the space between', spirituality is not more widely accepted as a 'fundamental pillar of the medical model in New Zealand'.[50]

Beginning to examine the differences between 'religion' and 'spirituality', the group noted that these 'common experiences' were often interpreted through lenses of 'belief' and faith' and by their absence. They saw religion as broadly associated with the group's Judaeo-Christian origins and identified it as an ideology, an organisation or community in which members share similar beliefs and values, moral rules and behaviours. Spirituality indicated a larger intuitively shared context, a shared relationship experienced uniquely with someone or something that transcends the individual, the self, and the ego. Client responses to spirituality, it was suggested, might be influenced by personal circumstances, 'spiritual understanding and beliefs might be activated by existential concerns'. Thus counsellors might explore pivotal moments in the lives of their clients in which crises occurs 'like birth and death and love … where change is negotiated, and existential meaning is highlighted'. These ideas correspond perfectly with Ronnie Janoff-Bulman's work on shattered assumptions in the face of the irrevocable experiences of trauma.[51]

The group brought together a number of concepts previously identified by the American Counseling Associations' Summit on Spirituality that describes spirituality as an actualising tendency that directs an individual 'towards knowledge, love, meaning, hope, transcendence, connectedness, and compassion … creativity, growth, and the development of a values system'.[52] The group, however, agreed that these 'spiritual aspects of ourselves are not often

48 Rose Pere, *Te Wheke: A Celebration of Infinite Wisdom* (Gisborne: Ao Ako Global Learning, New Zealand, 1997), 16.

49 Mason Durie, *Whaiora: Māori Health Development* (Auckland: Oxford University Press, 1994).

50 Melinda Webber, *Walking the Space Between: Identity and Māori/Pākehā* (Wellington: NZCER Press, 2008).

51 Ronnie Janoff-Bulman, *Shattered Assumptions: Towards a New Psychology of Trauma* (New York: Free Press, 1992).

52 Geri Miller, 'The Development of the Spiritual Focus in Counseling and Counselor Education', *Journal of Counseling and Development* 77.4 (1999): 498–501.

shared with colleagues or clients, and are even consciously withheld'. Thus any opportunity to bring them 'alongside aspects of ourselves as professional people' in conversation, 'bringing both the body and the head – being as fully present as possible' was to be welcomed. Discussion also highlighted how some participants had previously felt stigmatised and/or were aware that their belief systems could be regarded as professionally unconventional: 'I am mindful about which clients I talk to about it, which colleagues ... I am very cautious ... I respect others' belief systems'.

Clients, the group agreed, want counsellors to see them as whole people with resources that inform their wellbeing and provide healing.[53] Spirituality is a core component of a life experience, a cultural necessity, a positive resource for mental health or pathology.[54] Although deemed a vital element of any discussion between mental health clinicians and their clients, permission and safety are required to make it happen.[55] The group considered inviting clients to explore their fundamental spiritual concerns but were also interested in thinking about how they became the 'whole' people their clients expected them to be. The literature constantly remarks that, to be effective, counsellors should know themselves, value their spiritual journeys, and acknowledge and critique the impact of their beliefs, values and behaviours on clients as they proceed toward recovery; 'we must be grounded and balanced ... we need to know who we are before we help others to address their spiritual natures'.[56] This skill raised a significant point concerning professional training. One among the group stated that although she had been traumatically 'dismembered' by her experience of counsellor education and had 'been in recovery ever since ... Being so fragmented comes with a price but allows us to also be more fully exposed and known'. Another member, disclosing her attempt at suicide and other traumatic experiences in her life, explained how she 'knew' that be a counsellor meant undertaking her own difficult journey. As she explained, 'a number of things came up that I had just walked on from ... I hadn't done my grieving'. In other words, she had to work on herself first if she wanted to help others. Addictions work, the group duly noted, involves

53 Eugene W. Kelly, 'The Role of Religion and Spirituality in Counselor Education: A National Survey', *Counselor Education & Supervision* 33.4 (1994): 227–237.

54 Nelson, *Psychology, Religion, and Spirituality*; Harold G. Koenig, 'Research on Religion, Spirituality, and Mental Health: A Review', *Canadian Journal of Psychiatry* 54.5 (2009): 283.

55 Kelly, 'Role of Religion and Spirituality'; Bray, 'Naming Spirituality', 76–97.

56 Johanna Leseho, 'Spirituality in Counsellor Education: A New Course', *British Journal of Guidance & Counselling* 35.4 (2007): 441–454.

a sensitive balancing act holding similar and contradictory notions for counsellor and client.

Christina Grof reminds us that human beings have a fundamental desire for wholeness satisfied through their attachments to each other, their environment, and with Creation. She suggests that sacred and spiritual experiences and knowledge satisfy these important needs. 'The only way we successfully satisfy this elemental craving for wholeness or for God is through an ongoing relationship with a vast spiritual source'.[57] However, for many individuals, spirituality and drug use are not incompatible. Access to the spiritual can be quickly achieved through the use of substances rather than through deliberate training. Grof intimates that personally traumatic and alienating experiences can disrupt these meaningful attachments and subsequently become the drivers for behaviours that support addictions and create further isolation. In short, a significant link exists between the temporary fulfilment of addiction and the desirability of surrendering to spiritual wholeness. 'Standing on the edge of my new life ... I began to see that the dark years of my alcoholism had actually been an important stage in my spiritual journey'.[58] Grof also suggests that the human encounter with life and death can also be profoundly and positively activating in this painful but often rewarding journey towards wholeness. It is important to note here that drug use and spirituality are not antithetical.

The group went on to explore the idea that, due to their exposure, counsellors might be in danger of 'rationalising suffering and pain by positively projecting upon client experiences spiritual explanations that satisfy us that our work is worthwhile or that there are benefits to be derived from suffering?' However, one member countered that counsellors do not generally indulge in delusory ' "benefit-finding" or looking for "silver-linings" where there are none'. Although counsellor observation and experience justify arguing for post-traumatic growth, it is wrong to assume this in all cases, and even when 'clients choose to survive because they are not finished [with life]'.

> The paradox is that bad stuff is bad stuff and yet there is some good that comes out of it. I don't know if there is any alternative ... we have all had these situations where we have burdened clients ... and I've sat there and listened to their stories and thought, "They're right, it's hopeless." It's just the most horrible feeling ... unless we hold that piece that there has

57 Christina Grof, *The Thirst for Wholeness: Attachment, Addiction, and the Spiritual Path* (New York: HarperOne, 1993), 1.

58 Ibid., 4.

> to be something good, when actually in reality there is nothing, there is nothing that we can do ... What we might identify as spiritual are the moments of awareness, even in the most difficult and hopeless situations, where the client may glimpse however briefly a moment of peace ... There is something in our clients that desires it, is courageous enough to seek the right thing or something better. We admire our clients' ability in appalling adversity to reach out – to connect to something that supports them to perform the simple and the miraculous things for themselves. When clients find it hard to have a purpose in life, then as therapists we are stuck.

5 Admitting Spirituality into Practice

Given that counsellors or psychotherapists from diverse backgrounds hold spiritual beliefs not wholly inconsistent with those of the 12-step model it was encouraging that the group wanted to critically examine this area of their work and embed it in a broader experiential framework.[59] As one group member said expansively,

> You have got to walk the talk ... it comes with a lot of responsibility. That's why it is a vocation ... and even that sounds like a spiritual practice.

5.1 *How Much Do We as Counsellors Admit Spirituality into Our Work?*

As qualified professionals, group members were open to new ideas and had a depth of experience in the field. Examining their own spirituality, qualities that enable them to help others and influence their professional development, got them through addiction and other difficult life events seemed important to the group. For one member, psychotherapeutic training was like coming home. It answered and 'deeply validated' the questions raised by her spiritual worldview 'that nothing was impossible'. For another, the training was experienced as 'quite linear, clinical, and cold'.

In spite of the differences, the group agreed that, as clients do not have two dimensional existences, spiritual orientation still needs to be aligned with the therapeutic approach. Similarly, the group discussed extensively how member's diverse spirituality beliefs positioned them in the therapeutic relationship: 'If

59 Marilyn Freimuth, 'Psychotherapists' Beliefs About the Benefits of 12-Step Groups', *Alcoholism Treatment Quarterly* 14. 3 (1996): 95–102.

we regard spirit as something that originates in ourselves we might take a different position to that of believing that spirit originates beyond ourselves'. One counsellor took the view that spirituality itself constitutes a relational connection. She recounted her experience with a suicidal client who 'had lost the ability to carry on', and identified her client's spirituality as a 'thread that might help her to survive'. In these cases, the counsellor's role is to hold and nurture that fragile 'piece … when they can't. Until they are ready to pick it up again'.

Another clinician, discussing the therapeutic relationship, explained his ability to use intuition like a 'psychological radar' to 'send out energy and receive an inner response'. He describes human life 'as either individual atoms with nowhere to go but inwards, or fragments of a larger pattern in creation'. Another, introducing the notion of determinism into counselling, suggested that some counsellors and clients might believe that all encounters, including those in a past life, are part of a pre-designed package that implicates us in each other's destinies.

The discussion moved freely into the spiritual experience of counselling and empathic awareness. Reflecting on the synchronicities of connection with clients, one therapist described her altered energetic state of consciousness in sessions as 'wonderful'. Another suggested the existence of a 'dimension of [the therapeutic] relationship where intuition exists, that can provide access to mutually satisfying ways forward'. She felt that to be shut off from it would limit her effectiveness as counsellor. The group agreed that spirituality permeates all clinical practice, either as introduced by the therapist or provided by the experiences of the client.[60] Thus 'positioning with our client's consciousness is about awareness and accommodation' and 'expanding our consciousness'.

Some suggested that 'clients want to feel special', and to regard spiritual resources as a no-go area in professional practice diminishes the holistic power of their beliefs in their personal theory of change. Nevertheless, even as private individuals, the group confessed to rarely accommodating others' worldviews, acknowledging, 'I don't do this with my peers, my friends, and my family'. As a result, a professional question arose concerning professional boundaries: 'How much can I allow myself to disclose to others and how much this might restrict or permits client disclosure and development in this area?' Reflecting our own group process, members noted how they had reached different stages in their disclosure of spiritual beliefs and practices with clients. This led to significant exploration here as practitioners discussed their management of imbalances between their values and those that they interpreted as existing between the

60 West, *Psychotherapy and Spirituality.*

medical model and their professional codes of ethical practice. One counsellor accepted that, although it means accommodating two positions simultaneously, he must put his Christian belief structure aside whilst still maintaining a space for the client's spiritual beliefs and experiences.

Some also suggested that if we as a professional group were experiencing reluctance or resistance then permission, confidentiality, and trust might well be factors for our clients. One member suggested that before mutual sharing, there needs to be awareness, a space created where spiritual disclosure is allowed and honoured.

6 Competence

The group's concerns to address issues of spirituality in their work not only unconsciously touched upon a developing trend in mental health and addictions recovery literature noted above but in counselling practice too. Since 2009 the American Counseling Association, the ACA, has required its members to satisfy nine 'Competencies for Addressing Spiritual and Religious Issues in Counseling'[61] that assist them to develop a practice framework that allows them to understand and work effectively with clients' spiritual and religious lives. The competencies address four domains of counselling practice: knowledge of spiritual phenomena; awareness of one's own spiritual perspective; understanding clients' spiritual perspectives, and spiritually related interventions and strategies.[62] In Britain too there has been a cautious call to redress the imbalance caused by an overemphasis on the rational and to reintegrate spirituality into counselling theory and practice.[63]

6.1 *Counsellor Competence with Client Spirituality*

The majority of the group's therapeutic work includes daily client-centred individual and group processes blended with more directive clinical and psycho-educational programmes. Spirituality, admittedly, is at the core of counselling,

61 J. Scott Young, Marsha Wiggins-Frame, and Craig S. Cashwell, 'Spirituality and Counselor Competence: A National Survey of American Counseling Association Members', *Journal of Counseling and Development* 85.1 (2007): 47–52.

62 Currently, the American Spiritual Ethical and Religious Values in Counseling (ASERVIC) has 6 areas of spiritual concern with 14 competencies, viewed 19 August 2018, http://www.aservic.org/resources/spiritual-competencies/.

63 John McLeod, *The Counsellor's Workbook: Developing a Personal Approach* (Maidenhead: Open University Press, 2010); West, *Psychotherapy and Spirituality*, 17–18.

'a profound partnership between scientific empiricism and spiritual ways of knowing'.[64] Even Carl Rogers, an influential author of the person-centred approach to counselling, confessed that he had totally 'underestimated the importance of this mystical, spiritual dimension'.[65] Spirit-centred approaches to counselling, it is suggested, more than enhance 'the work we already do'.[66] Spirituality is central to Rogers' principle of empathy and his core conditions permit the counsellor to respond to the client's deep need for universal attachment and tendency to actualise.[67]

Perhaps not surprisingly, our group of therapists confessed to not having had any training in working with client's spiritual concerns and expressed criticism of training programmes that, by omission, seemed to deny a spiritual dimension of existence. They relied instead on their own convictions to guide their work with clients.[68] One member describing the spiritual dimensions of his practice, mentioned the importance for him of being active and intentional: 'I feel genuinely more connected with the people around me. Working with my intuition and naming things was a hundred percent accurate … like putting spiritual eyes on'. Participants also discussed the difficulties of using vocabulary associated with spiritual and religious ways of being in a medical context. They pointed out that assessments using language like 'faith' or having a 'Higher Power' can be challenging when completing conventional medical documentation.

In an institutional context, where spirituality is simply a component of mental health, and recovery is measured by observable and quantifiable changes and outcomes, the group valued the opportunity to discuss work that they believe instils hope in their clients. However, it was 'realistically' acknowledged that 'spirit-led' work in an institution that can be 'self-serving rather than client-serving' may not satisfy requirements or instil confidence. Although the institution has offered medical colleagues the opportunity to observe and to understand their approaches, 'time constraints' have made this infrequent. They have also shared that they feel professionally undervalued in a regime

---

64 Bray, 'Naming Spirituality, 76–97; Nelson, *Psychology, Religion, and Spirituality*; Brian Thorne, *Counselling and the Spiritual Journey* (Birkenhead: Time & Space, 1997); William West, *Spiritual Issues in Therapy: Relating Experience to Practice* (Basingstoke: Palgrave, 2004).

65 Carl R. Rogers, *A Way of Being* (New York: Houghton Mifflin, 1995), 130.

66 Keith Morgen, et al., *Strategies for the Competent Integration of Spirituality into Addictions Counseling Training and Supervision* (2010), viewed 19 August 2018, https://libres.uncg.edu/ir/uncg/f/C_Cashwell_Strategies_2010.pdf.

67 Rogers, *A Way of Being*, 134.

68 West, *Psychotherapy and Spirituality*.

where it is best 'not to make waves' and not 'reveal too much imagination or creativity'. Under these conditions professional supervisors are chosen carefully, and senior managers sympathetic to spiritually-centred approaches are like gold. Consequently, members of the group were careful about recording interventions that might reveal their 'utilising individual's faiths to strengthen them in their healing' or respecting a 'past-life experience' because they had been too readily misinterpreted.

Returning to an earlier theme, members of the group cautiously noted that their experience of addiction psychiatry practices, originating in the Kraepelinian model of mental disorders, made them realise that it can hold little regard for spiritual experiences and those that espouse them.[69] One ruffled soul remarked that 'Doctors are gods with a small "g" and they don't like the competition'. Consequently, members had not been able to 'publicly' reveal their spiritual experiences because taken out of context 'inexplicable experiences and psychic phenomena are often modified by [official] interpretations'. One member alluded to a local psychologist stood down because of his publicised beliefs about spiritual guardians, a particularly telling example as it re-emphasised the potential misunderstanding and literal thinking in this area of practice.

From their work in addictions group members realised that individuals are unique and can have rich experiences of the spiritual realm that do not always correspond to the culture of origin or other social signifiers. They explained that, meeting clients on 'many different levels', they sometimes feel unable to 'discuss with them and others the deeper and more holistic nature of [their] experiences'. Consequently they recommended that the counsellor's role must include sensitiveness to the spiritual material that clients present, appreciating its positive contribution to healthy mental and social functioning, and recognising when it begins to activate and shape pathology rather than resolve it.[70] The group identified that to work with a client's spiritual resources it takes trust in themselves, their intuition and self-care, timing and appropriateness, confidence in colleagues and the counselling process, and the capacity to raise client awareness. They regard their clients as survivors already on the road to recovery and making strong connections between their process toward wholeness, 'a sense of something better', and spirituality. One member pointed out that his clients often have a degree of resilience and a surprising, if unformed, familiarity with spirituality:

69 Galanter, 'Spirituality and Addiction', 287–288.
70 Koenig, 'Research on Religion', 289.

> They have more experience of distressing circumstances – developed spiritual muscles – and therefore have pushed to the line between the natural and the supernatural ... they have gone to places that have prepared their psyches to connect with the numinous.

In terms of assessment, the group were unclear about how to interpret, judge, or value some of their clients' symptoms and behaviours, if they were seen to have originated from spiritual sources; 'spirituality is separate from the job that we do – if you are unwell spirituality doesn't come into it. It's separate from the Western perspective – the DSM V'. Positioned in the medical model, they learn to seek symptoms in bio-organic origins or in an individual's response to external events, 'these are explainable and fit the medical analysis – this is the symptom, this is the diagnosis, and this is the drug'. 'Spiritual emergency' is a good example of an experience that does not quite fit a 'this-makes-sense' diagnosis.[71]

Activated by a moment of crisis, a spiritual emergency overwhelms the ego and loosens its control, which in turn opens a doorway to alternate perception. Spiritual emergencies can easily be diagnosed as a response to trauma and/or a form of psychosis.[72] In these instances, the individual sees the world in a different way and what they assumed about the world is no longer tenable. Although this rarely impairs day-to-day functioning it can be alarming, and clients require understanding and education to make sense and positive use of these intra-psychic experiences. Such experiences may also hold the potential for psychological growth. As clinicians, group members were open to this as a possibility, along with the need to make clear assessments: 'we are powerfully placed to broaden the scope of what is seen as either normal or safe for our clients'. They were also extremely conscious that 'spiritual experiences can [adversely] change their [clients'] label or diagnosis'. They felt genuinely challenged to find treatment pathways that respect the intangible nature of clients' experiential styles whilst simultaneously responding to the expectations of their institution. It was suggested that 'Either we are accused of being too cautious or unclear in our assessments or we only tick the boxes that enable us to be accountable'.

Members noted, in the context of working with vulnerable clients, that they can be 'acutely sensitive to our ability to understand them'. Thus 'tapping into' spirituality in the therapeutic relationship allows clinicians to be more

71 David Lukoff, 'The Diagnosis of Mystical Experiences with Psychotic Features', *Journal of Transpersonal Psychology* 17.2 (1985): 155–181.

72 Grof and Grof, eds., *Spiritual Emergency*.

present, enhances mutual understanding, deepens trust, strengthens and supports the client's resolve toward recovery. Additionally, members spelt out the importance to validate 'spirituality experienced in the body' as the burden of rational knowing can prevent a client from 'being fully immersed in their experience'. They also agreed that clients enjoy opportunities to explore the fullness of their spiritual natures through therapeutic conversations once 'barriers to a spiritual mode of communication are no longer a problem or exist'.

A further thread running through discussions concerned the capacity of the counselling relationship to generate its own energy, access 'spiritual' energy, and harness organismic intuition that consciously directs the process. Indeed, the ideas of engaging one's inner 'radar' or spiritual energy in ways that do not 'distinguish between the head and the body' resonated with our group's understanding of counselling relationships. Remarking on Jung's collective unconscious, one member stated, 'I see it as energy that permeates everything and everywhere and we can tap into that ... and it taps into me', suggesting that individuals do not have to be religious in order to be spiritual, and *vice versa*.[73] Another member described her intimate ability to receive client data in terms of intuitive and guiding impressions: 'I get things [pictures] in my head that don't belong to me'.

One counsellor encountered energy through an intuitive knowing that seemed to emerge in sessions when 'things are seamlessly unfolding – flowing, and there is little or no resistance'. But working from an intuitive place can challenge the therapist's groundedness. As counsellors 'we are privileged to know ourselves' and that presumes a degree of profound understanding which implies spiritual knowing. However, even counsellors can fear discussing such matters because of negative prior experiences or a lack of sufficient exposure to handle/approach/deal with the subject comfortably. Similarly, some argued that although clients' experiences of trauma and addiction impinge on their abilities to be 'grounded enough' the therapeutic container can 'provide the right conditions for intuitive sharing of spiritual perspectives'. One counsellor explained, 'getting in the flow of the spirit, rather than just being present in body and mind, can be focussing in terms of relationship and effective therapy but it's also consuming'. Another reflected that she was conscious of the process but not the outcome, noting, 'I want to understand by using all of my connections'. However, she did not feel compelled to guide it,

73 Pavel Rican and Pavlina Janosova, 'Spirituality as a Basic Aspect of Personality: A Cross-cultural Verification of Piedmont's Model', *The International Journal for the Psychology of Religion* 20.1 (2010): 2–13.

> You're in this intuitive flow and it's kind of only being revealed one step at a time ... so your kind of on the edge, and it's like that sensation of being pushed from behind and you take the next step, and the next step ...

Recognising spirituality as energy in the relationship one counsellor confessed that she was concerned about its origin. The depth and intensity in the client's condition, they suggested, can resonate with the therapists'. For example, 'in group I expand my awareness to get to how they [clients] are and not just what they are saying'. Another member observed, 'when clients bring "a dark aura" or "negative spiritual energy" ... that is nothing to do with me I need to protect myself from spiritual attack'. Thereafter a discussion addressed the need for a 'blessing or cleansing' from some 'darker energy that can exist within the client' or when 'the client [is] a receptacle or a conduit for it'

7 Trauma and Change

The phenomenon of psychological growth and greater consciousness that follow highly stressful life events commonly appears in the literature and in philosophical, spiritual and religious traditions and teachings. It also emerges as a central principle in humanistic and transpersonal psychologies. Concepts of 'actualisation', 'peak experience' and 'spiritual emergency' in the work of psychologists and educators including Carl Rogers, Viktor Frankl, Abraham Maslow,[74] and Stan and Christina Grof,[75] reflect an immense interest in understanding spirituality. The tendency toward growth in the wake of crisis has also been embraced by positive psychology's Stephen Joseph and Alex Linley, in their further interest in 'adversarial growth', 'stress-related growth', and 'benefit finding', as well as in Richard Tedeschi and Lawrence Calhoun's inventory and model of 'posttraumatic growth'.[76]

---

74 Carl Rogers, *On Becoming a Person: A Therapist's View of Psychotherapy* (London: Constable, 1961); Viktor Frankl, *Man's Search for Meaning: An Introduction to Logotherapy* (New York: Washington Square Press, 1963); Abraham Maslow, *The Farthest Reaches of Human Nature* (New York: Viking Press, 1971).

75 Originating in Grof's 'holotropic' model of the psyche, first detailed in Stanislav Grof, *Beyond the Brain: Birth, Death, and Transcendence in Psychotherapy* (New York: State University New York Press, 1985), 'spiritual emergence' and 'spiritual emergency' are the subject of Grof and Grof, eds., *Spiritual Emergency*; and Stanislav Grof and Christina Grof, *The Stormy Search for Self* (Los Angeles: J. P. Tarcher, 1990).

76 Stephen Joseph, *What Doesn't Kill Us: The New Psychology of Posttraumatic Growth* (London: Piatkus, 2012). For their review of the impact of benefit finding on health outcomes, see P. Alex Linley and Stephen S. Joseph, 'Positive Change Following Trauma and

The impact of traumatic life events and the importance of mental health CEPs, the misuse of drugs and alcohol and subsequent addiction, are all substantially linked and currently intensely researched.[77] The addictions literature now suggests that spiritual approaches to treatment might be substantially supported by staff working in the field and that spirituality is a recurring theme in client change and recovery as both protective and risk factors.[78]

7.1 *Does Trauma Hold the Potential for Growth-Promoting Change?*

Putting their ideas together, the group recognised trauma as a trigger to addiction: 'the damage is done ... you have arrived at a place where you can't go back. You can no longer be who you were'. They also suggested that the experience, and change to identity and the self, brought on by addiction is also likely to be traumatising for the individual 'when it creates something worse than the thing you are trying to avoid'. They described the recovery process as a need to make meaning, and its realisation as the beginning of their work in guiding the client in their journey from the 'false normal' of the addicted emotional self back to the rational self.

> There is a point where you [clients] are forced into, and must confront, the next piece. And the next piece is when they have to come and seek out helping professionals and work through managing losses, sense of self, all of the fractured bits and pieces, and then making meaning without drugs, and recreating a life without that ...

In the same way, Francesca Brencio and Kori Novak consider the potency of sharing traumatic experiences in similarly experienced populations, to establish a consensual historically normal baseline from which healing can begin to emerge.[79] The group broadly broadly agreed that counsellors help

---

Adversity: A Review', *Journal of Traumatic Stress* 17 (2004): 11–21; Richard G. Tedeschi and Lawrence G. Calhoun, 'The Posttraumatic Growth Inventory: Measuring the Positive Legacy of Trauma', *Journal of Traumatic Stress* 9 (1996): 455–471.

77 Keyser-Marcus, et al., 'Trauma, Gender, and Mental Health Symptoms'. 3–24.

78 Hansen, Ganley and Carlucci, 'Journeys from Addiction to Recovery', 265–266; Carlo C. DiClemente, 'Paths Through Addiction and Recovery: The Impact of Spirituality and Religion', *Substance Use & Misuse* 48 (2013): 1260–1261; Robert F. Forman, Gregory Bovasso, and George Woody, 'Staff Beliefs About Addiction Treatment', *Journal of Substance Abuse Treatment*, 21 (2001): 1–9.

79 See Francesca Brencio and Kori Novak's contribution to this volume, 'The Continuum of Trauma'.

clients to gather up the 'developmental pieces that have been useful to the person' and support them to work through their trauma and not to re-addict. They discussed the painful and uncertain struggles of clients who, at the beginning of their work 'have potential but frustratingly are unable to reach it'. As in a glass case, 'I can see what I want but I can't touch it ... I can understand the expectations, but I also understand how hard it is to break through the glass'. If the client returns to their pre-trauma environment then, 'It's like watching someone you care about going back into trauma. That's the hard bit'. They discussed the importance of acknowledging the steps that clients do make and resisting becoming too invested in their success or overwhelming them with too many expectations. 'We hold that potential for them that they may never see ... and that's our job ... if we didn't have that [passion] what would our work be like?' They stressed how critical it is that the counsellor has faith in the therapeutic process and believes that the client can achieve recovery.

Discussing the jarring effect on the client of undertaking rehabilitation on their own, and the self-sabotaging impact of unreal expectations, one therapist made a distinction between 'Trauma with a capital "T" and trauma with a small "t" '. The accumulation of repeated 'failures and relapses that affect the psyche' in the latter is just as traumatising as in the former. Acknowledging these long-term effects, another member saw a return to drug use as 'escapist', a self-soothing attempt to move out of the pain and closer to healing and spirituality, '[c]hanging realities – when coping strategies become dangerous'. Considering substance use in traditional cultures, they also understood that to return to any community that shares similar values, and where using drugs is ritualised could be attractive.[80] They debated the differences between 'non-drug induced spirituality', 'studied' use to achieve a greater consciousness, and unregulated 'gratuitous' use. In this instance, they firmly noted that while 'The doors to perception are opened', clients, especially those with co-existing conditions, are poorly equipped psychologically to manage, 'something that might cause more trauma ... [;] if it is a psychic opening it can be overwhelming and disturbing'.

The group clearly distinguished between those who are addicted and those who purposefully use addictive substances in a controlled way without becoming addicted. Animated by the subject, group members declared that 'no one knows where the line is between control and addiction'. They also questioned

80 Robin Room, 'Spirituality, Intoxication and Addiction: Six Forms of Relationship', *Substance Use & Misuse* 48 (2013): 1109–1113.

how 'controlled' the use of alcohol and substances can be when enjoyed as a reaction to an emotional stimulus or to manage a crisis event without formal support. Thus they shared that 'you may control what you take but you can't always control its affect', suggesting that being an addict can become a 'stuck place where … spirituality is numbed-out or disconnected rather than a place of continual enlightenment'. Some further observations were made about the culturally directed use of substances in rites-of-passage. However, the overwhelming experience of the group seemed to be that like 'Pandora's box, once it is open you may not be able to close it'.

> The drugs, whilst opening the Pandora's box of experience, also lower your resistance and ability to achieve actualisation … on the one hand you take something which enables you to enhance or to actualise and on the other hand you've crippled yourself by the very act of doing that because you are not ready to do that. You are not psychologically prepared.

Without understanding and training, the management of simultaneously experiencing inner and outer manifestations together with the 're-entry' to a material universe, especially after such subtle and complex connections with the cosmos, was also identified as a problem. Nevertheless, the group generally agreed that the metaphor of a spiritual journey is useful and does tend to unconsciously inform their work,

> I see them [clients] as having been off their pathway through drug use and alcohol abuse … I work quite hard to reconnect them to where they need to be right now to do what they need to do.

8 Trauma and Spirituality

At first the group aimed at creating a common-sense model of spirit-led practice that corresponded with members' experiences of spirituality in their work with trauma and addiction recovery. Presented with a draft pathway to recovery, originating in trauma and continuing into developing post-addiction opportunities, the group roughly articulated a way to practice.[81]

---

81 'Figure 3. An expanded model of PTG and psycho-spiritual transformation', in Bray, 'A Broader Framework', 302.

8.1 *Conceptualising Spirituality in Addiction's Counselling Practice*

The group conceived recovery as a survival process, equipping individuals to manage their behaviours and addictions that originate in, and are triggered by, traumatic events. Later they incorporated the idea of self-actualisation into this process and suggested that it is fuelled by spirit and facilitated in a spiritual dimension. They formulated the idea that trauma significantly disrupts or wounds the human organism's natural tendency to actualise and creates less effective pathways to achieving or to recovering the capacity to reach higher states of consciousness.

The group also saw addiction as a false, or unwelcome outcome of the struggle to meaning in a disrupted journey, and the process of recovery as a spiritual quest to recover and reconnect with lost potential, echoing Freud and Caruth's conception that trauma not only signals a breach but an interruption or detour in consciousness.[82] The group also agreed that even when problematic, the identification and naming of spiritual resources are a central element in the process of recovery. One clinician likened the process to a 'shamanic' journey beyond trauma:

> You have come through the pain. You have come through the experience and you have come back with the word and the knowledge and you know that there is a door – you know that there is a way out. You know the route.

The group identified the clinician's role as a guide who assists clients in their integrative process of re-attachment and re-alignment 'so that the journey can continue'. Therapy was seen as a 'space where informed choices are being made and actions are tentatively taken, disruptions are being challenged, and meaning and learning is happening'. The group acknowledged that for some the space was more complicated than for others, because 'the spiritual part of them [clients] is quite depleted when they come here'. As one member sympathetically stated,

> I experience the clients here as the more sensitive souls in the world. The substance has been a way to armour up. We don't have to go too far to find that … life is awful and the world is not a nice place … they absorbed all of the negative stuff in the family whilst others have managed to get above that somehow or do something different, but that person holds a

82 See Cassie Pedersen's contribution to this volume, 'Encountering Trauma "Too Soon" and "Too Late": Caruth, Laplanche, and the Freudian *Nachträglichkeit*.'

> lot of the family issues and uses alcohol, drugs or behaviour to manage and escape from that.

The group noted that, as they recover, clients eventually become unstuck and the outcomes are encouraging. Only then do clients regard their experiences as necessary and valuable. 'Clients are grateful for their addiction journeys because they can't hide from the insights they provide about themselves, who they once were, and how to relate again to the world'.

Importantly, the practitioners found that clients' responses to therapy did not always meet their counselling expectations, especially those borderline patients whose 'needs may be articulated through difficult behaviours rather than in self-consciously transparent language'. However, they also found that by 'making adjustments, synchronised or attuned with the spiritual character of clients, and accepting their views and aspirations', they could work with them as individuals and not judge them by their label of addict. One group member added realistically that, as human beings face major or minor disruptions throughout their development, addiction should be regarded as one of many possible responses to difficult life events: 'Some of us work through our trauma without addiction and some of us have got addiction as a way of coping'.

It was suggested that for some clients the experience of trauma is so all-encompassing that they are unaware of its true impact. Not until counselling reveals the deleterious effects can clients fully appreciate their woundedness. Another member thoughtfully concluded that addiction can be both a response to, and a cause of, trauma.

> Our work here is to look for what created the addiction, why that person needs to use substance ... when they come here they are already defined as being a dependent substance user. Some accept the diagnosis and some don't but the real struggle is to accept that they will need to be abstinent for the rest of their lives ... that they can never use substance again as a coping mechanism is the real trauma.

Clinicians and helping professionals hold the precarious space between the recovery institutions of our society and their professional obligations to honour and work with their clients' experiences. They recognise that the 'addict' is not the totality of the client, but rather a broken part searching to fulfil its seemingly insatiable appetites. Through their work, they understand that human beings desire wholeness, to be all that they can be, and that they can only finally resolve it in nurturing relationship with others in their communities and through life affirming and meaningful activities. Sadly, many recovering addicts will return to the places of their original traumas where they are challenged to continue in the company of those who may also require just as much support.

Nevertheless, in spite of the limitations of our society, counsellors and therapists, social workers and helpers do their work, to understand, and reintegrate the needy and vulnerable parts of clients with the whole. Together they engage in meaningful relational processes that positively draw upon profound personal resources to facilitate recovery and transformation.

Finally, a growing body of research, across a number of disciplines, overwhelmingly acknowledges the significant role that spirituality plays in integrating trauma, promoting positive health outcomes, developing wellbeing and psychological growth. For counselling and psychotherapy to successfully develop as fields that genuinely attend to the whole person, we will increasingly need to make way for conversations that share and examine the spirituality that lies at the centre of our professional day-to-day practices and caring relationships.

I am on the same journey as you are … and that changes our work hugely.

Acknowledgement

I would like to thank my colleagues whose permission, support, transparency, and enthusiastic participation in our Spirituality Special Interest Group has made this chapter possible. You do more than you know and your knowing is rich with common-sense and caring.

Bibliography

American Psychological Association. *Diagnostic and Statistical Manual of Mental Disorders*, 4th ed. Washington: American Psychological Association, 2000.

American Psychological Association. Dictionary of Psychology. Viewed 5 May 2109. https://dictionary.apa.org/twelve-step-program

American Spiritual Ethical and Religious Values. in Counseling (ASERVIC). *Spiritual & Religious Competencies. Competencies for Addressing Spiritual and Religious Issues in Counseling*. Viewed 19 August, 2018. http://www.aservic.org/resources/spiritual-competencies/.

Baroody, Alan N. 'Spirituality and Trauma during a Time of War: A Systemic Approach to Pastoral Care and Counseling'. In *Families Under Fire: Systemic Therapy with Military Families*, edited by R. Blaine Everson and Charles R. Figley, 165–190. New York: Routledge, 2010.

Bray, Peter. 'A Broader Framework for Exploring the Influence of Spiritual Experience in the Wake of Stressful Life Events: Examining Connections between Posttraumatic Growth and Psycho-Spiritual Transformation'. *Mental Health, Religion and Culture* 13 (2010): 293–308.

Bray, Peter. 'Naming Spirituality in Counsellor Education: A Modest Proposal'. *New Zealand Journal of Counselling* special issue (2011): 76–97.

Calhoun, Lawrence G., and Richard G. Tedeschi, eds. *Handbook of Posttraumatic Growth: Research and Practice.* Mahwah, NJ: Lawrence Erlbaum Associates, 2006.

Center for Substance Abuse Treatment. 'Anxiety Disorders'. In *Assessment and Treatment of Patients with Coexisting Mental Illness and Alcohol and Other Drug Abuse: Treatment Improvement Protocol (TIP) Series No. 9, DHHS Publication No. SMA 95–3061.* Rockville, MD: Substance Abuse and Mental Health Services Administration, 1994. Viewed 19 August, 2018. https://www.ncbi.nlm.nih.gov/books/NBK64659/.

Center for Substance Abuse Treatment. *Trauma-Informed Care in Behavioral Health Service: Treatment Improvement Protocol (TIP) Series No. 57, DHHS Publication No. SMA 14–4816.* Rockville, MD: Substance Abuse and Mental Health Services Administration, 2014. Viewed 19 August, 2018. https://www.ncbi.nlm.nih.gov/books/NBK207201/.

Cook, Christopher C. H. 'Addiction and Spirituality'. *Addiction* 99 (2004): 539–551.

DiClemente, Carlo C. 'Paths through Addiction and Recovery: The Impact of Spirituality and Religion'. *Substance Use & Misuse* 48 (2013): 1260–1261.

Doweiko, Harold E. 'Substance Use Disorders as a Symptom of a Spiritual Disease'. In *Addiction and Spirituality: A Multidisciplinary Approach.* Eds. Oliver J. Morgan and Merle Jordan, 33–53. St. Louis, MO: Chalice Press, 1999.

Durie, Mason. *Whaiora: Māori Health Development.* Auckland: Oxford University Press, 1994.

Durie, Mason. 'Counselling Māori: Marae Encounters as a Basis for Understanding and Building Relationships'. *New Zealand Journal of Counselling* 27.1 (2007): 1–8.

Forman, Robert F., Gregory Bovasso and George Woody. 'Staff Beliefs about Addiction Treatment'. *Journal of Substance Abuse Treatment* 21 (2001): 1–9.

Frankl, Viktor. *Man's Search for Meaning: An Introduction to Logotherapy.* New York: Washington Square Press, 1963.

Freimuth, Marilyn. 'Psychotherapists' Beliefs About the Benefits of 12-Step Groups'. *Alcoholism Treatment Quarterly* 14.3 (1996): 95–102.

Galanter, Marc. 'Spirituality and Addiction: A Research and Clinical Perspective'. *The American Journal on Addictions* 15 (2006), 286–292.

Galanter, Marc, Helen Dermatis, Stephen Post, and Cristal Sampson. 'Spirituality-Based Recovery from Drug Addiction in the Twelve-Step Fellowship of Narcotics Anonymous'. *Journal of Addiction Medicine* 7.3 (2013): 189–195.

Grof, Christina. *The Thirst for Wholeness: Attachment, Addiction, and the Spiritual Path.* New York: HarperOne, 1993.

Grof, Stanislav. *Beyond the Brain: Birth, Death, and Transcendence in Psychotherapy.* New York: State University New York Press, 1985.

Grof, Stanislav, and Christina Grof, eds. *Spiritual Emergency: When Personal Transformation Becomes a Crisis.* New York: G. P. Putnam's Sons, 1989.

Grof, Stanislav, and Christina Grof, eds. *The Stormy Search for Self.* Los Angeles: J. P. Tarcher, 1990.

Hansen, Mary, Barbara Ganley, and Chris Carlucci. 'Journeys from Addiction to Recovery'. *Research and Theory for Nursing Practice: An International Journal* 22.4 (2008): 256–272.

Heinz, Adrienne J., Elizabeth R. Disney, David H. Epstein, Louise A. Glezen, Pamela I. Clark, and Kenzie L. Preston. 'A Focus-Group Study on Spirituality and Substance-Abuse Treatment'. *Substance Use Misuse* 45.1–2 (2010): 134–153.

Hill, Peter C., Kenneth I. Pargament, Ralph W. Hood, Jr., Michael E. McCullough, James P. Swyers, David B. Larson and Brian J. Zinnbauer. 'Conceptualizing Religion and Spirituality: Points of Commonality, Points of Departure'. *Journal for the Theory of Social Behavior* 30.1(2000): 51–77.

James, William. *The Varieties of Religious Experience.* New York: Modern Library, 1929.

Janoff-Bulman, Ronnie. *Shattered Assumptions: Towards a New Psychology of Trauma.* New York: Free Press, 1992.

Joseph, Stephen. *What Doesn't Kill Us: The New Psychology of Posttraumatic Growth.* London: Piatkus, 2012.

Kelly, Eugene W. 'The Role of Religion and Spirituality in Counselor Education: A National Survey'. *Counselor Education & Supervision* 33.4 (1994): 227–237.

Keyser-Marcus, Lori, Anika Alvanzo, Traci Rieckman, Leroy Thacker, and Allison Sepulveda. 'Trauma, Gender, and Mental Health Symptoms in Individuals with Substance Use Disorders'. *Journal of Interpersonal Violence* 30.1 (2014): 3–24.

Koenig, Harold G. 'Research on Religion, Spirituality, and Mental Health: A Review'. *Canadian Journal of Psychiatry* 54.5 (2009): 283–291.

Langman, Louise, and Man Cheung Chung. 'The Relationship Between Forgiveness, Spirituality, Traumatic Guilt and Posttraumatic Stress Disorder (PTSD) Among People with Addiction'. *The Psychiatric Quarterly* 84 (2013): 11–26.

Leseho, Johanna. 'Spirituality in Counsellor Education: A New Course'. *British Journal of Guidance & Counselling* 35.4 (2007): 441–454.

Logrip, Marian L., Eric P. Zorrilla, and George F. Koob. 'Stress Modulation of Drug Self-Administration: Implications for Addiction Comorbidity with Post-Traumatic Stress Disorder'. *Neuropharmacology* 62 (2012): 552–564.

Linley, P. Alex, and Stephen S. Joseph. 'Positive Change Following Trauma and Adversity: A Review'. *Journal of Traumatic Stress* 17 (2004): 11–21.

Lukoff, David. 'The Diagnosis of Mystical Experiences with Psychotic Features'. *Journal of Transpersonal Psychology* 17.2 (1985): 155–181.

Maslow, Abraham. *The Farthest Reaches of Human Nature*. New York: Viking Press, 1971.

McGarrol, Andrew. '2014 Matua Raki Workforce Innovation Award' Unpublished Report, *Hawke's Bay District Health Board*, (2014): 1–17.

McLeod, John. *The Counsellor's Workbook: Developing a Personal Approach*. Maidenhead: Open University Press, 2010.

Mental Health and Addictions Service, 'Recovery Action Plan'. Unpublished document: 1–5.

Miller, Geri. 'The Development of the Spiritual Focus in Counseling and Counselor Education'. *Journal of Counseling and Development*, 77.4 (1999): 498–501.

Morgen, Keith. et al. *Strategies for the Competent Integration of Spirituality into Addictions Counseling Training and Supervision* (2010). Viewed 19 August 2018. https://libres.uncg.edu/ir/uncg/f/C_Cashwell_Strategies_2010.pdf.

Narcotics Anonymous. 'About the Narcotics Anonymous (NA) 12-Step Recovery Program'. Viewed 19 August, 2018. http://www.recovery.org/topics/about-the-narcotics-anonymous-na-12-step-recovery-program/.

Nelson, James M. *Psychology, Religion, and Spirituality*. New York: Springer, 2009.

Office of Applied Studies, Substance Abuse and Mental Health Services Administration (SAMHSA). 'Mental Health Screenings and Trauma-Related Counseling in Substance Abuse Treatment Facilities'. *The N-SSATS Report*, September 30, 2010.

Pere, Rose. *Te Wheke: A Celebration of Infinite Wisdom*. Gisborne: Ao Ako Global Learning, New Zealand, 1997.

Rican, Pavel, and Pavlina Janosova. 'Spirituality as a Basic Aspect of Personality: A Cross-Cultural Verification of Piedmont's Model'. *The International Journal for the Psychology of Religion*, 20.1 (2010): 2–13.

Reynolds, Martina, Gillian Mezey, Murray Chapman, Mike Wheeler, Colin Drummond, and Alex Baldacchino, 'Co-Morbid Post-Traumatic Stress Disorder in a Substance Misusing Clinical Population'. *Drug and Alcohol Dependence* 77 (2005): 251–258.

Rogers, Carl. *On Becoming a Person: A Therapist's View of Psychotherapy*. London: Constable, 1961.

Rogers, Carl. *A Way of Being*. New York: Houghton Mifflin, 1995.

Room, Robin. 'Spirituality, Intoxication and Addiction: Six Forms of Relationship'. *Substance Use & Misuse* 48 (2013): 1109–1113.

Savage, Julie, and Sarah Armstrong. 'Developing Competence in Spiritual and Religious Aspects of Counseling'. In *Handbook of Multicultural Counseling Competencies*. Eds. Jennifer A. Erickson Cornish, Barry A. Schreier, Lavita I. Nadkarni, Lynett Henderson Metzger, and Emil R. Rodolfa, 379–413. Hoboken, NJ: John Wiley, 2010.

Schafer, Ingo, Willemmien Langeland, Johanna Hissbach, Christel Luedecke, Martin D. Ohlmeier, Claudia Chodzinski, Ulrich Kemper, and Peter Keiper. 'Childhood Trauma and Dissociation in Patients with Alcohol Dependence and Drug Dependence, or Both: A Multi-Centre Study'. *Drug and Alcohol Dependence* 109 (2010): 84–89.

Shaw, Annick, Stephen Joseph, and P. Alex Linley. 'Religion, Spirituality, and Posttraumatic Growth: A Systematic Review'. *Mental Health, Religion, & Culture* 8.1(2005): 1–11.

Spencer, Herbert. *Alcoholics Anonymous: The Story of How Many Thousands of Men and Women Have Recovered from Alcoholism*. 4th ed. New York: A. A. World Services Inc., 2001.

Spiegel, Betsy Robin. 'The Use of the 12 Steps of the Anonymous Program to Heal Trauma'. *Journal of Social Work Practice in the Addictions* 5.3 (2005): 103–105.

Tedeschi, Richard G., and Lawrence G. Calhoun. 'The Posttraumatic Growth Inventory: Measuring the Positive Legacy of Trauma'. *Journal of Traumatic Stress* 9 (1996): 455–471.

Thorne, Brian. *Counselling and the Spiritual Journey*. Birkenhead: Time & Space, 1997.

Todd, Fraser C. *Te Ariari o te Oranga: The Assessment and Management of People with Co-Existing Mental Health and Substance Use Problems*. Ministry of Health: Wellington, 2010.

Walker, Robert, Theodore M. Godlaski, and Michele Staton-Tindall. 'Spirituality, Drugs, and Alcohol: A Philosophical Analysis'. *Substance Use & Misuse* 48 (2013): 1233–1245.

Walton-Moss, Benita, Ellen M. Ray, and Kathleen Woodruff. 'Relationship of Spirituality or Religion to Recovery from Substance Abuse: A Systematic Review'. *Journal of Addictions Nursing* 24.4 (2013): 217–226.

Webber, Melinda. *Walking the Space Between: Identity and Māori/Pākehā*. Wellington: NZCER Press, 2008.

West, William. *Psychotherapy and Spirituality: Crossing the Line Between Therapy and Religion*. London: SAGE Publications, 2001.

West, William. *Spiritual Issues in Therapy: Relating Experience to Practice.* Basingstoke: Palgrave, 2004.

Young, J. Scott, Marsha Wiggins-Frame, and Craig S. Cashwell. 'Spirituality and Counselor Competence: A National Survey of American Counseling Association Members'. *Journal of Counseling and Development* 85.1 (2007): 47–52.

Zavan, Valeria, and Patrizia Scuderi. 'Perception of the Role of Spirituality and Religiosity in the Addiction Treatment Program Among the Italian Health Professionals: A Pilot Study'. *Substance Use & Misuse* 48 (2013): 1157–1160.

Zinnbauer, Brian J., and Kenneth I. Pargament. 'Working with the Sacred: Four Approaches to Religious and Spiritual Issues in Counseling'. *Journal of Counseling and Development* 78.2 (2000): 162–171.

PART 2

Contemplating Trauma

CHAPTER 6

Transformative Shocks: War Trauma in David Rabe's *Sticks and Bones* and Sam Shepard's *States of Shock*

Aslı Tekinay

Abstract

In *Sticks and Bones*, David Rabe addresses horrors associated with the Vietnam War but taking place out of the battlefield. The play centers on the homecoming of a blinded and guilt-ridden veteran named David, who brings the war home after a traumatic experience during the Vietnam War. Much more than his body and physical vision, his cultural and spiritual vision has changed. David's eye-opening trauma renders him a stranger to his own family, country and values. It moves beyond sheer apathy, which dominates most homecoming veteran stories in American literature. It instigates a spirit of dissent in contradiction with the mainstream American rhetoric of narcissism that defines the United States in terms of superlatives like the most powerful, the most democratic, the most humanitarian and the most idyllic. The traumatised American warrior cannot adjust to the fantasy world of happy America. Likewise, his all-American family is not willing to accept him as the traumatised victim who accuses them of cruelty. Along similar lines, Sam Shepard's *States of Shock*, performed in 1991 after the Gulf War, brings the war home to the United States. The traumatic shock gives birth to a radical transformation in the demented veteran, which may be read as a nihilistic vision ironically resulting from awakening from an unquestioning American narcissism. In both plays, rhetoric of dissent exposes violence, racism, social hypocrisy, and the superficiality of the middle-class values.

Keywords

David Rabe – trauma – dissent – American – dream – narcissism – Vietnam War – *Sticks and Bones* – Sam Shepard – *States of Shock*

 | DOI:10.1163/9789004407947_008

The American myth of exceptionalism and the narcissistic love of everything American, as well as the denigration of the non-American, in time has constituted the predominant mainstream rhetoric in the United States. In the political realm, democracy has been championed as the greatest American value and associated with the mission of extending freedom to nations in the world, which need an outside power to rescue them from bondage or anarchy or totalitarian regimes. Needless to say, such totally subjective justification for interference in foreign affairs results from the unquestioning faith in the superiority of the American ideology. Despite the moralistic and humanitarian intent behind it, interference leads to wars outside the country – wars of violence and savagery where American values turn out to be too simplistic and inadequate. The experience is foreign to the American psyche, not equipped to deal with it.

Trauma means an injury, physically or emotionally inflicted. Medically a serious bodily injury, such a deeply shocking experience leaves permanent mental or emotional scars in the victim. Be it in individuals or societies, moments of trauma lead to the questioning of deep-ingrained values and eventually to deconstructing and denying them. Traumas commonly result in social aloofness, retreat to the self, transformation in the use of language and even suicide. Social conventions, religious convictions, faith, and language may lose meaning to such a degree that the victim starts living a life-in-death existence. Thus traumas bring about a re-assessment of value systems so far taken for granted and a subsequent loss of faith in them.

Often traumatic, times of war have shaken veterans so deeply that the before and after of the war drastically differ for them. In other words, wars have provided an invaluable subject matter for all arts including literature throughout history. In the twentieth century, America's involvement in several wars outside its own continent shattered the protected and secluded American life, simple middle-class values, and faith in American exceptionalism and benevolence in the face of violence, savagery, and primitivism witnessed in the war. Thus as they bring the war home, war veterans introduce a new rhetoric of dissent, which clashes with the conventional rhetoric of flowery exaggeration. The new rhetoric shows the hollowness of the deep-rooted mainstream American rhetoric in a potentially nihilistic process.

David Rabe's work bears the most obvious imprint of the Vietnam War on account of his own involvement in it as a soldier. For Rabe, the Vietnam War has always served as a departure point, which allows him to bring to the foreground the elements in the national life and consciousness shaped by, and giving shape to, the period during and after the war: rootlessness, drug culture, inevitability of violence, obsession with mechanical sex, superficiality of the middle-class value system, insincerity (not only of people but also of institutions of state and religion) and racism. Rabe does not see the irrational violence he witnessed in the Vietnam War as some localised anomaly but as a fundamental fact of life that permeates all current American experience. In other words, Vietnam has moulded Rabe's vision, but his writing does not simply focus on Vietnam; for Rabe shares with dramatists like Ibsen and Miller the moralist's devotion to exposing social hypocrisy. Through the sincere honesty that pervades his work, Rabe explores violence, racism, sex, death, the problematics underlying genuine communication and the American value system. A harsh critic of the middle-class and its pieties, Rabe has a keen perception of what it means to be a male in America's male world.

In *Sticks and Bones* (1971), Rabe addresses horrors associated with the war but taking place out of the battlefield. The play, centred on the homecoming of a blinded and guilt-ridden veteran named David, brings the war home. David has changed; much more than his body and his physical vision, his cultural and spiritual vision has changed. David is someone else now, a stranger, to his own family, country, and their values. As to the family he comes back to, it recreates the Ozzie and Harriet Nelson family of the 1950s television show *The Adventures of Ozzie and Harriett*, aired first on the American radio, then on TV from 1952 to 1966. According to Milton J. Bates,

> During the period between World War II and Vietnam, prime-time TV idealized and promoted the social experiment programs like *The Adventures of Ozzie and Harriett*. Once the prime-time family was accepted as authentic, it served to reinforce social conformity. A family that did not conform to the model was made to feel deviant.[1]

Naming the family members after the Nelsons, Rabe sets up this family as a microcosm epitomising the American ideals and values. The Nelsons encapsulate the American dream, into which David brings the war and all that is associated with the war. The play, however, does not focus on David but on the family and, through them, the culture that they represent. As Robert Brustein notes on this issue,

> Rabe employs David's physical condition and the new relationship with his family as a springboard for examining American values; the standards and assumptions by which we live, our motivation to go to war, what

1 Milton J. Bates, *The Wars We Took to Vietnam: Cultural Conflict and Storytelling* (Los Angeles: U of California P, 1996), 187.

> happens to those who go to war, the American ethos, and what hope we can have for the future.[2]

The war matters since it causes a re-evaluation of the conditions, attitudes and values of the family and, through them, American society. This all-American family symbolises the whole nation. As Bigsby ironically states, 'they [the family] come out of the world of Albee's T*he American Dream*; he [David] out of *Heart of Darkness*'.[3] The Nelson family, representing American society, happily welcomes their son, David, as the returning warrior; but they object to accepting him as a demented and confused victim who accuses himself and them of cruelty.[4] The play tries to show the impossible adjustment of the traumatised American warriors to the fantasy world of the happy America. Having lived the horrors of reality, the Vietnam veterans could not adapt to the world of dreams America represented.

Sticks and Bones concerns blindness: both the protagonist of the play, David, and his society are blind – the former literally, the latter metaphorically. Ironically, the society to which David returns is extremely content with its own blindness and desperately tries not to lose the bliss associated with that state, the ignorant state of bliss. In this context, sight is accompanied with knowledge – of the horrifying truth, of the harsh reality, and of everything that lies outside the merry fantasy world of peace. Such is Rabe's America: a country raised on fantasy and blinded to reality. Hence, the rhetoric of the blinded son challenges that of mainstream middle-class rhetoric.

In *Sticks and Bones*, Rabe plays on the image of the perfectly happy family and how people try to preserve that image. Anything that runs counter to those images is to be rejected. Ozzie, the father, has great difficulty in acknowledging that their son is being sent home to them:

> Sgt. Major- I have your son.
> Ozzie What?
> Sgt. Major- Your son.
> Ozzie No.
> Sgt. Major- But he is. I have papers, pictures, prints. I know your blood and his. This is the right address.[5]

2 Robert Brustein, 'The Crack in the Chimney: Reflections on Contemporary American Playwriting'. *Theater* 9 (1978): 22.

3 C.W.E. Bigsby, *Modern American Drama: 1945–1990* (Cambridge: Cambridge U P, 1992), 258.

4 Ibid., 258.

5 David Rabe, 'Sticks and Bones', *Two Plays by David Rabe* (New York: Viking, 1979), 127.

Not only Ozzie, but also David think some mistake has been made. This place 'doesn't feel right', David says. Later on, he screams out: 'Goddamn you, Sergeant, I am lonely here! I am lonely!'.[6] Even though David is as far removed as he may be from the war zone, he deeply feels the impact of trauma when he steps into his own house. This phenomenon may read as a case history of what Cassie Pedersen discusses.[7] According to Pedersen, trauma is irreducible to one specific event that took place in the past. Drawing on Freud's concept of *Nachträglichkeit,* she posits that the impact of trauma occurs belatedly in intrusive symptoms such as nightmares and flashbacks. For David, the blinded veteran in Rabe's play, trauma is indeed a missed encounter that re-emerges in the present. As Pedersen argues, trauma consists of a dual temporal structure not comprehended at the time of its arrival but rupturing conscious awareness afterwards. Physically blinded and mentally traumatised but morally and intellectually possessing a vision clearer than before, David is entirely unsuited to the ordinary lives of his parents and his brother, Rick. The family cannot accommodate David, either. Preserving the image of bliss matters most and the traumatised veteran's homecoming threatens it.

Artificiality is so explicit that these people no longer can use a genuine language to express themselves emotionally. Unable to accept the horrible facts David brings home from the war, the family can neither understand nor react to his pain. Harriet, his mother, asks him if he would like chocolate fudge. Rick acts as though nothing is wrong and Ozzie makes an empty dramatic speech filled with clichés:

> Ozzie — You look good. Good to see you. Yes, sir. I think, all things considered, I think we can figure we're over the hump now and it's all downhill and good from here on it. I mean, we've talked things over, Dave, what do you say? The air's been cleared, that's what I mean – the wounds acknowledged, the healing begun. It's the ones that aren't acknowledged – the ones that aren't talked over – they're the ones that do the deep damage. That's always what happens.
>
> Harriet — I've baked a cake, David. Happy, happy being home.
>
> Ozzie — And we've got pop and ice and chips, and Rick is going to sing some songs.

6 Ibid., 132.

7 Cassie Pedersen, 'Encountering Trauma "Too Soon" and "Too Late": Caruth, Laplanche et the Freudian Nachträglichkeit', in this volume.

Harriet	Maybe we can all sing along if we want.
Rick	Anything special you'd like to hear, Dave?[8]

The family responds with abhorrence to David's imperfection – his blindness – his ability to kill, his loving a Vietnamese girl, a woman of an *alien race*, and finally his refusal to integrate within the family's happy image-making process. His presence calls into question every assumption by which they define their family and themselves.

Ozzie	I say to myself, what does it mean that he is my son? How the hell is it that ... he ... is my son? I mean, they say something of you joined to something of me and became ... him ... but what kinda goddamn thing is that? One mystery replacing another? Mystery doesn't explain mystery.[9]

As David confides in his parents his relationship with a Vietnamese girl, Ozzie and Harriett's responses clearly attest to their limited, prejudiced, and racist vision. They have adopted the typical American rhetoric of aggressive language and cultural denigration aimed at all non-American people, particularly Asians and Africans:

Ozzie	I mean, what you mean is you whored around a lot. Sure. You whored around. That's what you're saying. You banged some whores ... had some intercourse. Sure, I mean that's my point. (David, turning away, seems about to rise.) Now Dave, take it easy. What I mean is okay, sure, you shacked up with. I mean, hit on. Hit on, Dave. Dicked. Look at me. I mean, you pronged it, right? Sure, attaboy. I mean it's like going to the bathroom. All glands and secretions. Look, Dave, what are you doing? (David, heading for the stairs, crashes into Ozzie.) Don't – goddamnit, don't walk away from me. What the hell do you think you're doing? It's what you did. Who the hell you think you are? You screwed it. A yellow whore. Some yellow ass. You put in your prick and humped your ass. You screwed some yellow fucking whore!

8 Ibid., 152.

9 Ibid., 148.

Harriet	That's right, that's right. You were lonely and young and away from home for the very first time in your life, no white girls around –
David	They are the color of the earth, and what is white but winter and the earth under it like suicide? (Harriet's voice is a high humming in her throat) Why didn't you tell me what I was? (And Harriet vomits, her hands at her mouth, her back turning. There is a silence. They stand. Ozzie starts towards her, falters, starts, reaches, stops.)
Ozzie	Why ... don't ... you ask her to cook something for you, David, will you? Make her feel better ... okay.[10]

The above-quoted conversation is a rather explicit attack on the typical American middle-class value system: its racist attitude, prejudiced outlook on life and lack of genuine compassion. Calling Zung *a yellow whore,* Ozzie uses obscene language, which contradicts David's lyrical language – *they are the color of the earth*. The shallowness and superficiality demonstrated by the discourse of the parents recur in the play. Rabe not only attacks the American middle-class value system but also Christian religion. Harriet invites Father Donald to talk to Dave, saying 'I feel ... his problem is he sinned against the sixth commandment with whores'.[11] The Father's remarks on a white man's involvement with a woman belonging to a different race reach the level of comic absurdity. The playwright's harsh criticism of the priest's racist discourse reads as follows:

> It was demonstrated beyond any possible doubt that people – soldiers – who are compelled for some reason not even they themselves understand to establish personal sexual relationships with whores are inferior to those who don't; they're maladjusted, embittered, non-goal-oriented misfits. The sexual acceptance of another person, David, is intimate and extreme; this kind of acceptance of an alien race is in fact the rejection of one's own race – it is in fact the rejection of one's own self – it is sickness, David.[12]

Father Donald adds to the string of ironies in the play: the priest is really non-Christian; only the blind David can see, the healthy family members are indeed

10 Ibid., 144–145.

11 Ibid., 179.

12 Ibid., 188.

sick, and the Vietnamese girl, labelled as a yellow whore, is really pure. This is the essence of Rabe's dissent rhetoric.

Rabe uses Zung – the Vietnamese girl David has guiltily left behind – as the surreal element in the play. Invisible, penetrating through the walls, Zung is an unseen force of not only David's but also Ozzie and Harriet's lives. From time to time she becomes visible. When she finally becomes visible to Ozzie he strangles her, thus creating one of the climaxes of the play:

> Ozzie — I'm not David. I'm not silly and soft ... little David. The sight of you sickens me. You hear me, David? Believe me. I am speaking my honest true feelings. I spit on you, the both of you; I piss on you and your eyes and pain. Flesh is lies. You are garbage and filth. You are darkness. I cast you down. Deceit. Animal. Dirty animal. (And he is over her. They are sprawled on the ground. Silence as no one moves. She lies like a rag beneath him.)[13]

The strangling of Zung and the sexual assault on her is followed by Rick's suggestion that David commit suicide. Rick had warned him before:

> Rick — Let Dad alone. Let him alone. He's sick of you. What the hell's the matter with you? He doesn't wanna talk anymore about all the stupid stuff you talk. He wants to talk about cake and cookies and car and coffee. He's sick at you and he wants you to shut up. We hate you, goddamn you.[14]

As Rick tells David 'I'd kill myself if I were you, Dave. You're in too much misery. I'd cut my wrists',[15] Ozzie and Harriet, the father and the mother, support him. The absurdity of the situation blends into the tragedy:

> Harriet — Go ahead, David. The front yard's empty. You don't have to be afraid. The streets, too ... still and empty.
> Rick — It doesn't hurt like you think it will. Go ahead; just take it, Dave.
> Ozzie — You might as well.
> Rick — That's right.
> Ozzie — You'll feel better.
> Rick — I'll help you now, Dave, okay?

13 Ibid., 217.
14 Ibid., 217.
15 Ibid., 221.

Harriet	I'll go get some pans and towels.
	…
	(Harriet has brought silver pans and towels with roosters on them. The towels cover the arms of the chair and David's lap. The pans will catch the blood. All has been neatly placed. David, with Ricky's help, cuts one wrist, then the other, as they talk.)[16]

Dave's killing by his family resembles a collective ritual. The family has arranged the sacrificial suicide, discarding the veteran son. The all-American family will finally be happy again:

Rick	Mom, I like David like this.
Harriet	He's happier.
Ozzie	We're all happier.
Rick	Too bad he's gonna die.[17]

Sticks and Bones offers a masterful attempt to capture the most accurate version of the Vietnam reality and its meaning for the American people. The prevalent rhetoric favoured in the American social and political domains proves too superficial, inadequate, xenophobic and prejudiced to deal with traumas of war. Its weakness initiates the need for a new rhetoric, a nihilistic one that requires clearing the ground first. In *Sticks and Bones*, Rabe aims to awaken the American audience to what he sees as the dishonesty in the national psyche. In an interview, he states 'we all agreed to have the same amnesia … the vets are welcomed back but they have to shut up'.[18] So the dramatist screams at America through the blinded veteran David, who – ironically – is silently killed by his own family who return back to their normal blissful life of chocolate fudge, music and TV.

War trauma as a transformative shock that alters the vision of the survivor also serves as the thematic concern of another American dramatist, Sam Shepard. In a letter he sent to Joseph Chaikin in 1983, Shepard wrote that he had been 'pondering the idea of being lost, of one's identity being shattered under severe personal circumstances – in a state of crisis where everything I've previously identified with in myself suddenly falls away'.[19] In that letter Shepard

16 Ibid., 221–222.

17 Ibid., 223.

18 Eric James Schroeder, *Vietnam, We've All Been There: Interviews with American Writers* (Westport, CT: Praeger, 1992), 208.

19 Frank Day, *Twayne's US Authors Series: Sam Shepard* (New York: Twayne, 1992), 133.

called this Pirandellian condition a shock-state and working together, Chaikin and Shepard dramatised this particular state of the human psyche in all its horror in *The War in Heaven* – a poetic monologue about an angel who dies on the eve of his birth and who, drifting aimlessly in the afterlife, has lost all sense of personal order and destiny:

> I died
> the day I was born
> and became an Angel
> on that day
> Since then
> there are no days
> there is no time
> I am here
> by mistake[20]

The War in Heaven focuses not on the trauma or shock itself but on the 'resulting emptiness or aloneness which ensues'.[21] Based on an extremely personal concept of a shock-state, the mood that emanates from the misty atmosphere of *The War in Heaven* bears on moral, cosmic and existential nihilism, individual lives as well as the cosmos utterly devoid of value and meaning. Reminiscent of Schopenhauer and his view of the universe as nihilistic, Shepard and Chaikin speak of the world as some penal colony or place of punishment and expiation for the crime of being born. Naturally, once seen in this way, the world does not condone the futile hope of happiness. In 1991, Shepard and Chaikin came together again to rework *The War in Heaven* for its New York premiere. This time, however, with the tense and heated political climate in the United States they must have felt obliged to widen the scope of the personal shock-state recounted in the play to speak for all of postmodern, post-Vietnam America, suddenly at war again. Their revisions resulted in a different and newly inspired reading of *The War in Heaven* by Chaikin at the American Place Theatre and an entirely new play by Sam Shepard, namely *States of Shock*. The Gulf Crisis sparking off, the US had sent its troops to the Persian Gulf to bomb Iraq. These current events contributed largely to Shepard's creation of *States of Shock* – a topical political play dominated by a nihilistic mood of despair. Shepard, like Turgenev's Bazarov, plays a nihilist's role in *States of Shock* and

20 Joseph Chaikin and Sam Shepard, *The War in Heaven* (New York: Penguin, 1987), 155.
21 Day, *Twayne's US Authors Series*, 133.

clears the ground that belongs to the United States at the beginning of the last decade of the twentieth century.

At the outset, *States of Shock* offers a political and philosophical reaction to the American government's military involvement in the Gulf War and its invasion of Iraq; at the same time it reacts to the American public's complacent attitude towards these things. The play goes on to strip American democracy of its glamour by presenting – in all their nakedness – the values on which it is founded. The myth of American superiority is debunked and replaced with absurdity.

Based on the relationship between a father and a youth, eventually revealed as his son, the play allows the two to assume socio-political dimensions and mythic proportions as the plot unfolds. A colonel, the archetypal military man, the father is a firm believer in the noble myths of war perpetuated by men like himself. He has faith in the uniqueness of the American experience and American ideology. Stubbs is a disabled veteran, a martyr-figure. The play explores the fragmented nature of reality. According to the Colonel's story, Stubbs is a war hero. He tried valiantly to protect the Colonel's son by shielding him with his own body against enemy fire but the missile went straight through him to kill the son. Stubbs is now partially paralyzed and confined to a wheelchair. The play takes place in a family café. The Colonel brings Stubbs from the hospital for a treat on the anniversary of his son's death. The truth gradually recalled by Stubbs, however, differs drastically from the Colonel's account. Stubbs is actually the Colonel's son whom he repudiated to protect his honor. The young man was shot by his own countrymen as he tried to flee from battle and abandoned on the field.

Both father and son function as victims of the American political system. The father clings tightly to the patriarchal, pre-Vietnam myth of a righteous American military. He cannot bring himself to acknowledge the bankruptcy of those timeworn myths although the shattered young veteran living the post-Vietnam reality of horror and trauma is his very son. Through his characters, Shepard presents – in a Nietzschean frame of reference – the hollow core of American socio-politics in the post-Vietnam era and the narcotising dreams or ideals propagated by the fathers:

> Stubbs Keep thinking of home. That's the way to pull through this. Fix a picture in your mind. A backyard. A tree house. A better time. Truman, maybe. Straight – Talkin' Harry. Think of station wagons! Country Fairs! Ferris Wheels! Think of canned goods and cotton candy! Home economics. Production lines! The Great Northern Railroad! Think of what we've achieved!
>
> …

> It's endless! A River of Victory in all directions! Flooding the Plains! Hold to an image! Lock onto a picture of glorious unending expansion! Don't let yourself slip into doubt! Don't let it happen! You'll be swallowed whole![22]

The teachings of the American fathers and the American government present a false picture. The Vietnam generation of sons, the generation to which Shepard belongs, has lived through the inglorious war and its brutal aftermath. During the Gulf War, on the other hand, the horrors of war are carefully avoided by media coverage of the events, which leads to the indifference of American youth or their ill-equipment to cope with the war. The young waitress in the play, Glory Bee, provides a good example for the innocence of the American youth:

> The thing I can't get over is, it never occurred to me that Denny's could be invaded. I always thought we were invulnerable to attack. The landscaping. The lightning. The Parking lot. All the pretty bushes. Who could touch us? Who would dare?
>
> ...
>
> When the first wave of missiles hit us, I kept studying the menu. I thought the menu would save me somehow. The pretty colored photographs of all our specials. The Catfish Dinner. The Chicken-Fried Steak. I worshipped the menu.[23]

As if to awaken the myopic American media and the insensitive public, Stubbs, the disabled veteran, wheels himself first to the white couple sitting in the café, then to the audience, trying to explain himself:

> When I was hit there was no sound.
>
> ...
>
> I was hit in silence.
>
> ...
>
> The middle of me is all dead.
>
> The core. I'm eighty percent mutilated. The part of me that goes on living has no memory of the parts that are all dead. They've been separated for all time. They'll never have a partner. You're lucky to have a partner.[24]

22 Sam Shepard, *States of Shock* (New York: Vintage, 1993), 38.
23 Ibid., 41.
24 Ibid., 15.

When Stubbs recalls the battlefield before he was shot, he defines its foreignness as non-American, for in such an alien setting he could not hold on to an image of home to narcotise oneself:

> I was here. Facing the green sea. I was smelling it. Through the smoke. It didn't smell American to me. It smelled like a foreign sea. The birds were not American birds. I wanted to have a feeling for home but nothing called me back. I wanted to have a memory. I prayed for a memory. But nothing came but smoke and the smell of dead fish.
>
> ...
>
> America had disappeared.[25]

Screaming at the world with all his might – 'My thing hangs like dead meat',[26] – Stubbs does not only refer to his physical impotence but also to the hollow core inside him. As Francesca Brencio and Kori Novak argue in their chapter in this book, trauma disturbs the 'ek-static' unity of temporality and when it enters into a person's life, everything changes as the traumatic event overwhelms the individual's ability to cope with, and find meaning in, life. In *States of Shock*, the mood is existentially nihilistic: human existence is pointless and absurd; life is riddled with disappointment, frustration and pain.

The tone of existential nihilism that dominates Stubbs' discourse is reminiscent of the lament Shakespeare put on the lips of Macbeth:

> Tomorrow, and tomorrow, and tomorrow,
> Creeps in this petty pace from day to day,
> To the last syllable of recorded time;
> And all our yesterdays have lighted fools
> The way to dusty death. Out, out, brief candle!
> Life's but a walking shadow; a poor player,
> That struts and frets his hour upon the stage,
> And then is heard no more; it is a tale
> Told by an idiot, full of sound and fury,
> Signifying nothing.[27]

The tone of Macbeth's soliloquy, striking a note of existential nihilism and presenting life as utterly devoid of sense and meaning, permeates *States of Shock*.

25 Ibid., 19–20.
26 Ibid., 34.
27 William Shakespeare, *Macbeth* (New York: Penguin, 1980), 105.

The Colonel tries desperately to narcotise himself with various illusions in order not to fall prey to nihilistic despair. His resolution to proclaim Stubbs as his son and his attempts at avoiding the truth through the image of a happy future he tries to reconstruct before his eyes:

> Stubbs? Are you there? Are you still there? Don't run out on me now. As soon as this is over, I'll take you back. I promise you. I will. I'll make it official. Look, stock and barrel. It's not too late for that. I'll proclaim it in public. Stubbs? Are you listening? You haven't left me yet? You haven't disappeared? Stubbs! – If you're very good, Stubbs – if you're very very good – I'll buy you two desserts. Anything you want. Hot fudge. Milky Ways. Anything your heart desires. I'll take you to the movies. How 'bout that? I'll take you to the park. We'll swing. We'll slide, anything your heart desires. Stubbs?[28]

The unrelievable tension between the human being's craving to feel at home in the world on the one hand and the world's strangeness and bitterness on the other creates in *States of Sh*ock a situation of existential nihilism. Stubbs represents reality in all its strangeness, bitterness and ruthlessness while all the other characters – the young waitress, the Colonel and the white couple – represent in different ways the desperate attempt to cope with the world. Each is narcotised in his/her way to avoid nihilistic despair. The Colonel holds onto illusions and myths of the past; the waitress is shielded in her naiveté in the sanctuary of Denny's; and finally the anaemic white couple, reverting to extreme egoism and insensitivity to the outside world, confine themselves in their own private cocoon.

States of Shock presents a godless cosmos, indifferent or even inimical to human concerns. As Stubbs tries to recall how he was shot, he clearly remembers the absence of God at a time when he needed Him most. His memories take him back to the time before he was shot, when he and a comrade were on the battlefield during intensive bombing around them:

> I could feel his spine trembling on my spine. There was nothing we could do about fear. We couldn't talk ourselves out of it. Neither one of us knew how to pray. We had no idea who God was. Who was God?[29]

The Colonel has no ready answer to this question. Saying 'we can reconstruct this later',[30] he manages to avoid the intolerable thought that there is indeed

28 Shepard, *States of Shock*, 46.
29 Ibid., 31.
30 Ibid., 31.

no God. The non-existence of God has been frequently associated with nihilism. In *The Specter of the Absurd,* Donald Crosby discusses how frequently atheism and nihilism come down to the same thing – that the only alternative to belief in God and adherence to traditional Western religious teachings boils down to nihilistic despair.[31] A necessary connection between belief in God and the meaning of life is assumed also by Kirillov, a character in Dostoevsky's *The Possessed*: 'I can't understand how an atheist could know that there is no God and not kill himself on the spot'.[32] Stepan Trofimovitch, another character in the same novel, also implies that

> the one essential condition of human existence is that man should always be able to bow down before something infinitely great. If men are deprived of the infinitely great, they will not go on living and will die of despair. The Infinite and the Eternal are as essential for man as the little planet on which he dwells.[33]

The cosmos in *States of Shock* is definitely bereft of a God, an Infinite and Eternal power before which man can bow down. If such a power indeed existed, would the universe still be a jumble of discordant events with no underlying unity, pattern or significance? The play forces this question into the mind. In a godless world, forlorn, abandoned individuals suffer both physically and mentally. Human lives – so vulnerable to devastating shocks, sorrows, disappointments and pains – cannot possible have any meaning in Shepard's world. He clears the ground of all illusions and imported meanings, using Nietzsche's terminology.

Frank Day calls *States of Shock* 'a play of non-conclusion'.[34] Shepard offers no conclusion to the loose plot. The play ends with a song; rhyming music is an attempt to fill the void. Stubbs, wearing a gas mask, stands at one corner of the stage, mumbling: 'Long live the enemy!!!'[35] The others are singing:

> Sometimes I live in the country
> Sometimes I live in the town

31 Donald A. Crosby, *The Specter of the Absurd: Sources and Criticism of Modern Nihilism* (Albany: State University of New York, 1988), 4.

32 Fyodor Mikhailovich Dostoyevsky, *The Possessed,* trans. David Magarschack (London: Penguin, 1953), 582.

33 Ibid., 624.

34 Day, *Twayne's US Authors Series, 133.*

35 Shepard, *States of Shock*, 46.

Sometimes I have a great notion
To jump into the river and drown
Irene, good night
Irene, good night
Good night, Irene
Good night, Irene
I'll see you in my dreams[36]

The lullaby dulls our senses and invites us to enter the trance-like state of death-in-life as Shepard directs his nihilistic rage at this human scene. The prologue he attaches to the play – the first stanza of Richard Hugo's poem *Degrees of Gray in Philipsburg* – takes on a wider meaning when reread after the play:

You might come here Sunday on a whim.
Say your life broke down. The last good kiss
you had was years ago. You walk these streets
laid out by the insane, past hotels
that didn't last, bars that did, the tortured try
of local drivers to accelerate their lives.
Only churches are kept up. The jail
turned 70 this year. The only prisoner
is always in, not knowing what he's done.
The principal supporting business now
is rage.[37]

In this morbid human scene, fathers and sons are at each other's throats, far beyond commonplace rivalries and generation gaps since murder is at stake. As Martin Tucker writes, 'in Shepard's earlier work, the father was at the core of the drama, but the father's role was subordinate to the son's leading character; here the father is the protagonist and the son is his foil'.[38] Tucker draws a parallel between Shakespeare's *Hamlet* and Shepard's *States of Shock* as both plays end with the son killing the father figure. In *States of Shock*, Stubbs 'grabs the Colonel around the neck in a stranglehold'[39] and, choking in Stubbs' stranglehold, the Colonel continues to paint an idyllic picture of their future together:

---

36 Ibid., 46.
37 Ibid., 3.
38 Martin Tucker, *Sam Shepard* (New York: The Continuum Publishing Company, 1992), 164.
39 Shepard, *States of Shock*, 46.

> If you're very, very good, Stubbs – if you're very, very good – I'll buy you two desserts. Anything you want. Hot fudge. Milky Ways. Anything your heart desires. I'll take you to the movies. How 'bout that? I'll take you to the park. We'll swing. We'll slide. Anything your heart desires.[40]

The father's suggested remedy for the tragic loss the son has suffered is a retreat to the sweet American world of chocolate fudge, candy bars, movies and parks. Clearly the narcotising effect of sweet desserts, movies, music, and games plays an integral role in the rhetoric of both *Sticks and Bones* and *States of Shock*. They function as metaphors for the shallowness and innocence of the American way of life. In both plays, the adherence to the joyful picture-perfect American world of innocence acquires such strength that it destroys everything in its pathway. The family in *Sticks and Bones* kills the veteran son who cannot fit into that picture, while the son in *States of Shock* is on the verge of killing the father who still expects him to be good in his own terms. Despising his own crippled son and forsaking him, the Colonel cannot bring himself to embrace Stubbs as his own son and to open his eyes to see the truth.

Both plays present the void beneath the American values of order and patriotism. What the sons experience abroad in the wars they were sent to negates the faith in the American values. When they come back home, they are confronted with the self-centredness of their loved ones: parents and brother in *Sticks and Bones* and father in *States of Shock*. At the end of the former, the son is killed, while the latter ends with the son and father frozen, with a sword in the son's hand. Thus both plays end with murder – infanticide and parricide. The blinded David and the crippled Stubbs, beaten and whipped, display horrifying images on the stage. Stubbs' refrain lines, 'I remember the day you forsake me and You invented my death',[41] attest to the tragic dimension of the American psyche, which – unable to penetrate into the truth – goes on swimming in a sea of narcotising narcissism.

The discourse of the Colonel, the waitress and the white couple at the café (who hardly have any other topic of conversation except the clam chowder they are waiting for) in *States of Shock*, as well as that of Ozzie, Harriett, and Rick in *Sticks and Bones* abound with references to all-American foods and empty clichés in contrast with the language of the war veterans. Like the powerful visual images on the stage – dark eye-glasses, cane, wound in the chest, and wheelchair – the language used by the veterans – curt, concise and shocking – has

40 Ibid., 46.
41 Ibid., 39.

the effect of an ear-piercing scream. David and Stubbs scream at the audience and in a thoroughly Artaudian fashion, try to awaken the audience from their sleep. In line with theories that Antonin Artaud formulated on the theatre of cruelty, Rabe and Shepard use the stage as a platform to shatter the American rhetoric of narcissism and expose its superficiality and hollow core. Both their plays posit the existence of broad humanitarian values, not only ignored but also contradicted by the faith in the superiority of America's national values. In Caldwell's words, 'We are human. They are not. It is the nationalist's classical justification for murder'.[42] Rabe and Shepard debunk this very rhetoric in their anti-war plays and, as they do so, they rely on the first-hand experience of war trauma as a figurative springboard that enables the veteran protagonists to expose the downsides of the American myth of exceptionalism.

Bibliography

Bates, Milton J. *The Wars We Took to Vietnam: Cultural Conflict and Storytelling.* Los Angeles: U of California P, 1996.

Bigsby, C.W.E. *Modern American Drama: 1945–1990.* Cambridge: Cambridge U P, 1992.

Brustein, Robert. 'The Crack in the Chimney: Reflections on Contemporary American Playwriting'. *Theater 9* (1978): 21–29.

Caldwell, Wilber W. *American Narcissism: The Myth of National Superiority.* New York: Algora, 2006.

Chaikin, Joseph and Sam Shepard, *The War in Heaven.* New York: Penguin, 1987.

Crosby, Donald A. *The Specter of the Absurd: Sources and Criticism of Modern Nihilism.* Albany: State University of New York, 1988.

Day, Frank. *Sam Shepard.* New York: Twayne, 1992.

Dostoyevsky, Fyodor Mikhailovich. *The Possessed.* Translated by David Magarschack. London: Penguin, 1953.

Rabe, David. 'Sticks and Bones'. *Two Plays by David Rabe, 125–223.* New York: Viking, 1979.

Shakespeare, William. *Macbeth.* New York: Penguin, 1980.

Schroeder, Eric James. *Vietnam, We've All Been There: Interviews with American Writers.* Westport, CT: Praeger, 1992.

Shepard, Sam. *States of Shock.* New York: Vintage, 1993.

Tucker, Martin. *Sam Shepard.* New York, The Continuum Publishing Company, 1992.

---

42 Wilber W Caldwell, *American Narcissism: The Myth of National Superiority* (New York: Algora, 2006), 142.

CHAPTER 7

'Pinned limb to limb by a ton of rocks': Annihilation in the Face of Captivity and Torture in Alan Cumyn's *Man of Bone*

Danielle Schaub

Abstract

Alan Cumyn's *Man of Bone* offers a powerful example of the traumatic impact that captivity and torture can afford on a human being. The novel narrates the nine-month-long period during which Bill Burridge, a Canadian diplomat, endures captivity and torture after a guerrilla faction kidnaps him on the imaginary South Pacific Island of Santa Irene. Hooded for most of the narration until his release, Burridge gives way to a wide range of responses, his narrative evoking the terror of uncertainty and life threat in its disjunctive presentation, hallucination, dream realm and stylistic fragmentation. Language narrows in on small details recorded in elliptical sentences, whose choppy structures convey suffocation and awe; to keep such devastating feelings at bay and distract his mind, the protagonist turns to repetitive patterns and flashbacks. Even when freed, Burridge persists with his fixation on details, dissociative flashbacks and exploitation of water imagery to convey the sense of distressed immersion, making it hard for the readers to determine the boundary between the real and the imaginary. His narrative keeps echoing his inability to disentangle himself from the obsessive thoughts that drive him outside himself and cause him to relive the experience in confused divided consciousness. The discussion of trauma from captivity and torture will call on psychoanalytical theories of Michael Balint, Wilfred R. Bion, Frances Tustin and Judith Mitrani.

Keywords

captivity – torture – disjunction – dissociation – textual reflection of traumatic experiences – fragmentation

 | DOI:10.1163/9789004407947_009

1 Introduction

Those subjected to trauma tend to inscribe their own chaotic experiences with disjunctive patterns even after freeing themselves from their most direct post-traumatic symptoms, for the life strategies adopted for survival still linger and inform the ways trauma pursues the person long after the event. When the trauma undergone lasts for an extended period of time as happens in captivity,[1] particularly with the added penalty of mental and physical torture inflicted haphazardly on a daily basis, the victim adopts what psychoanalyst Judith Mitrani names 'autistic manoeuvres [that] serve as a protective shell against the terrifying awareness of bodily separateness and dissolution into nothingness'.[2] The anxiety provoked proves so unbearable that the victim of captivity and torture focuses on sensations, thereby maintaining distance from the experience and becoming incapable of facing it so as to process it. As Mitrani notes, sensations 'provid[e] an illusion of safety, strength and impermeability, or … may have a numbing or tranquilizing effect upon the individual, which blocks out terrifying awareness'.[3] In other words, by using 'sensation-dominated delusions' the victim does not take in the experience, thereby disconnecting from the situation. Such detachment Mitrani considers the sign of 'unmentalized experience'.[4] To put it differently, the victim does not integrate the sensations mentally or view them as representative of the event, somehow regressing to a pre-symbolisation phase so that perceptions remain purely bodily realities without mental association for further use. The victim can therefore not store the experience, reflect on it or learn from it.

Writers attempting to capture life threatening events and their impact on human beings tend to convey them through stylistic/linguistic and poetic/narratological patterns that reflect the disjunction experienced. Such exploitation of writing techniques definitely characterises Alan Cumyn's *Man of Bone*[5] while highlighting the traumatic fissure undergone at the time of its occurrence by a Canadian diplomat named Bill Burridge. The novel narrates how, during his

1 In *Trauma and Recovery: From Domestic Abuse to Political Terror* (London: Pandora, 1992), Judith Lewis Herman notes that drawn-out traumas exist only in captivity whether the person is literally imprisoned or simply restrained 'by a combination of force, intimidation, and enticement' (74), coercion, dependency or subordination. In Burridge's case, physical captivity applies in the narrative present and subjection in childhood.

2 Judith L. Mitrani, 'On the Survival Function of Autistic Manoeuvres in Adult Patients', *International Journal of Psychoanalysis* (1992), 73: 549.

3 Mitrani, op. cit., 550.

4 Mitrani, op. cit., 550.

5 Alan Cumyn, *Man of Bone* (Toronto: McClelland and Stewart, 1998).

first post on the imaginary South Pacific island of Santa Irene, he falls in the hands of a guerrilla faction that keep him in captivity and torture him during nine months. Visually impaired on account of the hood imposed on him for most of the narrative until his release, Burridge gives way to a wide range of responses, during and after his imprisonment. In particular, the narrative relating his reactions and thoughts during captivity evoke the typical terror of uncertainty and life threat in its disjunctive presentation, hallucination, dream realm and stylistic fragmentation. To render his disempowerment, annihilation and disconnection, language narrows in on small details recorded in elliptical sentences, whose choppy structures convey suffocation and awe; to keep such devastating feelings at bay and distract his mind and distract his mind, the protagonist turns to repetitive patterns and flashbacks. Even when freed, Burridge persists with his fixation on details, dissociative flashbacks and exploitation of water imagery to convey the sense of distressed immersion, making it hard for the readers to determine the boundary between the real and the imaginary. The failed attempt to flee from his captors finds an echo in his failure to disentangle himself from the obsessive thoughts that drive him outside himself and cause him to relive the experience in confused divided consciousness. The discussion of trauma from captivity and torture that follows calls on psychoanalytical theories of Michael Balint, Wilfred R. Bion, Frances Tustin and Judith L. Mitrani to explain some of the patterns followed by the victim.[6]

2 Relevant Psycho-Analytical Theories

Balint's *The Basic Fault: Therapeutic Aspects of Regression* clarifies some of Bill Burridge's responses. While addressing Freud's reflections on narcissism, Balint notes that some patients withdraw 'from the world of normal – that is, triangular or Oedipal – relationships'.[7] On account of their regressive state, they require more understanding and attunement than others, which they can more easily secure in one-on-one relationships, as Balint observes.[8] Conversely, Balint would remark that the regressive state in captivity so characteristic of Bill Burridge stems from the primary caregiver's inability to protect the child against a domineering father. With memories of a father making him feel worthless, Bill has little positive parental support as emotional foundation to counterbalance the effects of sustained trauma. An example foreshadowing

6 I am indebted to Dana Amir for making me discover Judith Mitrani.

7 Michael Balint, *The Basic Fault: Therapeutic Acts of Regression* (London, Tavistock, 1968), 52.

8 Michael Balint, 'On Love and Hate', *International Journal of Psycho-Analysis*, 33 (1952): 355–362.

Burridge's susceptibility to traumatic experience, his parents proved so fascinated by news of catastrophic events on the television screen during his childhood that they could not provide him with answers to his questions and reassure him; in other words, his parents must have granted him little space and caused a form of second-hand traumatisation because the child could not fathom whatever he witnessed on the screen; as a result, at night his imagination haunted him with terrifying images that even the proximity of his mother's warm body could not obliterate. On account of past faulty primary love or reductive family object relationships, Bill succumbs to the iniquitous treatment meted out to him in captivity and falls into the abyss of human erasure. Since the environment does not secure harmony, he withdraws and holds onto sensations for survival, but these offer no alleviation. Securing no understanding or empathy, captivity fixes Burridge in terror and inhumanity so that, to ward off the evil eye, he utters clichés and sayings in elliptical form.

In this respect, Bion's article 'Attacks on Linking'[9] provides meaningful reflections as he ascribes the fragmentation and apparent meaninglessness of schizophrenics' thought and language to attacks on a link between objects as a result from failed primary caregiver's containment. Bion's claims that psychosis consists of attacks that break bonds with others and within oneself rather than creating them apply to Bill Burridge.[10] He certainly cannot connect his bodily sensations to any organised mental evaluation of the situation, for he cannot integrate them. Because the terror inspired by repeated torture and degradation leaves him helpless, Burridge does not apprehend reality meaningfully, the more so as he cannot fathom what the faction seeks and has no strong beliefs to feel less powerless. Attacking links, his mind wanders off on loose, disconnected sense impressions and flimsy memory tracks. In addition, as his captors keep him hooded for most of the time, Burridge cannot allocate to his perceptions any consequential evaluation, even less so for his disorientation causes him to sever the situation from the mental processes that reason and organise experiences.[11] The disconnected discourse of the novel underscores Bill's inability to link the senses to the mind as though he cannot contain the experiences, voice his most difficult feelings and then reflect them in a way

9 Wilfred R. Bion, 'Attacks on Linking', *International Journal of Psycho-Analysis,* 40 (1959): 308–315.

10 Wilfred R. Bion, op. cit., 308–315.

11 In *Space and Place: The Perspective of Experience* (Minneapolis: University of Minnesota Press, 1977), Yi-Fu Tuan notes that human beings achieve order and control through the organisation of their spatial perception (34–50). Place is space that an individual associates with familiarity and safety (29–33, 73, 136–148).

that does not harm him. As his childhood's sense of futility and uselessness resulting from his domineering father not containing his emotions but rather aggravating them, Bill Burridge's containing function resembles a sieve letting unorganised sensations slip through large holes like so many roasted peels separated from the nuts he cannot enjoy.

The disjunctive succession of fragments so characteristic of Bion's patients also bears similarity to the 'inconsequential' talk of Frances Tustin's patient in her article on 'Autistic Processes'.[12] She recalls his illogical flow of words as preventing her from concentrating. Her reflections on the 'consistency and regularity in the therapeutic setting'[13] oppose the lack of predictability behind the captors' visits to Burridge and his feelings of separateness as well as lack of nurturing support. Frances Tustin's considerations in 'The "Black Hole": A Significant Element in Autism'[14] bear on the hopelessness and helplessness that Burridge experiences. These feelings ensue from the lack of protection sensed while in captivity and under torture. The lack quite likely goes back to childhood since the novel reveals, as mentioned before, that he could not rely on a containing mother, let alone on a containing father; consequently, in captivity he feels terrorised as though amputated from the maternal container, indeed from any source of protection. Totally alone in seclusion, he can rely on no one; to secure protection, he shuts himself off the situation. Needless to say, as a subject of torture inflicted without any periodicity, he suffers from external and internal stimuli, the former induced by the captors, the latter by his terror of prospective torture. By disconnecting from the situation, he can also not assimilate the experience or articulate it in any fashion that would help him negotiate his sense of fear and panic so that he loses any sense of agency and vitality in the face of the black hole created for want of connection. At the same time, the separateness imposed by solitary confinement causes terror and Burridge tries to restrict his awareness of it by focusing on his bodily and sensorial experiences.

In this context, Judith L. Mitrani's considerations in her article 'On the Survival Function of Autistic Manoeuvres in Adult Patients' clarifies the process followed by Bill Burridge while in captivity and thereafter.[15] She claims that adult patients may resort to 'autistic manoeuvres' to protect themselves against 'dissolution into nothingness'.[16] The anxiety provoked by unexplainable

12 Frances Tustin, 'Autistic Processes', Journal of Child Psychotherapy, 2 (1969): 23–39.

13 Tustin, op. cit., 37.

14 Frances Tustin, The 'Black Hole': A Significant Element in Autism, *Free Associations*, 1 (1988): 35–50.

15 Mitrani, 'On the Survival Function of Autistic Manoeuvres in Adult Patients', 549–559.

16 Ibid., 549.

captivity and torture proves so unbearable that the victim focuses on sensations, thereby maintaining safe distance from the experience. By concentrating on sensations, Burridge obstructs the harrowing experience, which provides 'a numbing or tranquilizing effect'.[17] In other words, for the sake of surviving the experience and not succumbing to the 'overwhelming anxiety' it engenders, the victim uses 'sensation-dominated delusions', thereby disconnecting from the situation.[18] Such detachment Mitrani considers the sign of 'unthought experience'.[19] To put it differently, the victim does not integrate the sensations mentally or view them as representative of the event, somehow regressing to a pre-symbolisation phase so that perceptions remain purely bodily realities without mental association for further use. The victim can therefore not store the experience, let alone reflect on, or learn from, it.

3 Stylistic and Compositional Reflection of Trauma

Evoking Bion's theory in its stylistic characteristics, the novel starts with such a sensation-dominated passage reflecting the daily endurances faced by Bill Burridge that it also illustrates Mitrani's theory. The passage reads as follows:

> Black oil pit. Bands out to each side but there's no wall. No wall, no tree, no door, nothing solid. Just black, oily air. Can't move my head to see. I open my eyes but see only blackness. Take a step, can't keep my balance but don't fall either. Try to drop to my knees, crawl, feel something with my hands but can't, something holds me up. Try to yell but my voice won't work. No sound, just the smell of the oily black air. Have to hurry because of the noise from behind, don't know what it is, have to move move move or it'll get me. But where? Trying to run in slow motion, then stepping on snakes, a mass of them, try to pull out but it's too late, they bite at my leg, can't see them, pain shoots through me. Shake, thrash, try to cry out but there's no voice, hands can't move to rip them off. Writhe in panic, and they bite now up my calves, my thighs, tear now at my testicles, but my hands won't move to get them off. Tremble, scream, roll, no escape just oily black air ...[20]

---

17 Ibid., 550.

18 Ibid., 550.

19 Judith Mitrani, 'Toward an Understanding of Unmentalized Experience', *Psychoanalytic Quarterly*, 64 (1995), 109 For an elaboration of 'unmentalized experience', see Judith Mitrani, op. cit., 68–112.

20 Alan Cumyn, *Man of Bone* (Toronto: McClelland and Stewart, 1998), 7.

The report of inaptitude rendered in a virtually dehumanised voice for want of an expressed agent equates traumatic reality with a 'black oil pit', the very limy pit into which trauma throws the victim and from which he cannot disentangle himself. The passage points to multiple characteristics of trauma, such as the absence of spatial parameters, inability to move, voicelessness, darkness, unexplainable noises, threatening wild animals. Both the absent agent and the lack of strong verbs in the first four fragments reinforce the narrator's helplessness. Illustrating Bion's attacks on linking, fragments, juxtaposition of statements and asyndeton (or lack of coordination) transmit the staccato and violence of the experience from which Burridge wishes to disconnect. In the same vein, the deletion of the narrator's 'I' (first-person pronoun) or eye (the organ of sight) bar one instance deprives the human of existence, indeed overwhelmingly erases the human agent.[21] At the same time, the whirl of sensations evokes the narrator's inability to fathom the experience undergone in Mitranian terms.[22] Burridge can only succumb to dread as he cannot activate his brain. The passage conveys the reality confronting him through a series of images that render the experiential parameters of trauma, with its parallel external and internal spaces that collapse for want of accurate spatial markers and boundaries that would hinder the infiltration of chaos.

Given that, according to George Matoré's *L'Espace humain,*[23] humans tend to control chaos by delineating their spatial environment whether physically or linguistically, the narrative absence of boundaries and spatial determiners reinforce the devastating uncertainty caused by captivity and the threat of the unknown characteristically yielding the "chronic apprehension of imminent doom" that Judith Herman reports.[24] In this spatial void, even the strong verbs related to the subject in absence end up negated, manifesting the stark contrast between the wish to escape and its impossible realisation. Even the injunctive repetition 'move move move' remains ineffective as without the perception of spatial parameters, Burridge surrenders to the horror of imagination. While darkness, impeded vision and unaccounted for threatening noises characterise Burridge's deficient perception of the setting and its concomitant physical threat, the response they engender in the traumatised – voicelessness, paralysis, stress, terror and pain – entails the inefficient range of emotional and physical reactions.

21 Such erasure calls to mind Judith Lewis Herman's comment on the insidious erosion of personality, on the victim's not having a sense of self (op. cit. 86).

22 Mitrani, 'On the Survival Function of Autistic Manoeuvres in Adult Patients', 550.

23 Georges Matoré, *L'Espace humain: L'Expression de l'espace dans la vie, la pensée et l'art contemporains* [Paris: La Colombe (Sciences et techniques humaines, 2), 1962], 15–26.

24 Herman, ibid.

Pinned in unassimilable surroundings of highly graphic quality, Burridge gives way to panic-inducing imagination trapping him in further powerlessness.[25]

Following the description of the helplessness trapping the narrator, the beginning of the next paragraph changes the nature of the opening paragraph. With its initial one-word fragment – Awake – the passage makes the opening of the novel a clear oneiric representation rather than a description of lived experience. However, since dreams comprise elements of one's waking life and concerns, the initial opening contains some elements of reality that clearly point to the traumatic experience; Burridge's considerations after waking up signal that, at first, he tries to process the traumatic situation mentally by correlating elements from the dream and his situation:

> Awake. Now I'm awake, heart pounding, shit – awake. No snakes. There aren't any snakes. The blackness is the hood, the oily smell from the many layers of paint that keep out all light. My shackled legs. The needles of pain from this cramped position against the wall and floor – those were the snakes. Wet and cold, which is the night; hot like an oven would be day. I try to move my fingers. My arms are strapped behind my back but I can't feel them anymore. Neck and shoulders in constant pain, feet and legs too, but my arms have no feeling at all. I'm seized with the thought that I've lost them, they've been amputated. I rock back and forth. Something under my bum, a straw mat or my fingers. I try to breathe slowly, not give in to the panic. Mat? Fingers? Everything's in pain, but what wouldn't I give for pain in my fingers to show they're still there? Please God, I think, please God, whoever you are, please God, give me pain in my fingers![26]

Starting with equations comparing the dream with the conditions under which his captors keep Burridge, the paragraph shows that trauma has not

25 In her chapter on 'Transformative Shocks' in this volume, Aslı Tekinay also quotes the characters visually obscene language in Rabe's *Sticks and Bones*. Similarly, in his chapter on 'Body and Trauma in Chuck Palahniuk's *Haunted*' in this volume, Claudio Zanini comments on the graphic nature of the novel he discusses, remarking that at public readings, numerous members of the audience would faint or vomit at the vivid description of an adolescent character's intestinal content in a narrative by one of the wannabe writers. The same holds for Elwin Susan John's references to the deformities of the flawed bodies after exposure to chemical disasters in the novels she examines in her chapter 'I Used To Be Human Once', in this volume. Equally graphic, some passages from Nadeem Aslam's *The Wasted Vigil* in Gen'ichiro Itakura's chapter 'Writing Trauma, Writing Modern: Nadeem Aslam's *The Wasted Vigil* and Atiq Rahimi's *The Patience Stone*', in this volume offer gory descriptions of violence.

26 Cumyn, op.cit., 7.

yet interrupted his consciousness. Through the comparison, Burridge clarifies both the dream and the particulars of his captivity. However, in his survey, the sensations remain fragmentary, as though not connected to him, partly because of the ties that constrict him. Clearly in his attempt to decode the dream and its connection to his reality, he hops from one image and/or feeling to another as if the need to disconnect prevents him from creating a coherent picture. When he reflects on painful or benumbed parts of his body, he imagines the worst – amputation of the desensitised arms – and adopts a soothing foetal position, rocking like a baby. His imagination unleashes such distress that he even repeatedly invokes divine help to retrieve pain where his body lacks response.

In his endeavour to stay in control, Burridge then uses several strategies; to keep the traumatic experience at bay, he tries to maintain corporeal awareness by giving orders from his brain to his body as though he were monitoring the situation from a distance: 'Message from brain: Fingers, can you read me? Fingers, do you copy? Fingers, if you copy, give me a sign. Move, fingers. Scratch the floor. Scratch your bum. Fingers. Just flex. Fingers if you can read me …'[27] The series of imperatives mark the stress felt at losing feelings. Clearly at such times, Burridge loses the ability to secure cooperation between mind and body. He therefore tries to take leave of his own body in a Zen fashion by counting steamboats, by avoiding sleeping for fear of the snakes that people his dreams, by imposing other mental exercises.

Language marks the heightened burden and oppressiveness of sequestration. Rather than following some logical stream, Burridge's narrative hops from one thought to another, from one bodily sensation to another without clear logic, as in the initial dream, illustrating what Whitehead calls 'the hiatuses and dislocations which necessarily inhabit trauma'[28] or Bion's attacks on linking.[29] Figures of style, such as polysyndetons (or multiple coordination), asyndetons (or total lack of coordination), intentional fragments, comma splices, and run-ons, also disrupt the flow to reproduce the experiential confrontation with trauma. Polysyndetons stress the intolerable weight of the conditions that Burridge must sustain, as for instance in the following sentences: 'Hell is being shackled *and* hooded *and* handcuffed in a closet *or* basement *or* whatever it is *and* freezing at night *and* roasting in the day *and* smelling shit *and*

27 Ibid., 8.

28 Anne Whitehead, *Trauma Fiction* (Edinburgh: Edinburgh University Press, 2004), 5.

29 These recall the fissures discussed by Itakura in his analysis of Nadeem Aslam's *The Wasted Vigil* in this volume. As Marcus Caldwell attempts at working through the trauma he has suffered, his narrative abounds in disruptions that capture his confused state.

piss from your own pants'[30]; 'The first time I had to go, I held it *and* held it *and* yelled for someone, *but* there was no one, *and* then the cold *and* the smell *and* disgust'.[31] By piling the past participles, the polysyndeton in the first example emphasises the unendurable passiveness, whereas the piled gerunds convey the equally insufferable sensorial impact of the experience. The text abounds in soothing sayings mimicking normalcy, such as 'The longer you stay alive, the better your chances'[32], or orders pretending security exists, such as 'Don't panic',[33] 'Stay alert',[34] 'Focus yourself',[35] 'Dial 911'[36], as if the mind tries to take control of the situation, somehow recalling the uncomprehending responses of non-survivors to survivors' realities. As though it could help, Burridge invokes the lack of preparation for the experience – 'I've not been briefed for this. Williams do you hear me? I've not been briefed'[37]; clearly such invocation recalls the unforeseeable character of trauma that shakes the foundational belief in safety and concomitant trust. He mimics journalistic reports to sum up his experience, pointing to the large-scale aseptic minimisation of human realities so typical of a world seeking uniform normalcy; but it characterises his approach too as he holds a hypothetical phone conversation with his mother and explains the naïve impossibility of kidnapping.[38] Moreover the hypothetical conversation signals the need to return to the maternal for safety.[39] However, no comfort can ensue, for the mother cannot know how to deal with such abnormal situation. She can obviously offer no help, the more so as in the past her fascination for the action of the Front de Libération du Québec (FLQ) kidnapping and murdering opponents left no space for her son nor even for an explanation of the events, just fueled fear owing to her injunction not to go out without permission[40]; at the time, the parents could not disconnect themselves from the screen so that the child suffered from exposure to the unexplained images on the screen, his night peopled by devastating dreams of the invincible FLQ. The flashback of that important childhood experience indeed accounts for his own traumatogenic kidnapping. As Balint would claim, the

30 Cumyn, op. cit., 9; emphasis mine.
31 Ibid., 9; emphasis mine.
32 Ibid., 10.
33 Ibid., 9.
34 Ibid., 8.
35 Ibid., 9.
36 Ibid., 11.
37 Ibid., 11.
38 Ibid., 11–12.
39 The imaginary conversation calls to mind the need for connection affecting victims of captivity (Herman, op. cit., 81).
40 Cumyn, op. cit., 68–70.

lack of parental support in childhood – or basic fault – accounts for a person's response to a traumatic experience. Victims of trauma do not all suffer from post-traumatic stress disorder; only those who lacked proper care in childhood do.

Imagery accesses all the senses as in the following passage where fragmented perception evokes the terror of the unknown:

> Another sound and my heart hammers against my ribs. Not just traffic. A door. Footsteps. Heavy boots. Suddenly I feel my fingers, just like that, like they've been held on the burner, *God!* and then hands pull me out, my legs flaming in the pain of the movement, my neck jerked, screaming my throat raw. Pushed, I fall forward, but my hood doesn't choke me, they must've released it. The white pain from my eyes when they grab off the hood, I close them but it's still white, blinding. I turn my head but there's no escape, cruel whiteness everywhere.[41]

The mere change in sensory perception leads to drastic somatisation captured in full by the first sentence with a cause and effect relation, enhancing the devastating anticipation that noises must generate as further implied by the four following fragments. The importance of the sensorial perception recalls Mitrani's considerations of autistic manoeuvres and the focus on sensations. The anticipative impact takes its full significance the more so as the subsequent adverb 'Suddenly' and the phrase 'just like that' insist on the acute nature of the changed feeling. The constant switch between active sensations and passive endurance conveys the confusion resulting from unawareness of what to expect from one moment to the next, further rendered by the synaesthetic 'white pain' and the hypallagic 'cruel whiteness'. Synaesthesia, the figure of speech that involves cross-sensual perception, contrasts the obliterating darkness created by the hood that magnifies the ignorance and confusion of the threatened being at the time of experiential occurrence. The victim can obviously not avoid suffering from torture; the longer the exposure the more passive for sheer fear of retaliation.[42]

Apart from the meaningful imagery, Burridge resorts to nursery-like mantras, such as 'Bring the needle, bring the needle, bring the needle'[43] or 'Kill me. Kill me. *Kill me*'[44] or '*Shoot me! … Shoot me! Shoot me!*'[45], in the hope of

41 Ibid., 12.
42 Herman, op. cit. 90–91.
43 Cumyn, op. cit., 17.
44 Ibid., 44.
45 Ibid., 112.

escaping his situation through anaesthesia or death. Pervading the narrative, such exhortations address the readers because of the imperative structure; but as though bombarded, the readers cannot possibly help. Similar repetitions convey the relentless corporeal reactions over which Burridge has no control: 'Hammer hammer hammer'[46] or 'heart slams slams slams'[47] or 'Coughing, coughing, coughing'.[48] He also turns nouns into verbs to mark the passage from active to passive numbing as in the switch from chosen impassiveness – 'If I stay a puddle I can manipulate them. They don't know what to do with a puddle' – to the imposed loss of character and strength – 'You've puddled my body' – which clearly objectifies him.[49] Bill Burridge's illogical and haphazard statements recall the inconsequential talk of Tustin's patient and her feelings of confusion.[50] Burridge's flow of thoughts follows a totally idiosyncratic stream that requires particularly careful concentration on the part of the readers.

Burridge evidences maximised signs of stress. Hyper-vigilant, he listens to noises in fear and when he perceives one sound, his body, mind, breathing freeze. He cannot access his memory of time, of events, and questions his knowledge of the situation, for trauma shatters memory. Time and space vanish in the dissociation resulting from the traumatic experience. Giving in to the oppressors, Burridge ceases to fight, indeed expresses a death wish to shun the unbearable reality of captivity and torture; the low self-esteem afforded by the cumulative past trauma on account of his father's continuous deprecation reduces him through the enhanced trauma to a diminutive form of himself, to a regressive wish for reverse birth. Utter confusion characterises his interaction with the one human captor, the one that does not burn him with cigarettes or electrocute him or stare at him threateningly or kick him with his boots. Flashbacks of unpleasant situations parallel thoughts of potential torture through mock executions that cause 'the prisoners [to] dissolve in terror'.[51]

When his captors assign Josef, a survivor of destruction, to watch over Burridge, he feels an improvement in his treatment. As Josef knows all about trauma, having been 'burned till he could smell his own flesh cooking'[52] in an interrogation centre and having subsequently lost his entire family to destruction

46 Ibid., 111.
47 Ibid., 111.
48 Ibid., 137.
49 Ibid., 17.
50 Tustin, 'Autistic Processes', Journal of Child Psychotherapy, 2 (1969): 37.
51 Cumyn, op. cit., 24.
52 Ibid., 26.

of his village by political arson, he can recognise Burridge's trauma so that it makes all the difference. Josef's kindness keeps Bill alive but does not prevent nightmares or flashbacks from haunting him. Whatever he undergoes triggers memories of the past where violence breeds violence. Briefing notes and newspaper articles find their way into the narrative, as so many past instances of foreshadowing pointing to Bill Burridge's vulnerability. The more time passes by, the more sensation-dominated and unmentalised narration comes into play either to describe Burridge's reactions or the actual torture scenes. His helplessness in the face of the unpredictable encounters with his captors suffuses the narration time and again, as in the following passage that captures his contradictory, not to say paradoxical, feelings:

> Crying, sobbing most of the time. Nothing to do. Long stretches when they don't come back – when I don't want them to come back – but there's the fear and terror of the waiting. When they strap me again. Don't want to think about it but sometimes can't help myself. Burning, crackling, searing from inside, like everything ripped open. Different every time, but the same.[53]

Combining sensation-dominated, unmentalised relation à la Mitrani and linguistic disconnection in the vein of Bion's schizophrenics with numerous fragments even for the statement referring to the captors, the erased agent disappears under the impact of cumulative trauma. The same holds for the run-on sentence cum comma splices that technically flow into one another, presumably securing connection, but whose agent obliterates himself so that the potential link achieves nothing:

> Air ripping from me screeching rigid flailing like I'm skinless running from a burning building but not moving, can't move, just have to let the flames broil the air slamming in and out don't damn it don't damn it don't![54]

The bodily sensations and incoherent flow of words call to mind Tustin's comments on autistic speech. Statements merge and dislocate at once, rendering the experience disjointed and slimy.

Even when no longer in captivity, Burridge shows awareness of his body, looks at it and relates only to sensations, to the bodily symptoms of the trauma,

53 Ibid., 52.

54 Ibid., 74.

becoming 'breathing bone', an alliteration suiting the alliteration of his own name, Bill Burridge:

> Bone. It's all I have left. Rigid, fleshless, jutting bone. Man of bone. Breathing bone. Breathing man of bone. Hood off, shackles off, in the dark with the maggots and the mosquitoes, with my chills and aches, my brain going yammer yammer yammer. And these bones. Long, skeletal, wrapped in bags of deflated skin. Where there used to be muscles. Used to be sinews and what else? Flesh. I had flesh before. It wasn't discoloured like this crumply skin, with burn marks and bruises and running sores. My beard so itchy. A clever person would be able to tell from this beard how long they've held me. This is no svelte little beard. This is a months-long, lifetime kind of beard.
>
> Of course. That's how long: a lifetime. Several lifetimes. A month of Sundays. Ages since I've seen you. Rip van Winkle. Twenty years?
>
> Yammer yammer yammer.[55]

No longer in captivity, Burridge focuses on his body, considers its emaciation, defines it as bone, in the singular, not the plural, pointing to the reductive impact achieved by an unbearably long cumulative undermining of resilience and corporeal deterioration. Only bone remains, admittedly capable of breathing, but dry fleshless bone. Though freed, the body retains the marks left by the theatre of trauma, enhanced by the polysyndeton 'with burn marks and bruises and running sores' that insists on the devastating weight of the waste. Still fragmentary, the representation of the body brings to mind the inability to shake off the bodily reality experienced in the midst of trauma. The juxtapositions buzz like so many bumblebees threatening sanity. Even the repetition of 'yammer' conveys the mental intrusion of the experience, as though Burridge cannot possibly rid himself of it. Temporally and spatially invasive, the marks of the trauma supersede the previous corporeal reality in desolation.

In his rambling monologue, Burridge addresses the calamitous repercussions of trauma on both mind and body:

> Man of bone. Why can't I just make my brain still? That would be a consolation. *They captured me, but I learned to meditate. Actually, it was one of the most peaceful periods of my life.*

55 Ibid., 113.

> The thought is so ridiculous I start laughing. Strange, giddy, sobbing, painful laughter. I must have some broken ribs.[56]

Dried out physically, Burridge wishes for mental paralysis. The contrast between the fragment stating a fact and the question finds its reflection in the italicised statement inspired by Zen philosophy, which he tried to apply with mantras and sayings. In his reference to mantras and chants during captivity, he evidences the gap between what he would like to believe and reality, as nothing really prepares anyone for traumatic experiences. He indirectly addresses the Zen belief that life amounts to suffering and that one needs to find a balance to go through it, but in case of extreme suffering humans break. However, on hindsight, he underscores the preposterous quality of the statements through the multileveled, fragmentary characteristics of his laughter, merging the mental and the corporeal with the assumption regarding his ribs.

In the subsequent passage, Burridge jumps from his corporeal appearance and that of other survivors after cataclysmic trauma, probably in an attempt to shut off his own reality.

> Shoulderblades and jutting hips and ribcage stark against this bag of skin. Cheekbones, elbows, huge knobbly knees. Man of bone. Like Auschwitz. Like the Hong Kong prisoners. I remember the pictures. Those stark men of bone with the large blank eyes, trousers held up with ropes. Not blank eyes, no – a different kind of wisdom. From the reaches of hell.
>
> Here I am in the reaches of hell, indestructable [sic] man of bone. They can't kill me. *I can't be killed!* No, nothing so simple. I can be starved, beaten, shocked, humiliated, kicked, taunted, degraded, ground into gravel and taken away by the shovelful. But I can't be *killed!* I cannot die. Man of bone for all time, doomed and cursed to suffer with my eyes open.[57]

Polysyndeton and asyndeton in the first two statements combine to weigh down and axe the horror of the bodily reality at once. Rather than focusing on his emotions or even his own body, he steps back and considers how history repeats itself, how his looks recall those typifying previous men of bone coming out of 'the reaches of hell' whether out of the extermination camps in Germany or in Hong Kong. Again protecting himself with mantra-like statements, he piles up past participles whose destructive and demeaning reality he opposes

56 Ibid., 113.

57 Ibid., 113–114.

to death as though they do not mean death of emotions. He only manages to sum up his suffering in general words – 'Man of bone for all time, doomed and cursed to suffer with my eyes open'.

At night, the recent harrowing experience of torture haunts him; he relives the sensations he had while recalling the delayed onset of traumatic impact, the temporal afterwardness of trauma, Caruth 'double wound',[58] the wounding impact also a site of trauma lived over and over again. This recalls Cassie Pedersen's considerations of Freud's *Nachträglichkeit*.[59] The retroactive recurrence of the trauma not fully integrated haunts him long after the event, as he relives the sensations of the experience but cannot yet assimilate it. Evoking the stylistic reflections of Bion, Mitrani, and Tustin, the following passage hints at the devastated land of body and mind after lengthy traumatic endurance:

> My teeth clamp right through the flesh of my tongue. Body lifts off the table. Scream like the howl of a hurricane. Flesh burns from the inside. Try to turn to get away but the ropes. Scream and fucking scream. Everything shaken loose inside. Going to die. Any longer too long. Too long, too long, I'm going to fucking die! Try to reach my hands to rip the clamps away but can't reach, nothing can move. Next pulse worse, slams like an electric wall. Can't scream loud enough. Can't reach it!
>
> Die! Die! I think. Please God! Only place for safety. But can't reach. He won't let me. Burning out my body and brain from inside but too slow. All the shrieking in the world can't take me out. Burning again and again and I yell out I'll fucking sign anything! But can't reach can't stop.
>
> *Pleading sobbing wailing shrieking*. Stop it stop it stop it stop it stop it! But again and again. Teeth go through my tongue. Bloody mouth. I smell the fear and fire of it. Endless shriek cracks every nerve and bone.
>
> Die, please God, let me let me let me please. But no release. Again and again. No way from now. Yelling, shrieking, writhing, but more and more and more. Stop it! STOP IT! Every shriek of fear and pain brings only more

58 Cathy Caruth, *Unclaimed Experience: Trauma, Narrative and History* (Baltimore: John Hopkins University Press, 1996), 3–5.

59 Cassie Pedersen, 'Encountering Trauma "Too Soon" and "Too Late": Caruth, Laplanche, and the Freudian *Nachträglichkeit*', in this volume. Her grasping the paradoxical experience of trauma in different temporal zones bears similarities to the findings of Donald W. Winnicott in 'Fear of Breakdown' [*International Review of Psycho-Analysis*, 1 (1974): 103–107], an article positing that the traumatised fear trauma as an experience to come when in fact it has already happened, disrupting temporal and causal perceptions.

> and more. Feet now, throat, nipples, fingers. Stuffing fire in my mouth. No. *NO!* Can't survive this. Can't. *Won't!* Kill me, please God, please!
>
> *Stop it stop it stop it stop it stop!* I howl, as long as I can still form words.[60]

The first paragraph re-presents a range of corporeal reactions, helpless feelings and unendurable fear of the lived reality. The second paragraph with its weird combination of exhortations, prayer, inaptitude, godly refusal to comply, slow mental and bodily destruction, fear, imploration and final powerlessness echoes the throes and suffering still haunting the dried-out body. The third and fourth paragraphs combine the implorations of the second and the bodily hardships of the first, emphasising their unbearable quality. The inability to fathom what he went through, to step out of it and live normally hits him. He relives all the physical details in flashbacks, hallucinations and nightmares, realising the full repercussion of his prolonged trauma *a posteriori*, assimilating it somehow but still not knowing what belongs to reality as though he lives 'alternate realities'[61] from a distance. As such, he perceives the perfidiousness of the experience and the inability to share his anguish and distress with anyone, calling to mind Elie Wiesel's comments of his own encounter with trauma.[62] No one knows how to deal with him, for the non-traumatised cannot fathom what he lives and has lived. He relives the trauma in the presence of those who love him, still repeating chants, such as 'hammering, hammering, hammering'[63]:

> even if I survive it'll be with the knowledge that I did nothing – just accepted and suffered. That's who I am, the kind of person who allows this to happen to himself, who brings it on, does nothing to get out. What kind of life would that be? Spineless, haunted, trembling. Fighting nightmares every night. Shaking in the middle of the day, panicked at the slightest noise, losing my mind with the memory of it. End it now, I think. Better to have his fist go through me like cardboard than live as an insect.[64]

Blame kicks in as though he inflicted the trauma on himself and he feels as though still in captivity even though life has changed and comfort surrounds

---

60 Cumyn, op. cit., 136–137.

61 Ibid., 179.

62 Shoshana Felman quotes Elie Wiesel's words on the loneliness felt by survivors in her article 'Education and Crisis', *Trauma: Explorations in Memory*, Ed. Cathy Caruth (Baltimore and London: John Hopkins University Press, 1995), 15.

63 Cumyn, op. cit., 185.

64 Ibid., 159.

him, but his reality takes him back to the shed 'immobile, heart hammering, the minutes ticking over, not ticking, stalled. ... There's no escape ... at night there's no escape. Close your eyes or not'.[65] He cuts himself with a paring knife, bleeding with a 'surprising amount of blood for a man of bone', conscious that no one, not even his wife, understands that 'there's no escape'; he senses the illusion 'of heading toward safety and peace' as he boards the ambulance on a stretcher.[66]

4 Conclusion

With the final illusion Burridge utters, *Man of Bone* grasps the fissure in temporality and assimilation after incontrollable terror has taken hold of the traumatised. Rather than pointing to the resilience that Boris Cyrulnik refers to in *Un Merveilleux malheur*,[67] the narrative mirrors the frailty of the human experience when, in childhood, the child could not experience parental containment – the source of Balint's basic fault. It also reflects how, in the experience and its reliving afterwards, the human brain disconnects, attacks links as Bion argues and cannot mentalise the experience, thus reliving sensation-dominated experiences as Mitrani and Tustin observe, not yet capable of assimilating the experience as countless trauma theoreticians would contend. Burridge's fragmented perception of past and present realities, inability to articulate them in coherent discourse, sensorial focus, loss of security, all illustrate in mixed combination the theories of Balint, Bion, Tustin and Mitrani, enhancing the unutterable. Robbed of his vitality, Burridge succumbs to the scars inflicted by his captors, attempting to finish his suffering, for he has found no place to relocate the trauma and live with it.[68] Had he managed to relocate the trauma of captivity and torture spatially, he would have exerted control over the harrowing experiences by perceiving the feelings engendered in such a way as to comprehend them, just as Nicholas Quin Serenati in his working through the trauma of illness by locating illness spatially.[69]

65 Ibid., 184.

66 Ibid., 186.

67 Boris Cyrulnik, *Un Merveilleux malheur* (Paris: Odile Jacob, 2002).

68 In his deflated approach, Bill Burridge joins those victims in the Nazi concentration camps who lost 'the will to live', becoming 'the living dead' (Herman, op. cit., 85).

69 Nicholas Quin Serenati, 'Illness Is a Window: Reframing Leukaemia Through Dharma Art', in this volume. Serenati obviously managed to integrate the traumatic encounter with

With *Man of Bone* staying at ground zero, Cumyn obviously joins those 'trauma narrativists' who, as Vickroy notes in *Trauma and Survival in Contemporary Fiction,* 'immerse us in individual experiences of terror, arbitrary rules, and psychic breakdown so that we might begin to appreciate these situations'.[70] In so many ways, novels and literary pieces dealing with traumatic experiences address the absurd idealisation of normalcy for those not having endured trauma. As many human beings have faced trauma in a way or another, reading a novel like this can empower them to retrieve some of their own experiences in the face of trauma for better integration. They might perceive the inability of the traumatised to disentangle from the obsessive thoughts that drive them outside themselves and cause them to relive the experience in confused divided consciousness as happens with Bill Burridge. However, as witnesses of his incapacity, they might understand the need to find a way to relocate their own trauma from unstructured and threatening spaces to a place from which to observe, claim and integrate the various facets of the traumatic disruption so as to map and engage the experience towards creative growth.[71]

Bibliography

Balint, Michael. 'On Love and Hate'. *International Journal of Psycho-Analysis*, 33 (1952): 355–362.

Balint, Michael. *The Basic Fault: Therapeutic Aspects of Regression*. London: Tavistock, 1968.

Bion, Wifred R. 'Attacks on Linking'. *International Journal of Psycho-Analysis,* 40 (1959): 308–315.

Caruth, Cathy. *Unclaimed Experience: Trauma, Narrative and History*. Baltimore: John Hopkins University Press, 1996.

Cumyn, Alan. *Man of Bone.* Toronto: McClelland and Stewart, 1998.

Cyrulnik, Boris. *Un Merveilleux malheur*. Paris: Odile Jacob, 2002.

illness and to locate it in a place that opens creative channels for a deeper understanding of the unfathomable.

70 Laurie Vickroy, *Trauma and Survival in Contemporary Fiction* (Charlottesville: University of Virginia Press, 2002), 34.

71 Akin to Marie France Forcier's reflections on her choreographing post-traumatic realities in her chapter 'Creating and Contextualising Trauma-Related Contemporary Choreography', in this volume, such approach would engender healing for the traumatised and for those non-survivors would yield empathetic understanding.

Felman, Shoshana. 'Education and Crisis'. *Trauma: Explorations in Memory*. Ed. Cathy Caruth. Baltimore and London: John Hopkins University Press, 1995. 13–60.

Herman, Judith Lewis. *Trauma and Recovery: From Domestic Abuse to Political Terror*. London: Pandora, 1992.

Matoré, Georges. *L'Espace humain: L'Expression de l'espace dans la vie, la pensée et l'art contemporains*. Paris: La Colombe (Sciences et techniques humaines, 2), 1962.

Mitrani, Judith L. 'Toward an Understanding of Unmentalized Experience'. *Psychoanalytic Quarterly*, 64 (1995): 68–112.

Mitrani, Judith L. 'On the Survival Function of Autistic Manoeuvres in Adult Patients'. *International Journal of Psychoanalysis* (1992), 73: 549–559.

Tustin, Frances. 'Autistic Processes', *Journal of Child Psychotherapy*, 2 (1969): 23–29.

Tustin, Frances. The 'Black Hole': A Significant Element in Autism. *Free Associations*, 1 (1988): 35–50.

Vickroy, Laurie. *Trauma and Survival in Contemporary Fiction*. Charlottesville: University of Virginia Press, 2002.

Whitehead, Anne. *Trauma Fiction*. Edinburgh: Edinburgh University Press, 2004.

Winnicott, Donald W. 'Fear of Breakdown'. *International Review of Psycho-Analysis*, 1 (1974): 103–107.

CHAPTER 8

Writing Trauma, Writing Modern: Nadeem Aslam's *The Wasted Vigil* and Atiq Rahimi's *The Patience Stone*

Gen'ichiro Itakura

Abstract

Post-9/11 literature is a contested field. Once represented in fiction, trauma and suffering in post-9/11 Afghanistan are necessarily experienced individually and collectively across the globe. Local languages of victims and the cultural baggage behind those languages are translated, in most cases, into global languages of the literary market and professional psychiatry so that trauma and suffering are intelligible to a global readership. Such cultural translation often involves commodification of trauma and suffering as well as silencing of experiences irrelevant to narratives sanctioned by the dominant discourse of the global market. Novelists – especially those neither white middle-class nor native speakers of 'global' languages like English and French – are invariably caught in a dilemma of prioritising or sacrificing readability. Nadeem Aslam's *The Wasted Vigil* (2008) and Atiq Rahimi's *The Patience Stone* (*Syngué sabour*, 2008) seek to resolve this dilemma by their ecclesiastic use of modernist techniques. This chapter explores literary representation of trauma in the context of post-9/11 Afghanistan through analysis of these two texts. Set in post-9/11 Afghanistan, both novels choose to represent the protagonists' trauma and its locality or time-specific nature paradoxically by appropriating European modernists' textual strategies. In *The Wasted Vigil*, Aslam creates disruptions and displacements in the text like Joseph Conrad, T. S. Eliot and others to represent the kind of trauma and suffering rarely narrated. In *The Patience Stone*, Atiq Rahimi achieves this by his mixing-up of interior and exterior monologues and use of fragmented prose *à la* Imagists. By updating European modernist strategies, those writers extend the scope of post-9/11 literature and the possibility of literary representation of trauma and suffering.

 | DOI:10.1163/9789004407947_010

Keywords

post-9/11 fiction – literary representation of trauma – Nadeem Aslam – Atiq Rahimi – modernism – Afghanistan – war on terror

1 Introduction

'About suffering they were never wrong', writes W. H. Auden, 'The Old Masters'.[1] This apparently Euro-centric observation points to the ironical truth of our understanding of trauma. No matter where they take place or who experience them, suffering and trauma are recognised, evaluated or even 'ranked' according to the extent to which Western specialists identify with victims or overcome their – racial, ethnic, pathological – otherness.[2] Even if their sufferings survive this selection, they are rarely communicated directly to a wider audience. Suffering and trauma are more likely understood in the light of Western theory than in any other way and therefore translated into more 'universal' languages of psychiatry, sociology and politics than vernacular languages in which they are originally experienced and narrated.[3] Cathy Caruth's analysis of Alain Renais' *Hiroshima mon amour* (1959) exemplifies this trend. As Stef Craps points out, Caruth seeks to 'gloss over the lop-sided quality of the cross-cultural dialogue established in *Hiroshima mon amour*' when she argues that Renais' film helps Western spectators go beyond cultural differences and comprehend untold stories of Japanese, as a traumatised French woman and a traumatised Japanese man achieve a certain level of intimacy.[4] Nothing more than a narrative function, the Japanese man allows the French woman to narrate her own story. The Japanese man's untold story is somehow equated with

1 W. H. Auden, 'Musée des Beaux-Arts', in *Collected Poems*, ed. Edward Mendelson (London: Faber, 1976), 146.

2 Didier Fassin and Richard Rechtman, *The Empire of Trauma: An Inquiry into the Condition of Victimhood*, tr. Rachel Gomme, 282 (Princeton, NJ: Princeton University Press, 2009), 282; Stef Craps, *Postcolonial Witnessing: Trauma Out of Bounds* (Basingstoke: Palgrave, 2015), 13.

3 Arthur Kleinman, Veena Das and Margaret Lock, 'Introduction', in *Social Suffering*, eds. Arthur Kleinman, Veena Das and Margaret Lock, x (Berkeley, CA: University of California Press, 1997).

4 Craps, *Postcolonial Witnessing*, 18; Stef Craps, 'Beyond Eurocentrism: Trauma Theory in the Global Age', in *The Future of Trauma Theory: Contemporary Literary and Cultural Criticism*, eds. Gert Buelens, Sam Durrant and Robert Eaglestone (London: Routledge, 2014), 47; cf. Cathy Caruth, *Unclaimed Experience: Trauma, Narrative, and History* (Baltimore, MD: Johns Hopkins University Press, 1996), 56.

the French woman's, or a typical Euro-American trauma narrative of a young woman coming to terms with her own personal loss. His individual uniqueness, as well as the tremendous impact of the atomic bombings on Japanese people's collective memory, is dismissed as trivial or irrelevant. Caruth strives to demonstrate the validity of Western trauma theory by silencing or 'revising' non-Western experiences. In this respect, canons of trauma theory were 'never wrong' because all the 'irrelevant' experiences have been excluded or transformed into something more 'relevant'.

However, recent research has challenged this trend. In *Postcolonial Witnessing: Trauma Out of Bounds* (2012), Stef Craps criticises Caruth, Dominick LaCapra and other theorists for their Eurocentric bias in their reliance on a particular model and aesthetics. He interrogates a certain tendency among cultural theorists to use the individual and event-based model uncritically, even though psychologists have already begun to question it.[5] Instead, he turns to hitherto disregarded kinds of trauma or psychological pain suffered by silenced, disenfranchised non-Western people. In the colonial/postcolonial context in particular, he argues, trauma does not always result from 'a single, extraordinary, catastrophic event', but is experienced through ongoing, 'ordinary' forms of traumatising violence, persecution and oppression such as state violence and institutional racism.[6] Furthermore, Craps challenges trauma theorists' over-reliance on Western modernist aesthetics as a mere cultural construct. Given the similarities between modernist strategies and the psychic experience of trauma, he warns that other narrative forms and strategies – non-Western as well as Western lowbrow aesthetics – must not be automatically dismissed as insignificant or irrelevant.[7]

This chapter then investigates how contemporary literature has responded to hitherto underrepresented kinds of trauma in the non-Western, postcolonial, 'post-9/11' context. I will explore textual strategies representing trauma in Nadeem Aslam's *The Wasted Vigil* (2008) and Atiq Rahimi's *The Patience Stone* (*Syngué sabour*, 2008). Hailing from Pakistan and Afghanistan, Aslam and Rahimi may well be classified as 'new', 'postcolonial' writers who have chosen to write in English and French respectively.[8] These two texts are set in post-9/11 Afghanistan, the main theatre of great power game in the time of global civil war. Interestingly, both Aslam and Rahimi seek to appropriate textual strategies of Western modernists to varying

5 Craps, *Postcolonial Witnessing*, 24–28.

6 Ibid., 4–5, 52.

7 Ibid., 41.

8 Their first languages are Urdu and Persian (or to be more precise, Dari) respectively.

degrees. Indeed, neither Urdu nor Persian literary tradition has been immune to Westernisation. The 'Progressive Movement' of the 1930s has had a huge impact on Urdu-speaking intellectuals on the Indian subcontinent.[9] Saadat Hasan Manto, for instance, not only translated European novels into Urdu but also expanded the scope of Urdu literature.[10] Urdu intellectuals have known about appropriation of Western literary idioms long before the rise of new Pakistani literature in English characterised by its cosmopolitan outlook.[11] Modernism in Persian literature is perhaps familiar to a wider readership. Sadegh Hedayat's most influential work, *The Blind Owl* (*Boof-e koor*, 1936), praised by his contemporary Western writers such as André Breton, borrows and appropriates themes and aesthetics from European literature and cinema – E.T.A. Hoffmann's motif of the 'double', Robert Wiene's and F.W. Murnau's macabre fantasy and James Joyce's interior monologue.[12] Nevertheless, these two writers' use of modernist textual strategies warrants critical attention, as, given the immense impact of Western modernist aesthetics on medical and cultural discourses of trauma, they may end up formatting and commodifying their singular, non-Western narratives in a rather conventional way.

This chapter is divided into two parts. In the first two sections, I will analyse representation of trauma in *The Wasted Vigil* in relation to modernist aesthetics. Aslam represents his protagonists' – especially Marcus Caldwell's – trauma mainly in two ways: disruption and displacement. Marcus, an elderly

9 For further discussion, see Sobia Kiran, 'Modernism and the Progressive Movement in Urdu Literature', *American International Journal of Contemporary Research* 2.3 (2012): 179–181.

10 Manto surely helped broaden the trajectory of Urdu literature. His famous short story 'The Return' ('*Khol do*', 1947) explores the psychology of a man named Sirajuddin who instinctively welcomes the return of his daughter, Sakina, who has been raped and is therefore supposed to die in order to protect the 'honour' of the family. When the doctor tells his old assistant to open the window, saying 'Open it' ('*Khol do*'), Sakina opens her thighs and unfastens her clothes, as she has done when rapists say the phrase. Sirajuddin feels glad to know his daughter is alive, instead of getting indignant at her 'dishonourable' response. Saadat Hasan Manto, 'The Return', in *Bitter Fruit: The Very Best of Saadat Hasan Manto*, tr. Khalid Hasan (New Delhi: Penguin, 2008), 41.

11 Cf. Cara N. Cilano, *Contemporary Pakistani Fiction in English: Idea, Nation, State* (London: Routledge, 2013), 11. Cilano dedicates one chapter on post-9/11 Pakistani novels in English as well as another on novels on Muhammad Zia-ul-Haq's Islamisation, which allegedly transformed Pakistan into one of the global centres of 'political Islam'. However, I must mention the existence of a vast body of 'local' writings on the 1971 civil war.

12 André Breton, 'Les Capucines violettes', *Médium* 8.6 (1953): 68; Marzieh Balighi, 'Sadegh Hedayat, un écrivain francophone iranien de l'entre-deux-mondes', *Alternative Francophone* 1.8 (2015): 78–81.

Englishman, mourns for the death of his Afghan wife Qatrina and still wants to know what happened to their daughter Zameen. He always tries to 'work through'. His narrative is characterised by interruption and displacement as if to reflect his confusion. Such fissures in the text refer the reader back to modernist textual strategies. The last two sections will be devoted to *The Patience Stone*. Inspired by a true story, Rahimi created a quaint narrative mostly comprised of the unnamed female narrator's monologues, both interior and exterior. The narrator continues – or feels compelled – to tell her husband in a coma or her 'patience stone' about her suffering of the pain from the 'ordinary'. While she is talking, her interior and exterior monologues intermingle. In the meantime, the narrator's voice is only expressed in fragmented prose abounding with juxtaposed images, which recall Imagist poetry. By this appropriation of modernist strategies, these two texts provide non-confrontational ways to reconcile the actual, non-Western experience of trauma and the Western medical and cultural discourses of trauma.

2 Interrupted Amputation

In *The Wasted Vigil*, Aslam often disrupts the accounts of traumatic events, mostly narrated from the points of view of the traumatised subject, before they reach crucial moments. Sudden disruptions like these yield certain cinematic effects, as Aslam's attempt reminds the reader of the classic Hollywood cinema that avoids representation of extreme violence. However, he does not always refrain from graphic description of violence, as he provides such details as 'the bright blood-seeping flesh of the severed thigh that is still attached'.[13] Rather, he uses this technique as a response to the modern tradition of the trauma narrative that can be traced back to modernism.

Disruptions in Aslam's text often reveal the traumatised subject's reactions to the trauma through the contrast between absence and presence. This contrast can be found in a scene where Qatrina is forced by the Taliban to amputate Marcus:

> The gun was taken off her head and moved to Marcus's temple.
>
> 'Do it, or we'll kill *him*.'
>
> When the blade came towards him he stretched his fingers to touch her palm. The last act his hand performed for him.

13 Nadeem Aslam, *The Wasted Vigil* (London: Faber, 2009), 74.

> In the months that followed they entered a different geography of the mind altogether. She would not speak, or couldn't, kept her face to the walls, to the shadows. In any room she rushed towards corners. Or she wandered off into the burning noonday sun until he found her, fully expecting her eyes to have evaporated from their sockets in all that heat.[14]

As in the quotation above – narrated from Marcus's point of view except for the first two paragraphs – the scene of violence suddenly terminates and after a blank line, the novel resumes to describe Qatrina's mental disorders in the following months. The passage indicates various forms of absence. The scene of amputation is apparently missing. The synecdoche 'the blade' aptly conceals Qatrina's hand holding the scalpel, pointing to Marcus's suppression of her forced act of violence.[15] Unlike Qatrina's mental disorders, his changes are absent in the second half of the passage. All this suggests an enormous amount of effort with which Marcus manages to disguise his own trauma. Furthermore, what is present is revealing, too. Qatrina's severe psychological conditions signal the loss of her normal self and thus prepare Marcus – and by extension, the reader – for her physical death by stoning that he cannot even witness.[16] The 'last act' of his fingers (touching her palm) points to his intense attachment to Qatrina, which lasts even after her death. The vividness of his fingers' movement, as well as his memory of her '[clamping] the radial and ulnar arteries',[17] her tacit act of kindness, contrasts with the supernatural overtones with which residents of Usha, Kandahar, tell him of her death, which he is unable to witness himself.[18] In other words, Marcus's trauma is inscribed in this disruption of the text.

This kind of gap in Aslam's text compares to modernist aesthetics. In Joseph Conrad's *The Secret Agent* (1907), Stevie, a boy with intellectual disabilities, is convinced by terrorists into carrying the bomb to the Royal Observatory, Greenwich, but it detonates prematurely as he stumbles against the root of a tree. Conrad follows his unusual excitement – 'gesticulating

---

14 Ibid., 244.

15 Forced amputation also serves as a metaphor for the dismemberment of the country like the violent death of Benedikt, Lara's brother. Peter Childs and James Green, *Aesthetics and Ethics in Twenty-First Century British Novels: Zadie Smith, Nadeem Aslam, Hari Kunzru and David Mitchell* (London: Bloomsbury, 2013), 117.

16 Aslam, *The Wasted Vigil*, 265–267.

17 Ibid., 388.

18 Ibid., 267. For a further discussion of his 'absence', see Cilano, *Contemporary Pakistani Fiction in English*, 216.

and murmuring'[19] – and then gives a newspaper report of the explosion and the chief inspector's dispassionate account of the miserable condition of his shattered body, with particular emphasis on the 'shovel' with which his body is gathered, followed by the agitation of the dead boy's sister Winnie, who overhears the conversation.[20] In other words, Stevie's unimaginable agony is only inscribed in the total absence of a first-hand account of the event and in the presence of the boy's excitement in the previous day, the shovel and the sister's psychological disturbance.[21] This technique can be observed not only in high-modernist texts but also in 'war poems', generally known for their graphic description of shocking war details. In 'S.I.W'. (1918), Wilfred Owen moves from the soldier's deteriorating mental condition to the second stanza that begins with a patrol carrying his body apparently after having shot himself – an acronym for 'self-inflicted wound'.[22] Despite the poet's omniscience (he freely moves inside the soldier's mind), he chooses not to provide any detail of how the soldier commits suicide or how he must be feeling then. In an apparently more 'graphic' poem 'Dulce et Decorum Est' (1918), Owen carefully avoids describing the moment when the poet encounters the traumatic sight. Although the poet records his experience of witnessing a soldier 'drowning', he suddenly jumps to the nightmares he has suffered since this traumatic experience.[23] The vivid details of the dead body such as 'the white eyes writhing in his face' and 'the blood/[Coming] gargling from the froth-corrupted lungs' are only given in a counterfactual conditional clause ('If ... you too could ... watch ...'). Such disruptions, which characterise modernist aesthetics, express the inexpressibility of traumatic experience.

In this way, disruptions in Aslam's text read as his appropriation of a modernist strategy for representation of trauma. He chooses to borrow and revise the Western tradition of the trauma narrative rather than introduce indigenous narrative forms or magic realist elements that have characterised South Asian literature in English.

---

19 Joseph Conrad, *The Secret Agent: A Simple Tale* (Oxford: Oxford University Press, 2004), 41.

20 Conrad, *The Secret Agent*, 154.

21 For further discussion of the role of the shovel, see Sarah Cole, *At the Violet Hour: Modernism and Violence in England and Ireland* (Oxford: Oxford University Press, 2009), 115.

22 Wilfred Owen, 'S.I.W'., in *The Complete Poems and Fragments*, Vol. 1, ed. Jon Stallworthy (London: Chatto, 1983), 160.

23 Wilfred Owen, 'Dulce et Decorum Est', in *The Complete Poems and Fragments*, Vol. 1, ed. Jon Stallworthy (London: Chatto, 1983), 140.

3 The Lost Girl and the Lapis Lazuli

Like disruption, Aslam adopts displacement, a stylistic feature of the trauma narratives in modernist texts. He frequently inserts apparently irrelevant images and episodes in parts of the text narrated from the viewpoint of the traumatised subject. As with textual disruptions, it produces certain cinematic effects. Aslam's juxtaposition helps the reader create 'overtonal' or 'intellectual' associations often found in Soviet montage and French New Wave films.[24] His use of the technique, however, contains strategic and thematic resonances to modernist texts, especially their representation of loss and mourning.

In Aslam's text, the traumatic memory of loss is often juxtaposed alongside or replaced by inconsequential images. Lara's flashback to the day she lost her husband Stepan suddenly ends with a casual talk of the size of the Cosmos Oak.[25] Marcus's careless act of opening Virgil's *Aeneid* induces a flashback to the days he spent with his lost daughter Zameen.[26] His memory of the day he and Qatrina lost Zameen is disrupted by the details of the sunrise:

> The lapis lazuli of their land was always desired by the world, brushed by Cleopatra onto her eyelids, employed by Michelangelo to paint the blues on the ceiling of the Sistine Chapel, and, from the look of certain sections of the sky above Marcus and Qatrina as they came out into the garden, it could have been Afghanistan's heights that were mined for lapis lazuli, not its depth.[27]

The tragic memory of the loss of their daughter is linked, through the colour of the sky, to lapis lazuli and its uses in history. The reference to Cleopatra reveals what Zameen means to Marcus: her physical beauty and his apprehension of her tragic fate. By contrast, the reference to Michelangelo underlines the contrast between the tragic incident, which takes place at night, and the timeless, heavenly beauty of the sky, even though this timelessness is illusory.

Interestingly, the act of mining, not only evoked by the phrase 'lapis lazuli' but also mentioned here, is at once a conflation of Marcus's memory and a

24 For a theoretical discussion, see Sergei Eisenstein, 'The Fourth Dimension in Cinema', in *The Eisenstein Reader*, ed. Richard Taylor and trans. Richard Taylor and William Powell (London: Palgrave, 1998), 118–120.

25 Aslam, *The Wasted Vigil*, 146.

26 Ibid., 112.

27 Ibid., 18–19.

carefully chosen trope. Mining easily associates with his memory of the 'fossil hunt in the Cotswolds' during which Zameen finds an ammonite.[28] On another level, this mining of what can be deemed timeless compares to the raising of the statue of the Buddha found in Marcus's perfume factory.[29] Although he finds this head of the Buddha 'perishable' and the statue is going to be preserved as a valuable artefact under the protection of the British Army,[30] Marcus somehow tends to focus on the smile of the Buddha, or rather, what it symbolises.

> The stone face hangs from the twin-rotored military helicopter. As they hover and then move sideways and gain in height, Marcus looks down and catches glimpses of the head. The features smiling above the suddenly visible vista. His own body – the portion of earthly dust assigned him – feels insubstantial in comparison with all this.[31]

The physical presence of his own body is 'insubstantial', compared with the presence of the Buddha's smile. The smile of the Buddha, moreover, often associates with the 'perfect awakening' or '*bodhi*' that transcends time in the Buddhist tradition as well as in Western representation of the Buddha: the serene, smiling Buddha at *bodhi* attains 'vision, knowledge, wisdom, true knowledge, and light' according to the fifth book of the *Samyutta Nikaya*, or the connected discourses of the Buddha,[32] whereas this awakening is represented by the 'smile of simultaneousness above all the thousand births and deaths' in Hermann Hesse's novella.[33] In other words, Marcus tries to re-imagine his beloved daughter in this timeless, peaceful condition.

This displacement can also be read as Aslam's response to modernists' works. Freudian displacement, famously observed in the case of the 'Wolf Man', often engenders associations of apparently inconsequential memories. Whilst Freud's client's dreams of white wolves conflate his traumatic memory of watching his parents' copulation and his innocuous memory of sheepdogs,[34]

28 Ibid., 400.

29 Ibid., 22, 429–31.

30 Ibid., 431.

31 Ibid., 429.

32 Cited in Peter Harvey, *An Introduction to Buddhism: Teachings, History and Practices* (Cambridge: Cambridge University Press, 2013), 15.

33 Hermann Hesse, *Siddhartha*, trans. Hilda Rosner (London: Picador, 1974), 118.

34 Sigmund Freud, 'From the History of an Infantile Neurosis', in *The Standard Edition of the Complete Psychological Works of Sigmund Freud*, Vol. 17, ed. and trans. James Strachey (London: Vintage, 2001), 57–58.

Aslam's lapis lazuli sky connects Marcus's loss of his daughter to the family's peaceful days in a more stylised manner. The sudden appearance of the beautiful sky refers the reader back to that of a rainbow at the end of D. H. Lawrence's *The Rainbow* (1915). Having experienced a miscarriage, Ursula sees colliers with no life in their eyes and maimed soldiers but suddenly feels inspired at the sight of a 'faint, vast rainbow', 'great architecture of light and colour and the space of heaven'.[35] This rainbow appears primarily as a symbol of rebirth, but it also underscores the illusory nature of such hopes, as it cannot easily obliterate the shock value of what lies below the rainbow, or what Ursula tries not to see – the miserable state of the working class and demoralising physical trauma suffered by soldiers returning from the Great War.[36] This displacement is presented in a more explicitly modernist way in T. S. Eliot's *The Waste Land* (1922). The death of the poet's friend, Jean Verdenal, during the ill-fated military operation in Gallipoli is transformed into an ironic reference to the Roman victory over Carthage in Mylae during the First Punic War and the strange conversation: 'That corpse you planted last year in your garden,/Has it begun to sprout? Will it bloom this year?'[37] The tuber imagery evokes the notion of rebirth, but it hardly disguises the trauma of a friend's death, together with the shock at the news of soldiers' bodies buried like tubers. This points to the poet's desperate, impossible hope for rebirth or his defensive reaction to the traumatic experience. Although Aslam's text does not have the avant-garde, anti-narrative feel of high modernism, its theme and strategies certainly invite a reading of the text in this tradition.

The displacement in Aslam's text also recalls modernist representations of trauma. Even though he incorporates 'Asian' elements this time, he successfully connects the trauma suffered by individuals in Afghanistan since the Soviet-Afghan War to the more widely known, modernist tradition of the trauma narrative. Whilst modernists' strategies often contribute to the essentially anti-narrative nature of their texts, Aslam's strategies signal his indebtedness to the modernist tradition.

---

35 D. H. Lawrence, *The Rainbow* (Cambridge: Cambridge University Press, 1989), 458.

36 Even though Lawrence intended to set *The Rainbow* before World War I, Krockel detects this kind of anachronism in Lawrence's text. Carl Krockel, *War Trauma and English Modernism: T. S. Eliot and D. H. Lawrence* (Basingstoke: Palgrave, 2011), 42–43.

37 T. S. Eliot, 'The Waste Land', in *The Complete Poems and Plays of T. S. Eliot*, ed. Valerie Eliot (London: Faber, 1969), 63; Sarah Cole, *At the Violet Hour*, 73; Jean-Michel Rabaté, '"The World Has Seen Strange Revolutions Since I Died": *The Waste Land* and the Great War', *The Cambridge Companion to* The Waste Land, ed. Gabrielle McIntire (Cambridge: Cambridge University Press, 2015), 12–13.

4 More Than Just a Piece of Meat

Atiq Rahimi also appropriates modernist textual strategies to fictionalise traumatic experience in post-9/11 Afghanistan, though in different ways.[38] Inspired by the 2005 murder of a young Afghan poet, Nadia Anjuman,[39] Rahimi explores the psychology of an unnamed woman who keeps talking to her militant husband, now in a coma. Whilst Aslam's expatriate characters are tormented by the loss of their loved ones, Rahimi's heroine has a different type of suffering, the one that results from her constant, prolonged exposure to subtle forms of oppression, not always traumatising *per se*. As is the case with racism in the (post)colonial context, 'cumulative micro-aggressions' can trigger traumatisation.[40] In this novel, most aggressions are not so much predicated upon racism as machismo or revanchist urges to redeem patriarchy in post-9/11 Afghanistan. As the woman treats her husband in a coma like a 'patience stone',[41] she tries to tell him everything until she can set herself free from her pain and suffering. Her lopsided conversation or 'monologue' is at times inseparable from her interior monologue, as she supposedly tells everything that comes up to her mind, so that Rahimi's mode of writing is reminiscent of European modernists'.

The heroine's 'monologue' at times comes close to interior monologue in modernist novels both in technique and in contents. She tells her husband everything, including what she should hide from him – as if talking to her psychiatrist. The length of this 'monologue' puts the verisimilitude of the story into question; the reader may well wonder whether she actually says all those words placed between inverted commas or the reader just witnesses whatever comes up to her consciousness. Like stream of consciousness in Virginia Woolf's *Mrs Dalloway* (1922), Rahimi's heroine digresses freely and jumps

38 Technically speaking, the place is not specified. After the acknowledgement and the epigraph, Rahimi notes, 'Somewhere in Afghanistan or elsewhere'. Atiq Rahimi, *The Patience Stone*, tr. Polly McLean (London: Vintage, 2011), n.pag.

39 Jacques Perrin, 'Rancœurs de pierre', *Libération* (18 September 2008), para. 1, viewed on 24 January 2015, http://next.liberation.fr/livres/2008/09/18/rancoeurs-de-pierre_80475; Valérie Marin La Meslée, '"Syngué sabour. Pierre de patience", d'Atiq Rahimi: La voix des épouses silencieuse', *Le Monde* (2 October 2008), para. 4, viewed on 24 January 2015, http://www.lemonde.fr/livres/article/2008/10/02/syngue-sabour-pierre-de-patience-d-atiq-rahimi_1102119_3260.html; Elodie Bernard, 'Rencontre avec Atiq Rahimi', *La Revue de Teheran* 39 (2009), para. 11, viewed on 24 January 2015, http://www.teheran.ir/spip.php?article898#gsc.tab=0.

40 Craps, *Postcolonial Witnessing*, 26.

41 Rahimi, *The Patience Stone*, 74.

from the present to her childhood and vice versa.[42] At one point, she becomes suddenly unable to resist talking about her childhood secret: she sets free one of her abusive father's precious quails. Obsessed with quail fighting, he beats his wife and daughters after having lost in the quail fight. Finally he has to marry off his daughters to pay off his debts. As a young girl, the heroine sees him tuck one of his quails into his trousers, an episode which facilitates the equation between quails and masculinity.[43] She sets one of the quails free to let it be eaten by a cat. She describes the sensation she experiences in an elliptical sentence, 'A moment of pure delight'.[44] At one level, this refers to her triumphant feeling after having revenged herself on her abusive father; but at another, it indicates her delight in telling the story as her revenge on patriarchy or machismo that motivates both her father and her husband. Known as a 'hero', her husband supposedly fights for 'freedom' and 'Allah' but his obsession with war and the fetishistic 'pleasure of weapons' recalls her father's with quails.[45] Interestingly, she records a sudden change in her feelings at the sight of the cat eating her father's quail. Feeling 'jealous', 'frustrated' and 'desperate', she tries in vain to grab the quail back from the cat and then begins 'licking up those few drops of blood from [her] father's quail that dripped on to the floor'.[46] Her reaction points to her repressed sexual desire or appetite for sexual pleasure, which has not been satisfied by her husband or young soldiers who have treated her like a prostitute. As happens with Woolf's Clarissa Dalloway and James Joyce's Molly Bloom, interior monologue often allows to turn characters' sexually repressed feelings 'inside out'.[47] Significantly, this childhood episode of Rahimi's heroine refers to her aunt's assault on her father-in-law, who continues to rape her.[48] Ironically, the aunt manages to

42 The free moves of consciousness appear in the famous opening of *Mrs Dalloway*, where Clarissa Dalloway's mind wanders off from the present to her childhood. Septimus Warren Smith, a WWI veteran suffering from 'shell shock', also swings back to his traumatic experience of the war and loss of his friend Evans, for whom he probably has homoerotic feelings. Virginia Woolf, *Mrs Dalloway* (Oxford: Oxford University Press, 2009), 3, 59, 123.

43 Rahimi, *The Patience Stone*, 57–58.

44 Ibid., 59.

45 Ibid., 53–54, 56.

46 Ibid., 59–60.

47 Although she does not understand it clearly herself, Clarissa Dalloway harbours homosexual feelings for Sally Seton, which she has repressed. E.g. Woolf, *Mrs Dalloway*, 28. The 'Penelope' section of *Ulysses* (1922) comprises Molly's interior monologue with her thoughts moving swiftly, for instance, from her husband Leopold Bloom's atheistic worldview to her lover Boylan's 'tremendous big red brute of a thing'. James Joyce, *Ulysses* (London: Bodley Head, 1993), 611.

48 Rahimi, *The Patience Stone*, 86.

liberate herself from repression by telling her family her wish to commit suicide and ending up living in a brothel, i.e., experiencing a symbolic death and rebirth as a new individual.[49] Later in her life, the Hakim's order to copulate with a man to bear children at once traumatises the heroine and forces her out of the cosy realm of falsehood – where no one could challenge patriarchal myths such as male fertility – into a reality where she must survive by debasing herself to prostitution. Such episodes clearly fall into the category of disgraceful memories that should not be divulged to violent husbands. Whether she actually says all these things or not, her monologue can read as the externalisation of her repressed emotions.

Interestingly, this peculiar monologue of Rahimi's heroine adds a twist to modernist trauma narratives. Whilst modernist literature is characterised by what Patricia Rae calls 'resistant mourning' that involves a 'refusal to accept the acceptance of loss',[50] Rahimi's heroine responds in a more aggressive way to the loss – of her virginity, innocence and hope. Her aggressivity eventually drives her to kill her husband, who wakes up and tries to kill her. Unlike modernist responses to loss, her aggressive reactions are somehow rendered 'comprehensible' – if not predictable or socially prescribed – in the popular imagination. The reader is less likely shocked when, enraged, Rahimi's heroine hurls a diatribe at her intimidating husband, which can read as a critique of the male commodification of the female body in general:

> Your honour is nothing more than a piece of meat, now! You used to use that word yourself. When you wanted me to cover up, you'd shout, *Hide your meat!* I was a piece of meat, into which you could stuff your dirty dick. Just to rip it apart, to make it bleed![51]

Indeed, her word choice as well as male obsession with female virginity implied in the last sentence seems odd in contemporary Western culture and therefore indicates Asianness to some degrees,[52] but her rage is comprehensible in

---

49 Ibid., 86–87.

50 Patricia Rae, 'Introduction: Modernist Mourning', in *Modernism and Mourning*, ed. Patricia Rae (Cranbury, NJ: Associated University Presses, 2007), 16.

51 Rahimi, *The Patience Stone*, 112.

52 In the original version, Rahimi uses the phrase 'Ton honneur' (Your honour), an overt reference to the Islamic concept of *nāmūs* (ناموس) or moral law, especially one of female chastity. Atiq Rahimi, *Syngué sabour* (Paris: POL, 2008), 116; Hans Wehr, *A Dictionary of Modern Written Arabic*, edited by J. Milton Cowan (Urbana, IL: Spoken Language Services, 1994), 1099; Abbas Aryanpur-Kashani and Manoochehr Aryanpur-Kashani, *The Concise Persian-English Dictionary* (Tehran: Amir Kabir, 1978), 1293.

two ways. First, contemporary readers likely comprehend the consequences of long-term exposure to male oppression and find it unacceptable to see anyone reduce an individual human being into a 'piece of meat'. In *The Madwoman in the Attic* (1979), Gilbert and Gubar famously argue that Charlotte Brontë's 'madwoman', Bertha Antoinetta Mason, functions as the heroine's avatar or 'double' since the former's incendiary tendencies can be understood in relation to the latter's – or women's – 'flaming rages' against male rule.[53] This level of feminist criticism has been ushered into the popular discourse since the 1970s. Second, contemporary readers, Francophone or Anglophone, are familiar with the story of a woman's vengeance. In this respect, this scene can read as a post-9/11 Afghan version of Beckett's *Eh Joe* (1966), narrated from the female ghost's point of view. In Beckett's TV play, Joe strangles to death all the ghosts who have tormented him – a kind of imaginary murder he calls 'mental thuggee'[54] – except the one of a woman who eventually traumatises and drives him to suicide. In Rahimi's novel, the man tries to wring his wife's neck, only to be stabbed in the heart with a khanjar.[55] Whilst the man is cold-hearted and never traumatised – symbolically enough, not a single drop of blood comes from the chest when she stabs him[56] – she liberates herself from the oppression she has suffered all her life at a tremendous cost.

Rahimi's use of the 'monologue' foregrounds his indebtedness to European modernists, whereas his narrative differs from the typical trauma narrative circulated in the West. Unlike disruption and displacement, monologue, whether interior or exterior, is not a technique frequently associated with representation of trauma. In this respect, Rahimi experiments with this modernist textual strategy in a rather unconventional way.

5 Rain, Drips, Breaths

Rahimi's novel is also characterised by fragmented style, which also characterises certain modernist writers. Unlike the heroine's verbose monologue, the narrator's language is ostensibly economical. He only provides a minimum

53 Sandra Gilbert and Susan Gubar, *The Madwoman in the Attic: The Woman Writer and the Nineteenth Century Literary Imagination* (New Haven, CT: Yale University Press, 1984), 359–362.

54 Samuel Beckett, *Eh Joe*, in Cascando *and Other Short Dramatic Pieces* (New York: Grove Press, 1970), 37.

55 Rahimi, *The Patience Stone*, 135–136.

56 Ibid., 135.

amount of description as if writing stage directions. Halfway through the novel, paragraphs begin to fall short, made up of one sentence or an elliptical sentence. Towards the end, his prose comes close to Imagist poetry. Rahimi's choice of such a peculiar style does not only contribute to narrative economy and the construction of a somewhat allegorical note, but it also consolidates the link between his own prose and modernist aesthetics.

Indeed, the narrator reduces unnecessary lyricism as well as his own involvement by taking out adjectives and adverbs and, though less frequently, by leaving sentences incomplete. After pulling the feeding tube out of her husband's mouth, the heroine disappears from the scene, with solution drips falling on his forehead. Then, the narrator suddenly inserts the following description of urban combat:

> The sun is setting.
> The weapons awakening.
> Tonight again they will destroy.
> Tonight again they will kill.
> Morning.
> Rain.
> Rain on the city and its rubble.
> Rain on the bodies and their wounds.[57]

Ostensibly fragmented, the passage above made up of eight paragraphs, each one-sentence long, only contains 33 words (38 words in the French original). The passage reads like a musical phrase, but it does not perfectly conform to a traditional metrical structure like iambic pentameter or alexandrine. Despite the third and fourth lines of the quote, the passage concentrates on images without having recourse to ready-made poetic diction or craving for metaphysical depth. It does not even evoke anti-war sentiment, fear of death, the anxiety of being or any other idea worth exploring in the context. In this respect, Rahimi's prose resembles Imagist poetry. However, it produces quite an opposite effect. Whilst T.E. Hulme considers a poem a vehicle for sensory experience or small epiphanies derived from Bergsonian *images successives*,[58] Rahimi's juxtaposition of images does not convey feelings or intuitive, image-based

57 Ibid., 62. The original text is equally fragmented: 'Le soleil se couche./Les armes se réveillent./Ce soir encore on détruit./Ce soir encore on tue./Le matin'./Il pleut./Il pleut sur la ville et ses ruines./Il pleut sur les corps et leurs plaies. Rahimi, *Syngué sabour*, 70–71.

58 T. E. Hulme, 'A Lecture on Modern Poetry', in *Selected Writings*, ed. Patrick McGuinness (New York: Routledge, 2003), 54.

thoughts. Rather, it points to a desensitised consciousness or dissociative experience – 'de-realising' what one witnesses – commonly observed in people with PTSD.[59] In other words, Rahimi employs modernist aesthetics to an essentially different effect.

This quasi-Imagist juxtaposition of images culminates in the finale of the novel where the heroine is about to liberate herself from oppression. She stabs her husband in the heart and he strangles her neck. He eventually falls down on the floor, supposedly dead, while she is left with his body.

> The woman slowly opens her eyes.
> The breeze rises, sending the migrating birds into flight over her body.[60]

This signals her awakening to a new horizon, a new reality where she is free from oppression. The breeze and migrating birds encapsulate her transcendence. This reading is further confirmed by Rahimi's original phrasing in French. He puts a famous quote from Paul Valéry's 'Le Cimetière marin' (1920) in the first clause of the second sentence ('Le vent se lève').[61] In Valéry's poem, that sentence is followed by an apparently life-affirming sentence 'il faut tenter de vivre!' ('we must try to live!').[62] Read alongside Valéry, the three images here (the woman opening her eyes, the breeze and the birds), combined together, manage to convey a sensation the heroine experiences, a sense of life or vitality, which may help heal her psychological – though not physical – trauma.

As happens with the monologue, Rahimi appropriates modernist aesthetics much more freely than Aslam. While Aslam links hope to a subtly expressed hope in modernist writings such as *The Rainbow* and *The Waste Land*, Rahimi expresses it by juxtaposing images and a quotation.

6 Conclusion

Despite their differences, Aslam and Rahimi appropriate textual strategies used – or made famous – by Western modernists to create trauma narratives

59 *Diagnostic and Statistical Manual of Mental Disorders: DSM-5* (Arlington, VA: American Psychiatric Association, 2013), 272.

60 Rahimi, *The Patience Stone*, 136.

61 Rahimi, *Syngué sabour*, 137.

62 Paul Valéry, 'Le Cimetière marin', *Œuvres*, vol. 1, ed. Jean Hytier (Paris: Gallimard, 1957), 151.

in the post-9/11 Afghanistan context. In *The Wasted Vigil*, Aslam uses disruption and displacement effectively and thereby manages to place his story of expatriates living in Afghanistan in the modernist tradition of representation of trauma. Marcus' trauma is made comprehensible through Aslam's eclectic use of 'high modernist' techniques. An apparently more experimental text, *The Patience Stone* also accomplishes the same feat. Rahimi deliberately overloads the text with the heroine's monologue so that it can be indistinguishable from her interior monologue. Only through this characteristic are her – silenced women's – fear of domestic tyrants and trauma from long-term oppression are comprehensible. In the meantime, Rahimi prunes superfluous elements in the narrator's account *à la* Imagists to let the reader associate images and finally get a glimpse of hope, though a tiny glimmer of it. They write texts not so ostensibly experimental or dense as 'high modernist' works like *The Waste Land* and *Ulysses*. Their use of textual strategies is not so much motivated by their artistic enterprise as by their endeavour to make hitherto unheard voices heard in a more global context – the voices otherwise heard only in vernacular languages.[63]

Despite the clear socio-cultural difference in time and space, Western modernist experimentations turn out to be valid as strategies for literary representation of trauma in the contemporary Asian setting. This does not mean that such modernist aesthetics is uncritically exported to contemporary Asian contexts. Rather, inventive writers like Aslam and Rahimi keep it alive by recycling and appropriating modernists' stylistic features and narrative techniques so that their text could operate in – and the voices they want to spread among – a wider readership. It is perhaps wrong to assert, with no reservation, that the 'Old Masters' were 'never wrong' about suffering. However, Auden's statement holds true as long as new writers study them carefully and appropriate their techniques. The 'Old Masters' can be right about suffering – even suffering in post-9/11 Afghanistan – with a little help from 'new masters' from elsewhere.

Acknowledgement

This research has been made possible through the Japanese Grant-in-Aid for Scientific Research C (Grant no.: 26370342 and 17K02524).

63 Needless to say, there is another possibility. In the past decade, an urge to return to modernist aesthetics and its radicality has been observed in art. E.g. Nicolas Bourriaud, *The Radicant*, tr. James Gussen and Lili Porten (New York: Sternberg Press, 2010).

Bibliography

Aryanpur-Kashani, Abbas, and Manoochehr Aryanpur-Kashani. *The Concise Persian-English Dictionary*. Tehran: Amir Kabir, 1978.

Aslam, Nadeem. *The Wasted Vigil*. London: Faber, 2009.

Auden, W. H. 'Musée des Beaux-Arts'. In *Collected Poems*, edited by Edward Mendelson, 146–47. London: Faber, 1976.

Balighi, Marzieh. 'Sadegh Hedayat, un écrivain francophone iranien de l'entre-deux-mondes'. *Alternative Francophone* 1.8 (2015): 71–85.

Beckett, Samuel. *Eh Joe*. In Cascando *and Other Short Dramatic Pieces*, 33–42. New York: Grove Press, 1970.

Bernard, Elodie. 'Rencontre avec Atiq Rahimi'. *La Revue de Teheran* 39 (2009). Viewed on 24 January 2017. http://www.teheran.ir/spip.php?article898#gsc.tab=0.

Bourriaud, Nicolas. *The Radicant*, translated by James Gussen and Lili Porten. New York: Sternberg Press, 2010.

Breton, André. 'Les Capucines violettes'. *Médium* 8.6 (1953): 68.

Caruth, Cathy. *Unclaimed Experience: Trauma, Narrative, and History*. Baltimore, MD: Johns Hopkins University Press, 1996.

Childs, Peter, and James Green. *Aesthetics and Ethics in Twenty-First Century British Novels: Zadie Smith, Nadeem Aslam, Hari Kunzru and David Mitchell*. London: Bloomsbury, 2013.

Cilano, Cara N. *Contemporary Pakistani Fiction in English: Idea, Nation, State*. London: Routledge, 2013.

Cole, Sarah. *At the Violet Hour: Modernism and Violence in England and Ireland*. Oxford: Oxford University Press, 2012.

Conrad, Joseph. *The Secret Agent: A Simple Tale*. Oxford: Oxford University Press, 2004.

Craps, Stef. 'Beyond Eurocentrism: Trauma Theory in the Global Age'. In *The Future of Trauma Theory: Contemporary Literary and Cultural Criticism*, edited by Gert Buelens, Sam Durrant and Robert Eaglestone. 45–61. London: Routledge, 2014.

Craps, Stef. *Postcolonial Witnessing: Trauma Out of Bounds*. Basingstoke: Palgrave, 2015.

Diagnostic and Statistical Manual of Mental Disorders: DSM-5. Arlington, VA: American Psychiatric Association, 2013.

Eisenstein, Sergei. 'The Fourth Dimension in Cinema'. In *The Eisenstein Reader*, edited by Richard Taylor. Translated by Richard Taylor and William Powell, 111–23. London: Palgrave, 1998.

Eliot, T. S. 'The Waste Land'. In *The Complete Poems and Plays of T. S. Eliot*, edited by Valerie Eliot, 59–80. London: Faber, 1969.

Fassin, Didier, and Richard Rechtman. *The Empire of Trauma: An Inquiry into the Condition of Victimhood*, translated by Rachel Gomme. Princeton, NJ: Princeton University Press, 2007.

Freud, Sigmund. 'From the History of an Infantile Neurosis'. In *The Standard Edition of the Complete Psychological Works of Sigmund Freud*, XVII, edited and Translated by James Strachey, 3–124. London: Vintage, 2001.

Gilbert, Sandra, and Susan Gubar. *The Madwoman in the Attic: The Woman Writer and the Nineteenth Century Literary Imagination*. New Haven, CT: Yale University Press, 1984.

Harvey, Peter. *An Introduction to Buddhism: Teachings, History and Practices*. Cambridge: Cambridge University Press, 2013.

Hesse, Hermann. *Siddartha*. Translated by Hilda Rosner. London: Picador, 2013.

Hulme, T. E. 'A Lecture on Modern Poetry'. In *Selected Writings*, edited by Patrick McGuinness, 53–68. New York: Routledge, 2003.

Joyce, James. *Ulysses*. London: Bodley Head, 1993.

Kiran, Sobia. 'Modernism and the Progressive Movement in Urdu Literature'. *American International Journal of Contemporary Research* 2.3 (2012): 176–182.

Kleinman, Arthur, Veena Das and Margaret Lock. 'Introduction'. In *Social Suffering*, edited by Arthur Kleinman, Veena Das and Margaret Lock, ix-xxvii. Berkeley, CA: University of California Press, 1997.

Krockel, Carl. *War Trauma and English Modernism: T. S. Eliot and D. H. Lawrence*. Basingstoke: Palgrave, 2011.

La Meslée, Valérie Marin. ' "Syngué sabour. Pierre de patience", d'Atiq Rahimi: La Voix des épouses silencieuse'. *Le Monde* (2 October 2008). Viewed on 24 January 2017. http://www.lemonde.fr/livres/article/2008/10/02/syngue-sabour-pierre-de-patience-d-atiq-rahimi_1102119_3260.html.

Lawrence, D. H. *The Rainbow*. Cambridge: Cambridge University Press, 1989.

Manto, Saadat Hasan. 'The Return'. In *Bitter Fruit: The Very Best of Saadat Hasan Manto*, translated by Khalid Hasan, 39–41. New Delhi: Penguin, 2008.

Owen, Wilfred. 'Dulce et Decorum Est'. In *The Complete Poems and Fragments*, Vol. 1, edited by Jon Stallworthy, 140–161. London: Chatto, 1983.

Owen, Wilfred. 'S.I.W'. In *The Complete Poems and Fragments*, Vol. 1, edited by Jon Stallworthy, 160–61. London: Chatto, 1983.

Perrin, Jacques. 'Rancœurs de pierre'. *Libération* (18 September 2008). Viewed on 24 January 2017. http://next.liberation.fr/livres/2008/09/18/rancoeurs-de-pierre_80475.

Rabaté, Jean-Michel. ' "The World Has Seen Strange Revolutions Since I Died": *The Waste Land* and the Great War'. In *The Cambridge Companion to* The Waste Land, edited by Gabrielle McIntire, 9–23. Cambridge: Cambridge University Press, 2015.

Rae, Patricia. 'Introduction: Modernist Mourning'. In *Modernism and Mourning*, edited by Patricia Rae, 13–49. Cranbury, NJ: Associated University Presses, 2007.

Rahimi, Atiq. *The Patience Stone*. Translated by Polly McLean. London: Vintage, 2011.

Rahimi, Atiq. *Syngué sabour*. Paris: POL, 2008.

Valéry, Paul. 'Le Cimetière marin'. *Œuvres*, vol. 1, edited by Jean Hytier, 147–151. Paris: Gallimard, 1947.

Wehr, Hans. *A Dictionary of Modern Written Arabic*, edited by J. Milton Cowan. Urbana, IL: Spoken Language Services, 1994.

Woolf, Virginia. *Mrs Dalloway*. Oxford: Oxford University Press, 2009.

CHAPTER 9

Body and Trauma in Chuck Palahniuk's *Haunted*

Claudio Vescia Zanini

Abstract

Chuck Palahniuk's 2005 novel *Haunted* presents a group of wannabe writers confined for a retreat. The description of their interaction during confinement intertwines with the short stories they produce, and in both narrative levels, the writers invariably revisit memories of abuse, loss, social displacement and frustration. While confined, they spend part of their time inflicting pain and mutilation to themselves, aiming at the fabrication of new traumas, which they believe will increase the public's interest in their works and lives. I analyse the representation and fabrication of trauma in *Haunted* through the manipulation of the body via bruising, (self-inflicted) mutilation, gender and age bending, cross-dressing and exacerbated sexualisation, among others. Jean Baudrillard's concepts of simulation and hyperreality support the fabrication of trauma in the novel, whereas images of bodies changed by trauma are associated to the three phantasies that, according to Baudrillard, haunt the contemporary world: cancer, terrorism and transvestite.

Keywords

representations of trauma – body – *Haunted* – Chuck Palahniuk – Jean Baudrillard – simulation – hyperreality – cancer – transvestite – terrorism

In 2005, Chuck Palahniuk, American author better known for *Fight Club* (1996), published *Haunted: A Novel of Stories*. At the time, the author drew some attention to *Haunted* by capitalising on a phenomenon that came to be known as the 'Guts effect': in his American tour promoting the novel, Palahniuk delivered dramatic readings of its opening short story, entitled 'Guts', a first-person narrative of a teenager who describes in detail the loss of his intestines during a masturbatory experience underneath water while sitting on the pool's pump. Due to its graphic nature, and its detailed description of the narrator's

 | DOI:10.1163/9789004407947_011

intestines (and its contents, for that matter), the story is reported to have made over eighty listeners either faint or vomit.[1]

The novel's basic premise is built upon a group of strangers who have responded to an intriguing note left all over town, inviting people to put their lives on hold for three months so as to pursue their dreams of becoming successful writers. Not much is said regarding the location and the working conditions, except for the inclusion on food and lodging. The promise of leaving behind aspects of mundane life seduces nineteen wannabe poets, screenwriters, novelists and playwrights, who gather in order to join the writers' retreat. They do not go by their real names, but adopt pennames such as Mother Nature (a hippie masseuse), Chef Assassin (a man who lost his job as a chef after a bad review) or Agent Tattletale (a man whose job was to identify disabilities invented by people in order to collect pension from the government). In some cases, the penname includes a nobility title, such as Baroness Frostbite, the Earl of Slander or the Duke of Vandals. The multiple functions of these epithets include: a. dispossessing the members at the retreat of individuality until they produce their short stories, when they reveal core aspects of their past; b. in the cases of those pennames that include a nobility title, emulating, even if whimsically, nobility members from other haunting works of literature – Count Dracula, Lord Ruthven, Countess Carmilla Karnstein, for instance. As we shall see, this aspect is particularly important insofar as *Haunted* connects on many levels to Gothic literature; c. pointing out in an ironic fashion how far from nobility these wannabe writers actually are – Baroness Frostbite used to be a waitress, for instance; d. reminding themselves (and readers as well) of the traumatic experiences each of them has undergone until the presentation of their stories. For example, in Baroness Frostbite's story, entitled 'Hot Potting', we learn that she actually underwent frostbite, earning her not only the epithet but also a deformed face, that constantly exposes her darkened rotten gums.

Instead of enjoying the inspirational perks of an idyllic place as Wordsworth, Mary Shelley and Blake had before them, they end up locked up in an abandoned theater supplied with costumes and thematic rooms, such as the Italian Renaissance lounge, the French Louis XV lobby, the black mohair Egyptian auditorium, the Arabian Nights gallery, the red imperial-Chinese promenade, and, as one would expect, the Gothic smoking room. Eventually, confinement takes its toll, and as weeks pass, a frenzy of (self-inflicted) mutilations and

1 Palahniuk himself addresses the issue in a text available at <http://chuckpalahniuk. net/features/the-guts-effect>, Viewed 5 February 2016.

murders unfolds. Their main concern, we are constantly reminded, is to have a marketable story to tell, which would grant them literary success, money, and a considerable share of public attention.

In order to achieve such a goal, the inmates turn to their most traumatic memories throughout the writing process and do their best to make confinement as harsh as possible: they lock themselves up, waste their food supply, tamper with water and gas facilities, and ultimately mutilate others and themselves, as the following passage describes: 'Director Denial has already hacked off fingers. So has Sister Vigilante – plus some toes, using the same paring knife that Lady Baglady borrowed from Chef Assassin to slice off her ear.'[2] In spite of its nonchalant tone, the passage above retains the graphic nature found both in Palahniuk's oeuvre and in many of the works discussed in the chapters present in this section: it certainly applies to the novel analysed by Danielle Schaub, Alan Cumyn's *Man of Bone*, whose main character's highly sensorial captivity narrative involves the description of disgusting sounds, sensations and feelings; it is also something noticeable in David Rabe's play *Sticks and Bones*, whose characters eventually resort to obscenities and extremely violent actions, as Aslı Tekinay shows in her reading of the play; however, Gen'ichiro Itakura's analysis of Nadeem Aslam's *The Wasted Vigil* has a stronger resonance with *Haunted*, insofar as Itakura argues that Aslam employs the technique of using highly graphic images as a response to the modern tradition of trauma narrative traced back to modernism as a means to symbolise trauma and indicate disruptions and displacements. As my reading of Palahniuk's novel presented over the next pages will prove, the same happens in *Haunted*.

The approach to *Haunted* from the perspective of trauma studies presented here benefits from Leanne Dodd's framework in her chapter about crime fiction as trauma literature.[3] The description of trauma proposed by the Australian Psychological Society (APS) – 'very frightening or distressing events [that] may result in a psychological wound or injury – a difficulty in coping or functioning normally following a particular event or experience'[4] – emphasises what trauma does rather than what it is. Some of the trauma aftermaths identified by the APS brought by Dodd in her text – hyperarousal of the nervous system, intrusion of repetitive thoughts and memories, numbing responses such as addiction, self-harm and dissociation and undesirable behaviours ranging

2 Chuck Palahniuk, *Haunted: A Novel of Stories* (New York: Doubleday, 2005), 149–150.

3 See Leanne Dodd's chapter in this volume.

4 Australian Psychological Society, 'Understanding and Managing Psychological Trauma', Viewed 10 February 2016, <http://www.psychology.org.au/publications/tip_ sheets/trauma/>.

from withdrawal to violence – occur to the writers in *Haunted* throughout the retreat.

Haunted is indeed a narrative made of traumatic stories.[5] Besides the episodes of loss, murder, rape, abusive relationships, child abuse, accidental mutilation, and impairing disease that inspire the stories within the novel, the title clearly evokes ghosts, arguably the most efficient metaphor for trauma in literature and other means of storytelling. These writers decide to do what others have done before them, that is, to try to come to terms with their traumas by revisiting them through writing, in a process that allows a parallel to the metaphor of 'releasing a voice through the wound' proposed by Cathy Caruth in *Unclaimed Experience*.[6] On the other hand, reliving their traumas through writing and storytelling does not suffice: new traumas are sought, the writers generally believe that the public and the media will only embrace them in the future if they present visible and palpable trauma ('How they act inside here, it won't matter, but once those doors come open they'll need to be kissing and hugging every time a camera turns their way. People will expect a wedding. Maybe even children.').[7] Such belief explains the mutilation frenzy and consequent dismantlement of the human body so frequently perceived in Palahniuk's work and most particularly in *Haunted*. Indeed, Andrew Slade goes as far as to say that for the American author 'the practice of mutilation is the sublime figuration of survival',[8] and in this case, 'survival' entails coming to terms with the past.

The suffocating space and the absence of windows are apt metaphors for the inescapability of trauma, as well as for the characters' dislocation and alienation. The Gothic literary tradition, deeply rooted in devices to express trauma such as the return of the past and its materialisation into a monstrous character, is at first perceived in the novel due to its dark setting. As Fred Botting observes, darkness threatens the light of reason with what it does not know,[9] and by needing to confront darkness once again, the haunted narrative voices in the novel must make sense out of the situation somehow. Palahniuk's oeuvre – especially *Haunted* – presents a textual device that concomitantly

5 In the text referred to in note 1, Palahniuk points out that most stories in *Haunted* originate from real cases he heard either from friends or acquaintances, or while attending meetings for sex addicts as part of the research for his novel *Choke*.

6 Cathy Caruth, *Unclaimed Experience: Trauma, Narrative, and History* (Baltimore: The John Hopkins University Press, 1996), 2.

7 Palahniuk, *Haunted*, 149.

8 Andrew Slade, 'On Mutilation: The Sublime Body of Chuck Palahniuk's Fiction' (New York: Routledge, 2009), 71.

9 Fred Botting, *Gothic* (London: Routledge, 2004), 32.

evidences the absence of the 'light of reason' and serves as a tool to deliver criticism: the repetition to exhaustion of words, phrases and short structures until they become hollow maxims. Both novel and film versions of *Fight Club* are famous for the sentence '[e]verything is. ... A copy of a copy of a copy',[10] used by Jack/Tyler Durden in a critique of consumer's society. Although in *Haunted* that mechanism is part of social criticism as well, it creates a multidimensional, fragmented and delusional description of the confined writers' inner state. The narrative voice that describes the writers' interaction in the retreat – a 'we' that refers to all characters without referring to any of them specifically – frequently resorts to structures such as 'us against us against us'[11] when describing the construction and simulation of traumas. Nonetheless, the most recurrent repetition in *Haunted* is 'the camera behind the camera behind the camera';[12] despite its poor syntax and apparent absurdity, the structure is part of a criticism mechanism towards mass media, particularly applicable to yellow journalism and reality television. The writers/characters in *Haunted* seem well aware of how communication works and flows among the masses in postmodern times: in times of convergence culture, post-truths and the virulent spread of news, images are essential, and stories are shared with little or no critical thinking, and the more blatant and gruesome, the more powerful they are bound to be within certain niches. In Miss America's short story, entitled 'Green Room' (a reference to the room where people wait in television studios before going on air), she observes a young man who, like herself, is waiting to advertise products on a typical morning show: 'That's what this guy wants to be: the camera behind the camera behind the camera giving the last and final truth. We all want to be one standing farthest back. The one who gets to say what's good or bad. Right or wrong.'[13] Later on, when Comrade Snarky dies during the retreat, the narrative 'we' observes that she 'will not be the camera behind the camera behind the camera. We hold the truth about her in our hands. Wedged between our teeth.'[14] The repetition of words and phrases also abounds in Alan Cumyn's *Man of Bone*. Albeit with different purposes, character Bill Burridge also exploits that technique throughout the narrative recounting his memories of trauma.[15]

10 Chuck Palahniuk, *Fight Club*. (New York: W. W. Norton & Co., 1996), 11.

11 Palahniuk, *Haunted*, 27, 89.

12 Ibid., 27, 104, 255, 292, 328, 357.

13 Ibid., 51.

14 Ibid., 255.

15 See Danielle Schaub's chapter in this volume.

The complex narrative structure in *Haunted* comprises three different textures: the one that serves as a backbone for the entire book, in which the narrative 'we' describes the writers' life in the retreat and how they eventually lose their minds over confinement and face the return of traumatic memories. This narrative dimension intertwines with the short stories produced during the retreat, each preceded by an introductory poem describing the traumas that inspired such stories. In its structure and atmosphere, *Haunted* emulates classic works of literature, such as Chaucer's *The Canterbury Tales*, which also presents a group of storytellers whose nicknames refer to their social status rather than their individuality (for instance the Knight, the Nun and the Wife of Bath), Sade's *The 120 Days of Sodom*, where another group of confined people endure physical and psychological suffering, and Stoker's *Dracula*, whose main character inhabits a castle as secluded, broad and dark as the abandoned theater where the writers' retreat takes place. The connection between *Haunted* and classic Gothic literature is enhanced by a conversation the writers have in which they parallel their current situation to the mythic 1816 Villa Diodati episode – the gathering of Lord Byron, Percy Bysshe Shelley, Mary Shelley, Claire Clairmont and John Polidori, which resulted in *The Vampyre* (a short story written by Polidori that Stoker admittedly used as an inspiration for *Dracula*) and *Frankenstein*, published in 1818.

> It was a summer house party in 1816, where a group of young people spent most days trapped in a house because of rain. Some of them were married, some not. Men and women. They read ghost stories to each other, but the books they had were terrible. After that, they all agreed to write a story. Any sort of scary story. To entertain each other.
>
> (...) 'So what did they write?' Miss Sneezy says.
>
> Those middle-class, bored people just trying to kill time. People trapped together in their moldy-damp summer house.
>
> 'Not much,' Mr. Whittier says. 'Just the legend of Frankenstein.' Mrs. Clark says, "And Dracula".[16]

The construction – or in some cases the remembrance – of the setting for the short stories walks hand-in-hand with those traumatic memories: 'Evil Spirits', the story written by Miss Sneezy, takes place in a prison on an island where she was kept in isolation due to a contagious and lethal disease; 'Dog Years', one of the short stories by Mr. Whittier, unfolds in a retirement home from where he

16 Palahniuk, *Haunted*, 62–63.

cannot leave. Despite his appearance, Whittier is in fact a teenager who suffers from progeria, a rare genetic disorder materialising through early signs of body aging. Finally, the setting for Comrade Snarky's short story 'Speaking Bitterness' is a very small room filled with enraged women.

Within the settings in the novel 'are hidden some secrets from the past (sometimes the recent past) that haunt the characters, psychologically, physically, or otherwise at the time of the story.'[17] In Palahniuk's novel that happens through the stories written during the retreat and the reference to 'ghosts':

> 'Our ghost, again,' says the Baroness Frostbite. Saint Gut-Free's two-headed baby. [He gets his own sister pregnant by masturbating in the swimming pool, hence the fear of a defective baby] The Countess Foresight's antiques dealer. Agent Tattletale's gassed and hammered private detective. [Both the Countess and the Agent murdered people][18]
>
> To the Countess Foresight, the ghost is an old-man antiques dealer, his throat slashed with a straight razor. (…)
>
> To Saint Gut-Free, the ghost is an aborted two-headed baby, both heads with his skinny face.
>
> To the Baroness Frostbite, the ghost wears a white apron around his waist and curses God. (…)
>
> To Sister Vigilante, the ghost is a hero with the side of his face caved in. To Miss Sneezy, the ghost is her grandmother.[19]

The term 'ghosts' echoes Jean Baudrillard's 'phantasy' in his theory. Both terms translate identically in Brazilian Portuguese ('fantasma') and are symbolically similar, even though phantasies, as we shall see, are collective whereas 'ghosts' are representations of individual traumas. The interplay between the absence of trauma (it happened in the past) and its presence[20] (it is represented on the diegetic level, either through the ghosts in the retreat or through the writing of short stories) derives from the writers' need to tell their stories, even if they lack objectivity or an unbiased view, given their traumatic origin. The confusion perceived in the writers' storytelling identifies as a feature of the so-called

17 Jerrold E. Hogle, 'Introduction: The Gothic in Western Culture', in *The Cambridge Companion to Gothic Fiction*, ed. Jerrold E. Hogle (Cambridge: Cambridge University Press, 2002), 2.

18 Palahniuk, *Haunted*, 378.

19 Ibid., 196.

20 Gen'ichiro Itakura's chapter in this volume also deals with the simultaneous absence and presence of trauma in his reading of *The Wasted Vigil*.

postmodern Gothic, which frequently tells stories through 'a triptych of mirrors in which images of the origin continually recede in a disappearing arc',[21] and, in a way, it parallels the 'camera behind the camera behind the camera' repetition.

Haunted is classic in its references, postmodern when it comes to its awareness of communication, and timeless inasmuch as it deals with the therapeutic effects of writing about trauma. The combination of these elements leads to the reading presented in this chapter, namely, one that observes representations of trauma in a work of literature from a theoretical perspective focused on issues of the so-called postmodern times. In order to do so, the adopted framework is that proposed by French philosopher and cultural theorist Jean Baudrillard, particularly his notions of simulation and hyperreality, besides the three phantasies that, according to him, haunt the postmodern times – cancer, terrorism and transvestitism.

'Postmodernism' is a paradoxical and contradictory term, given that

> [t]he Postmodern would be that which, in the modern, puts forward the unpresentable in presentation itself; that which denies itself the solace of good forms, the consensus of a taste which would make it possible to share collectively the nostalgia for the attainable; that which searches for new presentations, not in order to enjoy them but in order to impart a stronger sense of the unpresentable.[22]

More complex than presenting the unpresentable is the reason why the unpresentable is sought: not for enjoyment, taste or fruition, but for impact, shock and extreme experiences – a notion that pervades *Haunted*, whose stories are naturally difficult to be put to representation because of their traumatic nature. As the novel unfolds, the concern displayed by the confined writers over the marketability of their stories becomes more blatant, which indicates that they might have embellished or invented some of the traumas. Still, Palahniuk's writers remain in tune with the postmodern possibilities of trauma representation, given that

> The question (overt or implied) now asked (...) is no longer 'Is it true?' but 'What use is it?' In the context of the mercantilization of knowledge,

21 Steven Bruhm. 'The Contemporary Gothic: Why We Need It', in *The Cambridge Companion to Gothic Fiction*, ed. Jerrold E. Hogle (Cambridge: Cambridge University Press, 2002), 262.

22 Jean-François Lyotard, *The Postmodern Condition: A Report on Knowledge*, trans. Geoff Bennington and Brian Massumi (Manchester: Manchester University Press, 1984), 81.

> more often than not this question is equivalent to: 'Is it saleable?' And in the context of power-growth: 'Is it efficient?'[23]

If postmodern fiction is fascinated with artifice, schlock and kitsch, it is fair to assume that part of postmodern culture is obsessed with 'ugliness' and 'poor taste' – after all, 'we greet both worst and best with the same fascination'.[24] Therefore, some questions arise: how do postmodern audiences deal with 'taste'? Is this a concern at all, consciously or otherwise? Is it fair to say that at least part of postmodern audiences have unorthodox, 'strange' taste? And if so, can we consider part of this fascination as directed towards reports of trauma?

Baudrillard somehow approaches these issues when he affirms that *reality is over*. That means that to represent anything we can depend only on images and processed ideas. For Baudrillard, simulation begins with an implosion of meaning.[25] Given that the postmodern world is characterised by 'a process of social entropy leading to a collapse of boundaries, including the implosion of meaning in the media and the implosion of media and the social in the masses',[26] simulation becomes the defining characteristic of contemporary society. No true reality exists, just a series of representations and simulations that perpetuate themselves as they are constantly reproduced. The more complete and frequent simulations become, the closer it feels to being immersed in reality,[27] leading to the establishment of 'a world of simulation, of the hallucination of the truth, of the blackmail of the real, of the murder of every symbolic form and of its hysterical, historical retrospection.'[28] The simulacra are the symbolic places where simulations emerge, and Baudrillard divides them into three orders:

1. The first order qualifies 'natural, founded on the image, on imitation and counterfeit', they are 'harmonious, optimistic, and aim at the restitution or the ideal institution of nature made in God's image',[29] represented in *Haunted* by the recurrence of copies and reproduction of behavior and images. However, for Baudrillard's definition to make sense, some terms

23 Ibid., 51.

24 Jean Baudrillard, *The Transparency of Evil: Essays on Extreme Phenomena*, trans. James Benedict (New York: Verso, 2002), 69.

25 Jean Baudrillard, *Simulacra and Simulation*, trans. Sheila Faria Gleiser (AnnArbor: University of Michigan Press, 1994), 31.

26 Steven Best and Douglas Kellner, *Postmodern Theory: Critical Interrogations* (New York: Guilford Press, 1991), 121.

27 Paul Hegarty, *Jean Baudrillard: Live Theory* (London: Continuum, 2004), 49.

28 Baudrillard, *Simulacra and Simulation*, 9.

29 Ibid., 121.

must be submitted to the writers' 'twisted aesthetics'. For them, the ideal image implies bruises, missing parts and scars. Within the small community they form, they completely distort the notions of 'harmonious' and 'optimistic', aiming at the destruction of the body – or, as Baudrillard points out, 'a chemical prosthesis, a mental surgery of performance, a plastic surgery of perception'[30] that characterises the postmodern world. The word 'counterfeit' suits the novel perfectly: the Duke of Vandals earns his living by copying works of art and killing artists, while Agent Tattletale is a detective who must identify people pretending disability to collect pension. Likewise, some writers pretend to be what they are not: Lady Baglady pretends to be homeless when in fact she is a millionaire, Mr. Whittier pretends to be an elderly man when in fact he is a teenager suffering from progeria and the Earl of Slander is a reporter who kills a decadent TV star and plants false evidence of suicide, in order to have a good story to write about.

2. The second order of simulacra states they are 'productive, productivist, founded on energy, force, its materialisation by machine and in the whole system of production';[31] in the novel, producing, advertising and selling appear in some of the short stories, such as Miss America's 'Green Room' and Chef Assassin's 'Product Placement', which toys with the idea of mass production and negative advertisement – the story consists of a letter the Chef writes to a cutlery industry describing how he uses their knives to kill people, and how easily he can destroy their reputation if he divulges that.
3. The third order of simulacra stipulates: 'Simulacra of simulation, founded on information, the model, the cybernetic game – total operationality, hyperreality, aim of total control',[32] characterising contemporary times. Examples of the third order abound in the novel, considering that that every event that takes place during the retreat is fake – simulations based on what the writers consider an irreversible trauma, therefore a marketable story.

Given the loss of referentials that characterises the postmodern world, there is no way to identify an authentic source of reality; thus, our models of the real are generated without a distinguishable origin or reality, they are based on processed and simulated images, leading to what Baudrillard calls the 'realer than real',[33] or hyperreality.

30 Baudrillard, *The Transparency of Evil*, 49.
31 Baudrillard, *Simulacra and Simulation*, 121.
32 Ibid., 121.
33 Ibid., 18.

As Baudrillard affirms, 'present-day simulators attempt to make the real, all of the real, coincide with their models of simulation.'[34] Such a fact is possible due to the absence of concrete referentials of reality, which is precisely what we see in *Haunted*: the theater is a symbolic simulacrum (the place that enables simulation), the events are all simulated, and the overall situation (the retreat, the recordings of the events and the (self-) infliction of bruises, for instance) constitutes the hyperreality they are immersed in.

The hyperreal depends on the elimination of the subjective point of view, the suppression of the look, the fact that the object of perception is always already there, already seen, thus preventing the act of seeing. This combination of elements allows them to resort to victimisation, something that comes naturally for them, due to the traumatic and personal origins of their stories. Such victimisation becomes a core element in the hyperreality they create, as evidenced in the following passage:

> Already, we were making matters worse. Exaggerating. We'd say how the place was freezing-cold. There was no running water. We had to ration the food.
>
> None of that was true, but it does make a better story. No, we'd warp the truth. Blow it up. Stretch it out. For effect.
>
> We'd create our own incestuous orgy of people and animals for the world to gossip about.[35]

Though based on individual trauma episodes, the stories produced during the retreat (and the retreat itself, for that matter) aim at calling an intended audience's attention. In a way, it is as if these people wanted to share what haunts them so as to haunt their viewers/readers as well in a process that implies relying on a haunting code that mixes timeless, profound fears and aspects of contemporary life. In Baudrillardian terms, these 'phantasies' pervade the most varied areas of human relations. *Cancer*, *transvestitism* and *terrorism* are the direct consequence of the indifferentiation, emptiness of information, violence, neurosis and loss of referentials that characterise the world.

> These forms, terrorism, transvestitism, and cancer, all reflect excesses – on the political, sexual and genetic levels respectively; they also reflect

34 Ibid., 2.

35 Ibid., 84.

> deficiencies in – and the consequent collapse of – the codes of the political, sexual and genetic realms.[36]

Cancer is a phantasy based on the idea that both an individual's organism and society are vulnerable to silent, massive and dangerous threats. Its effects influence our modes of conceiving and perceiving communication, information, art and interpersonal relationships. This phantasy manifests itself in the stories and characters in *Haunted* in four main ways, namely, emptiness in communication and information (in association to the notion of *virulence*); the banalisation of aesthetics and art; the 'artificial sterilisation' of the environments and the people; and the massive presence of body diseases and the decay they bring.

The destruction of bodies associated to cancer as a disease somehow echoes in the novel through the massive presence of other diseases and conditions with equally destructive consequences. Four writers have illnesses or deformities prior to the retreat: Saint Gut-Free (missing part of his intestines), Mr. Whittier (progeria), Miss Sneezy (a rare and highly contagious virus) and Baroness Frostbite (missing part of her mouth because of frostbite). In addition, the unfolding of the retreat and the environment in which it takes place invite to vicious behaviors and attitudes that also lead to body decay.

Transvestitism, on the other hand, is the phantasy related to the excesses and deficiencies in our sexual codes. It happens because the fascination exerted by these forms is, according to Baudrillard, 'viral', and their virulence is 'reinforced by their images, for the modern media have a viral force of their own, and their virulence is contagious.'[37]

Crossdressing and gender performance appear in short stories with a background pervaded by trauma. 'Punch Drunk' presents two US Air Force members, Flint and Webber, who plan to crash an airplane somewhere in the Middle East. In order to raise the necessary money, they dress as famous female singers in motorcycle runs, rodeos, boat shows and country fairs, in order to allow people to spank them, leaving them with a few marks of their own:

> Webber looks around, his face pushed out of shape, one cheekbone lower than the other. One of his eyes is just a milk-white ball pinched in the red-black swelling under his brow. His lips, Webber's lips are split so deep in

36 Baudrillard, *The Transparency of Evil*, 36.

37 Ibid., 36–7.

> the middle he's got four lips instead of two. Inside all those lips, you can't see a single tooth left.[38]

'Speaking Bitterness', written by Comrade Snarky, presents Miranda, a transsexual that crafted herself to the image of someone like La Cicciolina. The story describes Miranda's attempt to participate in a meeting held at a club for women only – a 'women-only safe space'.[39] The bitterness in their conversations at the club, highlighted by the title, essentially focuses on experiences with men. At the very beginning of the story, the narrative voice states that 'To men, a woman is either a virgin or a slut. A mother or a whore.'[40] Prior to the story, we are introduced to Comrade Snarky's childhood background, such as her parents' divorce and the fear her mother instilled in her that her father would rape her someday. That never took place, but it had some impact on her, as Snarky herself admits: ' "Instead of all that," ' (…) "my father took me to the zoo."/He took her to the ballet. He took her to soccer practice./He kissed her good night. (…) "But, for the rest of my life, I was always ready [to defend herself from a rapist]" '.[41]

The women in 'Punch Drunk' prefer beating super feminine crossdressers, whereas the ones in 'Speaking Bitterness' are uncomfortable with Miranda. Indeed, her efforts to look female end up forming an over-the-top, stereotypical image: a lizard-skin pocketbook, long, pink fingernails; a rainbow-coloured scarf and a complementary fur coat on a cropped silk blouse covering big breasts. The narration goes on, defining Miranda as 'a total sex-doll fantasy, the kind of woman only a man would become.'[42] She eventually epitomises the excess of reality, or the hyperreal.

The gathering unfolds until the women force Miranda to undress and they abuse her, as a sort of symbolic vendetta against all men that have harmed them in the past. 'The women in the group, we look at each other. To have a man here taking orders. Some of us were molested. Some of us, raped. All of us, ogled, groped, undressed by male eyes. It's our turn, and we don't know where to begin.'[43]

Obviously, Miranda's efforts to become a woman are all based on a superficial, toxic and pornographic femininity, and perhaps because of that the

38 Palahniuk, *Haunted*, 182.
39 Ibid., 258.
40 Ibid., 258.
41 Ibid., 257.
42 Ibid., 259.
43 Ibid., 265.

women in the group speak bitterness to her. The rejection of Miranda's status as a woman is evident in the recurrence of the pronouns 'he' and 'his' throughout the story whenever they refer to Miranda, even after they discover she has undergone a sex reassignment surgery. When the group of women call Miranda a 'sex-doll fantasy', it is only the first step in their 'decoding' process of Miranda's physical femininity. The conclusion of their analysis comes with harsh words:

> Here's every male fantasy brought to life in a kind of Frankenstein monster of stereotypes: The perfect big round breasts. The hard muscle of long thighs. The mouth, a perfect pout, greasy with lipstick. The pink leather skirt too short and tight for anything but sex. He speaks with the breathy voice of a little girl or a movie starlet. A huge gush of air for what little sound comes out. It's the kind of whispery voice Cosmopolitan magazine teaches girls to use, to make listening men lean closer.[44]

The excerpt highlights the mouth, 'greasy with lipstick'. Previous passages mention the blush put on top of more blush, mascara on top of mascara, somehow emulating the distortion mantra 'the camera behind the camera behind the camera' through the manipulation of images and Baudrillard's hyperreality, where things are 'more real than real'. While unfolding, the story clarifies that the embargo on men derives from past traumatic experiences each of these women have endured: 'husbands who won't pick up dirty socks. Husbands who slap us around, then cheat on us. Fathers disappointed that we're not boys. Stepfathers who diddle us. Brothers who bully us. Bosses. Priests. Traffic cops. Doctors.'[45]

The destruction of every single device Miranda employs to become a woman leads to her deconstruction as a woman and also as a Baudrillardian transvestite. All the elements that form her physical femininity are destroyed or altered somehow, leading to a pitiful result:

> Whatever he is, 'Miranda' is crying. Caught up in his little drama, all his eye makeup and blusher mixed with his foundation and coming down his cheeks to each corner of his mouth. He's almost naked with his stretched pantyhose webbed between his ankles, his feet still in gold-elegant high-heeled sandals. His blouse is gone, and his pink lace bra is open and hanging off his shoulders. His firm, round breasts shiver with each sob. He's on

44 Ibid., 260.

45 Ibid., 260–261.

> the conference table this way. His fur coat on the floor, kicked off into a corner, his blond hair falling down. His own little horror story.[46]

Miranda is raped by the women in the group, which represents not only a moment when the traumatised perpetrate trauma but also a rite of passage of sorts. The ending of the story insinuates that after being abused, Miranda can finally understand what it feels like to be a woman, such as the other members of the group. In reality, the final words of the story match exactly the opening words, 'From the minute she sat down, we tried to explain. We don't allow men. This is a women-only safe space. The purpose of our group …'[47] In spite of the anatomic details, the transphobia and the sexual abuse, 'Speaking Bitterness' also epitomises the non-sexual aspect of Baudrillard's notion of transvestitism; indeed, Miranda is a 'sex doll', the women in the group have suffered sexual violence and later on, they perpetrate sexual violence against Miranda. However, not even all those aspects related to sexual codes make the characters deeply involved with sex and its procedures. As Baudrillard observes, "Sexed beings, we certainly are (…) but sexual? That's the question. Socialized beings, we are (and sometimes, by force), but social? It's still to be seen. Realized beings, yes – but real? Nothing is less certain."[48] Therefore, sex and its determinants are twisted in the story to show positions of power and separation of groups, but above all, to show that Miranda – the sex doll, the Frankenstein creature, the monster, the made-up sex robot – is not sexual, merely 'sexed'. She, like the women in the group, is aware of the sexual codes and sexual determinants. By turning herself into a woman made to the image of cheap porn stars, Miranda displays what Baudrillard calls an 'excess of reality, this hyperreality of things.'[49] She demonstrates her talent in representing, in producing an image with a well-set objective. There lies the main difference between her and the other women, who state that '[b]eing a woman is special. It's sacred. This isn't just some club you can join.'[50] The twist of sexual determinants comes through once more, when, right before the abuse takes place, the feminine 'we' that narrates the story expresses itself in a stereotypical masculine fashion, probably mimicking the way abusive men would express themselves:

> It's obvious. This poor, sad, misguided fuck, he's using us. The way a masochist goads a sadist. The way the criminal wants to be caught. Miranda

46 Ibid., 265.
47 Ibid., 268.
48 Baudrillard, *The Transparency of Evil*, 54.
49 Ibid., 29.
50 Palahniuk, *Haunted*, 262.

> is begging for it. This is why he's shown up here. It's why he's dressed this way. He knows this shorty-short skirt, these big casaba boobs, they drive a real woman wild. In this case, 'no' does mean 'yes.' It means 'Yes, please.' It means, 'slap me.'[51]

All things considered, Miranda embodies the idea Baudrillard proposes when he comments on the child-prosthesis: everyone performs an appearing act, and for it everyone needs the right look: 'So it is not: I exist, I am here! But rather: I am visible, I am an image – look! Look!'[52]

Finally, terrorism is based on the premise that 'everything is political'. Baudrillard affirms that we are living at the age of the 'transpolitical', and that '[t]errorism in all its forms is the transpolitical mirror of evil. For the real problem, the only problem, is: where did Evil go? And the answer is: everywhere – because the anamorphosis of modern forms of Evil knows no bounds.'[53] The irony lies in the fact that we ourselves have spread evil everywhere precisely by trying to avoid it at all costs, as it happens for instance in David Rabe's play *Sticks and Bones*.[54] The efforts made by Ozzie and Harriett (named after a happy couple from a television series, as Tekinay aptly observes) to erase the war horrors from their household imply a symbolic erasure of their son David, a war veteran, as well. Like the writers/characters in *Haunted*, David must deal with traumas, both those inflicted upon the mind and those inflicted upon the body.

Terry Eagleton agrees with Baudrillard about the status of evil as something contemporary societies have tried to banish by arguing that '[i]f the word "evil" is not listed in the dictionary of political correctness, it is because it is thought to imply a particular theory of wrongdoing, one springing from metaphysical rather than historical causes.'[55] This issue is approached by Mark Callaghan in his discussion regarding governmental initiatives in Northern Ireland to alter mural images that could either mark the division between different social communities or remind people of a bellicose past. In order to refer to this 're-imaging' scheme Callaghan uses the term 'whitewashing', a term also present in Baudrillard theory. For the French philosopher, the desperate attempt of sterilising the world of negativity (which Baudrillard calls *prophylaxis*) leads to a hyperprotected space, where all defences are

51 Ibid., 264.

52 Baudrillard, *The Transparency of Evil*, 23.

53 Ibid., 82.

54 See Aslı Tekinay's chapter in this volume.

55 Terry Eagleton, *On Evil* (New Haven: Yale University Press, 2005), 115.

lost.[56] Positivity in excess leads to repression, and repression leads to infinite simulation. To this chain of events Baudrillard gives the name *operational whitewash*:

> we are doomed in consequence to a whitewashing of all activity – whitewashed social relations, whitewashed bodies, whitewashed memory – in short, to a complete aseptic whiteness. Violence is whitewashed, history is whitewashed, all as part of a vast enterprise of cosmetic surgery at whose completion nothing will be left but a society for which, and individuals for whom, all violence, all negativity, are strictly forbidden.[57]

The erasure of negativity, although seemingly a good thing, originates in an imbalance that interferes with individualities and differences. Forms, faces, personalities: everything must be submitted to corrections and compulsive remodeling, which is symbolised by the notion of the surgical face[58] in *Haunted*, where only faces are surgical, but also bodies; however, due to the writers' twisted aesthetics, the aim is not to 'look good and feel gorgeous', but to display severed limbs, bruises and scars. In order to corroborate his ideas about the negative consequences of prophylaxis, Baudrillard resorts to a parallel between the social sickness (collective neurosis against negativity) and diseases that epitomise postmodern times

> Total prophylaxis is lethal. (…): it [medicine] treats cancer or AIDS as if they were conventional illnesses, when in fact they are illnesses generated by the very success of prophylaxis and medicine, illnesses bred of the disappearance of illnesses, of the elimination of pathogenic forms.[59]

Baudrillard brings terrorism and cancer together by emphasising the virulent spread of news and the presence of invisible threats, thus removing the spotlight from the physical violence and directing it towards terror. In Palahniuk's novel we perceive that in stories such as 'Product Placement', in which Chef Assassin instills terror into the owner of Kutting Blok through a series of innuendoes related to a possible killing spree involuntarily 'sponsored' by the Kutting Blok top-quality knives. He has the targets in sight – critics who have written bad reviews about his cooking – and the tools to perform

56 Baudrillard, *The Transparency of Evil*, 62.
57 Ibid., 44–45.
58 Ibid., 45.
59 Ibid., 64.

the service. Not one blood drop is shed in the story, but terror and fear pervade it, as the atmosphere of the letter hints that murders might take place any time. In addition, Chef Assassin cleverly uses the power of media and its contaminative capacity, given that '[t]he contagiousness of terrorism, its fascination, is every bit as enigmatic as the contagiousness of these other phenomena.'[60]

The title of the novel prevents us from forgetting that terrorism is necessarily implicit in the process of being haunted. As the writers deal with their traumas/ghosts, some of them verbalise their fears and anxieties in ways that make the connection between haunting and terrorism clear. As he comments the downsides of his masturbatory experiences in the swimming pool, Saint Gut-Free affirms in 'Guts' that '[t]hat used to be my worst fear in the world: my teenage virgin sister, thinking she's just getting fat, then giving birth to a two-headed retard baby. Both the heads looking just like me. Me, the father AND the uncle',[61] which indeed happens at the end.

The terrorism in Palahniuk's work is related to his characters' awareness of the world: it is their perceptions and knowledge of how their society works and responds to events that lead them to act in excessive and overdramatic ways. There is even an element that might be called meta-terrorism: in their attempt of creating an ideally terrifying story, the writers feel anxious and frustrated when certain elements are missing, which might be ultimately interpreted as the fear of not having fearful enough embellishments. 'Swan Song' describes how the Earl of Slander murdered former TV star Danny Wilcox and planted fake evidence of Danny's paedophilia and zoophilia, in Palahniuk's most evident criticism towards the yellow press.

In that sense, 'Swan Song' works as a micro-mirror of the writers retreat that backbones *Haunted*, whose narrative describes how the players of the story manipulate it to the point of transforming it in a transvestite of itself. Once again, it is important to point out the utilitarian aspect and usefulness of such enterprise. Stephen King asks in *Danse Macabre*: 'Why do you want to make up horrible things when there is so much real horror in the world?'.[62] The answer he gives echoes the unconscious motivation for the Earl of Slander in his short story and for all the characters in *Haunted* to come to terms with their traumatic pasts: '[t]he answer seems to be that we make up horrors to help us cope with the real ones.'[63]

60 Ibid., 38.

61 Palahniuk, *Haunted*, 16.

62 Stephen King, *Danse Macabre* (New York: Berkley Books, 1983), 13.

63 King, *Danse Macabre*, 13.

Bibliography

Australian Psychological Society. 'Understanding and Managing Psychological Trauma'. Viewed on 10 February 2018. <http://www.psychology.org.au/publications/tip_sheets/trauma/>.

Baudrillard, Jean. *Simulacra and Simulation.* Translated by Sheila Faria Gleiser. Ann Arbor: University of Michigan Press, 1994.

Baudrillard, Jean. *The Transparency of Evil: Essays on Extreme Phenomena.* Translated by James Benedict. New York: Verso, 2002.

Best, Steven and Douglas Kellner. *Postmodern Theory: Critical Interrogations.* New York: Guilford Press, 1991.

Botting, Fred. *Gothic*. London: Routledge, 2004.

Bruhm, Steven. 'The Contemporary Gothic: Why We Need It'. In *The Cambridge Companion to Gothic Fiction*, edited by Jerome E. Hogle, 259–276, Cambridge: Cambridge University Press, 2002.

Caruth, Cathy. *Unclaimed Experience: Trauma, Narrative, and History.* Baltimore: Johns Hopkins University Press, 1996.

Eagleton, Terry. *On Evil.* New Haven: Yale University Press, 2010.

Hegarty, Paul. *Jean Baudrillard: Live Theory*. London: Continuum, 2004.

Hogle, Jerrold E. 'Introduction: The Gothic in Western Culture'. In *The Cambridge Companion to Gothic Fiction*, edited by Jerrold E. Hogle, 1–21. Cambridge: Cambridge University Press, 2002.

King, Stephen. *Danse Macabre*. New York: Berkley Books, 1983.

Lyotard, Jean-François. *The Postmodern Condition: A Report on Knowledge*. Translated by Geoff Bennington and Brian Massumi. Manchester: Manchester University Press, 1984.

Palahniuk, Chuck. *Fight Club.* New York: W. W. Norton & Co., 1996.

Palahniuk, Chuck. *Haunted: A Novel of Stories.* New York: Doubleday, 2005.

Slade, Andrew. 'On Mutilation: The Sublime Body of Chuck Palahniuk's Fiction'. In *Reading Chuck Palahniuk: American Monsters and Literary Mayhem*, edited by Cynthia Kuhn and Lance Rubin, 62–72. New York: Routledge, 2009.

CHAPTER 10

'I Used To Be Human Once': Trauma and Reconfigurations of the Body in Chemical Disasters

Elwin Susan John

Abstract

The chaos or the disorder initiated by a traumatic experience/event leaves visible scars on the selves reminding one about a painful lived experience. The human body becomes a space and canvas for the expression of such sufferings. These incidents strike both physical and mental markings on a body and it results in an explosion of questions. Writers in fact consider the body as a tool to communicate the misery and agony of the victims. In this chapter, an attempt is made to identify and record the 'identities' that have emerged out of the incidents that have left a mark on the Indian psyche. Narratives on the Bhopal Gas Tragedy and the Endosulfan Tragedy in Kerala are chosen for this study. More than a comparative study of these two incidents, I try to make sense of the physical transformations of the individual bodies that accompanied these tragedies and the resulting identity formations. On one hand, the emerging images of the victims are considered to be ugly and monstrous and they are treated as outcasts in society. Or are we sympathetic towards such individuals? On the other hand, these victims try to live their lives by compromising on a lot of things. My study will explore the strategies employed by the victims to move forward with their lives and obtain justice, and the scheming done by the State. In a larger framework, the presence of such figures in society questions our own existence. The notion of being normal and a life without defects is an abnormality to these people. In such a context, these people find their own ways to fit in which are articulated in the narratives selected for this study. I will be drawing on trauma theory, body criticism and postcolonial theories to substantiate my arguments.

Keywords

body – trauma – activism – memory – disaster

 | DOI:10.1163/9789004405431_010

1 Introduction

The year is 1984.[1] A central figure in Indian politics was assassinated on 31st October 1984 – Mrs Indira Gandhi. In the following month, November 1984, the Republic of India witnessed one of its most violent episodes of the century, the anti-Sikh riots killing thousands of people, as a response to the assassination of Indira Gandhi by her Sikh minder. Adding on to the miseries of 1984, on the night of 2 December 1984 a massive leak of Methyl Isocyanate from the Union Carbide[2] company's plant in Bhopal (capital of the Indian state of Madhya Pradesh) took thousands of lives from the sleeping city. The deadly gas quickly spread, leaving incalculable damages on the environment and the social life of the people. The death toll rose higher every week with its impacts lasting for years. In short, 1984 bid adieu to India with an invitation for torrential compassion from the world.

As if the Bhopal Gas Tragedy set a benchmark to all the disasters in the country, Indian environmentalists addressed the Endosulfan victims of Kasargod (northern district in the Indian state of Kerala) as 'silent Bhopals', an example of slow poisoning. Endosulfan is a pesticide banned in more than 80 countries around the world. The intensive aerial spraying of Endosulfan over the cashew plantations in the district of Kasargod from 1976 to 2001 resulted in irreversible health defects. The Endosulfan Tragedy caused a very obvious transgression of medical vocabulary due to the multiplicity of novel conditions appearing as an outcome of this disaster. The tragedy clearly blurred the line between the victims and survivors withthe latter category still on the cusp of becoming tomorrow's victims.

By collating the academic inquiries on Bhopal gas tragedy and Endosulfan tragedy (BGT and ET respectively) one could imagine multiple reasons behind them. S. Ravi Rajan's[3] study on BGT proposes that improper storing facilities, poor maintenance and negligence of authorities resulted in the massive leak of this poisonous gas. Mahapatro and Panigrahi's[4] commentary on ET critiques the inappropriate use of technology. The Union Carbide India Limited (UCIL)

1 The quotation in the title of this paper comes from Indra Sinha's *Animal's People*. The line suggests that he/she is no more considered a human being and thus becomes relevant as it chronicles the probable reconfigurations of such bodies. Indra Sinha, *Animal's People* (New York: Simon & Schuster, 2007), 1.

2 Union Carbide India Limited (UCIL) was a subsidiary of the US based chemical company, Union Carbide (now Dow Chemical Company) established in India prior to the Indian Independence. The company's plant in Bhopal used to manufacture and store batches of highly poisonous Methyl Isocyanate.

3 S. Ravi Rajan, 'Disaster, Development and Governance: Reflections on the Lessons of Bhopal', *Environmental Values* 11.3 (2002): 369.

4 G. K. Mahapatro, 'The Case for Banning Endosulfan', *Current Science* 104.11 (2013): 1477.

contended that an act of sabotage caused the leak whereas it was a corporate crime in the eyes of many Indians.

2 The Human Body and the Discourse of Disaster

The list of reasons and discussions abound, but rarely do they provide any help to the survivors of both tragedies. To clarify the trajectory of this chapter's progress, I borrow cultural anthropologist Allen W. Batteau's distinction between an accident and a disaster. He says, 'what distinguishes a disaster from an accident is this: accidents and natural events such as hurricanes and earthquakes claim lives and damage property, but disasters damage, sometimes fatally, entire communities, industries or political regimes'.[5] The United Nations' global report on human settlements defines disaster as,

> a serious disruption of the functioning of society, causing widespread human, material or environmental losses which exceed the ability of the affected society to cope on its own resources. A disaster is a function of risk processes. It results from a combination of hazards, human vulnerability and insufficient capacity or measures to reduce the potential negative consequences of risk.[6]

Following these definitions, to a greater extend both BGT and ET count as chemical *disasters* that have scarred the Indian psyche.

The existing academic discussions about these disasters include questions on class, gendered readings, environmental justice, ethics, struggle of the victims, inappropriate application of technology etc. Satinath Sarangi's[7] commentary on BGT accuses the indifference of the legal system in providing justice to the victims of BGT whereas Betwa Sharma[8] notes that new victims have emerged through groundwater pollution, again a consequence of BGT.

5 Allen W Batteau, 'Aggressive Technology in a Century of Industrial Disasters', *Practicing Anthropology* 23.4 (2001): 28.

6 *Enhancing Urban Safety and Security: Global Report on Human Settlements* (Un-Habitat (London: Earthscan, 2007): 168.

7 Satinath Sarangi, 'Bhopal Disaster: Judiciary's Failure', *Economic and Political Weekly* .46 (1995): 2907–2909.

8 Betwa Sharma, 'Bhopal Gas Tragedy: New Victims', *Economic and Political Weekly* 41.17 (2006): 1613–1616.

Priyanka Pulla[9] reports on the plight and predicament of the female victims of ET. From Rajiv Lochan's[10] study on the health issues of BGT, we can derive the existence of an obvious transgression in medical vocabulary due to the multiplicity of novel conditions that have appeared as an outcome of the disaster.

In this chapter, I explore the reconfigurations of the body when it comes face to face with an industrial disaster. The human body has become a category for analysis in contemporary academia. In Humanities and Social Sciences, 'body'[11] functions as a buzzword that incorporates techniques of production, consumption, marketing, commodification etc and debates on gender, empire, fashion, sports, health, medicine, hygiene, eroticism etc. Within the premise of industrial disasters, the human body serves as a space and a canvass for the expression of sufferings. Such incidents strike both physical and mental markings on a body, resulting in an explosion of questions. Writers consider the body as a tool to communicate the misery and agony of the victims. They thus attempt to identify and record the 'identities' that have emerged through these incidents.

The two most immediate associations made with the discourse of the body concern health and disease. The identities I focus on in this chapter are products of health related 'imperfections'. This chapter progresses through a close analysis of the select narratives on BGT (Indra Sinha's *Animal's People* and Anjali Deshpande's *Impeachment*) and ET (*Enmagaje* by Ambika Sudhan Mangadu).

Indra Sinha's *Animal's People* narrates the story of a 'beastly boy' who happens to be a victim of the Bhopal gas tragedy. The story develops in the form of tape recordings between the boy and a journalist. The boy is called, or rather prefers to be called, 'Animal' because he walks on all fours. The readers get the sense that the poisonous gas released on the night of the tragedy was responsible for Animal's inability to walk on two legs. On the night of the tragedy he was only a few days old and orphaned. The novel tells how Animal tries to cope with the 'normal' life of others and he wonders how it would feel to be 'normal'. Animal's desire to get his back fixed coupled with his premonition

9 Priyanka Pulla, 'Kerala's Endosulfan Tragedy: Did It Really Happen?', *Open Magazine*,153 (1 June 2013), viewed on 29 September 2014. Priyanka Pullais a freelance journalist. <http://www.openthemagazine.com/article/nation/kerala-s-endosulfan-tragedy>.

10 Rajiv Lochan, 'Health Damage Due to Bhopal Gas Disaster: Review of Medical Research', *Economic and Political Weekly* 26.21 (1991):1323.

11 'Body' is a category analysed and studied across multiple disciplines today. For example, Deborah Lupton in *Medicine as Culture: Illness, Disease and the Body* (London: Sage Publications, 1994) gives a detailed framework to the ongoing discussions about body outside the realm of medicine.

that an impossible task lingers throughout the novel. Animal's life centres on his dog Jara and his fantasies about the local musician's daughter. He is also dragged into the scams and plots surrounding a free clinic opened by an American doctor in their village. It is an interesting narrative as it gives an insider and outsider outlook of the tragedy.

Impeachment by Anjali Deshpande portrays the power dynamics within the Indian legal system with regard to the Bhopal gas tragedy. A group of friends – journalists, lawyers and NGO members – narrate the disaster through the eyes of the Carbide victims and their own experiences. The novel takes a stand on how the State sees the issue. Although the educated FOB group (Friends of Bhopal) tries to fight for justice for the victims, the said survivors find it difficult to live their lives due to their own lack of legal knowledge and poor financial backing.

The ill-effects of Endosulfan that raised a huge uproar in Kerala are portrayed in the Malayalam novel *Enmakaje* by Ambikasuthan Mangad. Bearing the name of a village in the Kasaragod district mostly affected by pesticide overuse, the novel progresses with its two main characters, Neelakantan and Devayani, abandoning all human contact from city life and planning to start a new peaceful life in one of the hills in the village. They are completely oblivious about the nature of the village and the medical conditions of the villagers. Neelakantan was practising a vow of silence and by living in the jungle, they can take up the life of jungle dwellers without any traces of their previous existence in another world outside the forest. Only by chance do they encounter the various human conditions in this village never seen before: kids who could not grow up, people with huge heads, kids with lost limbs, crippled individuals, people with strange mental sicknesses etc. Nestled in the language of myth and folklore, the narrative incorporates the attempts of activism initiated by Neelakantan and his friends.

3 Memories, Relics and Display Bodies

Although BGT and ET occurred in two different spatial and temporal boundaries of the country, the chaos and the disorder initiated by them incidents cannot be side-lined or underestimated. The experience of trauma links both these disasters according to the definition of the American psychiatrist Judith Lewis Herman: 'Traumatic events are extraordinary, not because they occur rarely, but rather because they overwhelm the ordinary human adaptations to life'.[12] Both BGT and ET have disrupted the social, economic and political

12 Judith Lewis Herman, *Trauma and Recovery: From Domestic Abuse to Political Terror* (New York: Basic Books, 1992).

well-being of the people affected by them. Traumatic experiences and events, they have left visible scars on the selves whose cultural representations are explored in this chapter.

Every culture goes through its own irregular patterns of forgetting and remembering so that trauma related discussions inevitably connect to the discourse of memory. Without any doubt, one can say that the reminiscence of a traumatic past affects the quality of the present. Julian Barnes in *The Sense of an Ending* says, 'history is that certainty produced at the point where the imperfections of memory meet the inadequacies of documentation'.[13] Such a history points out the images that may not have received sufficient recognition and attention through the discourse of trauma writing. Many of these images still remain as memories in the minds of the survivors. As Suroopa Mukherjee suggests, 'the most powerful media-generated images of the disaster are faces of men and women staring blankly at the uncertain future'.[14] Reminders of the past also instil fear among people that such an incident could happen again and the blankness on their faces indicates their helplessness at the thought of undergoing a similar trauma.

The spirits of memory are rekindled through visual agencies. The horrific images and photographs of industrial disasters force individuals to relive the traumatic past over and again. The photograph of a child with hydrocephalus (also known as 'water in the brain' or an enlarged brain condition where the head appears much bigger than the body) is the mostly circulated image of ET. It symbolises the face of ET just as Pablo Bartholomew's photo of a half-buried child under the wreckage of BGT. These images leave such powerful impacts that even those who have not experienced the incidents feel that they are witnessing it. In short, a cultural consequence of such tragedies lies in the creation of display bodies. People, scenes and conditions exhibited, displayed and talked about become like some caged animals to be looked at. Such cultural transgression projects humanity's endurance to embrace spectacles of suffering.

The trauma inducing scenes of the surroundings and people captured from the locations evidence what really happened. Visual media intensifies pain through such frozen moments. Photographs not only reintroduce traumatic images into a cultural sphere, but might also act as gap-fillers. Ulrich Baer's research offers an interesting contribution to this connection between trauma and photography. More than considering trauma as a theme for photography,

13 Julian Barnes, *The Sense of an Ending* (London: Jonathan Cape, 2011), 17.

14 Suroopa Mukherjee, *Surviving Bhopal: Dancing Bodies, Written Texts and Oral Testimonials of Women in the Wake of an Industrial Disaster* (New York: Palgrave Macmillan, 2010), 2.

Baer illustrates how both trauma and photography 'arrest' moments and memories through experience and technology respectively. According to Baer, 'because trauma blocks routine mental processes from converting an experience into memory or forgetting, it parallels the defining structure of photography, which also traps an event during its occurrence while blocking its transformation into memory'.[15] In this respect, M. Candace Christensen engages trauma resulting from gender-based violence through photovoice and generates hope among victims.[16] The repeated circulation of such photographs could even remove the trauma associated with the incident. The bodies displayed could demystify the event itself. In an age where science, media and its related discussions detach the element of mystery from everything, humans try to unveil secrets in order to present the raw form of things, causing the victimisation of the human body. To illustrate this, I point out the advent of digital technology and its offshoots like the *Visible Human Project*.[17] There is a recurring tendency to know more and an urge to explore the hidden, which explains that the dissection and display of photographs from a traumatic event. Apart from capturing a memorial, such photographs commodify 'the bodies' in consumer culture.

Animal in Indra Sinha's *Animal's People* is approached by a journalist through a middle man by the name Chunaram. Sinha illustrates the probable attitude of the victims repeatedly questioned about the incident and verbally made to relive the night every time they are asked about it. At one point, Animal says, 'on that night it was poison, now it's words that are choking us'.[18] His outburst to the journalist is worth quoting here.

> Actually, Jarnalis, I was trying not to show that I was laughing at you. After that, what else, I talked. Your tape crawled. Then you were happy, this is what you had come for. You were like all the others, come to suck our stories from us, so strangers in far off countries can marvel there's so much pain in the world. Like vultures are you jarnaliss. Somewhere a bad thing

15 Ulrich Baer, *Spectral Evidence: The Photography of Trauma* (Cambridge, MA: MIT Press, 2005), 9.

16 M. Candace Christensen's 'Engaging Trauma Resulting from Sexual Violence Through Photovoice', in this volume.

17 The project undertaken by the National Library of Medicine has produced three-dimensional representations of the male and female human bodies with human cadavers allowing to record anatomically detailed illustrations. Viewed on 26 October 2015 <https://www.nlm.nih.gov/research/visible/visible_human.html>.

18 Indra Sinha, *Animal's People* (Britain: Simon & Schuster, 2007), 3.

> happens, tears like rain in the wind, and look, here you come, drawn by the smell of blood. You have turned us Khaufpuris into storytellers, but always of the same story. Ousraat, cette nuit, that night, always that fucking night.[19]

One might see that even if their intentions are genuine the repeated questioning of the victims and the circulation of images from the incident surpasses the actual trauma behind the incident. It just makes the disaster some kind of a 'story' for the media.

> Jarnalis says it's a big chance for you. He will write what you say in his book. Thousands will read it. Maybe you will become famous. Look at him, see his eyes. He says thousands of other people are looking through his eyes. Think of that.[20]

This excerpt maintains an overshadowing vagueness about whose 'eyes' the author is talking about – Animal's or the journalist's or the author's? What stands out is how the villagers were in a mad rush to find opportunities even in the midst of trauma and suffering.

4 Survival, Activism and Struggling Bodies

Another cultural impact expressed in these narratives concerns the creation of 'struggling bodies'. The victims live a struggle in every possible realm. They struggle to survive, their bodies unhealthy; they cannot go to work and are thus stuck at their homes. They struggle for justice to have their rights recognised. They struggle to sustain life with the poor medical attention they receive and thus visiting a health centre every day is part of their daily routine. In effect, the limits of their bodies are pushed to the extremes.

Suroopa Mukherjee's seminal study on BGT proposes that activism on the streets was a learning experience to the victims because their 'learning had to negotiate the space between the 'lived' experience and the 'reconstruction' of reality through words'.[21] In her study to analyse activism, she uses the metaphor 'dancing in the streets'[22] suggesting that '*dancing* shows how words

19 Ibid., 5.

20 Ibid., 7.

21 Mukherjee, *Surviving Bhopal*, 162.

22 Ibid., 159.

get interlaced with bodies, used as expressive tools for self-expression and resistance'.[23] Holding strikes and staging hunger strikes is an age old practise of announcing displeasure against decisions at the national and domestic levels. The victims of BGT and ET also staged protests in real life, their reflections appearing in the select narratives too. Anjali Deshpande's *Impeachment* describes the life long struggle of the victims of BGT. In *Animal's People*, Zafar plans to go on a hunger strike against the anticipated deal between the government and the Carbide. In *Enmagaje*, under the leadership of ESPAC (Endosulfan Spray Protest Action Committee) awareness classes, demonstrations and strikes are conducted. Interestingly, in all the narratives the 'body' holds a unique status of being what is affected and also of being a tool for protest.

Strikes, an extreme form of struggle and protest achieve none of the expected results in the three narratives studied here. While the fight for justice by the victims happen on one side, the novel *Impeachment* criticises that the government earned much at the expense of the people of Bhopal. Avidha, a journalist in the novel, storms at her friends who represent the Government and candidly criticises them in her outburst,

> You did. You people. You built your careers. You even got funds to participate in our struggles. And you feel you have done something very glorious. Sorry, but we don't exist to supply you material for your glory. You sold us to international seminars and to journals. You sell everything we have. Our experience, our diseases, therapies, cures, our hopes, our disappointments. You sell our lives. You are worse than Carbide. At least it is openly an enemy. You are an enemy that is difficult to recognise. I tried, you know, to smash that conceit of yours. But no amount of stone-throwing can smash that complacence. You people protect yourselves rather well.[24]

Avidha's violent flow of emotions also marks the crack in the flawed system that does not care for the wellbeing of people. Instead it categorises the victims and enables a national sell-out. According to the *Open Magazine* writer Priyanka Pulla, bogus ET cases emerged with people struggling to get onto the list of victims so that they would receive the financial support from the government.[25] Suroopa Mukherjee also documents a similar instance in

23 Ibid., 163.

24 Anjali Deshpande, *Impeachment* (Gurgaon, India: Hachette, 2012),358.

25 Pulla, 'Kerala's Endosulfan Tragedy: Did It Really Happen?'.

the case of BGT. The measures for rehabilitation, empowerment and disaster management are submersed in petty bureaucratic measures. In effect, even the survivors who require assistance are pushed behind the shadows of corruption.

> Interestingly enough, the discourse of rehabilitation and disaster management asks for systems of registration and classification by name, age, gender, and place of residence. It is this specificity that gets pitched against the mammoth anonymity of an industrial disaster. How many dead, how many ill, and how many rendered destitute remain a matter of statistics and official record. The individual is caught in the crossfire between the public and the personal. Therefore, his/her need to speak out is always in the context of monolithic systems of silencing.[26]

The extent of the victims' struggle also closely relates to their tolerance level and their beliefs. In the novel *Enmagaje*,[27] people attribute their ill fate to the curses of gods, 'this place will be saved only when the ghost of *Jadadhari*[28] is pacified',[29] the novel reiterates. Deeply rooted in mythical stories and illiteracy, these people cannot envisage the possibility of a multinational company trading people's health and basic rights. They blame the anger of *Jadadhari* until the disclosure of the real villain, namely Endosulfan. Chris Gabbard[30] suggests three paradigms to understand a medical condition: firstly, as a sign of divine intervention/warning/indicator of a bad moral conduct; secondly, a medical condition due to the attack of a pathogen; thirdly, a problem created by society. The novel demonstrates how denisens of Enmagaje are trapped with the first paradigm until social initiative programmes reveals the truth about the pesticide, a reflection of reality.

According to Dr. Elli in *Animal's People*, the residents of Khaufpur tolerate so much that she hates the way people think and put up with everything. They

26 Mukherjee, op.cit., 160–161.

27 The title of the novel refers to Enmagaje, a village in the Kasargode district of the Indian state of Kerala, one among the many places affected by Endosulfan spraying.

28 Jadadhari is part of the local folklore in Enmagaje. According to the stories, Jadadhari was locked inside a pot through special mantras and prayers, but escaped and its anger encroaches upon the lives of the people in that village.

29 Ambikasuthan Mangad, *Enmagaje* (Kottayam: DC Books, 2009):17.

30 A spokesperson for the inclusion of disability studies programmes with the regular courses, Chris Gabbard has taught a course titled 'From Wonder to Error: Defect and Deformity in British Literature' at the University of North Florida, viewed on 3 November 2015, <http://enlightanddis.wordpress.com/>.

treat problems as normal and they do not respond to issues, which irritates her throughout the novel.

> People tolerate it. This is the strangest thing of all about Khaufpur that people put up with so much. Take a look. It's not just blacked out streets and killer traffic, people in this city tolerate open sewers, garbage everywhere, poisoned wells, poisoned babies, doctors who don't do their jobs, corrupt politicians, thousands of sick that no one seems to care about. But wait, let someone come along with an open-hearted offer to help, these same citisens can't tolerate it, in fact find it so intolerable they must mount a boycott. People in this city must be either blind or mad. I don't get the way Khaufpuris think.[31]

Dr. Elli speaks from her own experience with the people of Khaufpuri, who do not bother to respond or react to their problems, simply ignoring issues that matter, treating everything casually and moving on with a slow life. Hence the struggle to reclaim their lost rights does not reach any results.

5 Visible Deformities and Disabled Bodies

To quote a few lines from Terry Allan's 'Flames Not Flowers':

> Dow has a history, several claims to fame
> It was their Napalm set Vietnam aflame.
> Agent Orange causes birth defects
> And using Dursban has nasty side-effects
> Dioxin squirts from every mother's breast
> Worldwide from north to south, east to west.
> But you corporate men in your ties of silk
> Can't know the horror of mothers feeding toxic breast milk
> To our beautiful babies, our new-born innocents
> This ain't no way to start their life experience.
> You invade our bodies knowingly
> Thanks to Dow, we're living poisoned daily.[32]

---

31 Sinha, *Animal's People*, 151.

32 Among the many narratives that came out on BGT, Terry Allen's poem 'Flames Not Flowers' has gained popular attention. Viewed on 12 February 2016, <http://poetry-praxis.blogspot.in/2008/12/bhopal-disaster-poetry.html>.

The atrocities that ensued from BGT and ET cannot be subsumed into these lines but the artistic expressions that have brought the trauma of these disasters to mainstream media cannot be forgotten. The most obvious reconfiguration of the body manifests in 'D' bodies – disfigured and disabled bodies making them dependent bodies. *Enmagaje* records such characters extensively throughout the novel. In it, a child's entire body is filled with blisters, a woman with Macroglossia (condition characterised by an enlarged tongue, making it difficult to speak, eat and in some cases even to close one's mouth), a girl with Hydrocephalus (enlarged brain condition), kids with Rett syndrome (condition typified by decelerated growth rate), a boy with Aniridia (absence of iris in the eyes), a kid with Bladder Exstrophy (condition where part of the urinary bladder is outside the body), brittle bone disease, and a numerous other neurological disorders. From his limited knowledge about the situation Animal recollects, 'the Kampani stood accused of causing the deaths of thousands on that night, plus it ran away from Khaufpur without cleaning its factory, over the years the poisons it left behind have found their way into the wells, everyone you meet seems to be sick'.[33] Dependent on the rest of the population, the sick turn out to be a burden to others.

These sick bodies tend to be misfits in the 'real world', their bearers thereby cast out as social misfits. From such reality emerges another strand of thought, the 'myth of body perfect', which can create 'insiders' and 'outsiders' in a society. Generally subjugated, outsiders are characterised as alien figures, for society tends to see a diseased person as deviant, infectious and abnormal. An individual with an imperfect body is an outsider when compared to an insider, an individual with a perfectly healthy body. Literature records the insider/outsider division based on the medical state of the body, evidencing the close relationship between literature, medicine and human nature. The flawed body generally tries to cross the frontier of imperfection and reach the so-called stage of flawlessness. Along with the incompleteness of their bodies, they are outsiders in the real world either because they are unaware of its existence or because they simply do not fit in, like the villagers in *Enmagaje*. To some extent, the presence of such misfit characters questions the overwhelming inscrutability of reality itself.

For the victims, the tragedies leave them with a distorted perception about themselves and the world around. The notion of being normal and a life without defects is an abnormality to these people. But some individuals do hope for a normal and better tomorrow like Indra Sinha's Animal. Animal always wonders how it would feel to walk on two legs, be normal and live with a woman. His hope about the future alternates between a faith in Dr. Elli's treatments and a remorse for thinking about a cure.

33 Sinha, *Animal's People*, 33.

> This very morning she took my x-ray, tomorrow she will send it to Amrika. Soon a reply will arrive. It will say come for an operation. This fucking hope grows wilder every day. When I return to Khaufpur after my operation, I will walk up and down the Claw. Nisha will not recognise me. She will see a young stranger, upright and handsome, there and then she'll fall in love. She'll forget Zafar, phhht, he's gone. She will be besotted with her new love, desperate to marry him. Only one regret, in some part of her mind she will be wondering, what happened to my dear and faithful Animal, where has he gone? She will mourn for Animal who's vanished no one knows where, but he will never return.[34]

The extract also indicates Animal's own dilemma about getting cured. The thought of walking on two legs terrifies him: 'it struck like a hurricane, surged up my spine like electricity, changed everything, the wild, stupid, unforgivable hope that she might cure me'.[35]

The plight of these people and their perceptions about themselves become more ambiguous with every social situation. Their deformities and disabilities have reached a level where they find it difficult to get suitable spouses. According to Priyanka Pulla, the ET victims do not get suitable life partners because of the stories that their genes are tainted and they cannot sell their lands or move out as their soil is poisoned.[36]

6 Resistance Strategies and Bodies of Natural Existence

The struggle continues and so do the options of resistance measures. With strikes, protests, boycotts, letters to the Prime Minister, interventions by NGOs and more. One among the startling observations with regard to the resistance measures culled out from the selected texts for this study concerns the hope for a future. The novels indeed offer a shimmering light of hope, akin to Rousseau's myth of the Noble Savage.[37] Accordingly, the hope for a future suggests the creation of certain bodies – the bodies of natural existence.

34 Ibid., 187.

35 Ibid., 141.

36 Pulla, 'Kerala's Endosulfan Tragedy: Did It Really Happen?'(2013).

37 I have adapted thoughts from a lecture delivered at University of Oregon on 'Rousseau and the Noble Savage Myth' viewed on 4 January 2016, <http://pages.uoregon.edu/jboland/rousseau.html>.

In *Enmagaje*, Neelakantan and Devayani abandon the civil society for the second time to live in the jungle. From then on, they are called as man and woman by being detached from their lawful names. They end up in a cavern in the jungle where many animals and birds live with them. Marked with elements of magic realism, the novel suggests that the cavern asks them to strip away the shackles of civilisation. The description of their new beginning calls to mind the image of Noah's floating ark. Their vision of the future critiques the lack of alternatives offered by modernism in the Indian context. ET and BGT could have been avoided with better foundation groundwork in the use of technology in India. In *Animal's People*, Animal finally decides to continue his life on all fours in spite of the cure promised by Dr. Elli. He prefers to live like an animal, unbound by the rules of society that do not apply to an animal. Animal's words concerning medical intervention calls for reflection:

> if I have this operation, I will be upright, true, but to walk I will need the help of sticks. I might have a wheelchair, but how far will that get me in the gullis of Khaufpur? Right now I can run and hop and carry kids on my back, I can climb hard trees, I've gone up mountains, roamed in jungles. Is life so bad? If I'm an upright human, I would be one of millions, not even a healthy one at that. Stay four-foot, I'm the one and only Animal.[38]

Questioning the success rate of an operation, Animal prefers to be healthy and four legged rather than becoming a weak two-legged man with a stick. In *Impeachment,* Avidha finally realises the irrelevance of their struggle, as she hopes that the victims will survive without the interim relief from the state, intimating the need for a space allowing the victims to resuscitate. She also recommends not to treat them as outcasts, but as fellow human beings, and to choose better terms to designate them. As Zafar tells Animal, he is 'especially-abled' and not 'dis-abled'[38].

This vision of a new beginning might sound like an attempt to create an ideal state with optimal preparations for growth and development or as an experiment to gloss over the monstrous atrocities of these disasters. Either way, the survivors have to move on with their limited options in their specific cultural locations. As Brencio and Novak argue in their chapter 'The Continuum of Trauma' in this book, any traumatic episode can result in grave outcomes when left unaddressed. Hence, the only way to deal with trauma would be to break its possible continuum whether it concerns psychological or biological afflictions. In the Indian context, the various forms of resistance discussed in the previous pages evidence a strategic approach to rupture the cycle of trauma.

38 Sinha, *Animal's People,* 366.

7 Conclusion

By tracing the probable re-configurations of the body through the narratives on chemical disasters, I have suggested that four specific cultural patterning of identities – namely display bodies, struggling bodies, 'D' bodies and bodies of natural existence – have emerged through these incidents. Such classification serves as a tool to read the narratives on chemical disasters in the Indian context.

Now in the Bhopal and Kasargod of 2018, the blame game still continues. The *Yes Men*[39] hoax of 2004 that the Dow Company is providing relief funds to victims also gained global attention. The man accused and associated with BGT, Warren Anderson, passed away in 2014, apparently haunted by his responsibility in the case[40]. As for the survivors, their sufferings and oral narratives continue, leading one to revisit the artistic hypothesis mentioned in the earlier pages, namely whether the most favourable solution lies in bodies of natural existence.

Bibliography

Baer, Ulrich. *Spectral Evidence: The Photography of Trauma.* Cambridge, MA: MIT Press, 2005.

Barnes, Julian. *The Sense of an Ending*. London: Jonathan Cape, 2011.

Batteau, Allen. W. 'Aggressive Technology in a Century of Industrial Disasters'. *Practicing Anthropology* 23.4 (2001): 28–32.

Deshpande, Anjali. *Impeachment*. Gurgaon, India: Hachette, 2012.

'Dow Does the Right Thing'. *The Yes Men*. Viewed on 2 February 2016. http://theyesmen.org/hijinks/bbcbhopal.

Enhancing Urban Safety and Security: Global Report on Human Settlements. Un-Habitat. London: Earthscan, 2007.

39 A group of people engaged in bringing the dehumanising and corrupt activities of people and organizations to the general public. 'Dow Does the Right Thing' *The Yes Men*, Viewed on 2 February 2016, <http://theyesmen.org/hijinks/bbcbhopal>.

40 The following articles all viewed on 17 February 2016 support this statement.
a) Douglas Martin, ' Warren Anderson, 92, Dies; Faced India Plant Disaster' *The New York Times*, 30 Oct 2014. Viewed on 17 February 2016. <http://www.nytimes.com/2014/10/31/business/w-m-anderson-92-dies-led-union-carbide-in-80s-.html?_r=0>
b) 'Warren Anderson: Obituary', *The Telegraph*, 3 Nov 2014. Viewed on 17 February 2016. <http://www.telegraph.co.uk/news/obituaries/11205397/Warren-Anderson-obituary.html> and
c) Allan Dodds Frank, 'The Haunted CEO', *The Daily Beast*, 19 July 2010. Viewed on 17 Feb 2016. <http://www.thedailybeast.com/articles/2010/07/18/union-carbides-warren-anderson-life-in-exile.html>

Enlightenment and Disability: British Literature and Culture. Viewed on 3 November 2015. http://enlightanddis.wordpress.com/.

Frank, Allan Dodds. 'The Haunted CEO'. *The Daily Beast.* 19 July 2010. Viewed on 17 February 2016. http://www.thedailybeast.com/articles/2010/07/18/union-carbides-warren-anderson-life-in-exile.htm.

Herman, Judith Lewis. *Trauma and Recovery.* New York: Basic Books, 1992.

Lochan, Rajiv. 'Health Damage Due to Bhopal Gas Disaster: Review of Medical Research'. *Economic and Political Weekly* 26.21 (1991): 1322–1324.

Lovett, Julia. *Poetry and Praxis* blog. Viewed on 12 February 2016. http://poetry-praxis.blogspot.in/2008/12/bhopal-disaster-poetry.html.

Lupton, Deborah. *Medicine as Culture: Illness, Disease and the Body*. London: Sage Publications, 1994.

Mahapatro, G.K and Madhumita Panigrahi. 'The Case for Banning Endosulfan'. *Current Science* 104.11 (2013): 1476–1478.

Mangad, Ambikasuthan. *Enmagaje*. Kottayam: DC Books, 2009.

Martin, Douglas. 'Warren Anderson, 92, Dies; Faced India Plant Disaster'. *The New York Times.* 30 October 2014. Viewed on 17 February 2016. http://www.nytimes.com/2014/10/31/business/w-m-anderson-92-dies-led-union-carbide-in-80s-.html?_r=0.

Mukherjee, Suroopa. *Surviving Bhopal: Dancing Bodies, Written Texts and Oral Testimonials of Women in the Wake of an Industrial Disaster.* Basingstoke: Palgrave Macmillan, 2010.

Pulla, Priyanka. 'Kerala's Endosulfan Tragedy: Did It Really Happen?' *Open Magazine* 153 (1 June 2013), viewed on 29 September 2014. http://www.openthemagazine.com/article/nation/kerala-s-endosulfan-tragedy.

Rajan, S. Ravi. 'Disaster, Development and Governance: Reflections on the Lessons of Bhopal'. *Environmental Values* 11.3 (2002): 369–394.

Sarangi, Satinath. 'Bhopal Disaster: Judiciary's Failure'. *Economic and Political Weekly* 30.46 (1995): 2907–2909.

Sharma, Betwa. 'Bhopal Gas Tragedy: New Victims'. *Economic and Political Weekly* 41.17 (2006): 1613–1616.

Sinha, Indra. *Animal's People.* New York: Simon & Schuster, 2007.

The Visible Human Project. Viewed on 26 October 2015. https://www.nlm.nih.gov/research/visible/visible_human.html.

US Political Thought: Rousseau and the Noble Savage Myth. Viewed on 4 January 2016. http://pages.uoregon.edu/jboland/rousseau.html.

'Warren Anderson: Obituary' *The Telegraph.* 3 November 2014. Viewed on 17 February 2016. http://www.telegraph.co.uk/news/obituaries/11205397/Warren-Anderson-obituary.html.

CHAPTER 11

Painting over the Past: Political Palimpsests in Northern Ireland and the Complexities of the 'Whitewash' Initiative

Mark Callaghan

Abstract

Northern Irish murals function as internal dialogues within two disparate communities, whilst also operating as memorials to 'volunteers', celebrations of heritage and affirmations of identity. They also serve as territorial markers, often aggressive in their nature, depicting masked gunmen and paramilitary emblems. These political murals are the subject of much debate. Authorities have been trying to replace unwelcome reminders of violence for a number of years. Community groups, residents, artists and local politicians have been involved in consultations and some of the more bellicose images have been replaced with depictions of less contentious history. The replacement of murals – carried out under the 'Re-imaging Communities' scheme – has, though, caused a division within Loyalist and Republican communities, including historians who consider the paintings part of their history, their identity, and the collective and individual trauma of the past, whilst some residents, journalists and politicians regard the old wall paintings as intimidating and therefore approve of the new ones. This war over memory offers particularly rich scope for analysis. It raises several questions, including the concern that the 'Re-imaging Communities' scheme initiates a 'whitewash' with all political murals expunged, and that a process designed to facilitate individual and societal healing has, in some cases, resulted in the opposite. Paying attention to these issues, this chapter focuses on the central questions of what it means to censor and sanitise the history of Northern Ireland's trauma. Is there a case for maintaining strident images of trauma? Do such changes reflect a transitional society and a post-conflict culture, or do the new murals represent the social truth of irreconcilable differences despite their apparent lack of belligerence? The chapter also pays considerable attention to the history of the Northern Irish political mural and its proneness to change and resistance in the urban landscape, including murals that appear to reflect the political climate, specifically the cease-fire period of 1994 and The Good Friday Agreement accord of 1998.

 | DOI:10.1163/9789004407947_013

Keywords

murals – political – trauma – paramilitary – censorship – terrorism – social memory – consensus – post-conflict

1 Introduction

The Northern Irish mural has origins dating back to 1908, though its significance increased during The Troubles, a thirty-year period of conflict that began in 1969, resulting in the deaths of more than 3,700 people. During this time, murals became more bellicose, more sectarian, and served increasingly as territorial markers in divided Belfast and Derry.[1] They still adorn the gable walls of working class areas; nearly all political, most can be identified to one of two sides – the Republican, Nationalist community, generally of Catholic heritage, or the Loyalist, Unionist Community, generally of Protestant heritage. Broadly, the Republican, Nationalist community have campaigned to be part of a united Ireland, and therefore part of the Republic of Ireland,[2] whereas, the Loyalist, Unionist community believe Northern Ireland should remain part of The United Kingdom.[3] For this reason, it is common to see Irish tricolours in Republican, Nationalist districts, and conversely, British Union symbols in streets where Loyalist, Unionists live.

The Troubles officially came to an end in 1998, as a corollary of The Good Friday Agreement – a bilateral treaty, signed by most of Northern Ireland's political parties, that fixed the status of Northern Ireland, meaning it could only

1 After the British government banned the broadcasting of the actual voice of supporters belonging to Republican and Loyalist paramilitary groups, mural paintings increasingly became an easy way to convey the invisible presence of the gunmen [Bill Rolston. *Drawing Support: Murals in the North of Ireland. Murals in the North of Ireland.* (Dublin: Beyond the Pale Publications, 1992), 16].

2 Northern Ireland was created in 1921 by an Act of the British Parliament, which subsequently led to The Irish Free State and then The Republic of Ireland. Ireland was partitioned due to the independence movement in Dublin and the south but the north remained British, as the majority of its unionist population wanted to remain part of Britain [Paul Bew, *The Politics of Enmity* (1798–2006) (Oxford: Oxford University Press, 2007), 14].

3 The UDA (Ulster Defence Association) is the largest Loyalist paramilitary group, with up to 40,000 members in the 1970s. However, the UVF (Ulster Volunteer Force), which has origins dating to 1912, represents the origins of Loyalism. Many of its members fought for the British in the First World War. Their commitments to Britain is often represented in their murals. By 2007, both groups had officially disbanded [Peter Taylor, *Loyalists* (London: Bloomsbury, 2000), 29].

become part of the Republic of Ireland if consensus is met in both Northern Ireland and the Republic of Ireland.[4] Due to this momentous change, I reflect on the way that political murals transformed during the late twentieth century, overlapping into the new century. I analyse differences in style, content, and location, what observable alterations in strategy were underway during this time, and ultimately, how the urban landscape of Belfast and Derry became a canvas for expressing multiple voices that expanded into new locations. Essential to these discussions is the Re-Imaging Communities programme, which began in 2006 with the aim of replacing aggressive sectarian murals with paintings that celebrate respective heritages that are outside of politics.[5]

As the mural serves as social memory, helping us to stifle through the confusion of the past for evidence that might serve to substantiate existing beliefs, including changes in attitude leading up to and since The Good Friday Agreement, I consider visual responses to political change that either reflect that accord or contradict it. In doing so, this chapter also analyses the use of specific locations that enhance the meaning of the mural and the extent to which this is a reciprocal relationship between place and the image being painted. This chapter also examines the consequences of the Re-imaging Communities scheme, asking whether the replacement of bellicose images with less contentious ones is a true reflection of post-trauma Northern Ireland, and also looking at how communities have re-imaged their streets and districts through their own changes instigated outside of the scheme.

2 The Northern Irish Political Mural: an Overview of Narrative in Space

As the death-toll rose during The Troubles, murals became memorials to paramilitary 'volunteers', and victims of terrorism.[6] This includes what Anthony

4 Dermot Keogh, *Northern Ireland and the Politics of Reconciliation* (Cambridge: Cambridge University Press, 1994), 17.

5 The first Re-imaging communities programme ran from 2006–2008 with a budget of £3.8 million. The Building Peace Through the Arts: Re-Imaging Communities Programme ran from 2012 October 2015 with a budget of £1.5m which supported 32 projects, and is due to evaluate this phase during 2016. The programme is currently closed; the Arts Council with its key partners will be exploring alternative funding schemes, partnerships and opportunities to continue the programme. Information provided by Noirin McKinney, Director of Arts Development on 16 February 2016.

6 Not until the early 1980s did murals become a prominent form of street display in Republican, Nationalist areas and the brush joined the Armalite and the ballot box as a facet of

FIGURE 11.1 A 'terrorist' mural. East Belfast. March, 2016.
IMAGE COURTESY OF MARK CALLAGHAN.

Buckley defines as the 'soldier hero' and 'the terrorist', representations of combatants that came to prominence in the 1970s and 1980s, and remain common today – the 'soldier hero' being the proud, sometimes smiling freedom fighter, now more familiar to Republican, Nationalist areas, and the 'terrorist', being the hyper-masculinised balaclava-wearing figure, that one can still see in Loyalist, Unionist parts of Belfast (Figure 11.1).[7]

Since The Good Friday Agreement, which brought relative peace, there is officially, a post conflict, Northern Ireland.[8] Murals, though, are still easily

---

political strategy. Numerous murals and political slogans appeared across nationalist Belfast; curbstones and lamp-posts were painted; streets were renamed in Irish; and the tricolour flag flew freely to assert a permanent and visible, political and cultural dominance over the area [Neil Jarman, "Painting Landscapes: The Place of Murals in the Symbolic Construction of Urban Space," in *Symbols in Northern Ireland*, ed. Anthony D. Buckley (Belfast: Institute of Irish Studies, Queen's University of Belfast, 1998), 4].

7 Anthony Buckley, *Symbols in Northern Ireland* (Belfast: Institute of Irish Studies, Queen's University of Belfast, 1998), 158.

8 Despite The Troubles having ended, 'The New IRA' still operate, detonating a car bomb in March 2016. 'Prison officer injured in New IRA car bomb attack in Belfast dies'. www.theguardian.com/uk-news/2016/mar/15/belfast-prison-officer-dies-targeted-new-ira-car-bomb-attack-adrian-ismay. 15.3.2016. Accessed 30.3.2016.

FIGURE 11.2 The mural known as 'The Memorial to Women Volunteers and Victims of the Occupation'. Ballymurphy, Belfast. March, 2016.
IMAGE COURTESY OF MARK CALLAGHAN.

assigned to different communities, be it through religious emblems and strident declarations of pride in their respective culture, or in some cases, continued animosity and belligerence toward historic and, in other instances, enduring adversaries. Large social housing estates across Belfast and Derry remain punctuated with murals in many forms – from portraits of Republicans who died of hunger strike in 1981, to declarations of allegiance to the British Crown in Loyalist, Unionist districts.[9] In Republican Belfast, murals include the 'Memorial to Women Volunteers and Victims of the Occupation' (Figure 11.2), whilst in Loyalist parts of the city one can expect to see murals dedicated to those who fought for one of their paramilitary organisations.[10]

9 Murals are, of course, akin to a form of propaganda in themselves. This is how they have been used for political purposes in other countries such as Guatemala, Mexico, Spain, Cuba and Russia. In Northern Ireland, they are a community's declaration to itself and proclamation to others entering the area [Oona Woods, *Seeing is Believing: Murals in Derry* (Londonderry: Guildhall Press, 1995), 16–18].

10 One might assume that memorials are unlikely to solicit the same 'sacredness' experienced at the physical grave or physical vernacular memorial site, but the maintenance of them – often repainted every six months – evidences their status as almost consecrated walls of remembrance.

Urban areas include dedications to those who suffered under British rule, and, conversely, those killed by the Irish Republican Army, the IRA. These streets are, as Maria Turmakin coins the term, 'traumascapes', places across the world marked by traumatic legacies of violence, suffering and loss in which the 'past is never quite over'.[11]

Beyond the binary of identifying the respective community represented by each mural are many unknowns; a story far less immediate than the image one sees. It is often undisclosed, for instance, who the painter was, who endorsed the mural, and to what extent the image remains germane.[12] Though their social power cannot be measured, the importance of the mural is evidenced by their sheer number, their strategic positioning (often lining the main arteries that link respective areas to the city centre), the way in which murals often change to reflect the political climate.

3 The Good Friday Agreement and Post-Conflict Northern Ireland

The Good Friday Agreement (officially, The Belfast Agreement) is a bilateral treaty, which became effective on 2 December 1999, though agreed on 10 April 1998. It is a multi-party agreement by most of Northern Ireland's political parties, and an international agreement between Great Britain and the Republic of Ireland. The agreement sets out the status of Northern Ireland within the United Kingdom, stating that Northern Ireland can only become part of the Republic of Ireland if a consensus is met in Northern Ireland *and* the Republic of Ireland. The agreement committed all parties to peaceful means of solving political differences.[13]

Among several considerable inclusions in the Agreement, the creation of a Northern Ireland Assembly established power-sharing between previously

11 Maria Turmakin. *Traumascapes* (Melbourne: Melbourne University Press, 2005), 9.

12 Although they have become an internationally recognised signifier of Belfast and Derry, it is not true to say that these paintings are loved by all those who live locally. In fact murals attract opposition from two quarters: from within and from without. The opposition from without has been well documented: murals have often become prominent targets for destruction from paint bombs and graffiti. The defacing of Republican paintings has, on occasion, been carried out by members of the security forces (Rolston 1991), and paintings in both communities which express support for paramilitaries have been the target of graffiti from the other side [Neil Jarman. "Commemorating 1916, Celebrating Difference: Parading and Painting in Belfast" in *The Art of Forgetting*, Ed. Adrian Forty, Adrian. (London: Berg, 1999), 18–27].

13 Paul Bew. *The Making and Re-Making of the Good Friday Agreement* (Dublin: The Liffey Press, 2007), 16–18.

un-cooperative political parties representing disparate communities.[14] The Agreement also granted all citizens the right to identify themselves as Irish or British, which meant that Republicans would no longer face punitive measures for flying the Irish tricolour or for including Irish symbols in their murals.[15] For the Agreement to have credibility as a peace initiative, it had to include the pledge that paramilitaries would de-commission their arsenals. This vital part of the accord took far longer than hoped for, though stockpiles of weapons were close to being fully de-commissioned by 2009.[16] The most contentious part of the new contract was the early release of all prisoners convicted of terrorist offences.[17] Those sentenced to more than five years would serve one third of their term, and prisoners given life sentences would now serve terms comparable to someone not sentenced for terrorist-related crimes, *and* minus one third of that time.[18]

The Good Friday Agreement was ratified after 71.1% of Northern Ireland's electorate voted in favour of the proposals, and 94% declaring their support in a simultaneous referendum conducted in the Republic of Ireland. Though the outcome was one that ostensibly endorsed the Agreement with a clear majority, it is significant that 53% of the Loyalist, Unionist electorate voted in support of the Agreement, which therefore expressed a less decisive approval in

---

14 Dermot Keogh. *Northern Ireland and the Politics of Reconciliation* (Cambridge: Cambridge University Press, 1994), 18.

15 The Irish tricolour was banned in Northern Ireland, until that ban was officially overturned in the late 1980s. However, the ban was usually ignored by Nationalists, who used the Irish flag anyway. Though fines were sometimes issued, the RUC tended to ignore the ban because when enforced it would often lead to rioting. Of more danger was the threat from Loyalists. In 1980, a 16-year-old was shot dead while painting Republican slogans on a wall [Neil Jarman, *Material Conflicts: Parades and Visual Displays in Northern Ireland* (Oxford: Berg Publishers, 1997), 232].

16 The IRA began to de-commission in October 2001, formally ending its campaign in 2005. By 2009, nearly all Loyalist paramilitaries had completed their de-commissioning, apart from the UDA (Ulster Defence Force), which had only just begun to permit the confiscation of its stockpiles [Diarmaid Ferriter, *The Transformation of Ireland 1900–2000* (London: Profile Books, 2005), 162.

17 The release of prisoners convicted of terrorist offences began in September 1998. By 2000, 428 terrorists, including 143 serving life sentences, had been released. Those released early included one of the most notorious Republican prisoners, Patrick Magee, responsible for the 1984 'Brighton bomb', the attempted assassination of British Prime-minister Margaret Thatcher. On the Loyalist side, infamous prisoners released early included Jonny Adair, sentenced to 16 years [Kieran McEvoy, *Paramilitary Imprisonment in Northern Ireland* (Oxford: Oxford University Press, 2001), 133].

18 Peter Taylor. *Brits: The War Against the IRA* (London: Bloomsbury Publishing, 2002), 158.

that community.[19] Opposition to the Good Friday Agreement within Unionism was focused primarily on the perceived 'appeasement' of Irish republicanism by the British Government in allowing 'IRA terrorists' into the new devolved assembly and executive.[20] Nonetheless, the settlement was supported with a clear majority thus recognising the legitimacy of both Loyalist, Unionist aspirations and those of Republican, Nationalists, too.[21]

4 The Cease-Fire Period

In August 1994 the IRA formally declared a 'complete cessation of military operations'. The announcement followed eighteen months of secret talks between the British Government and Republicans. Two months later Loyalist paramilitaries urged to follow suit also broadcast their intention to suspend hostilities. These breakthroughs would eventually lead to the Good Friday Agreement.[22]

As images murals are always open to multiple interpretations, but as artefacts in public space they are also open to multiple forms of use, re-use and abuse. As images they always have had a functionality: as propaganda, as rhetoric, as ideological and symbolic markers. But as artefacts their use is potentially more varied. While on one level it is primarily the image that is being used and transformed, on another level it is the physical artefact, fixed in space, which is the subject of activity; taken still further it is the public space in which the

19 Cillian McGrattan. *Northern Ireland 1968–2008: The Politics of Entrenchment* (London and New York: Palgrave MacMillan, 2010), 165.

20 One of the most controversial appointments, former IRA member Martin McGuinness became Deputy First Minister in 2007.

21 This has since led to the perception of relative peace, but this must be tested against an increase in the building of 'peace walls' that separate Loyalist and Republican communities and also the recent controversy over the flying of the Union Flag at Belfast City Hall, now restricted to four days per year, which further demonstrates the enduring sensitivity of such symbols also prevalent in the murals. As Charles Purdick described the period, with the conflict so recent and no concrete political progress for several years, the period was more 'an end to a war but not quite peace' [Michael Cox. *A Farewell to Arms? Beyond the Good Friday Agreement* (London and Dublin: Liang, 2007), 18].

22 The IRA ceasefire ended on 9 February 1996 when it planted a huge bomb in London's Docklands. It killed two, injured more than 100 and caused more than £85m of damage. A new ceasefire was finally announced in July 1997. The future of the IRA's weaponry was one of the dominant and unresolved issues of the peace process. Republicans argued that the arms could only be dealt with as part of a solution leading to "all the guns being removed from Irish politics" – giving equal weight to IRA weapons and the presence of the British military [Richard English, *Armed Struggle: The History of the IRA* (London: PAN, 2012), 94].

artefact is sited that is changed.[23] As artefacts all murals are site-specific; their power as political statements and as symbols is enhanced by their location. Their significance of the murals is generated by a semiotic dynamic which involves the images taking meaning from their location and the location in turn having a differing significance because of the paintings. In the following examples, relating to the cease-fire period, one can understand why muralists and their patrons chose specific locations and their corresponding images that relate to the change in the political climate.

For painters the site is always of importance; if permission is given to paint a wall – usually granted by paramilitaries – then all is well and good, but without acquiescence then prime sites were, and still are today, claimed and painted. A site on Newtownards Road, east Belfast, exemplifies this with its location in a major thoroughfare in a predominately Loyalist, Unionist area of the city, significantly close to the only Republican, Nationalist neighbourhood of this area. It has, then, been an ideal location for Loyalist paramilitary groups to assert their presence – a situation found in other parts of Belfast where Republican, Nationalist murals line neutral streets in areas with a preponderance of Republicans. During the cease-fire period of the mid-90s, murals in such non-aligned streets were either re-painted, enlarged, or created anew in order to show the continued presence of paramilitaries.[24] In other words, despite the cease-fire, both Loyalist and Republican paramilitaries were determined to remind public and media alike, not only that they continued to exist and would take up arms again, but also that their dominance of locations would be expressed in neutral thoroughfares.

The pertinence of location is also demonstrated in areas vehemently partisan whilst also visible to public, media and politicians who would not encroach into these areas of Belfast. A case in point during the cease-fire period is the Mount Vernon district of north Belfast and the painting of the 'Prepared for Peace, Ready for War' mural, which depicts two masked men brandishing machine guns. Whilst the message of this Loyalist mural is axiomatic – paramilitaries had agreed to a cease-fire but the prospect of decommissioning was fanciful – its location meant it was more than an internal discourse and a topical declaration for the residents of Mount Vernon. Painting this mural on the largest available wall in the district was part of the political mural paradigm. Its location – an elevated position facing the often congested M2 motorway,

23 Neil Jarman, 9. *Material Conflicts: Parades and Visual Displays in Northern Ireland* (Oxford: Berg Publishers, 1997). 9.

24 Graham Dawson, *Making Peace with the Past: Memory, Trauma, and the Irish Troubles* (Manchester: Manchester University Press, 2007), 166.

however, pointed to an audience other than those living in Mount Vernon. Those who commissioned and painted the mural showed a clear interest in taking their message far beyond the boundaries of the Mount Vernon district. In turn, by association, Mount Vernon itself pledged a commitment to a cessation of hostilities with a warning that this might only be a hiatus in their armed fight against the IRA.

Paradoxically, even after Loyalist paramilitary groups declared a ceasefire in October 1994, the paramilitary iconography held centre stage, with their slogan 'no surrender' becoming more prevalent. According to Bill Rolston, this was designed as a message not only to the opposing community, but also to Unionist politicians, warning them not to move too far beyond the paramilitary groups from which they emerged and not to give away too much in negotiations.[25] Yet the message conveyed by murals was typically diverse. In Derry (officially known as Londonderry to the Loyalist, Unionist community), a mural devoid of images and consisting of the words 'Londonderry West Bank Loyalists. Still Under Siege. No Surrender' (Figure 11.3) appeared at a location that signaled to a new role for the Northern Irish political mural.[26] Facing the celebrated seventeenth-century *Derry Walls* that encircle the old town, the mural succeeded in attracting media attention whilst informing the city's tourists of Loyalist feelings at this time. As such, this rather uncomplicated mural used the city's most famous landmark to gain awareness of Loyalist stoicism and thus to draw a clear distinction between the ceasefire and the notion of submission. But the re-appropriation of this space with one of the least aesthetically accomplished of murals has a complex, historic meaning. It refers to the famous 'Siege of Derry' of 1689, when, for three months, Irish protestants refused to surrender to Catholic King James II's forces, using the city walls to defend themselves from attack.[27] By painting this mural in this location, directly opposite the city's famous walls, Loyalists re-appropriated not only part of the

25 Bill Rolston, *The War of the Walls* (Dublin: Beyond the Pale Publications, 1998). 4.

26 This, like many murals, has been re-painted several times, with different font styles, but always the same wording.

27 James II was ousted from power in England and Scotland in 1688 by Protestant William III (of Orange), known to Loyalist, Unionists as 'King Billy', and his wife Mary II. Subsequently, Catholic James II looked to mostly Catholic Ireland to muster support to regain his kingdom. Taking control of Derry was central to his plans. 8,000 of the city's 30,000 protestants died, many due to warfare, whilst thousands died from disease and starvation, as James II's forces blocked all supplied to the city. The blockade was breached after 105 days of the siege and the Protestant defenders claimed victory. The following year James II was defeated at 'The Battle of The Boyne' [John Graham, *A History of the Siege of Londonderry* (Birmingham: Nabu Press, 2005), 124].

FIGURE 11.3 The Loyalist West Bank mural, as seen from the *Derry Walls*. March, 2016. IMAGE COURTESY OF MARK CALLAGHAN.

historic space but also the origins of the city's Protestant resistance, drawing comparisons between the most renowned example of their defiance (which ultimately led to victory) and their contemporary situation. Despite its lack of imagery and apparent complexity, the Derry mural is more ambiguous than the aforementioned 'Prepared for Peace, Ready for War' mural in Belfast. Instead, the Derry mural suggests victimisation rather than a community primed for a return to belligerence. It speaks of indomitability rather than cease-fire.

During the cease-fire period, Republican, Nationalist murals maintained their show of weapons but began to make significant changes that, unlike many Loyalist murals, did not make immediate statements about the on-going truce. Typical of this time, the mural on Beechmount Avenue situated at the heart of Republican west Belfast uses like the majority of murals a space visible to all who travel through a main thoroughfare, in this case, anyone moving south along the Falls Road (Figure 11.4).

Like the Loyalist murals created during this time, this Republican murals does not make a direct statement about the cease-fire and instead features the derivation of their armed struggle, in this case against the British. It depicts a scene of the 1916 'Easter Rising' when the Irish Republic was proclaimed and Dublin's General Post Office (the neo-classical building in the mural's

FIGURE 11.4 The Loyalist West Bank mural, as seen from the *Derry Walls*. March, 2016.
IMAGE COURTESY OF MARK CALLAGHAN.

backdrop) was seized by Irish combatants.[28] The commemorated event thus provides the historical legitimacy, and indeed the ideology, for the contemporary Republican movement, as well as justifying the IRA's continued struggle. Like other murals, it used the Gaelic language as a title – in this case, simply *The Easter Rising 1916* – furthering the Irish identity of this Belfast region, thus, with the context of the cease-fire in mind, asserting their intention to be part of a united Ireland despite the armistice.[29] Equally, in relation to the cease-fire period, comes the mural's lack of a contemporary figure, be it 'the terrorist' or 'the solider hero', as it depicts a generic fighter from the past, and a proud, contradictorily non-aggressive one at that. This complies with the willingness of the IRA to participate in a cease-fire whilst reminding all who see the mural that weaponry and the martyrdom of volunteers are the foundations of the Republican cause.

28 The Easter Rising, an armed insurrection launched by Irish republicans against British rule, was led by poet and schoolmaster Patrrick Pearse, and by James Connolly at the head of the Irish Citizen Army. After five days, the British Army suppressed the uprising. Nearly 500 people died in the Easter Rising. Its leaders, including Pearse and Connolly, were executed by the British. This British reaction caused much sympathy for the rebels among Irish citizens.

29 Nearly all streets in Republican Belfast have dual English and Gaelic titles.

5 Re-Imaging Communities

The way in which murals often change to reflect the political climate also shows through more official means, coming by way of the Re-Imaging Communities scheme, which has, so far, replaced eighty-four aggressive murals with less confrontational ones. A positive initiative, it has though raised issues concerning the replacement of paintings, regarded by some as part of Northern Ireland's history and identity, and also the collective and individual trauma of the past. Ironically, the Re-Imaging Scheme has revealed similar views in otherwise polarised communities – with a process meticulous in gaining approval from residents for the replacement of murals, but also, in some cases, exposing less formal objections, including the satirical epithet given to the scheme: the 'whitewash campaign'.[30] Opposition is sometimes discordant, with one Republican muralist famously stating that replacing murals is 'akin to Bulldozing Auschwitz'.[31] Here I endeavour to look behind such comments and consider the case for maintaining hostile images, and in tandem, highlighting the argument for the Re-Imaging programme's continuation.

The scheme commenced in 2006, and through consultation with local residents, has replaced sixty-one murals in Loyalist, Unionist districts, and twenty-three in Republican, Nationalist areas.[32] This ratio of nearly 3:1 is best explained by the aforementioned prevalence of the 'terrorist' figure in Loyalist estates, some of which have been expunged as part of the scheme. Both communities have expressed an interest in changing the appearance of their respective neighbourhoods. Indeed, as a Director of the initiative argues, one of the main strengths of the programme lies in the empowering of communities vis-à-vis decisions about their own shared common spaces – that is, to decide if they wished to live with the history of a very troubled past, or to change the space occupied by long-standing murals into representations more relevant and meaningful to their contemporary realities.[33]

A most significant example is the replacement of the 'Grim Reaper' mural in a Loyalist, Unionist stronghold of Belfast, with an equestrian painting of William III, a seventeenth-century monarch, referred to by this community as 'King Billy' (Figure 11.5). A skeletal, masked, and clearly armed figure, has been substituted with a regal presence – a sign of cultural origins instead of an

30 www.belfasttelegraph.co.uk/news/is-it-time-to-whitewash-northernirelands-paramilitary-murals-28530284.html. Accessed 9.1.2016.

31 Ibid.

32 interview with Noirin McKinney, Director of Arts Development, 16 Feb. 2016.

33 Ibid.

FIGURE 11.5 A 'King Billy' mural, Sandy Row, central Belfast. March, 2016. IMAGE COURTESY OF MARK CALLAGHAN.

axiomatic warning of death to enemies of this sect. Of further significance is the change from a seemingly contemporary character to one from an entirely different era. A machine gun has been replaced by a weapon of a bygone era – a sword. Whilst this contrast results in a far less intimidating street, it is still, arguably provocative, as 'King Billy' was the Protestant King who defeated the Catholic King James II in 1690, a victory that consolidated British rule over the whole of Ireland, and as a result, is a portrait often viewed as an affront to the Republican, Nationalist community. Even the ostensibly apolitical Titanic – of which there are six extant murals – is not without its potential to be odious. Built in Belfast, the Titanic is promoted as a symbol of Northern Irish craftsmanship, but with many craftsmen of Catholic heritage, the knowledge of many forbears' exclusion from the famous project causes its perception as a symbol of the socioeconomic deprivation lived through during the twentieth century.[34]

So despite the constructive aims and achievements of the Re-Imaging Scheme, no guarantee exists that new murals will show pictures of trust and

34 Charles River Editors, *Building the RMS Titanic: The Construction of the World's Most Famous Ship* (London: Create Space Publishing, 2014), 119.

shared understanding. Whilst paramilitary culture is unwelcome to those who petitioned the erasure of the 'Grim Reaper', one cannot possibly ascertain whether murals dating back to the 1970s and 1980s reflect community consensus more than the new, less belligerent ones. Not everyone is prepared to formally speak in favour of maintaining the old murals, usually concerned that such opinions could be misunderstood as wishing for a return to violence and support for the paramilitaries.[35]

Painting over the scars of the Troubles is not accepted by all. Some muralists object to the Re-Imaging programme on the grounds that it signals the beginning of the end for the political mural. This concern has some validity if one considers the scheme's interest in replacing the so-called family murals, which depict paramilitary 'volunteers' and their families, painted memorials with visible, not hooded faces of combatants. Whilst the Re-Imaging scheme would only replace such murals with approval from residents, the long-term intent appears to cause some unease. The so-called family murals, in memory of particular individuals who died in the troubles, however remain a sensitive issue, with a spokesperson for the Re-Imaging scheme saying, 'We won't be able to replace those for a number of years', which expressed a long-term interest in doing so.[36]

Additionally, just as the Re-Imaging programme dealt with painting over images of men in balaclavas, new murals depicting near-identical terrorists were being created. One such example, the 2011 militant Loyalist mural in East Belfast revealed how sectarian issues are still at the forefront of the city's consciousness and how some still struggle to come to terms with the peace process. This mural prompts the question of whether it is a closer reflection of today's climate than the Re-Imaging productions – or at least as relevant? Do the less menacing replacements convey the reality of a supposedly post-conflict country? Are the replacements, as some fear, sanitised representations of today's Northern Ireland? Furthermore, given the long history of violence between these communities, one has to wonder whether newly painted, more passive murals, connect to one of their original functions as territorial markers that caused people to feel protected rather than fearful.[37]

---

35 Interview with William Kelly, one of the Bogside artists.

36 'Whitewashing Northern Ireland's Notorious Murals' 22.7.2010. http://observers.france24.com/en/20100722-whitewashing-northern-ireland-notorious-murals-troubles-belfast-derry. Accessed 14.2.2016.

37 Graham Dawson, *Making Peace with the Past: Memory, Trauma, and the Irish Troubles* (Manchester: Manchester University Press, 2007), 114.

As an outsider, I also raise queries concerning the consequences of painting over the past. The sectarian, aggressive murals, could, for instance, act as a visible reminder of how relative peace in Northern Ireland could easily switch back to a time of reprisal killings. As part of this, one should remember that some victims do not wish for peace and remain embittered by a perceived lack of justice. During the Troubles, the bereaved would sometimes wish for paramilitaries to take action, openly expressing their hope that terrorists would alleviate their suffering through revenge. Whilst some victims find relief by talking of their bitter feelings, others do not cope with their past in this way and instead articulate concerns about state-organised forgetting, evidence of which found in the changes to murals. Graham Dawson's *Making Peace with the Past*, cites among many others a victim who proclaims that she 'hates peace', a mark of her continued animosity and her refusal to forgive.[38]

Conversely, since violent imagery can evidently cause violent behaviour, and in other examples, induce trauma, we might reflect on whether some murals serve to influence continued hatred between communities. One can argue that such a martial environment will perpetuate what so many of the murals depict. There also exist reminders of a three-decade period that many would prefer to forget, which might explain the endorsement of less provocative murals, and more recently, proposals that only hint at past conflict, such as a mural which shows two children shaking hands, each representing one of the two communities. As Cathy Caruth writes of the comforting 'cure' of mainstream melodramas, such works posit trauma against its reality as a discrete past event, locatable, representable and curable, a symptom of a culture's need to 'forget' traumatic events while representing them in oblique form.[39] As Bill Rolston warns with regard to the Re-Imaging scheme, politics is potentially lost, because even the most offensive murals are undeniably political: 'A political position is being stated on the wall. But now there is a fear of politics, a fear of mentioning the Troubles'.[40] In this respect, the replacement murals point to a form of censorship, even self-censorship.

The notion that art can reflect reality is no longer limited to the field of academic criticism. Media portrayals of the conflict in Northern Ireland have consistently used murals as indicators of the political climate at a given time. Murals are an art form as well as a public expression of feeling and identity,

38 Ibid. 136.

39 Cathy Caruth, *Unclaimed Experience: Trauma, Narrative and History* (London and New York: John Hopkins University Press, 1993), 6.

40 Bill Rolston, *Politics and Painting: Murals and Conflict in Northern Ireland* (Cranbury, New Jersey, and London: Associated Universities Press, 1991), 76.

more dynamic than political commentary and, to a larger extent, freer from the constraints of censorship and control.[41] What is at risk is a reduction, or even loss, of the mural's multitude of expressions, and its indicator of the political climate. Conversely, the replacement of sectarian murals, though caused by a new form of control – an official government-sponsored programme, as opposed to commissions by paramilitaries – could indeed reflect a need to move away from visual reminders of hostilities.

Some, however, suspect that the logical outcome, if not the intention, of the state-down intervention is to remove the politics from the mural tradition to provide pleasant pictures which, even if artistically sound, say little of the identity and beliefs of the communities in which they appear.[42] One of the world's leading art experts, Martin Kemp, echoes their concerns by questioning the murals' destruction. Kemp argues that the murals represent some of the most important public images of our time and need preserving.[43] They are, I would argue, cultural relics, whereby the suffering and the response to it belong to the historical record. This includes both the need to paint over the past and also those who feel the need to paint new images depicting 'the terrorist'. But we should remember that mark change; beneath nearly every mural lies at least one other, different image.

6 Changes to Murals, Independent of the Re-Imaging Scheme

Prior to the Re-Imaging Communities Scheme, changes to murals included the modification concerning depictions of firearms. What became observable was an unofficial 're-imaging' that at least represented the interests of paramilitaries who wished to portray a more benign image connected to the changing political climate. Of the murals painted during and soon after the Good Friday Agreement, the most significant change from a Republican, Nationalist perspective was the apparent decision not to paint new murals that included guns, unless, as previously discussed, the mural referred to the origins of their cause. The removal of masked visages replaced by generic or actual faces of combatants was a simultaneous development toward the end of the century.

41 Oona Woods, *Seeing is Believing: Murals in Derry* (Londonderry: Guildhall Press, 1995), 69.

42 Bill Rolston, *Politics and Painting: Murals and Conflict in Northern Ireland* (Cranbury, New Jersey, and London: Associated Universities Press, 1991), 84.

43 Rob Sharp. 'Fading Fast, the murals that illustrate the story of the troubles'. 5.8. 2011. http://www.independent.co.uk/news/uk/home-news/fading-fast-the-murals-that-illustrate-story-of-the-troubles-2332678.html. Accessed 19.4.2016.

No announcement was made by the known muralists, or even by representatives of Belfast's Republican, Nationalist communities, but the move away from intimidating paramilitary imagery had begun. New murals began to focus on what Bill Rolston calls the 'cultural base of nationalism', which means that Republican, Nationalist murals became spare of hooded combatants and instead depicted scenes from Irish history or dedicated more space for those who had died during The Troubles, thus creating further murals classifiable as memorials.[44]

In Republican, Nationalist Belfast, the 'soldier hero' took precedence over the 'terrorist'. This seemed to reflect a feeling of confidence amongst those who commissioned and painted murals that the future for this community would no longer be founded on violence and antipathy toward the British, that Republicanism could now be represented by the historic roots of the cause and those who sacrificed themselves rather than an enduring hostility and apparent pride in the threat posed by the IRA. The changes appeared to correspond with the political settlement, which would grant Republican, Nationalists political, legal and cultural influence of a status hitherto unrecognised and arguably quixotic. More cynically, with murals intrinsically linked to propaganda, the self-determined re-appraisal of images was arguably designed to convey a new self-image, particularly in locations where few, if any, visitors would go.

Nowhere is the re-appraisal more evidenced than in the Ballymurphy estate in west Belfast, an urban landscape that epitomises the IRA's motivation for reprisal killings, the demographics of its membership, and all victims of The Troubles. Seen as the 'cockpit of nationalist resistance' throughout The Troubles, Ballymurphy has been the location for riots (the most notable being a clash between Loyalists in 1970, which subsequently led to fighting between residents and British soldiers); open gun-fire between Loyalists and Republicans, and the Loyalist bombing of Kelly's Bar, which injured sixty-three Ballymurphy residents. Ballymurphy has been the location for the deaths of twenty-nine IRA volunteers (the majority were killed by the British Army, some by the RUC, whilst six died as a result of premature explosions when making bombs); the deaths of eighty-five residents (Loyalist paramilitaries are believed responsible for more than a third of these killings, with the British Army accountable for at least twenty-one deaths, including, in 1971, the shooting dead of 11 civilians known as the 'Ballymurphy Massacre').[45] And, during The Troubles, this

44 Bill Rolston, *Drawing Support: Murals in the North of Ireland* (Dublin: Beyond the Pale Publications, 1992), 145.

45 Of several riots, the most notable was a clash between Loyalists in 1970, which subsequently led to fighting between residents and British soldiers.

one district of Belfast witnessed the deaths of twenty-six British soldiers, all killed by the IRA.[46]

One of the dead, IRA volunteer Tommy Tolan, painted a mural that shows the evolution of Republican, Nationalist imagery since the Good Friday Agreement. Tolan, a popular resident of Ballymurphy, was shot dead in 1977. The first mural to feature him was known as 'The Safe House Mural', which depicted a smiling Tolan before a background of three accompanying volunteers and their mothers willing to house them. Painted four years after the signing of the Good Friday Agreement, this Republican mural was in keeping with the changing representation of Republicanism with non-hooded or unmenacing Republican combatants that began during the cease-fire period (two of the other depicted volunteers even smiled). Yet it still presented an image of contemporary warfare. Tolan was shown holding an automatic rifle, he wore black leather gloves (one symbol of IRA membership) and behind him, on a table, were rifles and boxes of ammunition. Given the year this mural was painted, 2001, the combination of depicting heroicised volunteers who died in the 1970s, whilst still presenting a show of weaponry can read as relating to the then de-commissioning process, which the IRA had agreed to follow but would not complete for a further four years. Due to the Good Friday Agreement, this district of Belfast had become prone to curious tourists and journalists who felt safe to venture into streets previously no-go zones. It is plausible, then, that the mural was painted with a wider, new spectator in mind, which might explain the paradox of the mural's happy-faced armed men.

The contrast between the original mural and that which replaced it in 2003 – during the de-commissioning process, which would last for a further eighteen months – was unmistakable. Whilst the re-painted mural was nearly identical, the figure of Tolan now stood without a rifle and wore a three-piece suit rather than combat attire. The mural itself was in the process of de-commissioning; they were altering the history; Tolan, not even the 'solider hero' anymore, was now a presentable, friendly former resident of Ballymurphy who died during The Troubles. Those unfamiliar to the estate might wonder what role he played in the Troubles. Was he one of the civilian victims?

In 2014 the mural was re-designed (Figure 11.6), with all weaponry and even the reference to 'volunteers' removed, leaving the Irish tricolour as the only reference to Republicanism. The 'soldier hero' had now completed a transformation into a class hero, as the mural is known as 'The Working Class Heroes'. Several residents of Ballymurphy join the 'soldier hero', including those pictured

46 Ciaran de Baroid, *Ballymurphy and the Irish War* (London: Pluto Press, 2000), 390–394.

FIGURE 11.6 The new 'Safe House Mural', Ballymurphy, Belfast. March, 2016.
IMAGE COURTESY OF MARK CALLAGHAN.

in circular frames denoting the deceased. Whilst the residents of the estate would no doubt apperceive the violent history behind some of those pictured here, the mural brings about a striking change in the self-image of the represented, undeniably positive and overtly peaceful whilst also omitting their specific role as IRA members during The Troubles. Deep into the Ballymurphy estate, the location of the mural acquires significance for not being part of the tourist routes that opened five years after the signing of the Good Friday Agreement. To the inquisitive who endeavor to investigate these urban areas, the mural would, in effect, significantly reduce Ballymurphy's significance to the Republican armed struggle. Its location, however, relates the murals to an internal discourse that represents the end of The Troubles and a desire, at least by the sponsors of this painting, to reframe the conflict as one relating to social and economic status. Pride is still visible but it expresses respect for the community and its non-referenced history rather than a tribute to its violent past.

In contrast, murals in Loyalist, Unionists streets communicated very different feelings. Sinister, threatening murals were maintained and new confrontational ones appeared, reflecting an apparent insecurity due to the increasing voice of Sinn Féin – the political wing of the IRA. One cannot ascertain if these changes directly responded to Northern Ireland's new constitutional status, but surveys evidence that the Loyalist, Unionist community believed that Republican Nationalists had benefited from the Good Friday Agreement much more than they had.[47]

Criticism of the Good Friday Agreement was also expressed in a mural that included no military emblems but rather the words: 'Nothing about us without us is for us. …'. This collage, featuring a selection of residents from the Loyalist, Unionist community is unusual in Loyalist murals for its more developed aesthetic that still conveys a clear message to all who see it – that they must be consulted as part of Northern Ireland's future, that politicians should heed this warning when they make concessions.

7 The Bogside Artists

As the programme developed, the Re-Imaging Scheme approached a trio of muralists in Derry, known as the Bogside Artists, though the group did not wish to participate in the programme, as they argued it was burying the past.[48]

The Bogside Artists are responsible for more than a dozen murals, including one of the most famous murals in the world, *The Petrol Bomber*, painted in 1994. The mural uses a photograph of an event from 1969, known as the Battle of the Bogside (Figure 11.7). The mural, a photorealist presentation of a young boy in a gas mask, thus adds to the range of mural paintings, moving from the previously cited, arguably crude renderings, to this more accomplished work that makes permanent a scene from a real event. Although the mural depicts an act of violence, the boy is defending himself from CS gas, used by the RUC, the Northern Irish police. The masked face ascribes a much more complex significance to the image, as its anonymity suggests the child functions as a stand-in for any child as well as for Ireland, as signified by the badge on his shirt. As such the boy represents every Irish citizen and, in turn, Ireland as a whole.

Though previous examples might cause one to oscillate between the issues, the prospect of replacing this mural is less complicated. As one of its painters argues, this purely historical and commemorative work strives to enhance own understanding and experience. Its focus on the individual signals to the importance of every single person, regardless of their role in the Troubles, or

47 Answering the question "Nationalists benefitted a lot more than Unionists after the Good Friday Agreement". It shows that, in 1998 "Nationalists Benefits A Lot More Than Unionists After GF Agreement" was 19% v 1% re: same question re: Unionists; and it rises, year on year, going to 28% v. 1% in 2000; and 33% in 2002; and 34 % v 2% in 2004. www.ark.ac.uk/nilt/2002/Political_Attitudes. Accessed 19.7. 2016.

48 Interview with William Kelly, one of the Bogside artists. 17.1.2016.

FIGURE 11.7 *The Petrol Bomber* mural, Bogside, Derry. March, 2016.
IMAGE COURTESY OF MARK CALLAGHAN.

any conflict.[49] This mural, unlike others mentioned before, does not transform horrors into clichés with a limited range of symbolism. It causes one to wonder whether paramilitary murals would lose their impact, not by being painted over, but by being juxtaposed to more inventive, meaningful examples, such as *The Petrol Bomber* – a mural that does not expurgate the past, nor celebrate it.

Though the Bogside murals are, it would seem, ironically permanent, the Re-Imaging Scheme continues to support the replacement of murals, should a consensus be established, thus promulgating significant changes in the post-Troubles landscape of Northern Ireland. Whether one fully endorses the initiative or not, the programme has made the political mural increasingly complex, prompting new questions about an often one-dimensional art-form. The Re-Imaging Scheme leads one to re-appraise the purpose of the political mural, be it the consequences of leaving them untouched, or the effects and principles of painting over the past. As narratives change, these *aide-memoire* relate to multiple issues concerning power relations in communities, vicarious memory, generational disagreements, the role of the mural in terms of political, popular and collective memory, and perhaps the social truth of irreconcilable differences still represented on hundreds of walls despite the apparent success of the Good Friday agreement. The legitimate concerns outlined in this paper – be it the sanitisation of history, the question of whether murals convey the on-going reality of a post-Troubles society or the need to move away from the conflict by removing images of it – illustrate the subjective dimensions of conflict transformation in post-conflict Northern Ireland. The mural has a multiple role, including to celebrate, to complain, and to convince, but also to express aspirations and fears. Usually the topicality of murals reflects the period they address. In this respect, the Re-Imaging scheme has caused ambivalence where there used to be clarity.

8 Dialogue with other Work in the Volume

Leanne Dodd's chapter, 'Transcending Genre: Narrative Strategies for Creating Literary Crime Fiction as a Subset of Trauma Literature', highlights Cathy Caruth's point concerning the representation of trauma, as outlined in my chapter. Caruth writes of the comforting 'cure' that mainstream depictions attempt to deliver, which posit trauma as a discrete past event, representable and

49 Ibid.

seemingly curable. As I argue, one of the potential issues with the Re-Imaging programme is the removal of images that directly represent past trauma and the Northern Irish conflict, despite their aggressiveness and contrast to peace initiatives, particularly since the Good Friday Agreement. Though counter-arguments support the removal of belligerent murals, Caruth reminds us that the indirect representations of trauma can be symptomatic of a need to 'forget' them. Such form of censorship could result in the concealment of trauma with respect to the painful, visual reminders of the past having no role in the country's post-conflict exploration of its own trauma, as though the murals had no impact in any such regard. Dodd's chapter, which argues that crime fiction can be therapeutic, is especially important for also alerting us to another reality. She takes up an important line of inquiry that applies to the case of Northern Ireland. Indeed the most visible, publicly accessible of artforms, the mural also poses the question of whether its most harsh and direct imagery, depicting the pain of others and also those who inflicted violence, could also empower large audiences with empathetic knowledge of trauma, be they members of the divided communities or visitors to Belfast and Derry.

Bibliography

Primary Sources

Interview with William Kelly, one of the Bogside Artists. Conducted by Mark Callaghan. 12 January 2016.

Interview with Noirin McKinney, Director of Arts Development. Conducted by Mark Callaghan. 16 February, 2016.

Secondary Sources

Bew, Paul. *The Making and Re-Making of the Good Friday Agreement.* Dublin: The Liffey Press, 2007.

Bew, Paul. *The Politics of Enmity (1789–2006).* Oxford: Oxford University Press, 2007.

Buckley, Anthony. *Symbols in Northern Ireland.* Belfast: Institute of Irish Studies, Queen's University of Belfast, 1998.

Caruth, Cathy. *Unclaimed Experience: Trauma, Narrative and History.* London and New York: John Hopkins University Press, 1993.

Coogan, Tim Pat. *The Easter Rising.* London and Dublin: W&N, 2005.

Cox, Michael. *A Farewell to Arms? Beyond The Good Friday Agreement.* London and Dublin: Liang, 2007.

Dawson, Graham. *Making Peace with the Past: Memory, Trauma, and the Irish Troubles.* Manchester: Manchester University Press, 2007.

De Baroid, Ciaran. *Ballymurphy and the Irish War.* London: Pluto Press, 2000.

English, Richard. *Armed Struggle: The History of the IRA*. London: Pan, 2012.

Ferriter, Diarmaid. *The Transformation of Ireland (1900–2000)*. London: Profile Books, 2005.

Graham, John. *A History of the Siege of Londonderry*. Birmingham: Nabu Press, 2005.

Jarman, Neil. "Commemorating 1916, Celebrating Difference: Parading and Painting in Belfast" in *The Art of Forgetting.* Ed. Adrian Forty. London: Berg, 1999.

Jarman, Neil. *Material Conflicts: Parades and Visual Displays in Northern Ireland.* London: Berg, 1997.

Keogh, Dermot. *Northern Ireland and the Politics of Reconciliation*. Cambridge, Cambridge University Press, 1994.

McEvoy, Kieran. *Paramilitary Imprisonment in Northern Ireland.* Oxford: Oxford University Press, 2001.

McGrattan, Cillian. *Northern Ireland 1968–2008: The Politics of Entrenchment.* London and New York: Palgrave, 2010.

McKearney, Tommy. *The Provisional IRA: From Insurrection to Parliament.* London: Berg, 2011.

McKittrick, David, and McVea, David. *Making Sense of the Troubles: A History of the Northern Ireland Conflict.* London: Penguin, 2001.

McLiam Wilson, Robert. *Eureka Street.* London and New York: Secker and Warburg, 1996.

River Editors, Charles. *Building the RMS Titanic. The Construction of the World's Most Famous Ship*. London: Create Space Publishing, 2014.

Rolston, Bill. *The War of the Walls*. Dublin: Beyond the Pale Publications, 1998.

Rolston, Bill. *Drawing Support: Murals in the North of Ireland.* Dublin: Beyond the Pale Publications, 1992.

Rolston, Bill. *Politics and Painting: Murals and Conflict in Northern Ireland*, Cranbury, New Jersey, and London, Associated Universities Press, 1991.

Taylor, Peter. *Brits: The War Against the IRA*. London: Bloomsbury, 2002.

Taylor, Peter. *Loyalists*. London: Bloomsbury Publishing, 2000.

Turmakin, Maria. *Traumascapes*. Melbourne: Melbourne University Press, 2005.

Woods, Oona. *Seeing is Believing: Murals in Derry.* Londonderry: Guildhall Press, 1995.

Web-Sites and Press Sources

Rob Sharp. 'Fading Fast, the murals that illustrate the story of the troubles'. 5.8. 2011. http://www.independent.co.uk/news/uk/home-news/fading-fast-the-murals-that-illustrate-story-of-the-troubles-2332678.html. Accessed 19.4.2016.

www.belfasttelegraph.co.uk/news/is-it-time-to-whitewash-northernirelands-paramilitary-murals-28530284.html. Accessed 9.1.2016.

'Whitewashing Northern Ireland's Notorious Murals' 22.7.2010. http://observers.france24.com/en/20100722-whitewashing-northern-ireland-notorious-murals-troubles-belfast-derry. Accessed 14.2.2016.

Adrian Ismay. 'Prison officer injured in New IRA car bomb attack in Belfast dies'. www.theguardian.com/uk-news/2016/mar/15/belfast-prison-officer-dies-targeted-new-ira-car-bomb-attack-adrian-ismay. 15.3.2016. Accessed 30.3.2016.

www.ark.ac.uk/nilt/2002/Political_Attitudes. Accessed. 4.4.2016.

CHAPTER 12

Transcending Genre: Narrative Strategies for Creating Literary Crime Fiction as a Subset of Trauma Literature

Leanne Dodd

Abstract

The subject matter of crime fiction makes it an ideal vehicle for representing trauma as a subset of trauma literature, which provides an opportunity for crime fiction to offer therapeutic benefits to readers. However, the ongoing debate about the definition of 'literature' has meant that crime fiction is positioned hierarchically lower in the cultural field than trauma literature. This paper will dispute widely-held beliefs that crime fiction cannot be literary or therapeutic by presenting a framework of trauma theory and its relationship to literature, followed by an analysis of how narrative strategies used in trauma literature that mimic the symptoms of trauma align with the fast-paced narrative and literary devices typical of crime fiction. Through a case study and critical reflection of how writers have engaged with trauma in contemporary fiction, this argument supports an emerging theory positing the literary quality of crime fiction when it includes an authentic representation of trauma, and therefore serves similar therapeutic purposes as trauma literature. The re-writing of the traumatic past in crime fiction offers an opportunity to empower large audiences with empathetic knowledge of trauma, transform perceptions, remove stigmas and assist in combating the marginalisation that impedes recovery for trauma survivors. It also provides a safe narrative space for readers to confront their own fears, brought on by exposure to traumatic events in more graphic and perilous ways. This investigation will be informative for crime fiction writers, particularly those aiming to engage with trauma survivors and attempting a more authentic representation of trauma in their work. It will also provide a foundation for writing strategies that transgress the boundaries between mass genre fiction and literary fiction, thereby leading the way for further research into the power of narrative to evoke psychological and emotional growth and its therapeutic benefits for a genre fiction audience.

Keywords

trauma – trauma theory – trauma literature – crime fiction – literary crime fiction – fragmentation – repetition – characterisation – resolution

1 Introduction

Trauma literature has been defined as 'fictional narratives that help readers to access traumatic experience'.[1] Traumatic experience is frequently linked with events of a criminal nature, such as acts of violence or negligence,[2] and criminal events form the key subject matter of crime fiction. These associations suggest that crime fiction functions as an ideal vehicle for representing trauma, which provides an opportunity for crime fiction to offer therapeutic benefits to readers. However, the ongoing debate about the definition of 'literature' has traditionally positioned crime fiction lower in the cultural field than trauma literature,[3] which may explain its limited use in therapy. This paper contests the hierarchies of literature by proposing that the narrative strategies that mimic trauma in the crime novel render it *literary*.

Within a framework of trauma theory and its relationship to literature, crime fiction can portray narratives of trauma with similar literary devices to those used in novels classified as trauma literature. An analysis of the literary mystery novel *The Lake House* by Kate Morton and genre crime novel *Red Dragon* by Thomas Harris together with the narrative strategies used in trauma literature, including fragmentation, repetition, characterisation and resolution proves they match the fast-paced narrative style and literary devices typical of crime fiction. This study offers crime writers tools to mimic the effects of trauma and a method that produces similar therapeutic benefits to those credited to trauma literature. By moving beyond the prevailing conventions of crime fiction to incorporate the well-being benefits of trauma literature, a form of literary crime fiction may emerge as a subset of trauma literature that has the potential to bring transformative benefits to its readers.

---

1 Laurie Vickroy, *Trauma and Survival in Contemporary Fiction* (Charlottesville: University of Virginia Press, 2002), 1.

2 Australian Psychological Society, 'Understanding and Managing Psychological Trauma', viewed 11 January 2016, http://www.psychology.org.au/publications/tip_sheets/trauma/.

3 Laura Marcus, 'Detection and Literary Fiction', *The Cambridge Companion to Crime Fiction*, ed. Martin Priestman (Cambridge: Cambridge University Press, 2003), 245–268.

2 The Relationship between Trauma and Literature

As grounding for this discussion, it is useful to understand what trauma is and how trauma literature delivers therapeutic benefits to readers. The Australian Psychological Society (APS) describes trauma as 'very frightening or distressing events [that] may result in a psychological wound or injury – a difficulty in coping or functioning normally following a particular event or experience'.[4] The focus lies not so much on what trauma is, but what trauma does. The APS lists some of the prevalent effects of trauma as hyperarousal of the nervous system, intrusion of repetitive thoughts and memories, numbing responses such as addiction, self-harm and dissociation and other undesirable behaviours ranging from withdrawal to violence.[5] The issue faced by survivors is that the trauma remains hidden but the resultant behaviours can sever their connections with other human beings.[6]

Freud first studied the latent effect of trauma, in 1895 writing

> Trauma is characterised by a lack of integration into consciousness at the time that the event occurs; it can only be assimilated belatedly, in its insistent and literal return [as nightmares and intrusive thoughts].[7]

In the 1990s, Caruth expanded upon these concepts, claiming that literature 'opens a window on traumatic experience because it teaches readers to listen to what can be told only in indirect and surprising ways'.[8] Modern psychology emphasises the importance of narrative, encouraging sufferers 'to learn to cope with memories by cognitively processing emotional content ... to understand their trauma and make it meaningful'.[9] As a therapeutic method, bibliotherapy aims to do this with 'guided reading of written materials [that offer] understanding and solving problems relevant to a person's therapeutic needs'.[10] Bearing witness to trauma testimonies, either real or fictional, can

4 'Understanding and Managing Psychological Trauma', op. cit.

5 Ibid.

6 Judith Herman, *Trauma and Recovery: The Aftermath of Violence – from Domestic Abuse to Political Terror* (New York: Basic Books, 1992), 2–3.

7 Sigmund Freud and Josef Breuer, *Studies on Hysteria* (New York: Basic Books, 2000), 174.

8 Cathy Caruth, *Trauma: Explorations in Memory* (Baltimore: John Hopkins University Press, 1995), back cover.

9 Nora Du Buiteleir, 'Losing the Plot? The Veteran as Murderer in Bettina Balaka's *Eisflustern*', *Journal of War and Cultural Studies* 6 (2013), 322.

10 Richard J. Riordan and Linda S. Wilson, 'Bibliotherapy: Does it Work?', *Journal of Counseling and Development* 67 (1989): 506.

assist trauma survivors to recognise their own issues and work through traumatic experience to reconnect with self, memory, and community. Testimony also provides a safe narrative space for readers to confront their own fears and acquire empathy to support trauma survivors.[11] Before examining specific narrative strategies used in writing practice, attitudes surrounding the 'literariness' of crime fiction are explored.

3 Literary Fiction vs Crime Fiction

Proponents of bibliotherapy contend that fiction should be realistic and of literary merit to gain therapeutic benefit.[12] This poses a problem for crime writers as critics continue to draw a culturally defined line between supposedly *literary* fiction and crime fiction, labelling crime fiction as 'artistically suspect' and 'low brow'.[13] The prevalence of traumatic events in crime novels, however, establishes parallels with the subject matter of trauma literature. King characterises crime fiction as a narrative with 'crime at its core'[14] whereas trauma literature has trauma at its core. However, many traumatic and criminal events are linked. The APS lists events that can lead to traumatic experience as acts of violence such as armed robbery, war or terrorism; interpersonal violence such as rape, child abuse, or murder; or involvement in accidents such as serious motor vehicle or workplace accidents that may bear some form of criminal negligence.[15] My fellow contributors in this section of the book discuss traumatic content that falls into these categories, in particular acts of war and terrorism, which may widen the context and provoke further thoughts on the material presented in this chapter.

Both crime and trauma genres also display parallels in their duality as they contain two interlinked stories. The first story handles an event that happened in the past: the traumatic event in trauma literature and the criminal event in crime fiction. The second story attempts to reconstruct the memory of that

11 Vickroy, *Trauma and Survival*, 1; Rachel E. Goldsmith and Michelle Satterlee, 'Representations of Trauma in Clinical Psychology and Fiction', *Journal of Trauma & Dissociation* 5 (2004), 43, 54.

12 Jonathan J. Detrixhe, 'Souls in Jeopardy: Questions and Innovations for Bibliotherapy With Fiction', *Journal of Humanistic Counseling, Education and Development* 49 (2010): 65.

13 Du Buiteleir, 'Losing the Plot?', 315.

14 Michelle Spring and Laurie King, *The Arvon Book of Crime and Thriller Writin,* (London: Bloomsbury Publishing, 2012), 172.

15 'Understanding and Managing Psychological Trauma', op. cit.

event to resolve the symptoms in trauma literature[16] or solve the crime in crime fiction.[17] These parallels create a good point of entry for developing a mode of crime fiction that fits into the definition of trauma literature. This characteristic alone, however, does warrant that a novel be characterised as literary.

Many classic literary novels have crime at their core. Consider, for example Du Maurier's *Rebecca*[18] incorporating the murder mystery of the first Mrs de Winter, Dickens' *Oliver Twist*[19] set in London's criminal underbelly, and Dostoyevsky's *Crime and Punishment*[20] and its pre-meditated murder plot. The question that begs is what characteristics these novels possess that categorise them as literary, while others are labelled as genre fiction.

Oxford Dictionaries define literature as 'written works, especially those considered of superior or lasting artistic merit'.[21] The answer, then, lies in what constitutes 'artistic merit'. Distinguishing features of *literary* works proposed by critics include

1. they break from convention and are innovative in terms of form
2. are subversive in terms of content, that is 'difficult' to understand, displaying complexity and ambiguity
3. focus more on ideological themes than on plot
4. explore some part of the human condition by focusing on character[22]

Trauma literature fits the definition of artistic merit by way of its innovative form, subversion of plot and its focus on character by exploring the human condition through trauma. It uses narrative strategies that distort time to mimic the way trauma is not fully integrated into consciousness. Expanding earlier definitions, trauma literature is associated with a structural and thematically fragmented form that simulates the temporal disruption caused by

16 Anne Whitehead, *Trauma Fiction* (Edinburgh: Edinburgh University Press, 2004), 161–162.

17 Carl D. Malmgrem, 'Anatomy of Murder: Mystery, Detective, and Crime Fiction', *Journal of Popular Culture* 30 (1997), 121.

18 Daphne Du Maurier, *Rebecca* (New York: Avon Books, 1971).

19 Charles Dickens, *Oliver Twist* (Oxford: Clarendon Press, 1966).

20 Fyodor Dostoevsky. *Crime and Punishment* (New York: Modern Library, 1947).

21 *Oxford Dictionaries*, s. v. 'Literature', viewed 17 January 2017, https://en.oxforddictionaries.com/definition/literature.

22 Wendy Roy, 'Misreading the Literary Evidence in Carol Shield's Mystery Plots', *English Studies in Canada* June/September (2008), 121–122; Stephen Knight, 'Poetry and Gore and More', *Arena Magazine* 107 (2010), 37–41; Helen Oakley, 'Disturbing Design: Nabokov's Manipulation of the Detective Fiction Genre in Pale Fire and Despair', *Journal of Popular Culture* 36 (2003), 480–496; Paul Cobley, 'The Reactionary Art of Murder: Contemporary Crime Fiction, Criticism and Verisimilitude', *Language and Literature* 21 (2012), 286–298.

trauma.[23] Fellow-contributor Danielle Schaub gives examples of this in her chapter.[24] She illustrates how Cumyn uses stylistic and linguistic patterns that reflect the disjunction of traumatic experience and repetitive patterns in his novel. The use of flashbacks disorient readers between the realms of reality and the imagined, and the employment of attacks on linking, juxtaposition of statements and asyndeton (or lack of coordination) give way to a whirl of sensations that create disorder and chaos, adding complexity and ambiguity. She demonstrates how this succession of disjunctive fragments can add to the innovation and thereby the artistic merit of the novel.

Crime fiction consequently receives little literary credit largely for formulaic and conventional reasons, namely its lack of innovativeness in form. It customarily begins with a crime, includes a second narrative about the investigation, and ends with justice and a return to order.[25] Furthermore, because this formula guarantees readers closure, crime fiction is not 'difficult' to understand. Ordinarily action-based, it focusses more on plot than theme or character. How, then, might a crime novel transcend to the category of 'literary' crime fiction so that it may be deemed suitable for therapeutic use?

4 Rite of Passage

Some critics argue that writers can achieve the *literary* crime novel by breaking with the conventions of traditional crime writing, while maintaining crime at the core of the novel. Todorov has studied the conventions of crime fiction, suggesting that to break with those norms 'is to write "literature" '.[26] Introducing narrative strategies into crime fiction similar to those used in trauma fiction can break with convention and make the crime novel more innovative so it fits within the definition of literature. Means to achieve this will be explored by examining the narrative strategies used by Kate Morton in her literary mystery novel *The Lake House*[27] in comparison with those used by Thomas Harris in his genre detective novel *Red Dragon*.[28]

23 Collins, 'The Ethics and Aesthetics of Representing Trauma', 9.

24 Danielle Schaub, '"Pinned limb to limb by a ton of rocks": Annihilation in the face of captivity and torture in Alan Cumyn's *Man of Bone*', in this volume.

25 Roy, 'Misreading the Literary Evidence', 113.

26 Tzvetan Todorov, *The Poetics of Prose* (Oxford: Wiley-Blackwell, 1977), 43.

27 Kate Morton, *The Lake House* (Crows Nest, Australia: Allen & Unwin, 2015).

28 Marla Harris, '"You Think It's Possible to Fix Broken Things?": Terror in the South African Crime Fiction of Margie Orford and Jassy Mackenzie', *Clues: A Journal of Detection* 31 (2013).

The recipient of several coveted literary awards, Morton includes numerous reviews for the novel in the front matter of her novel. *Literary Journal* confirms that 'Morton has quickly established herself as a master'. The novel is described as 'finely crafted' by Book'd Out and 'masterful' by the *Sun Herald*. Although the novel is not marketed as crime fiction, other reviews point to its parallels with the crime genre, *Canberra Times* defining it as 'a page turner', Barnes and Noble as a novel 'that mixes mystery [and] murder'.[29] Like a crime novel, it has a crime at its core, a detective and an investigation. *The Lake House* follows an informal investigation led by police detective, Sadie Sparrow, on leave in Cornwall when she stumbles upon the unsolved case of the disappearance of eleven-month old Theo Edevane, who local police suspect was murdered seventy years prior. In her review, fellow author Kate Forsyth states 'with this one she takes a step closer to the crime genre',[30] although this statement alludes that this novel remains somehow distinct from genre crime fiction.

As a sub-genre of literary fiction, trauma literature characteristically has a fragmented narrative structure.[31] *The Lake House* fits more aptly the definition of trauma fiction as it depicts the testimonies of several traumatised characters, and closely replicates the literary strategies associated with trauma literature through the non-chronological fragmentation of the plot between the 1930s and present-day Cornwall in 2003. Partly set after the patriarch of the Edevane family, Anthony, returns from fighting in the First World War, it reveals the symptoms of his post-traumatic stress disorder, or shell shock as it was then termed, and the impact this has on his wife and family. It also delves into the traumatic effects of long-term guilt. Anthony's daughter, Alice Edevane, now an elderly spinster, has lived a solitary life dictated by her guilt, believing that she was partly responsible for Theo's disappearance. The detective, Sadie Sparrow, is haunted by the guilt of giving a child up for adoption when she gave birth at the age of sixteen. The plot works toward the characters resolving the effects of these traumatic experiences.

While Harris's *Red Dragon* has been rated at the apex of its genre, it has never been categorised as anything but a genre crime novel. Edward Guthmann of the *San Francisco Chronicle* claims 'there's trash and there's trash with a pedigree' and 'the 1981 Thomas Harris novel that introduced Hannibal

29 Morton, *The Lake House*, i.

30 Kate Forsyth, 'Review: The Lake House by Kate Morton', *Kate's blog* (blog), viewed 27 January 2016 www.kateforsyth.com.au/kates-blog/review-the-lake-house-by-kate-morton.

31 Jo Collins, 'The Ethics and Aesthetics of Representing Trauma: The Textual Politics of Edwidge Danticat's The Dew Breaker', *Journal of Postcolonial Writing* 47 (2011), 9.

Lecter to the world … falls solidly into the second category'.[32] *Red Dragon* similarly follows an investigation, led by FBI investigator Will Graham on the hunt for a serial killer, revealed early on to readers as film laboratorist Francis Dolarhyde. It also includes traumatised characters, as many crime novels do, revealing that Francis Dolarhyde's mother and grandmother treated him poorly, that he was bullied as a child due to a lip disfigurement, and Will Graham's life was shattered after being knifed by the serial killer Hannibal Lecter in a previous case. So what characteristics lead to the categorisation of *The Lake House* as a literary novel and *Red Dragon* as a genre novel? Frow suggests a novel can take other genres into itself, 'enriching its own texture by drawing upon their structural force'.[33] While containing some elements of crime fiction, the additional employment of narrative strategies in trauma literature plays a significant role in *The Lake House's* categorisation as a literary mystery novel.

Having considered the broad context of trauma and its relationship to literature, some specific narrative strategies employed in trauma literature are now examined and compared with those used in genre crime fiction using these two novels as case studies. The study does not provide an exhaustive list of strategies but attempts to generate tools of use to writers in creating literary crime fiction carrying therapeutic benefits.

4.1 *Fragmentation*

Fragmentation is one strategy employed to 'convey the fracturing of time, self and reality that … accompanies traumatic episodes or recall'[34] using literary devices such as analepsis (or flashbacks), non-linear narrative, delayed narrative or textual gaps. Morton manages to engage with and subvert the conventions of crime fiction by employing fragmentation in *The Lake House*. The crime drives the narrative forward in a fast-paced linear manner through Sadie's investigation, which follows conventional crime fiction strategies, but its subversion lies in using analepsis to move the reader between the 1930s and 2003. The investigation is persistently frustrated by digressions into the past where characters reveal family secrets, creating complexity and ambiguity that the reader must interpret and reconstruct. Knight argues that subversion

---

32 Edward Guthmann, 'Dragon' has no Bite/All-Star Cast Fails to Make 'Silence of the Lambs' Prequel Appetizing', *San Francisco Chronicle*, Friday 4 October 2002, viewed 12 January 2016, www.sfgate.com/movies/article/Dragon-has-no-bite-All-star-cast-fails-to-2765306.php.

33 John Frow, *Genre* (London: Routledge, 2006), 40.

34 Goldsmith and Satterlee, 'Representations of Trauma', 45.

makes it impossible to reach 'true meaning'[35] so it breaks with the conventions of the traditional crime plot. This complexity and ambiguity is evidenced in some reader reactions with one calling the novel 'engaging' although 'complicated and a bit hard to follow', and another stating she did not finish it because it 'jumps back and forth between multiple time periods and characters [like] someone trying to tell me a story that cannot stay on track'.[36] In their critical reviews, these readers have unwittingly provided support that *The Lake House* meets one of the criteria for being categorised as literary fiction, namely its 'difficulty' to be understood. Whether a reader then persists to interpret and reconstruct the story is a subjective endeavour.

The non-linear narrative in *The Lake House* flashes back to revelations by Theo's mother, Eleanor, about her husband Andrew's war-induced post-traumatic stress disorder, his unpredictability and violent episodes she conceals from the family, and his reaction to an affair she was engaged in with the gardener, Ben. These revelations serve as clues to position Andrew as suspect in the investigation, aligning it with the conventions of crime fiction but this must be interpreted alongside the testimony of Alice, their daughter, who firmly believes Ben abducted Theo for ransom. This technique appropriates the crime fiction device, the 'red herring',[37] to plant false clues, creating further parallels with crime fiction conventions.

Going beyond these conventions, Morton uses analepsis to mimic the way the traumatic recall surrounding events affects the characters' lives, allowing readers to bear witness to their torment. Alice harbours the guilt of firstly sharing her novice kidnapping story with Ben as a teenager, believing he has carried it out but it went awry leading to Theo's death. Secondly, she carries the guilt of her ongoing silence for seventy years as an adult. Alice was 'sick with the secret she hadn't been able to make herself tell, the guilt she'd nursed deep inside ever since'.[38] Sadie reflects upon an unexpected letter she has received from the child she gave up for adoption. 'Fifteen years in which she'd focussed on moving forward … all her efforts to build a barrier between then and now, it only took one letter to bring it down'.[39] The novel is further complicated, as Morton steps beyond the confines of time found in the formulaic crime novel by delivering flashbacks to traumatic events in characters' lives

35 Knight, 'Poetry and Gore', 41.
36 Goodreads. 'The Lake House', viewed 13 January 2017, http://www.goodreads.com/book/show/21104828-the-lake-house.
37 Spring and King, *The Arvon Book of Crime*, 214.
38 Morton, *The Lake House*, 90.
39 Ibid., 57.

non-chronologically. Readers must reconstruct these memories out of order in their attempt to fill in the textual gaps she creates. Du Buiteleir contends that this structure creates a story that 'does not so much unfold as fall open, refold and double back on itself, presenting a sense of disorientation' symptomatic of trauma.[40] Fellow-contributor Gen'ichiro Itakura's chapter offers examples to supplement and extend those presented in this chapter.[41] Itakura describes the novel as characterised by interruption and displacement that reflects the characters' confusion.

Morton inserts these memories into the narrative by using triggers. Many of Alice's flashbacks are prompted by Sadie's requests to interview her in relation to Theo's disappearance. Alice describes Sadie's first letter to her as 'charged with delivering such a potent detonation from the past' as 'images fell inside her mind, one after the other, like cards dealt from a pack' although she had 'done everything she could to avoid ever going back to that place, that time'.[42] Andrew's violent outbursts are sometimes provoked by the cries of baby Theo, which he mentally associates with danger based on an incident he experienced in the war. Schaub discusses in her chapter how victims cannot always integrate traumatic events but retain the bodily sensations without the mental association to make sense of them.[43] Morton utilizes this strategy in the way Andrew reacts without understanding that the cries are those of his own son. These strategies further mimic the way that associated events can trigger traumatic memories, both mentally and bodily.[44]

In comparison, the structure of *Red Dragon* lies in its predominantly fast-paced linear narrative that drives the investigation forward in the formulaic manner of the crime novel. The first eight chapters focus primarily on the investigation of the crime and collection of clues by FBI investigator Will Graham. The reader is not introduced to the villain Francis Dolarhyde until Chapter Nine where he appears in his everyday world; 'Seven hundred miles to the southwest, in the cafeteria at Gateway Film Laboratory of St. Louis, Francis Dolarhyde was waiting for a hamburger'.[45] While Harris uses analepsis at times, flashback scenes depart momentarily from the narrative to reveal clues in the way that the generic crime formula uses double movement to

40 Du Buiteleir, 'Losing the Plot?', 321.

41 Gen'ichiro Itakura, 'Writing Trauma, Writing Modern: Nadeem Aslam's *The Wasted Vigil* and Atiq Rahimi's *The Patience Stone*', in this volume.

42 Morton, *The Lake House*, 89–90.

43 Schaub, op.cit.

44 Vickroy, *Trauma and Survival*, 30.

45 Thomas Harris, *Red Dragon* (New York: Berkley Books), 88.

shift backward toward revelation, and forward toward resolution.[46] The author presents these chronologically as the story progresses. He depicts traumatic events through brief flashbacks, including one on Dolarhyde bullied as a child due to his lip disfigurement and one with Lecter knifing Graham, but the narrative is not fragmented in a way that mimics trauma or subverts the plot. The linear structure of *Red Dragon* prevents the novel from being innovative in terms of form or content, so it cannot be considered as 'difficult'. Thereby, it does not fit the definition of artistic merit.

4.2 *Repetition*

As a strategy in trauma literature, repetition mimics the repetitive intrusion of traumatic memory in combination with mirroring and recurring motifs.[47] The motif of 'secrets' central to *The Lake House* reflects the effects of trauma in their persistent intrusion into the linear mystery plot.

Sadie hides the reason for her leave at her grandfather's country Cornwall property. Her enforced leave stems from her overzealousness in a case in which a mother has allegedly abandoned her young child and Sadie leaks classified information to the press in her bid to prove foul play. This undesirable behaviour results from parallels in her life, and her reaction to the letter she has recently received from the teenage child she secretly adopted out at birth. Sadie's guilt over the harm she may have caused her child in abandoning her causes her to shut out the traumatic event by returning the letter from her birth daughter unread, marked *No longer at this address*. 'Without the letter clouding her judgment, she'd be able to let the ... case go once and for all, and creep out from whatever madness it was that had cloaked her.[48] This secret, however, provokes Sadie's relentless investigation into the cold case of Theo's disappearance. Sadie's secret investigation, driven by the influences of her past, further disrupts the traditional crime novel formula in which there would normally be official police activity.[49] Oakley suggests that a 'lack of a rational problem-solving presence'[50] inverts the structure of the crime novel by taking the emphasis away from the detective and placing it on the victim. Theo and his family members become the dominating consciousness of the novel.

---

46 Oakley, 'Disturbing Design', 486.

47 Whitehead, *Trauma Fiction,* 120.

48 Morton, *The Lake House*, 66.

49 Anne Jones, 'The Blackshaw Chord, Crime Fiction, Literary Fiction: Why the Demarcation?' (PhD diss., University of Southampton, Faculty of Humanities, 2013), 267.

50 Oakley, 'Disturbing Design', 481.

Sadie's secret echoes the family secrets kept by the Edevanes. Initially, the suspected harm to Theo by his father mirrors Sadie's guilt for the harm she believes to have inflicted in abandoning her own child. This secret, reflected through her emotions of loss and guilt, is later mirrored by Eleanor's loss and guilt for giving up her own child when it is eventually revealed that she gave Theo to a childless couple to protect him from Anthony's unpredictable violence, lamenting 'Anthony was worse than ever. Theo was in danger … this plan, this sickening, unthinkable plan, was the only way to stem disaster's flow'.[51] Further mirroring of loss and guilt appears when the author reveals that Eleanor's mother, Constance, has also kept a secret about giving birth to a stillborn child. The use of repetition in this way makes the novel innovative in form. These strategies, with their focus on ideological themes and the human condition, break with the conventions of the genre crime novel to aid in the novel classified as literary.

Harris employs repetition in *Red Dragon* but in a form inherent to crime fiction through the formulaic model. Fellow-contributor Claudio Zanini presents in his chapter, the Baudrillardian notion that reality is never true, but a succession of simulations constantly reproduced.[52] Readers can trust exposure to the narrative of crime and death because they know from repeated experience of these simulations that crime novels carry them through to a safe resolution.[53] A reading of Mark Callaghan's contribution helps us to imagine how visual images can also reinforce simulation.[54]

Red Dragon's primary dramatic interest is entrenched in the crime and its solution by FBI investigator, Will Graham. The following scene, although graphically told, can be assimilated by the reader because it repeats the type of scene often encountered in crime narratives. It leads to the resolution of the crime by bringing the villain to justice after he attacks Graham.

> … she shot him in the face as he slid down the door facing and she shot him in the face as he sat on the floor and she ran to him and shot him twice in the face as he sprawled against the wall, scalp down to his chin and his hair on fire.[55]

51 Morton, *The Lake House*, 546.

52 Claudio Zanini, 'Body and Trauma in Chuck Palahniuk's Haunted', in this volume.

53 Rose Lucas, 'Anxiety and its Antidotes: Patricia Cornwell and the Forensic Body', *LIT: Literature Interpretation Theory* 15 (2004), 210.

54 Mark Callaghan, 'Painting over the Past: Political Palimpsests in Northern Ireland and the Complexities of the 'Whitewash' Initiative', in this volume.

55 Harris, *Red Dragon*, 433.

This style of crime fiction also capitalises on the propensity of some readers to associate graphic and shocking experiences with enjoyment, which Zanini suggests may be explained by our libidinal forces and death drive that push readers toward a fascination with 'poor taste'. Callaghan additionally warns against violent imagery that in some cases may induce violent behaviour or trauma. These forms of repetition focus more on plot than the ideological themes of literary fiction.

The serial killer, Dolarhyde, exhibits further repetitive behaviours across crime scenes, such as placing mirrors in the victims' eyes, but their purpose is to provide clues that lead to the crime's solution and the killer's demise, ultimately restoring the world to order. This practice of employing formulaic repetition places genre crime fiction outside the definition of artistic merit.

4.3 *Characterisation*

Karlin and Bruneau suggest that for a novel to be therapeutic, it needs to reveal the origins of emotional reactions.[56] Dealing with individuals, particularly revealing their angst and flaws, can move the focus of a crime novel from plot to character.[57] Fellow-contributor Aslı Tekinay discusses in her chapter how the war has provided a horde of subject matter for literature that enables an exploration of attitudes and values about family and society, and the traumatic effects of war.[58] Morton's novel takes up this subject and extends it to the multitude of emotional after-effects that the cast endure as a result of Andrew's war-induced trauma. The strategy aligns *The Lake House* with the criteria for literary fiction, as it is as much a novel that explores the human condition of trauma as it is a mystery. Morton believably portrays details of the effects of trauma suffered by the characters who are casualties of the crime, and the impact it has on their lives.

The main female characters, Sadie, Alice and Eleanor are all strong women with flaws. Sadie is committed to the ethics of right and wrong to the extent that she puts her policing career on the line to prove a woman's innocence when accused of abandoning her child, yet she shies away from meeting her own abandoned child due to guilt and fear of reprisal. 'The letter inside was her own personal time-bomb, tick-tick-ticking while she worked out how to

56 Andrea Karlin and Odette Bruneau, 'Child Abuse: Helping Children through Bibliotherapy' (paper presented at the Annual Meeting of the Texas State Council of the International Reading Association, Texas, 14–16 March 1985).

57 Knight, 'Poetry and Gore', 37.

58 Aslı Tekinay, 'Transformative Shocks: War Trauma in David Rabe's *Sticks and Bones* and Sam Shepard's *States of Shock*', in this volume.

defuse it. She needed to defuse it. It made a mess of everything'.[59] The plot circles around Alice's secret from the first page when she buries her incriminating novel as a teenager, 'There was no one she could tell, no way to fix it, no way they would ever forgive her. The only thing left was to bury the evidence'[60] until nearer the end where she digs it back up as an elderly woman and her 'heart had begun to trip along when she saw it',[61] still wracked with guilt until she discovers Theo is alive. Eleanor shows great conviction in keeping her vow to remain with and support her husband, Anthony, and in keeping her promise not to reveal his mental illness to anyone to the point that she gives up Theo, her long-awaited son, rather than break that promise. Engaging in an affair with the gardener, Ben, exposes her weakness. She describes her love for her husband as 'keeping the patched-up ship from sinking in the storms' but her relationship with Ben as 'a little rowboat in which one floated calm above it all'.[62] When she realises that Ben is Theo's biological father her 'guilt, long suppressed, began to stir. She'd been wrong to betray Anthony ... her dear love'[63] and as a fitting punishment she avoids the garden at Loeanneth she has always loved in order to avoid Ben. The characters' imperfections allow readers to identify and empathise with their traumatically driven plights. In this way, the novel explores the human condition by focusing on character, thereby meeting the criteria for artistic merit.

Jones states that 'it is not the remit of the standard detective story to deal with the psychological damage done to the survivors of the crime'.[64] Harris does not develop any narrative around the victims of the crime beyond their function to solely die and provide clues to set the investigation in motion. Harris also fails to portray Dolarhyde's childhood traumatic experiences in a sympathetic way, painting his character as a villain rather than a victim of trauma. The narrative does not delve deeply into the effects of these traumatic experiences, as the scene between the young Dolarhyde and his step-siblings at his mother's house demonstrates.

> "He's sick because of your ugly face," Ned said. ... Ned grabbed Francis by the ears and held him close to the mirror over the dressing table. "That's why he's sick!" Ned slammed his face into the mirror. "That's why he's

59 Morton, *The Lake House*, 64.
60 Ibid., 1.
61 Ibid., 558.
62 Ibid., 485.
63 Ibid., 489.
64 Jones, 'The Blackshaw Chord', 283–284.

> sick!" Slam. "That's why he's sick!" Slam. The mirror was smeared with blood and mucus. Ned let him go and he sat on the floor. Victoria looked at him, her eyes wide, holding her lower lip between her teeth. They left him there. His face was wet with blood and spit. His eyes watered from the pain, but he did not cry.[65]

The scene ends abruptly here without developing the effects of the trauma Dolarhyde suffered from his childhood bullying. Four pages later, the author briefly mentions that he had lived at his mother's house only a month, having been raised by his Grandmother, and 'was sent away at the age of nine for hanging Victoria's cat'.[66] In the science of behaviour profiling, the FBI have consistently found it common behaviour for serial killers to begin torturing and killing animals as children',[67] so although this information provides some foundation for the characters' subsequent behaviour, the reader is left to make the causal connections on their own. Harris does not privilege readers with an inner journey into the workings of his characters' traumatised minds, as Morton does in *The Lake House*. Plot-driven, *Red Dragon* does not fully explore the human condition so that it cannot claim artistic merit.

The lake house, Loeanneth, appears as much a character in Morton's novel as its inhabitants. For Alice, Loeanneth produced 'a great swelling of affection. … For as long as she could remember, she'd been aware that the house and gardens of Loeanneth lived and breathed for her'.[68] Writers of literature often employ place as a character motif. Manderley, the mansion, in Du Maurier's classic novel *Rebecca,* easily comes to mind. The use of a recurring location that takes on a life of its own provides readers with a vantage point to gain access to the traumatic event.[69] Morton exploits this strategy in *The Lake House* to allow readers to return to the location of Theo's disappearance, Loeanneth, repeatedly in the characters' recurrent intrusive flashbacks. Using grim and threatening imagery to construct this character motif further assists to evoke traumatic memory.

---

65 Harris, *Red Dragon*, 272.

66 Ibid., 276.

67 Mark Griffiths, 'What Drives People to Torture Animals?', *Independent*, Friday 7 November 2014. Viewed 16 January 2017, http://www.independent.co.uk/life-style/health-and-families/features/what-drives-people-to-torture-animals-9844721.html.

68 Morton, *The Lake House*, 15.

69 Ulrich Baer, 'To Give Memory a Place: Holocaust Photography and the Landscape Tradition', *Representations* 69 (2000): 48.

> The summer had ripened and rotted so that autumn when it fell was thick and sullen. With it, an interminable grief settled over Loeanneth, as if all hope that Theo would be found had died with the warmer season.[70]

Morton continues to paint a bleak picture of Loeanneth throughout the novel when she depicts the property in the recall of Alice and Eleanor's traumatic memories of Theo's disappearance, so that the house and its surrounding woods take on sinister characteristics. This is reinforced in the strange ominous feeling that overcomes Sadie when she happens upon the abandoned and dilapidated house seventy years later, personified with its 'windows wink[ing] conspiratorially',[71] and it taking on 'a sullen cast like a spoiled child who enjoyed being the centre of attention and now wasn't happy being ignored'.[72] Crime fiction, as Lloyd observes, 'is typically depicted through landscapes … which are grim, threatening places, hiding darkness the detective … must penetrate in order to survive',[73] so this strategy serves to align the novel with the crime fiction genre while the stylistic language used to personify Loeanneth as a character sets the novel apart from popular genre fiction.

In *Red* Dragon, there is no dominant place in which readers can repeatedly return to the site of traumatic events. The fast-paced linear narrative of the genre crime novel moves the reader rapidly from crime scene to crime scene, and between the characters' various workplaces and homes. Places are not personified to act as a character motif in the novel but are purposed as a setting in which the action takes place. This grim description of the first crime scene is given from Graham's investigative view.

> Graham had studied the detectives' report at Atlanta Homicide for most of the day and early evening. … Now he stood in the doorway of the master bedroom. He could see faintly without the flashlight. A digital clock on a nightstand projected the time on the ceiling and an orange night light burned above the baseboard by the bathroom. The coppery smell of blood was strong. Eyes accustomed to the dark could see well enough. The madman could distinguish Mr. Leeds from his wife. There was enough light for him to cross the room, grab Leeds's hair and cut his

---

70 Morton, *The Lake House*, 282.

71 Ibid., 39.

72 Ibid., 44.

73 Joanne R. Lloyd, 'Talking to the Dead – the Voice of the Victim in Crime Fiction', *New Writing: The International Journal for the Practice & Theory of Creative Writing* 11.1 (2014): 105.

> throat. What then? Back to the wall switch, a greeting to Mrs. Leeds and then the gunshot that disabled her?[74]

Characterisation strategies that reveal angsts and flaws, or use place as a character motif, therefore offer a way for writers to explore themes of trauma and render the crime novel of therapeutic benefit.

4.4 *Resolution*

Resolution in the formulaic model of the crime novel, which restores order, stands outside of the definition of 'artistic merit'. Cobley suggests that fidelity to reality, where endings are not always resolved neatly and justice is not always served can break with the conventions of crime fiction and make the crime novel literary.[75] While this would seem at odds with the goal of therapeutic gains, Detrixhe proposes that vague, and even unpleasant endings, can have a place in bibliotherapy as they can open up deeper reflection leading to alternative solutions for the reader.[76] In *The Lake House*, the solution to the mystery is not as anticipated at the beginning of the novel. Sadie and Alice pursue their investigations into Theo's disappearance, all the while expecting to discover the resting place of his body and the identity of the murderer. Instead, they discover that Theo is alive, partially resolving some of the guilt that has burdened the now elderly Alice throughout her life, convinced of her responsibility for Theo's death. However, there can be no punishment or atonement for the crime because the perpetrators are deceased. The resolution focusses on the discovery that Sadie's grandfather is, in fact, the adopted child Theo. There is no attainable justice for the years the family members have lost with Theo, leaving a portion of the story forever unresolved. Cobley claims that 'lack of resolution more closely imitate[s] life in the mode of realism or, at least, constitute[s] 'good art''.[77] This form of resolution therefore fits the definition of artistic merit.

In contrast, Harris follows the formulaic structure of crime fiction in *Red Dragon* to bring the novel to a predictable and comforting ending where the world is restored to order. The FBI investigator, Will Graham, investigates the crime and gathers clues that assist him to track down and identify the serial killer, Francis Dolarhyde, then justice prevails when Dolarhyde is shot dead. This resolution meets the expectation of dedicated crime readers; however,

---

74 Harris, *Red Dragon*, 13.
75 Cobley, 'The Reactionary Art of Murder', 289.
76 Detrixhe, 'Souls in Jeopardy', 66, 68.
77 Cobley, 'The Reactionary Art of Murder', 289.

Morton's use of the strategy of partial resolution confirms the potential to satisfy the reader's need for resolution in crime fiction while also contributing to the artistic merit of the crime novel, demonstrating potential for therapeutic use.

5 Conclusion

The preceding analysis provides a framework for transcending genre and breaking down barriers preventing crime fiction from being considered for therapeutic use. Employing strategies to represent trauma in ways that serve similar purposes to trauma literature offers an opportunity for crime fiction writers, particularly those aiming to engage with trauma survivors and literary institutions, to attempt to portray a more authentic representation of trauma in their work. This may enable such works to be sited in the literary category as a subset of trauma literature and open up opportunities for the use of crime fiction for therapeutic purposes such as in bibliotherapy.

This approach has the capacity to bring transformative benefits to readers and empower large audiences with empathetic knowledge of trauma, which may transform perceptions, remove stigmas and thereby assist in combating the marginalisation that impedes recovery for trauma survivors. In addition, it provides a safe narrative space for readers to confront their own fears, as they are exposed to traumatic events in more graphic and perilous ways in today's world. This investigation provides a foundation for writing strategies that transgress the boundaries between genre and literary fiction and leads the way for further research into the potential that narrative has to evoke psychological and emotional growth in treating psychological conditions brought on by trauma.

Bibliography

Australian Psychological Society. 'Understanding and Managing Psychological Trauma'. Viewed 11 January 2016. http://www.psychology.org.au/publications/tip_sheets/trauma/.

Baer, Ulrich. 'To Give Memory a Place: Holocaust Photography and the Landscape Tradition'. *Representations* 69 (2000): 38–63.

Caruth, Cathy. *Trauma: Explorations in Memory*. Baltimore: John Hopkins University Press, 1995.

Cobley, Paul. 'The Reactionary Art of Murder: Contemporary Crime Fiction, Criticism and Verisimilitude'. *Language and Literature* 21 (2012): 286–298.

Collins, Jo. 'The Ethics and Aesthetics of Representing Trauma: The Textual Politics of Edwidge Danticat's The Dew Breaker'. *Journal of Postcolonial Writing* 47 (2011): 5–17.

Detrixhe, Jonathan J. 'Souls in Jeopardy: Questions and Innovations for Bibliotherapy with Fiction'. *Journal of Humanistic Counseling, Education and Development* 49 (2010): 58–72.

Dickens, Charles. *Oliver Twist.* Oxford: Clarendon Press, 1966 [1837].

Dostoyevsky, Fyodor. *Crime and Punishment.* New York: Modern Library, 1947 [1866].

Du Buiteleir, Nora. 'Losing the Plot? The Veteran as murderer in Bettina Balaka's *Eisflustern*'. *Journal of War and Cultural Studies* 6 (2013): 313–327.

Du Maurier, Daphne. *Rebecca.* New York: Avon Books, 1971 [1938].

Forsyth, Kate. 'Review: The Lake House by Kate Morton'. *Kate's blog* (blog). Viewed 27 January 2016. www.kateforsyth.com.au/kates-blog/review-the-lake-house-by-kate-morton.

Freud, Sigmund and Josef Breuer. *Studies on Hysteria.* New York: Basic Books, 2000.

Frow, John. *Genre.* London: Routledge, 2006.

Goldsmith, Rachel E. & Michelle Satterlee. 'Representations of Trauma in Clinical Psychology and Fiction'. *Journal of Trauma & Dissociation* 5 (2004): 35–59.

Goodreads. 'The Lake House'. Viewed 13 January 2017. http://www.goodreads.com/book/show/21104828-the-lake-house.

Griffiths, Mark. 'What Drives People to Torture Animals?'. *Independent*, Friday 7 November 2014. Viewed 16 January 2017. http://www.independent.co.uk/life-style/health-and-families/features/what-drives-people-to-torture-animals-9844721.html.

Guthmann, Edward. 'Dragon' has no Bite/All-Star Cast Fails to Make 'Silence of the Lambs' Prequel Appetizing'. *San Francisco Chronicle*, Friday 4 October 2002. Viewed 12 January 2016. www.sfgate.com/movies/article/Dragon-has-no-bite-All-star-cast-fails-to-2765306.php.

Harris, Marla. '"You Think It's Possible to Fix Broken Things?": Terror in the South African Crime Fiction of Margie Orford and Jassy Mackenzie'. *Clues: A Journal of Detection* 31 (2013): 122–131.

Harris, Thomas. *Red Dragon.* New York: Berkley Books, 2009 [1981].

Herman, Judith Lewis. *Trauma and Recovery: The Aftermath of Violence: From Domestic Abuse to Political Terror.* New York: Basic Books, 1992.

Jones, Anne. 'The Blackshaw Chord, Crime Fiction, Literary Fiction: Why the Demarcation?'. PhD Dissertation, University of Southampton, Faculty of Humanities, 2013.

Karlin, Andrea and Odette Bruneau, 'Child Abuse: Helping Children through Bibliotherapy'. Paper presented at the Annual Meeting of the Texas State Council of the International Reading Association, Texas, 14–16 March 1985.

Knight, Stephen. 'Poetry and Gore and More'. *Arena Magazine* 107 (2010): 37–41.

Lloyd, Joanne R. 'Talking to the Dead: The Voice of the Victim in Crime Fiction'. *New Writing: The International Journal for the Practice & Theory of Creative Writing* 11.1 (2014): 100–108.

Lucas, Rose. 'Anxiety and its Antidotes: Patricia Cornwell and the Forensic Body'. *LIT: Literature Interpretation Theory* 15 (2004): 207–222.

Malmgren, Carl D. 'Anatomy of Murder: Mystery, Detective, and Crime Fiction'. *Journal of Popular Culture* 30 (1997): 115–135.

Marcus, Laura. 'Detection and Literary Fiction'. *The Cambridge Companion to Crime Fiction*, edited by Martin Priestman, 245–268. Cambridge: Cambridge University Press, 2003.

Morton, Kate. *The Lake House.* Crows Nest, Australia: Allen & Unwin, 2015.

Oakley, Helen. 'Disturbing Design: Nabokov's Manipulation of the Detective Fiction Genre in *Pale Fire* and *Despair*'. *Journal of Popular Culture* 36 (2003): 480–496.

Oxford Dictionaries, s. v. 'Literature'. Viewed 17 January 2017, https://en.oxforddictionaries.com/definition/literature.

Riordan, Richard J. and Linda S. Wilson. 'Bibliotherapy: Does it Work?', *Journal of Counseling and Development* 67 (1989): 506–508.

Roy, Wendy. 'Misreading the Literary Evidence in Carol Shield's Mystery Plots'. *English Studies in Canada* June/September (2008): 113–129.

Spring, Michelle and Laurie King. *The Arvon Book of Crime and Thriller Writing.* London: Bloomsbury Publishing, 2012.

Todorov, Tzvetan. *The Poetics of Prose.* Oxford: Wiley-Blackwell, 1977.

Vickroy, Laurie. *Trauma and Survival in Contemporary Fiction.* Charlottesville: University of Virginia Press, 2002.

Whitehead, Anne. *Trauma Fiction.* Edinburgh: Edinburgh University Press, 2004.

PART 3

Engaging Trauma

CHAPTER 13

Illness Is a Window: Reframing Leukaemia through Dharma Art

Nicholas Quin Serenati

Abstract

In 1978, *Illness as Metaphor* emerged from author Susan Sontag inspiring agency in challenging the existence of institutionalised metaphors present in illness discourse. From the concept that life is complex and burdensome in its dual citizenship with death, Sontag writes '[t]he metaphor implements the way particularly dreaded diseases are envisaged as an alien 'other', as enemies are in modern war'.[1] Sontag's position calls for the dismissal of illness metaphors that occupy this negative connotation and propagate discouragement, silence and/or shame in the mind of the patient. This chapter is intended to challenge that systemic thinking and offer a new alternative to established metaphors pervading illness discourse. Based on my personal journey with Acute Myeloid Leukaemia (AML), the intention of this discourse is to illustrate a re-contextualisation of my illness experience through a dharma art practice. Concentrated on diagnosis, treatment, and healing, a meditative practice is intricately woven with creative production to provide a documented articulation of the liminal spaces found in the memory of my illness. In this research, the process of aesthetising illness promotes healing and unearths a new metaphor to consider for illness discourse. Metaphors are similar to maps, providing an understanding of one kind of experience in terms of another.[2] As a map, the metaphor charts an intellectual terrain that shifts the perspective of experience from *here* to *there*. In employing poetry, photography, and video, a visualisation of process communicates a reframed experience with illness and maps the process of healing – my transformation from *here* to *there*. In producing a body of research that blends spirituality with creativity, a sophisticated response to my illness is located. As an empowered and impassioned voice, this presentation offers a new, positive metaphor for illness discourse intended to inspire and heal – *illness is a window*.

1 Susan Sontag, *Illness as Metaphor* (New York: Farrar, Straus and Giroux, 1978), 99.
2 George Lakoff and Mark Johnson, *Metaphors We Live By* (Chicago: University of Chicago Press, 1980), 158.

 | DOI:10.1163/9789004407947_015

Keywords

metaphor – illness – re-contextualisation – dharma – art – meditation – window – healing – transformation

On November 10th, 2000, I was diagnosed with Acute Myeloid Leukaemia (AML). Over the course of an 80-day treatment, I endured physical trauma brought about by an inversion of chromosome 16. The inversion process of chromosome 16 can be explained as an interference created in the production of normal blood cells. During this process, abnormal white blood cells in the bone marrow spawn, and begin to latch on and devour healthy cells. After 26 weeks and 4 misdiagnoses, the AML had a stake on my life. Left in the wake of the illness' path, my body was compromised by oppressive anaemia, countless blood transfusions, organ collapse, a life-threatening fungal infection in both

FIGURE 13.1 *Window* © 2011.
COURTESY OF NICHOLAS QUIN SERENATI.

lungs, and an experimental white-blood cell transfusion that if my body rejected, would have rendered me dead.

In coming to terms with illness experience, the personal narrative functions as a critical source for knowledge. The experience of an acute illness is a life-changing phenomenon. In one respect, illness can be thought of as an intricately demoralising and/or dehumanising endeavour of the human body. Illness attacks the body from a vantage point that renders the patient powerless, wherein lies the problem. A shift in power from patient to illness complicates the experience of being ill. The illness's encroachment ravages the body of its healthy cells – forcing the body to decay. Further, the illness distorts the patient's perception of himself or herself. It results in a direct offensive on the patient's identity prior to illness. The illness's intrusion challenges the patient's understanding of the self – mind, body and spirit – forcing the patient into a position of marginalised power.

Vital to this discourse is a call for agency in illness studies. As a survivor of AML, I am concerned with ways patients are able to be empowered by personal trauma. For me, methods of creative expression are critical to interpretation, understanding, knowledge building and claiming voice. From a lens of art-making, the creative renderings mediate the relationship between patient and illness while offering communication and understanding to others. To enable the patient with creative authorship of their experience signifies to resist the power of illness and claim their experience with illness, therefore, reclaiming the individual's voice over the illness.

My illness intended to victimise me – marginalise my life in the path of its all-consuming mutation. However, the transformation of my body led to the transformation of my mind. As a critical inquiry into locating one's self post-illness, my creative research employed poetry, photography, video, and mixed-media sculptures. In exercising these modes of expression, I managed to engage my illness and contextualise the experience. Illness challenged the nature of my being and mobilised my thinking toward charting a life-long trajectory of personal healing.

The concept of healing can be a controversial theme within the study of trauma. Within the discourse of this book, perspectives of how trauma impacts social, cultural, political and artistic frameworks have been engaged. At the intermediary of this thinking is either a direct or indirect consideration of healing being achievable. From the perspective of the artistic, documentation through sound, video, photography, dance, etc., aide in a process of confronting trauma, and/or the work of recovery and healing from it. In this realm, the work from the scholars in this volume profoundly contribute to the inquiry. To understand it more deeply, I look toward Candance Christensen and her work to organize community-based photovoice as a means of protest against gender-based violence, or Marie France Forcier's 'Creating and Contextualising Trauma-Related Contemporary Choreography', which demonstrates the importance of contemporary dance as a means of telling stories of trauma, and the body as a conduit for healing the mind. In Christensen's and Forcier's chapters, the intersection of trauma and the potential of healing is situated for the reader to consider. From the perspective of this particular discourse, healing from a trauma is a slow process of transformation. Through this process, mindfulness is necessary in order to ensure that transformation through an artistic practice can provide true meaning.

Taking experience and transforming it into meaning is at the root of the text entitled *True Perception: A Path to Dharma Art,* by meditation master Chögyam Trungpa. An organic philosophy about the transcendence of suffering illuminates Trungpa's path of awareness centred on employing a 'unique training practice in how to believe as an inspired human being. That is what is meant by being an artist'.[3] The *dharma*, as Trungpa teaches the word, means 'norm' or 'truth', and *art* 'all the activities of our life',[4] including the creative expressions by which we communicate. Dharma functions as the path that one may traverse in order to uncover a truth about one's self. The art is our entire being in expression – our light upon this path. Further, dharma art amounts to a type of material thinking formed from an awakened mind. 'It is an attitude of directness and unselfconsciousness in one's creative work'.[5] The artist must focus to go beyond the treacherous terrain found in the human experience. In weaving meditation with creative expression, a practice rooted in understanding the capacities of *being* and *doing*, allows for thinking to move from *here* to *there*.

The practice of dharma art entails a perpetually growing process in appreciation of the surroundings in life.[6] Agency through dharma art begins with the identification of *dukkha* in our lives.[7] *Dukkha*, or suffering, in a broad and encompassing definition includes such emotions as pain, dissatisfaction, anguish, loneliness, stress, anxiety, illness, and so forth. The Four Noble Truths in Buddhism frame the understanding of suffering: the existence of suffering, the causes of suffering, the cessation of the causes of suffering, and the path that leads to the cessation of the causes of suffering. Through these Four Noble Truths, one may learn the practice of embracing suffering through the mind

3 Chögyam Trungpa, *True Perception: The Path of Dharma Art* (Boston: Shambhala, 2008), 10.
4 Ibid., xiii.
5 Ibid., 1.
6 Ibid., 27.
7 Ibid., 21.

and body.[8] The practice of dharma art involves learning and teaching one's self about *being* with our humanness. Forcier's investigation into choreography as a lens for examining trauma through dance bears similarity to Trungpa's thinking as well. Dance not only functions as a method of storytelling, but also as a way of becoming closer to our bodies – to the thinking that our bodies communicate. The important aspect to the practice of dharma art lies in the ability it offers to craft a deeper relationship with our humanness – while shaping a creative rendering of that inquiry.

Being human and *being* with illness create a perplexing relationship, with illness unique to each individual. In 1978, a manuscript entitled *Illness as Metaphor* by Susan Sontag circulated and quickly became a hallmark in illness discourse. In it, Sontag reaches the depths of personal experience to share the difficult subject of the self as a form of exhibition. Sontag states:

> Illness is the night-side of life, a more onerous citizenship. Everyone who is born holds dual citizenship, in the kingdom of the well and in the kingdom of the sick.[9]

Sontag impresses upon the reader an unshakable perspective of what it means to be human – possessing citizenship. Her distinction of the 'dual citizenship' constructs a specific concept of place – 'kingdom' – that holds the terms of life: health and illness.[10] Though Sontag's thinking presents a sobering perspective on the mortality of being human, in my opinion it does not suffice to simply construct huge containers for illness experience. Rather, a deeply engaged sense of self is needed, combining the relationship one has with illness and the path one traverses toward empowerment and healing.

The negative connotations of language frustrated Sontag's experience with illness. For example, she mentions the metaphor of *war*, classic to the canon of illness metaphors, whose complexity lies in its reference to violence with the objective of only one victor. She therefore suggests to remove metaphors that wrap war and the 'war-makers' into illness experience from our discourse.[11] Sontag states,

> War-making is one of the few activities that people are not supposed to view 'realistically'; that is, with an eye to expense and practical outcome.

8 Gill Farrer-Halls, *The Illustrated Encyclopedia of Buddhist Wisdom* (Old Alresford: Godsfield Press, 2001), 14–15.

9 Sontag, *Illness as Metaphor*, 3.

10 Ibid., 20.

11 Ibid., 94–95.

> In all-out war, expenditure is all-out, unprudent – war being defined as an emergency in which no sacrifice is excessive.[12]

Sontag claims that the war metaphor in illness discourse suggests a mark of limitless destruction. In illness, loss and despair carve out the terrain, and in order to fend off causalities, medicine must engage in an effort of sacrificial force, which directly relates to medical procedures involving chemotherapy, experimental procedures and radiation in the treatment of cancers. In order to eradicate cancer, these forms of treatment exert a force that deteriorates the body. With my illness, the experience involved two intense rounds of chemotherapy that shut my system down from producing cells for 3 weeks. During that time, my lungs became infected with an acute fungus. The life-threatening situation with the fungal infection spurred an effort to attempt an experimental white-blood cell transfusion, which had not been approved. If my body had rejected the white-blood cell transfusion, I would have died. Working with the medical staff and physicians, I noticed a recurring theme; the language used to communicate the circumstances to me abounded with metaphors that pivot the idea of triumph with that of failure. In other words, metaphors used in situations such as mine possess a win/lose scenario. Words such as *battle, fight, struggle* create a 50/50 ratio. Sontag refutes the characterisation and defeatist tone present in language that refers to war to categorise illness experience.

Sontag's argumentative position challenges established metaphors in medical discourse and calls to action. This action starts with an interrogation of these and their ability to create otherness: as Sontag remarks 'The metaphor implements the way particularly dreaded diseases are envisaged as an alien 'other' as enemies are in modern war'.[13] Her claim situates a fascinating problem with war metaphors. Specifically, the problem arises immediately with the diagnosis of an illness. As the patient occupies the position of otherness, he/she becomes the illness. For Sontag, the materiality of assigning metaphor to illness (whether negative or positive) experience engenders a reduction of the experience and does not benefit the patient.

Sontag calls for the dismissal of illness metaphors charged with negative connotation and propagate discouragement, silence and/or shame in the mind of the patient. From an empathetic point-of-view, my experience was imbued with metaphors that embodied negative ideologies and imagery.

12 Ibid., 99.

13 Ibid.

Such language projected a thinking engrained in concepts of *war, battle, violence, confrontation, alienation,* and failed to define – or contextualise – my experience. The established metaphors misinterpreted my reality with illness.

Language begets perception; for Sontag, established metaphors have socially constructed an authoritative influence on illness experience. Sontag deepens her views on metaphor by claiming the injustice of the creative and imaginary. As suggested, the value and reasoning of the arts, such as poetry, that attempt to 'aestheticize the disease', Sontag believes, entails an unimaginable task.[14] Sontag's position reads as a rejection of a process aimed to empower the individual that is ill. In this vein of thinking, the concept of aestheticising disease as a mystifier creates a delusion of reality. According to Sontag, 'the most truthful way of regarding illness – and the healthiest way of being ill – is one most purified of, most resistant to metaphoric thinking'.[15] Her assertion proposes the patient relinquish the will to envision their illness experience in terms of a metaphor, which to my mind foregoes the opportunity to re-contextualise illness experience. I find Sontag's claims devalue the power to reframe and claim illness experience.

The process of recontextualization – or reframing – illness experience offers an opportunity. The individual has the power to harness this opportunity as agency. For example, in re-contextualising illness experience, the individual may have recourse to meditation, a central aspect to the arts-based research methodology. Specifically, the work that yields creative renderings must function to unearth metaphorical language that encourages the strength of mind to transcend or transform suffering. Mark Epstein exemplifies this idea in his essay 'Sip My Ocean', where he explains the process of meditation in art practice – the connection of the heart and mind suynchronised with creative production. Epstein claims,

> Buddhism offers something more than an analytical breakdown of objective reality. It has a process, conveyed through meditation, that affirms something essential about the making, and experiencing, of art.[16]

Drawing from Epstein's thinking, I find that dharma art practice enables the mind and heart to work in harmony. To aestheticise illness makes meaning

14 Ibid.

15 Ibid., 3.

16 Mark Epstein, 'Sip My Ocean', in *Buddha Mind in Contemporary Art*, ed. Jacquelynn Baas and Mary Jane Jacob (Berkeley: University of California Press, 2004), 30.

while claiming a voice. The process provides opportunity to locate one's place along the path of the experience; therefore, a map of the self can be shaped.

Metaphors act as maps. These maps illuminate ways of *seeing* illness – they construct the experience and move thinking from *here* to *there*. Positive metaphors in illness discourse allow the production and communication of complex concepts. In his article 'A Conceptual Structure of Visual Metaphor', Daniel Serig states, 'Perception flows from sensory experience and includes observation, classification, and conceptual thinking. The structure of metaphoric thinking is described as conceptual blending'.[17] Conceptual blending results from making meaning through the interaction of intention and emotions within a particular framework – a concept similar to dharma art practice. In this light Serig states,

> If the cognitive view of metaphor relies on the blending of concepts, and concepts derive from the play of the affective with the intellectual, then this appears to set art practice as an arena for the study of metaphor.[18]

Serig connects to the practice of dharma wherein the meditation and the act of making material function as the play between the affective and intellectual. The metaphor surfaces organically through the process of meditation, creative production and analysis. Therefore, to claim illness experience through a process of meaning-making – or aestheticizing illness – empowers the individual and produces experiential knowledge.

Aestheticising disease brings forth a dialogue that moves outside of conventional discourses occupied by the medical and academic institutes. Aestheticism performs a materiality in illness, a power by the maker that generates a performativity of the subject. True to this thinking, video and digital photography involve dynamic and rich art practices that embody the contemporary technology of time-based media that I find necessary to express myself. Similar to this position, the work of Danielle Schaub in 'Reading Myself and Worlds: Coping Strategies in the Face of Cumulative Trauma' examines closely personal childhood trauma through the practice of bibliotherapy, phototherapy and scriptotherapy.[19] Performing an interdisciplinary practice of trauma

17 Daniel Serig, 'A Conceptual Structure of Visual Metaphor', *Studies in Art Education* 47.3 (2006): 229.

18 Ibid., 230.

19 Danielle Schaub, 'Reading Myself and Worlds: Coping Strategies in the Face of Cumulative Trauma', *What Happened? Re-Presenting Traumas, Uncovering Recoveries*, edited by Elspeth McInnes and Danielle Schaub (Leiden: Brill, 2018), 158–186.

recollection and reframing, Schaub investigates the power of unconscious influence in creative retelling. In such fashion of scholarship, a creative medium's potential to examine theoretical frameworks can achieve new knowledge in the field of trauma as well as healing for the author.

Margaret Morse's essay 'Video Installation Art: The Body, the Image, and the Space-In-Between' examines the theoretical functionality of the image and image-production. Morse argues that people in general 'lack the vocabulary for kinaesthetic "insights", for learning at the level of the body ego and its orientation in space'.[20] In other words, Morse finds a difficult obstacle in building discourse about the image as a moving 'insight' into the characteristics of the body in given spaces. I argue that the image serves as an experience that under a certain context centres on the study of the body. In other words, central to understanding illness lies the notion that the body is where human culture begins and ends. Thus the image works as the extension of the body: an extension of the mind's creativity, and the hand's execution of the exposure trigger that assists in building the vocabulary in engaging theoretical concepts.

The concept of video as a fine art is informed by the practice of an image-culture documenting lived experiences as a form of contemporary communication. Not only does the practice of video consider the technology of image-capture and image processing, but it also takes into account the cultural reflection or mirroring that it performs on the subject. According to Morse, 'The designation video installation is not an accurate guide to what is undoubtedly the most complex art form in contemporary culture'.[21] The reason behind this thinking rests with the concept of the *space-in-between*. More specifically, a painting that hangs in a space can be freed of the placement, therefore, becoming exchangeable or changing into a commodity. In contrast, a video installation suggests an art 'ephemeral and never to be utterly severed from the subject, time and place of its enunciation'.[22] To that extent, the art exists when installed – with space-in-between – so that individual bodies can engage the work physically, intellectually and emotionally. The spatial relationship of an artwork offers a path for the audience to negotiate when reading the work as a text.

In my research, the image encompasses a *reflection* of my illness experience. My use of the word *reflection* relies on Rebecca Garden's 2010 essay, 'Telling

20 Margaret Morse, 'Video Installation Art: The Body, the Image, and the Space-In-Between', in *Illuminating Video: An Essential Guide To Video Art*, ed. Doug Hall and Sally Jo Fifer (New York: Aperture/Bay Area Video Coalition, 2005), 153.

21 Ibid., 154.

22 Ibid.

Stories about Illness and Disability: The Limits and Lessons of Narrative', where she defines it as a careful exploration into the shaping of literary categories such as 'recovery narratives' and 'caregivers'.[23] As Garden points out, individuals stricken with illness or disability look toward opportunities to see a reflection of their experience, or themselves, in culture. Culture, represented in an artistic form such as video, acts as a mirror in which community is established and grown from for the purposes of a sustained mission. In my thinking, the moving image as reflection of illness is a place where human culture can be measured with a beginning and an end because it constitutes a study of the body.

In thinking about the theoretical positions of Morse and Sontag, I am moved to find a creative outlet to open up the dialogue about the representation of the body and the occupation of metaphor in illness. Bill Viola, a recipient of 9 honorary degrees (Doctor of Fine Art), and over 40 selected solo exhibitions, has held captive the imagination and creative organization around many complex ideas.

Viola began his career with video as an intricate investigator of the medium's potential. His studies were geared toward the ways video and sound can be formed to function as an augmented reality. Since the 1990's, Viola's work has become more concentrated on profound ideas around birth, life, illness, and death. These areas of study are not only critical to the discussion laid out in this chapter, but also quite inspiring when pondering over these ideas within Viola's work. His research into these areas began with the passing of his mother in 1991. During this traumatic experience, Viola used his art practice as therapy 'to control the world that was around him'.[24] He recorded his mother as she lay comatose from a brain aneurysm. The project resulted in *The Passing* (1991), which centres on life and death. Viola created a map to situate the space of human experience, thus transforming it into a significant place in one's personal history. To ground this concept, I turned to Yi-Fu Tuan's 1977 book, *Space and Place: The Perspective of Experience*, which gives a theoretical framework to explain how spaces evolve into places through human experience. Tuan's theory, based on the study of human constructed geographies, suggests that human experience is initially an experience of space. Most importantly, Tuan's theory stresses the

23 Rebecca Garden, 'Telling Stories about Illness and Disability: The Limits and Lessons of Narrative', *Perspectives in Biology and Medicine* 53.1 (2010): 121.

24 *Bill Viola: The Eye of the Heart*. Directed by Mark Kidel. Performed by Bill Viola. 2005: 25:31-26:45.

reoccurrence of experience, or the prolonging of an experience itself. His theoretical framework thus transforms the notion of a space into an identifiable place in personal history.

Tuan's theory applies to Viola's *The Passing,* which as mentioned before documents a traumatic and profound life experience – the passing of his mother. In working creatively with this life experience, the process of documenting and turning the footage of his mother's slow death into visual examination provides an identification of Viola's personal space in this experience, and offers an opportunity to claim it as a significant place in his personal history. This transformation into place results from revisiting locations – geographically speaking – through the reflexive nature of video.

Rooted in my research, the inquiry into the transformation of space into place can theoretically apply to illness experience. Illness is a space initially foreign to the individual; therefore, how can a patient claim the experience – turning space into place? For example, I lacked the knowledge or experience to encounter a space such as illness. Over time, I learned the idiosyncratic nature of being ill. In my research I attempt to revisit my illness experience (the space) through meditation and art-making in order to identify and claim the places of my illness experience. In doing so, I suggest that one can move these *spaces* of experience toward *places* in one's personal history. These *places* become significant landmarks in our memory, and thus become a part of our personal identity, forming experiential knowledge.

To understand my theoretical claim, I would like to examine Tuan's theory further. First, Tuan states that space and place are tenets that share the common distinction of area. Yet humans recognize place as a form of security, and space as an unstructured form. As Tuan states, 'we are attached to the one and long for the other'.[25] The optimum goal is to locate the experiences of illness as a place. The process validates specific aspects/scenarios/moments of the illness as meaningful and deeply transforming.

If one wants to map out their life on a piece of paper, one may use a long horizontal line to express the scope of their life. On that line, one can place hash marks to indicate specific moments in time deemed impactful. For example, in magnifying aspects of my own life, I would consider illness to occupy a hash mark on my life's timeline. Further, significance can be placed on that particular moment in time with illness understood as space. In studying the space of my illness, I use meditation and the production of creative renderings

25 Yi-Fu Tuan, *Space and Place: The Perspective of Experience* (Minneapolis: University of Minnesota Press, 1977), 3.

to support the distinctive process of reflection and transformation – memory into creative renderings, or *spaces* into *places*.

In drawing Tuan's theory into the context of this research, I believe that place and the human experience with illness can be achieved by intellectual mapping. I suggest that in recalling illness experience and situating it into an artistic context, as Viola in his work, the artist takes a *space* of experience and gives it a significant *place* in personal history. Through creative rendering, the process of intellectual mapping provides a way to engage the matters of trauma, and an opportunity to give meaning to such experiences.

The Passing would not be the last project of Viola's that embodies the theory of transforming space into place. Investigations of birth, life, illness and death evolved further with his 1992 work, *Heaven and Earth*. Designed as a dynamic dual single-channel video installation, Viola situated two monitors vertically adjacent to each other. The first monitor – or bottom monitor – exists as a looping video track of Viola's newborn second child's face. The point of interest in this video rests on the eyes of the child as he witnesses the first moments of light. The second monitor – or top monitor – exists as a looping video track of Viola's mother during the last moments of her life. Viola notes that the monitors for both videos have a glass face that allows for a reflection of the images. With these two glass monitors facing each other in a vertical format – conceptually suggesting the position of Heaven and Earth – the reflection of his mother can be seen in the first moments of his son's eyes as they open.

In considering the meticulousness of Viola's work, I find a distinct connection between the theoretical underpinnings of Viola's creative practice and Susan Sontag's thinking. When considering Viola's work, I refer directly to Sontag's writing in *At the Same Time: Essays and Speeches*. Here, Sontag states,

> However much art may seem to be a matter of surface and reception by the senses, it has generally been accorded an honorary citizenship in the domain of 'inner' (as opposed to outer) beauty ... beauty is deep, not superficial; hidden, sometimes, rather than obvious; consoling, not troubling; indestructible, as in art, rather than ephemeral, as in nature. Beauty, the stipulatively uplifting kind, perdures.[26]

Sontag intimates that art possesses a valid accessibility to uncover the interiority of the subject. Beauty within the work of challenging and complex art is not

26 Susan Sontag, 'At the Same Time ... (The Novelist and Moral Reasoning)', *English Studies in Africa* 48.1 (2005): 4.

defined by the attributes on the surface, witnessed or expressed. Conversely, beauty is found in the meditative focus on subject and the unrestrained, unrelenting pursuit to disclose its context to others.

In my opinion, when Sontag refers to the act of aestheticising disease as unimaginable, I believe her concern lies in the way glamorised or sensationalised images influence our society. In other words, she is concerned by ways of representing the reality of illness and how images can dilute or even falsify the complexities of being ill. Her concern has led Viola's work to shine as foundational to the study of video art and illness narratives.

Viola pursued the ideas of birth, life, illness and death even further with another project produced in 1992, *Nantes Triptych*, in which he presents a three-way split screen containing the images of a woman giving birth, a fully clothed man floating limply beneath the surface of a pool of water, and Viola's mother lying on her deathbed. Viola states,

> I guess I felt these are the great universal experiences. They happen to be the most private personal experiences, and the camera is the embodiment of the invasion of privacy which is where the tension comes in … [b]ut, I also look at the camera as an open eye. Part of spiritual practice and spiritual training is to re-teach yourself how to see. So, [the brain] isn't making all the judgments on what you are seeing, but you are experiencing the world, and the image, in the pure form, in the open form.[27]

For Viola, this tension – the idea of the camera – brings a level of ambiguous pressure to viewing his work. He understands the role of the camera as much more organic and connected to his own place of spirituality.

One of the more significant pieces, *The Crossing* (1996), resonates deeply with the work that I have embarked upon. In this video, Viola plays with the complex notion of a man on fire. He explores through slow-motion – or the over-cranking of his camera – the movements of fire, the physical engagement of the man and the consuming force of the fire at centre screen, all taking place in this vast area of black nothingness. The connection I share with Viola's work centres on the study of the individual's interiority. For me, the interior factor consists in my illness experience. In setting the figure of the human on fire, or drenching the figure with water, by using an over-cranked camera mechanism (slow motion) to film the subject, the maker causes the audience to consider dramatically the action upon the human. The action is the inner self – a

27 *Bill Viola: The Eye of the Heart*, 30:17- 31:40.

burning desire, or subconscious conflict – performed through exterior representations. Like models of this concept were on display at the Getty Centre during his 2003 exhibition entitled *The Passions: Bill Viola*. This series of work explores similar ideas of birth, life, illness and death through recorded physical performances that express suffering. The ideas of birth, life, illness and death also play their role in pieces such as *Man of Sorrows* (2001), *Four Hands* (2001), *Surrender* (2001), and *Quintet and Astonished* (2000).

Contemporary artist Marie France Forcier's work in choreographed dance, specifically her 2015 presentation, *Scars are All the Rage,* bears similarities with Viola's work.[28] Forcier's trauma-related art is expressed through choreographed movements situated in a form of realism. Viola uses video as a tool to capture the essence of the performance and to work through the stresses of a post-traumatic existence. Forcier uses live performance as the tool, and through that channel, the artistic and theoretical impact produces a different result for an audience.

In the work of Viola I find the bridging of video art, performance and installation with important dialogues around the construction of conceptual metaphor. My interest in visual imagery as a signifier parallels the ways Bill Viola approaches the process of creating imagery. In his book, *Reasons for Knocking at an Empty House*, Viola writes,

> My interest in the various image systems of the cultures of the world involves a search for the image that is not an image. This is why I am not interested in 'realistic' rendering. Sacred art seems very close because of its symbolic nature. Its intrinsic interwoven meaning on other planes makes it more 'conceptual'. I am interested not so much in the image whose source lies in the phenomenal world, but rather the image as artefact, or result, or imprint, or even wholly determined by some inner realization. It is the image of that inner state and as such must be considered completely accurate and realistic.[29]

The very notion that Viola expresses about the symbolic nature of sacred art speaks to the direction that I anticipate my creative renderings to move toward. My work is not so much made for galleries or art houses, but rather, for

28 Marie France Forcier, 'Creating and Contextualising Trauma-Related Contemporary Choreography', in this volume.

29 Bill Viola, *Reasons for Knocking at an Empty House: Writings 1973–1994*, ed. Jean-Christoph Ammann, and Robert Violette (London: Anthony D'Offay Gallery, 1995), 85.

the mind of the individuals who encounter the work as a deeper process of creative rendering in illness narrative, and process-oriented healing.

With respect to creative renderings and process-oriented healing, M. Candace Christensen's work engages the public with an outlet for creating photographs in order to empower personal voice in matters of trauma. Specifically, her research on gender-based violence calls upon the engagement of members to use photography as a method of communicating concerns about a topic within their own community. Through this process, we can understand in another way Viola's thinking of the image as an artefact that represents a realization of the inner self within an exterior condition. The photograph, as a communicator, offers ways for others to see the maker as a being in a situation. This use of community not only strengthens ties within a public, but it also reinforces the importance of art-based research and communication as a means of understanding. Christensen's work, like mine, builds upon the dialogue in trauma-related issues with a public for the sake of social change.

My illness experience as a subject focuses on the premise that such experience becomes a way of *being* and a way of *seeing*. In the construction of video and photography as a method of creative explorations, I examine simultaneity of diagnosis, treatment and recovery during my creative process through my execution of *time, place* and *space* within the image. The *time* factor encompasses the span of experience from the onset of diagnosis to present day – illness through post-illness. In deepening this duality, the occupation of *place* emerges. I consider my body as a blank canvas where the convergence between normal and abnormal cells occurred. Finally, *space* is the centre of time and place that is cross-wired to form a new meaning of the illness experience. Another way of considering this process is to think of the creative process weaving a meditative concentration, while simultaneously constructing an image.

The physical and meditative performance of my creative research process reinforces a persistent movement to continually re-examine the body as a source of knowledge. The claim is further explored in Richard Shusterman's essay 'Thinking Through the Body, Educating for the Humanities: A Plea for Somaesthetics' where he makes a call for the recommitment to the study of the body. He states,

> The body is an essential and valuable dimension of our humanity … it should be recognized as a crucial topic of humanistic study and experiential learning.[30]

30 Richard Shusterman, 'Thinking Through the Body, Educating for the Humanities: A Plea for Somaesthetics', *The Journal of Aesthetic Education* 40.1 (2006): 1.

Shusterman's claim highlights the body as important material for examination, and calls for contemporary intensive study into the body as a way for gaining an understanding and methodology of articulation. His thinking can be further understood through the work of Elwin Susan John in 'I Used To Be Human Once: Trauma and Reconfigurations of the Body in Chemical Disasters', in this volume. John offers another example of how the body is a vital element for understanding our humanness in a post-traumatic existence. Whether the residue from a traumatic experience can be visibly located on the body, or resides primarily in the memory, the narratives that emerge from trauma studies offer a dynamic source of deep learning about our humanness. What is necessary for maintaining the value of this area of research lies in how the narrative is communicated to an audience, which explains the vital power of video and photography. As an artistic artefact the image possesses a universal language that transcends borders, becoming the bridge figure of all human language.

For an image-oriented art to be the staple by which I examine my illness experience and construct a new metaphor, I must unpack an array of formal elements for method justification. I would consider image art as a presence of focus – concentrated on meditation and image-making. The image represents my body and mind during illness experience. To call Shusterman back into the conversation, the role of 'sensory-aesthetic appreciation' allows my body to operate as a central figure of translation; it is the locus of experiential knowledge. Though this counters Sontag's stance of the aestheticisation of illness, my body serves as the central fuse for the materiality that informs the framework of my research. Further, Shusterman states that the body is 'a sensing, sentient soma' that represents a duality of status, 'object and subject'.[31] Being a matter of object, my body is the source *from which* and *through which* the research directly becomes conscious. As I examine my body through a meditative practice, and through art-making, a record of performance emerges, becoming my window in space.

Moving deeper into the reasoning for these preferred methods I examine Viola's essay, 'Sight Unseen: Enlightened Squirrels and Fatal Experiments' from his book *Reasons for Knocking at an Empty House*. Viola writes,

> We usually don't think of the idea that knowledge exists between each and every person, waiting to be released by some trigger mechanism, rather than just *out there* somewhere.[32]

31 Ibid.,4.

32 Viola, *Reasons for Knocking*, 92.

I believe that to connect people with knowledge happens through sight – or the see-able. Whether in photography, video, or in the real time and space, the visual organizes a meaning. Viola beautifully pens the phrase '[v]ision as transmission'.[33] Here, I find Viola to mean knowledge is most effectively exchanged in what and how information and ideas are expressed and seen – consumed and understood.

Viola's philosophical and theoretical concepts contrast what Sontag challenges as a wrong approach to illness experience, namely aestheticizing for the purposes of understanding. I find art an extremely important agent in realizing my illness experience. If I am able to place my experience into a context through artistic renderings, then I have worked toward containing my illness experience in a way that works for me. It is a delicate process to think how art can issue metaphor to my illness experience. From the position of artist and survivor, I assume the responsibility of contributing to my communities' new ways of understanding.

There are many challenges to being ill. Beyond the physical, mental and emotional toll that one experiences, one's way of living is put into question. I am currently engaged with ways of metaphorising my illness experience. In this, I find Arthur W. Frank's illuminating text *At the Will of the Body: Reflections on Illness* (2002) useful. Frank remarks:

> Illness takes away parts of your life, but in doing so it gives you the opportunity to choose the life you will lead, as opposed to living out the one you have simply accumulated over the years.[34]

This choice of life as outlined by Frank – the way in which to experience illness – requires a significant consideration of the language selected to name, locate and contextualize the body and the illness as *subject* – into a *position*. In the case of my illness, the inversion of chromosome 16 positioned Acute Myeloid Leukaemia into my body. The metaphor *illness is like a window* captures a complex and meaningful attempt at understanding my illness experience. The *window* provides a theoretical opportunity to suggest illness as a way of seeing the experience differently. The subtext of this metaphor suggests a philosophical position of shifting illness experience from pain and misery toward opportunity.

---

33 Ibid., 93.

34 Arthur W. Frank, *At the Will of the Body: Reflections on Illness* (Boston: Houghton Mifflin, 1991), 1.

Frank's perception of illness experience offers an insight toward locating one's self within illness discourse. Frank writes, 'To talk about illness you must go elsewhere'.[35] The work carried out for this project simply does that, goes elsewhere. The analysis and contextualization engage the matter of location – or the *elsewhere* – as a creative place for shaping expressive renderings for understanding illness experience.

As a foundational device for society to contain and realise the human condition, language helps form a cultural understanding. Working from prescribed established illness metaphors, Sontag calls for the concept of illness to become 'de-mythicize[d]'[36] – referring to the idea of separating concepts that present a false reality of illness experience to society. People experiencing illness may choose to only understand their condition through medical language, and nothing else. Though some patients concur with Sontag on this notion, I believe there exists a demand for other ways – a different language – to situate a contextual understanding of illness experience. I believe that not having language accessible to understanding the situations of illness experience is problematic to the individual and the totality of the experience. Resources that allow for a better understanding of illness experience – especially through the lens of others who have experienced illness (Sontag, Cousins, Frank, Prosser, Serenati, etc.) – contribute to the opportunity for a productive dialogue in community-building.

Metaphors matter greatly because they act as visualising agents of an idea for others to connect and understand certain situations. Jon Prosser discusses the complexities of mediating illness experience through visual imagery in his essay 'Visual Mediation of Critical Illness'. Complexities take form 'at the intersection' where the 'physical, psychological and the social'[37] converge to create images that allow for an understanding of illness experience. With this intersection in mind, the organisation of a mental, physical and emotional context derived from the experience can directly influence the types of metaphors assigned to illness. The metaphors that assume a bio-militarist approach have a detrimental impact. Bio-militarism infused metaphors act as an invisible ceiling – a limitation – upon the patient. This type of organisation becomes the architecture of the experience, or the effect of negative mind building. The invisible ceiling becomes a language-based disadvantage that specifically weakens the mental, physical, emotional and spiritual energy

35 Ibid., 15.

36 Sontag, *Illness as Metaphor*, 7.

37 Jon Prosser, 'Visual Mediation of Critical Illness: An Autobiographical Account of Nearly Dying and Nearly Living', *Visual Studies* 22.2 (2007): 185.

of the ill. By convoluting the mindset with negative or bio-militarism metaphors, an unnecessary idea of how illness will be experienced forms within the patient.

To move beyond established illness metaphors, there must exist material that works to shift the conventional paradigm. Prosser claims that visual imagery is a part of that converging intersection. Visual imagery offers a way of conceptualising – and/or mediating – the illness experience by drawing upon determined aesthetic precepts to constitute meaning.[38] In constructing visual content, metaphors operate as a substantial device to situate complex thinking. More specifically, the metaphor functions as a bridge. This bridge provides the access for individuals who may not have experienced illness directly to associate a particular conceptual understanding.

Illness experience is traumatic to an individual and can have a significant impact on their perception of life. Held closely by that trauma, illness experience possesses a theoretical terrain that offers countless possibilities for metaphorical construction or assignment. For me, using photography and video affords me the freedom to create. Andrea Duncan's article 'Humanscape: Image-Metaphor-Narrative: A Collaboration in Hemato-Oncology' examines how to establish an understanding of the images' potential to represent illness experience metaphorically. The metaphoric narratives, or cross-wirings as she calls them, 'connect various phenomena of perceptual experience'[39] and in doing so create a recognition and connection to the experience.

Duncan's perspective on metaphor construction through image-arts is boundless with the technological abilities of digital image processing. The work of digital applications to manipulate, shift, change and reform image 'creates an analogous language structure'[40] with which, she claims, can synthetically place the component parts of these cross-wirings together and create a seamless metaphoric narrative whole. Duncan's theoretical position centres on language constructed in clinical and culturally related spaces. In expanding upon this complexity, the exterior cross-wiring initiates a cross-wiring of the interior. More specifically, the exterior cross-wiring is the experience of the audience, while the interior cross-wiring is the experience of the artist. The artist becomes informed by the interaction of the audience with the work.

38 Ibid.

39 Andrea Duncan, 'Humanscape: Imagemetaphor-Narrative: A Collaboration In Hemato-Oncology', *Leonardo* 37.4 (2004): 278.

40 Ibid., 279.

My research and art practice dwell upon cross-wiring, or intersubjectivity. I am interested in how cross-wiring can be displayed or expressed through the process of the autobiographical examination of illness experience. From my working space, to cross-wire means to use multiple mediums to represent an idea or a series of interrelated ideas. My project performs a cross-wiring of photography, video, poetry, sound, and mixed-media to articulate my illness experience as reflected upon by intense meditative sessions. Through this process, I identify wires that cross in such a way as to encourage the emergence of a metaphorical sign.

The objective of cross-wiring is to find the ways in which the work functions at a rigorous and cohesive level of investigation (narrative and artefact(s)), and operates as a bridge for others to access its potential meaning(s). To that extent, my use of images (moving and still), poetry, sound, mixed-media, etc., offer lenses that represent and communicate my illness experience. To add to this cross-wiring approach, I immerse myself in meditation through which to produce a performance – one that encompasses a meditation and art making process – centred on addressing my illness experience, transforming it into a healing process and work of art.

My arts-based research project has engaged in a year-long performance with dharma art. I investigated the potential of awareness meditation and material-making through the reflection of illness experience. The framework for this research consisted of a daily 20-minute meditation session in a nearby meadow. During the meditations, a concentration on posture and breath invited a relaxed mind and a reflection on my illness. I placed a camera and recorded my practice. After a year of research, I spent 6-months reviewing, analysing, and writing about the material in order to contextualise the matters that emerged during this practice.

One of my most significant materials produced was the work *Misconceptions* – a poetic narrative juxtaposed with a window hanging in the forest. Critical to the piece is the use of the opening two lines that repeat from verse to verse: 'There are misconceptions about illness … to speak of it is to go elsewhere'.[41] For me, the two lines perform a choreographed reflection on illness as movement – a suggestive shift. The lines function as a philosophical place along the path of *seeing* and *being* with illness.

In the first verse, I present a setting that distinguishes the importance of *place*. *Place*, for the purposes of this piece, articulates mental and spiritual presence. 'The forest remains',[42] alludes to the concept of environment beholding

41 *Misconceptions*, dir. Nicholas Quin Serenati Saint Augustine, FL: RFJH Films, 2012, DVD.

42 Ibid.

individual experience. The environment – that forest – is 'irreducible'.[43] *Place* employs a juxtaposition of physical bodies that occupy space: nature and environment, illness and my body.

The 'window' in *Misconceptions* serves as a metaphorical mediator between illness and life after illness. For example, the line 'In the distance – a way of seeing'[44] refers to the mediator as an object of transformation. The window questions the ways of *being* and *seeing* illness experience. To further this point, the window is a physical function within the world – the state of *being* – swaying from side to side. The window is aesthetically plotted into *place*, magnifying the relationship – whether ambiguous or specific – of my body amidst the treacherous terrain of illness. The window as a way of *seeing* performs an embodiment of clarity. The window is fraught with residue and sections of broken glass, weathered and deteriorating – a preoccupation with suffering. The idea that the window is burdened by the lack of clarity throws light on my experience with illness as an opportunity rather than an otherness. *How* we see has a great deal to do with *how* we understand.

As in the practice of dharma art, the work of re-contextualising illness is intended to bridge the self with inner strength and understanding, thus, arriving at some form of healing. Bruce Moon addresses the importance of experimentation and self-discovery during art therapy in his seminal text *The Role of Metaphor in Art Therapy*. Vital to Moon's theoretical position are the creative renderings of his patients. For Moon, the patient must be aware that they are in power of their own healing. The process of creative production amounts to translating experience metaphorically. In that respect, the creator authors the metaphorical understanding of the experience.[45] For Moon, visual metaphors are attempts by artists to overtly or covertly provide description or definition of him or herself derived from experience.

Illness can unravel and chaotically deconstruct an individual's life. In my case, I am the ill and the therapist, the audience are my receivers, and my renderings are the source of the message. The process of dharma art embodies experiential thinking and provides agency that resonates a communicative power to heal. In reframing illness experience, a theoretical shift of moving from *here* to *there* occurs – new knowledge. My illness is a window – and I am healing.

---

43 Ibid.

44 Ibid.

45 Bruce L. Moon, *The Role of Metaphor in Art Therapy: Theory, Method, and Experience* (Springfield, IL: Charles C. Thomas, 2007), 3.

FIGURE 13.2 *Misconceptions* © 2012.
COURTESY OF NICHOLAS QUIN SERENATI.

Misconceptions

There are misconceptions about illness.
To speak of it is to go elsewhere ...
This forest remains,
Remarkably quiet.
Irreducible.
It stands awake.
Between the pillars of the live oaks,
Through the dense pockets of sugar pines,
Space for mindfulness.
Thoughts traced by the vulnerability of confusion,
Coloured by harmony – peace.
To move is to engage with intention.
These passages laid by a walking meditation – an engagement with illness.

There are misconceptions about illness.
To speak of it is to go elsewhere ...
Early morning sun shimmers across this landscape,
Air moistened by the dawn's rainfall.
Dew rolls down the bended back of grass tips.

I – walk – by.
Above treetops – sky – marbleized by shades of autumn; orange and pearl-gray.
The shifting sky calls for the presence of
Wind – it bellows,
Carrying the voices of the forgotten.
Their whispers graze my skin like a gentle feather.
Cessation.
In the distance, a way of being.
I – walk – through.
A serene meadow padded with ankle-high Bahia grass.
Centred, a hassock made from pine needles and oak branches.
Light stretches past the waving leaves.
I stand witness.
Eyes refocus.
In the distance – a way of seeing.
A window hangs.
I – walk – toward.

There are misconceptions about illness.
To speak of it is to go elsewhere …
There – a way of being.
Engraved on the skin of a live oak, I once wrote,
'Much like this window, illness'.
A journey that starts nowhere from here,
One must – be – in the moments of
Perfect disease – perfect health.
This window – weathered.
This path – travelled.
Textures – splintering wood – decaying form
Fractured experience – defines knowledge.
Contact.
Home are the woodlands that hold the memory.
Location of here and there; this window the mediator.
There – a self lost in translation.
Here – a place that I am present.
This window hangs elegantly – a way of being.

There are misconceptions about illness.
To speak of it is to go elsewhere …

Here – a way of seeing.
Glass broken
Clarity seeps in – only where it's empty.
Shards of glass – pieces of me – cover the ground.
My steps are careful when I walk over me.
Illness is an opportunity.
One that does not blend itself easily into the folds of our lives.
This window – a way of seeing.
Glass distorted
Residue clings – coarse to the touch
A personal history impressed upon the glass of sight.
To see through it is to see the other side,
To understand illness.
Changing poison into medicine
Awake – a way of seeing.

There are misconceptions about illness.
To speak of it is to go elsewhere …
To consider illness – what it is – might be what it is not.
Illness, like this window, a way of being, a way of seeing.
Never withdrawn
Suffering becomes transformative – becomes enlightenment.
This doorway, beside this window, is open.

Bibliography

Carter, Paul. *Material Thinking: The Theory and Practice of Creative Research*. Carlton, VIC: Melbourne University Press, 2004.

Dewey, John. *Art as Experience*. New York: Minton, Balch & Company, 1934.

Duncan, Andrea. 'Humanscape: Imagemetaphor-Narrative: A Collaboration in Hemato-Oncology'. *Leonardo* 37.4 (2004): 278–279.

Epstein, Mark. 'Sip My Ocean'. In *Buddha Mind in Contemporary Art*, edited by Jacquelynn Baas and Mary Jane Jacob, 29–35. Berkeley: University of California Press, 2004.

Farrer-Halls, Gill. *The Illustrated Encyclopedia of Buddhist Wisdom*. Old Alresford: Godsfield Press, 2001.

Frank, Arthur W. *At the Will of the Body: Reflections on Illness*. Boston: Houghton Mifflin, 1991.

Garden, Rebecca. 'Telling Stories about Illness and Disability: The Limits and Lessons of Narrative'. *Perspectives in Biology and Medicine* 53.1 (2010): 121–135.

Lakoff, George, and Mark Johnson. *Metaphors We Live By*. Chicago: University of Chicago Press, 1980.

Moon, Bruce L. *The Role of Metaphor in Art Therapy: Theory, Method, and Experience*. Springfield, IL: Charles C. Thomas, 2007.

Morse, Maragret. 'Video Installation Art: The Body, the Image, and the Space-In-Between'. In *Illuminating Video: An Essential Guide to Video Art*, edited by Doug Hall and Sally Jo Fifer, 153–167. 1st ed. New York: Aperture/Bay Area Video Coalition, 2005.

Prosser, Jon. 'Visual Mediation of Critical Illness: An Autobiographical Account of Nearly Dying and Nearly Living'. *Visual Studies* 22.2 (2007): 185–199.

Schaub, Danielle. 'Reading Myself and Worlds: Coping Strategies in the Face of Cumulative Trauma'. *What Happened? Re-presenting Traumas, Uncovering Recoveries: Processing Individual and Collective Traumas.* Eds. Elspeth McInnes and Danielle Schaub. Leiden: Brill, 2018, 158–186.

Serenati, Nicholas. 'The Reframing of Leukemia: Metaphor, Dharma Art and Illness experience'. PhD diss., Union Institute & University, 2014.

Serig, Daniel. 'A Conceptual Structure of Visual Metaphor'. *Studies in Art Education* 47.3 (2006): 229–247.

Shusterman, Richard. 'Thinking Through the Body, Educating for the Humanities: A Plea for Somaesthetics'. *The Journal of Aesthetic Education* 40, no. 1 (2006): 1–21.

Sontag, Susan. *Against Interpretation: And Other Essays*. New York: Dell Pub., 1966.

Sontag, Susan. 'At the Same Time ... (The Novelist and Moral Reasoning)'. *English Studies in Africa* 48.1 (2005): 5–17.

Sontag, Susan. *Illness as Metaphor*. New York: Farrar, Straus and Giroux, 1978.

Sontag, Susan. *Styles of Radical Will*. New York: Farrar, Straus and Giroux, 1969.

Suzuki, Shunryū. *Zen Mind, Beginner's Mind.* Edited by Trudy Dixon. New York: Walker/Weatherhill, 1970.

Trungpa, Chögyam. *True Perception: The Path of Dharma Art*. Boston: Shambhala, 2008.

Tuan, Yi-Fu. *Space and Place: The Perspective of Experience*. Minneapolis: University of Minnesota Press, 1977.

Viola, Bill. *Reasons for Knocking at an Empty House: Writings 1973–1994*. Edited by Jean-Christoph Ammann and Robert Violette. London: Anthony D'Offay Gallery, 1995.

Filmography

Bill Viola: The Eye of the Heart. Directed by Mark Kidel. Bristol: Calliope Media, 2005.

Heaven and Earth. Directed by Bill Viola. USA, 1992. Accessed 2016.

Misconceptions. Directed by Nicholas Quin Serenati. Saint Augustine, FL: RFJH Films, 2012. DVD.

Nantes Triptych. Directed by Bill Viola. http://www.billviola.com/ordering.htm.

The Crossing. Directed by Bill Viola. http://www.billviola.com/ordering.htm.

The Passing. Directed by Bill Viola. USA: RaroVideo, 1991. DVD.

The Passions: Bill Viola. Directed by Bill Viola. Getty Center, Los Angeles, 2003.

Exhibition Material: Man of Sorrows (2001), Four Hands (2001), Surrender (2001), and Quintet and Astonished (2000).

CHAPTER 14

Engaging Trauma Resulting from Sexual Violence through Autoethnography and Photovoice

M. Candace Christensen

Abstract

This chapter illustrates how I use an autoethnographic lens and photovoice research methods. These methods act as a tool to engage trauma I experienced resulting from sexual violence. Autoethnography methodology situates the researcher as both the investigator and subject of a given project. As the subject, the researcher reflects on and documents their experience of a specific phenomenon (e.g., sexual violence). The outcome is to create a story-like narrative that shows the researcher's unique point of view and connects this expertise to wider cultural understandings of the topic. Photovoice is a community based participatory research method that engages community members in taking photographs to illustrate community problems and potential solutions to these problems. Photovoice is not intended to address individual issues like trauma. However, in this chapter, I demonstrate how an autoethnographic approach to photovoice could be used to engage trauma using concepts from Briere and Scott's basic philosophical approach to trauma treatment. Through this framework, I examine how autoethnography and photovoice foster the intrinsic processing of trauma and cultivate a hopeful outlook on being present with the trauma. The chapter begins with a presentation of my photovoice project. Next, I describe the concepts and methods involved with autoethnography and photovoice. The third section is comprised of a scientific context for sexual violence and trauma. After which I link Briere and Scott's articulation of intrinsic processing and hope to an autoethnographic approach to photovoice methods. I end the chapter by demonstrating how my photovoice project promotes the intrinsic processing of trauma and generates hope.

Keywords

autoethnography – photovoice – trauma – sexual violence

 | DOI:10.1163/9789004407947_016

1 The Story

Part I: Somebody gives us a ride to his house, his father's house. The house is mid-century modern, with a dark wood exterior, surrounded by trees. It sits in a valley by a creek. Giant windows overlook the cascading water. We are eating dinner from Wendy's. I am proud of myself for choosing a dinner that does not have meat. His sister walks in and says, 'Ew ... what is that?!' While pointing, I proudly own my meal: 'Baked potato with broccoli and cheese'. The sister screws up her nose and whines, 'That Velveeta crap is so bad for you. It's disgusting'. I feel frightened and angry ... His sister thinks I am a junk-food eater. He must be ashamed of me.

His sister leaves. It is late. We do not know what to say to each other. We kiss. He pulls me to his bedroom. I find him sexy. He takes my clothes off; we get into bed. We kiss. I say, 'Thank you for not guilting me into having sex with you'.

He rapes me.

FIGURE 14.1 'Velveeta'.

Three separate items: baked potato, broccoli, Velveeta (melted in a dish). I associate the sister's disgust over my food choice with his choice to rape me. Maybe the sister's condemnation of my food choice is a condemnation of his decision to date me. She makes her disgust so clear, how could he not internalise that disgust and dehumanise me as punishment. To process this experience, I turn these ingredients into a photo composition; I transform these objects into a deconstruction of his sister's disgust. While I do feel objectified by the sister and him, I am objectifying their judgment of me. I turn their judgment into an item worth scrutiny. With that scrutiny, I dismantle the harms their judgments inflicted on me. I am taking control over my memory of the experience. I am reshaping this memory into a carefully composed photograph with which I can add filters, highlights, shadows, and intensity. The creative control I am claiming over this image soothes the disturbing emotions that come with this memory.

Part II. He finishes. I start to cry. I sob. I wail. He does not know what to do. He throws a blanket on me. I stop crying and put my clothes on. He borrows a car and drives me back to my dorm. I am 18. He is the second person with whom I have had sex. We had sex one time before.

FIGURE 14.2 'The Ride Home'.

I am reflected in the car window. Behind me a tree branching out. This image represents me, as a 45-year-old woman, who actively engages in sexual violence prevention. My scholarship focuses on transforming campus rape culture. Looking back on this memory, I am no longer trapped in that car with him. I have left the car and him inside, where he cannot harm me. In this new scenario, I am not alone; I have a lush, healthy, strong tree beside me. This tree withstands rain, wind, and unbearable heat. I am like the tree.

Part III. I tell my best friend what happened. She says, 'What, who?! No way. I'm sure he just didn't understand'. I tell a friend in my dorm. She responds, 'Wow. That sounds like date rape. I think you could take legal action'. I tell another friend. Her only words, 'I never liked him'.

FIGURE 14.3 'Everybody Has an Opinion'.

With this image, I create a rumpled, comfortable bed with three books lying where I usually lay. Each book examines and critiques the social forces that promote the acceptability of rape. When I revealed the rape to my three friends, they each had a different reaction. I think this experience with my friends is common. Most people do not know how to react to disclosures of sexual violence. With this image, I want to show the comfort and safety that my half-made bed brings to me. But, when I introduce these sophisticated and powerful critiques about the roots of sexual violence, it reminds me that I cannot stay too comfortable. Even though I want to curl up under those covers and let the world keep going, I must to transform rape culture. It is up to all of us to dismantle the social forces that make rape acceptable.

Part IV. Why did I not push him away? Tell him to fuck off? Punch him in the face? Twist his balls off? I am weak.

FIGURE 14.4 'The Rib Cage'.

In this photo, I am holding the rib cage of a deer that my dog found. While walking through the woods, my dog often discovers wildlife remains. Luna has a remarkable sense of smell, and locating dead animals is one of her favourite activities. Once she discovers a carcass, she will circle the body and then roll in the stinky decomposition. After rolling she grunts, puffs, and prances around the body, a beautiful ritual to witness. Bearing witness to Luna's luxurious savouring of what most would consider abject reminds me potently that we cannot avoid the 'terrible'; instead we must learn to embrace it. With respect to my self-blame, I want to forgive myself for not fighting back. I am conquering now. The process of doing this autoethnography photovoice is triumphant. Even though the rape happened almost 30 years ago, I am circling the bones, smelling and rolling in the decaying flesh, and reclaiming this experience as mine. I am in full control now.

As I write this story and compose these photos, stress, fear, and self-loathing re-emerge. I did not have compassion for myself immediately after the rape. I struggle to feel compassion for myself now. I fear to extend empathy to myself. I do not want it to dampen my anger.

Part v. I am linking the past to the present. A recent trip to the ocean.

FIGURE 14.5 'Naked on the Beach'.

I am standing on the beach embracing my partner. The sky, ocean, and sand blend into each other through colour and gentle textures. We stand in the middle of the frame, flesh pillars holding the sky. Standing naked signifies the embodiment of vulnerability. Sexual violence colonises our body and vulnerability. It can be difficult for a survivor to re-embody that vulnerability after the violence. I transgress the violence by encircling my partner with my naked body within a limitless horizon. The ocean, sand, and clouds possess us. My flesh connects to the earth again.

Part VI. I am not a survivor of sexual violence. I am a warrior, a sexual violence prevention scholar. I dismantle patriarchy with my writing and activism.

FIGURE 14.6 'The Warrior'.

A cat faces me, presenting a bundle of deer antlers. A fire fills my chest; I bend my head and look elsewhere out of deference to the creatures who shed their horns. Humans have been hunting deer for thousands of years, just as men have been perpetrating sexual violence against women for thousands of years. In response, I grow antlers on my head. I stand with grace and elegance while feeling my fear. I walk forward with my crown of horns and I look patriarchy in the eyes.

2 Background

The first part of this chapter consists of an autoethnographic photovoice examination of an experience I had with sexual violence, illustrating how autoethnography and photovoice can foster the intrinsic processing of trauma resulting from sexual violence and cultivate a hopeful outlook. Autoethnography consists of a systematic approach to observe, examine, and document a personal experience so as to connect the personal experience to broader cultural phenomena.[1] Photovoice involves documenting an individual's perceptions on a given topic through composing and taking photographs.[2] These approaches strive to address the power imbalance between the researcher and the 'researched' found in traditional positivist methods. In the case of photovoice, researchers use the methods as a means to both generate community-based data and teach the community how to advocate for social policy change.[3] The methods do not provide treatment but help alleviate the traumatic experience. In this chapter, I use my own experience to illuminate how an autoethnographic approach to photovoice engages trauma so as to disrupt the pain and illuminate possibilities for the future.

Autoethnography. This methodology centres on using the self as both the tool and subject of a research project. Such an approach dismantles the notion of the researcher as an objective outsider. Instead the researcher brings their own experiences, perceptions, and values into the research process. The

---

1 Carolyn Ellis, Tony E. Adams, and Arthur P. Bochner, 'Autoethnography: An Overview', Forum Qualitative Sozialforschung/Forum: Qualitative Social Research, 12.1, Art. 10, January 2011, viewed 3 January, 2018 <http://www.qualitative-research.net/index.php/fqs/article/view/1589/3095>.

2 Caroline C. Wang, 'Photovoice: A Participatory Action Research Strategy Applied to Women's Health', *Journal of Women's Health* 8.2 (1999): 185–192.

3 Caroline C. Wang and Mary Ann Burris, 'Photovoice: Concept, Methodology, and Use for Participatory Needs Assessment', *Health Education & Behavior* 24.3 (1997): 369–87; Wang, 'Photovoice', 186.

effort produces an intensely reflexive and personal engagement with a given research topic by lending a multi-dimensional lens to the research process. The issue under investigation is viewed from the inside-out (as also shown in the chapters by Jacqueline Linder and Nicholas Quin Serenati in this volume as well as by Danielle Schaub).[4] The postcolonial strand of ethnography influences autoethnography, which seeks to draw attention to how traditional research practices perpetuate discrepancies with power, trust, and ownership.[5] Autoethnography decolonises traditional research practices by emphasising researcher reflexivity as to how the relationship to the research subject influences the process and outcomes. Autoethnography also develops counter-narratives to oppressive cultural scripts, controlling stereotypes, or taken-for-granted assumptions.[6] For example, Linder's chapter in this volume uses her experiences with childhood sexual abuse (CSA) and a phenomenological examination of clinical research on CSA to act as an exemplar. Linder juxtaposes first-person narratives with findings from traditional research projects that by comparison break down the binary between researcher and researched. Using the self as subject generates results both grounded in personal experience and relevant to a larger, academic conversation about issues such as CSA or sexual violence.[7] As another example, Serenati develops a counter-narrative about illness through his personal experience with Acute Myeloid Leukaemia. He uses dharma art practice to aesthetise the illness experience by generating new metaphors for illness discourse.[8] The supposition is that through autoethnography the researcher can create knowledge that does not already exist. As a person that has experienced multiple forms of sexual violence, I can speak to survivorship in a way that differs from someone who does not have the experience. Also as a trained researcher, I am ideally situated to observe, document, and critically analyse my own experience.

4 Jacqueline Linder, 'Through the Looking Glass: Child Sexual Abuse from the Inside-Out', in this volume; Nicholas Quin Serenati, 'Illness as a Window: Reframing Leukaemia through Dharma Art', in this volume. Danielle Schaub, 'Reading Myself and Worlds: Coping Strategies in the Face of Cumulative Trauma', *What Happened? Re-presenting Traumas, Uncovering Recoveries: Processing Individual and Collective Traumas,* eds. Elspeth McInnes and Danielle Schaub (Leiden: Brill, 2018), 158–186.

5 Peter Collins and Anselma Gallinat, *The Ethnographic Self as Resource: Writing Memory and Experience into Ethnography*, (New York: Berghahn Books, 2013); Ellis, Adams, and Bochner. 'Autoethnography: An Overview', 1/1.

6 Tony E. Adams, Carolyn Ellis, and Stacy Holman Jones, *Autoethnography*, (Oxford: Oxford University Press, 2015), 68–98.

7 Linder, 'Through the Looking Glass', in this volume.

8 Serenati, 'Illness as a Window', in this volume.

I have the skills necessary to translate my experience into research findings, not to generate more 'truthful' knowledge but to illustrate how a person with a given experience creates a critical, empirical contribution by documenting their unique perceptions, values, and context.[9] The unique creation adds to a broader understanding of a given cultural phenomenon.

An autoethnographic approach can generate a therapeutic experience for the researcher. The process of engaging in creative self-reflection can create a sense of catharsis, empowerment, and growth. Taking the emotional and psychological risk of re-examining the traumatic events can cultivate healing insights. Writing and telling a story about distressing past events can open old wounds; it can also nurture the energy and hope necessary for healing. For example Schaub uses scriptotherapy to narrate the path she took from traumas experienced as a child to learning to experience and sustain pleasure as an adult.[10] Constructing the story promotes the integration of what has happened in the past with the person we have become in the present.[11]

Photovoice, a community-based participatory research (CBPR) method, strives to generate positive change in communities by engaging community members in articulating their point of view on a given phenomenon through photographs, narratives, and dialogue with stakeholders. The pictures are used to spark the critical consciousness of the participant-researcher into thinking about how the photo represents an oppressive reality or an empowered alternative reality.[12] Scholars developed photovoice methods in response to the ontological, epistemological, and axiological limitations of positivist and post-positivist research.[13]

Photovoice is meant to elicit community-based descriptions of a social problem (through photographs and narratives) that can act as the impetus for social change.[14] One foundational tenet for photovoice is that images teach.

---

9 Adams, Ellis, and Holman Jones, *Autoethnography*, 21–45.

10 Schaub, 'Reading Myself and Worlds', op.cit. 158–186.

11 Ellis, Adams, and Bochner, 'Autoethnography: An Overview', 1/1.

12 Claudia Mitchell and Susan Allnutt, 'Photographs and/as Social Documentary', in *Handbook of the Arts in Qualitative Research*, eds. Gary Knowles and Ardra Coles (Thousand Oaks, CA: Sage, 2008), 251–263.

13 Carolyn Ellis and Arthur P. Bochner, 'Autoethnography, Personal Narrative, Reflexivity: Researcher as Subject', *Handbook of Qualitative Research*, eds. Norman K. Denzin and Yvonna S. Lincoln (Thousand Oaks, CA: Sage, 2000), 733–768; Aline Gubrium, Krista Harper, and Marty Otañez. *Participatory Visual and Digital Research in Action* (Walnut Creek, CA: Left Coast Press, Inc., 2015); Wang, 'Photovoice', 185–86; Paulo Freire. *Pedagogy of the Oppressed* (New York: Herder & Herder, 1970), 125–147.

14 Wang, 'Photovoice'., 186–87.

Images contain both implicit and explicit messages, which influence our understanding of reality. Using pictures as the primary form of data can also express meaning across languages, cultures, and learning levels.[15] Another core tenet for photovoice concerns the use of photographs to advocate for social policy.[16] A community can generate inductive, accessible data to show how a community experiences a given problem and believes taking pictures and telling stories can resolve it. With the guidance of researchers, community members can use the photovoice data as a tool to advocate for social change. Implementing a public display of the photos and narratives acts as a forum where the community members can engage in a dialogue with decision makers. For decision makers, viewing the photographs and hearing stories allows them to understand how the community perceives and experiences a given problem.[17] The intimate exchange makes the individual community members appear as multidimensional, beings worthy of compassion and respect.[18]

While researchers developed the photovoice method as a tool to influence structural change, such as social policy, photovoice concepts and practices could be used to address psychological health issues, such as trauma. The process of producing pictures, deriving meaning from the images, and sharing the photos with a supportive social network may have a positive impact on trauma symptoms. As a reference, Serenati illustrates how developing aesthetic metaphors (images and poetry) for trauma resulting from illness, fosters self-discovery, builds internal strength, and promotes psychological healing.[19] Also, through her photograph entitled 'Reading myself and worlds', Schaub portrays the duality between bearing witness to ways she has been damaged and ways she has thrived.[20] With this depiction, she reveals the emotional process of acknowledging how trauma can both fragment our sense of a whole self and create pathways for revitalisation. Tools used to

15 Moshoula Capous Desyllas, 'Using Photovoice with Sex Workers: The Power of Art, agency and Resistance'. *Qualitative Social Work: Research and Practice* 13.4 (2013): 477–501; Wang and Burris 'Photovoice', 369–87.

16 Wang, 'Photovoice'., 186.

17 Jill Chonody, Barbara Ferman, Jill Amitrani-Welsh, and Travis Martin, 'Violence Through the Eyes of Youth: A Photovoice Exploration', *Journal of Community Psychology* 41.1 (2012): 84–101; Mitchell and Allnutt, 'Photographs and/as Social Documentary', 251–263; Wang, 'Photovoice'., 186–87.

18 Desyllas, 'Using Photovoice', 477–501; M. Brinton Lykes, 'Silence(ing), Voice(s) and Gross Violations of Human Rights: Constituting and Performing Subjectivities through PhotoPAR', *Visual Studies* 25.3 (2010): 238–54.

19 Serenati, 'Illness as a Window', in this volume.

20 Schaub, 'Reading Myself and Worlds', illustration 9.7, op. cit. 185.

cultivate this aesthetic processing of the trauma include: a) choosing a topic of personal interest, b) critically reflecting on one's experience with the topic, c) writing reflexive memos (or journal entries) that illustrate the experience, d) constructing the experiences into a story, e) composing photographs that illustrate the story, f) taking the photographs, and g) sharing the story and photos with one's community.

Sharing experiences serves as a vital step in the research and healing process. From a research perspective, we must disseminate the results of our research so that our findings can influence knowledge and practice on given topics. Linder and Forcier provide examples of how sharing our stories through creative means invites our community to learn and empathise with us as individuals and with others who have experienced similar traumas.[21] By sharing her own experiences, Linder illustrates the benefits of survivors sharing their stories as a tool for educating the public. But, Linder contends, the people must create the emotional space to understand these stories. Forcier reflects her experience surviving a street assault, coerced abortion, and an abusive relationship through choreographing a dance composition. She choreographed the performance to portray realistically how she processed the trauma resulting from the violence, creating discomfort for the dance company who promoted the piece. However, the discomfort itself generates community learning and growth.

3 Sexual Violence and Resulting Trauma

Amongst others, autoethnography and photovoice research and document the broader context in which a given issue operates. Evidence shows that my experience with college date rape is not unique. Researchers find that 26% of women, 30% of LGBTQ individuals, and 6% of men attending institutions of higher education in the United States report experiencing non-consensual sexual contact during their time as a student.[22] These data mean that 1 in 4 women, 1 in 3 LGBTQ persons and 1 in 16 men will be a victim of sexual violence during their time in college. The World Health Organization (WHO) defines sexual assault as 'any sexual act, attempt to obtain a sexual act, unwanted sexual comments or advances, or acts to traffic or otherwise directed against a person's sexuality

21 Linder, 'Through the Looking Glass'; Marie France Forcier, 'Creating and Contextualising Trauma-Related Contemporary Choreography', in this volume.

22 David Cantor et al., *Report on the AAU Campus Climate Survey on Sexual Assault and Sexual Misconduct* (Washington, DC: Association of American Universities, 2015).

using coercion, by any person regardless of their relationship to the victim, in any setting, including but not limited to home and work'.[23] The definition encompasses coercive sexual experiences that occur between two individuals on a date.

Sexual violence causes a complex trauma that affects all aspects of the survivor's health. Physical consequences include injuries to the genitals and other body surfaces, sexually transmitted infections or diseases, and unintended pregnancy. Psychological effects can result in posttraumatic stress, often accompanied by depression, anxiety, or adjustment concerns. Social traumas frequently experienced by the survivor include victim blaming and stigmatisation by peers, family, partner, or community members. Sexual violence, a ubiquitous social problem, includes a spectrum of sexual behaviours, often with destructive physical, psychological, and social consequences for the survivors.[24] For college students, the psychological and social trauma can result in decreased academic performance or withdrawal from school.[25]

Briere and Scott define trauma: 'an event is traumatic if it is extremely upsetting, at least temporarily overwhelms the individual's internal resources, and produces lasting psychological symptoms'.[26] This definition captures a multi-dimensional, complex response to having experienced sexual violence[27]; it is broader than the Diagnostic and Statistical Manual [DSM] V definition, which focuses on trauma resulting from physical injury.[28] Given the widespread nature of sexual violence, the significant incidence of traumatic symptomology, and the far-reaching psychological consequences for survivors undertaking a multi-dimensional, personal examination of trauma resulting from sexual violence is justifiable.

---

23 World Health Organization, *Understanding and Addressing Violence Against Women* (Geneva: World Health Organization,2012).

24 Ibid; Centers for Disease Control. *Sexual Violence: Consequences.* Atlanta, GA, Centers for Disease Control, 2017.

25 Cantor et al., 'Report on the AAU' 28–34.

26 John N. Briere and Catherine Scott, *Principles of trauma therapy: a guide to symptoms, evaluation, and treatment* (Los Angeles: SAGE, 2015), 10.

27 Laura S. Brown, *Cultural Competence in Trauma Therapy: Beyond the Flashback* (Washington, DC: American Psychological Association, 2009), 131–152; Stephanie M. Hoover, Andrew F. Luchner, and Rachel F. Pickett, 'Nonpathologizing Trauma Interventions in Abnormal Psychology Courses'. *Journal of Trauma & Dissociation* 17.2 (2015): 151–64.

28 American Psychiatric Association. *Diagnostic and Statistical Manual of Mental Disorders: DSM-5*. Washington: American Psychiatric Publishing, 2014.

Trauma resulting from sexual violence is standard, with 17% to 65% of those victimised reporting symptoms.[29] Trauma challenges a survivor's view of the world as inherently trustworthy so as to leave the survivor perceiving the world as unsafe and overwhelming. Specific to survivors of sexual assault, trauma often takes the shape of self-blame. The U.S. has a long history of blaming victims of sexual assault for their own victimisation.[30] Victim-blaming is an entrenched part of patriarchy because it prevents the perpetrators from being held accountable for their violations.[31] Survivors often internalise the victim blaming and often believe they were at fault for the violence.

4 Conceptual Approach to Addressing Trauma

For this book chapter, I use the concepts of 'intrinsic processing' and 'hope' developed by Briere and Scott to illustrate how an autoethnographic approach to photovoice can engage trauma symptoms. Briere and Scott have published research on therapeutic practices for trauma treatment for decades. Their efforts have culminated in an evidence-based approach to trauma treatment, which integrates psychoeducation, cognitive, and mindfulness therapeutic approaches. Briere and Scott's basic philosophical framework for treating trauma includes four concepts: a) intrinsic processing, b) respect, positive regard, and compassion, c) hope, and d) the pain paradox.[32] For this project, I illustrate how autoethnographic photovoice methods create a mechanism for sexual trauma survivors to engage with intrinsic processing and hope. The procedures involved with creating the photovoice story (at the beginning of this chapter) allowed me to perform the intrinsic processing of my trauma and cultivate hope that I can make peace with the trauma resulting from the sexual violence undergone.

---

29 Rebecca Campbell, Emily Dworkin, and Giannina Cabral, 'An Ecological Model of the Impact of Sexual Assault on Women's Mental Health'. *Trauma, Violence, & Abuse* 10.3 (2009): 225–246; Nicole P. Yuan, Mary P. Koss, and Mirto Stone, 'Current Trends in Psychological Assessment and Treatment Approaches for Survivors of Sexual Trauma', Harrisburg, PA: VAWnet, a project of the National Resource Center on Domestic Violence/Pennsylvania Coalition Against Domestic Violence, last modified April 2006, Viewed 26 December 2017, https://vawnet.org/material/current-trends-psychological-assessment-and-treatment-approaches-survivors-sexual-trauma.

30 Joanna Bourke, *Rape: A History from 1860 to the Present* (London: Virago, 2007), 5–50.

31 Emilie Buchwald, Pamela R. Fletcher, and Martha Roth, eds. *Transforming a Rape Culture* (Minneapolis, MN: Milkweed Editions, 2005), 5–10.

32 John Briere and Catherine Scott, *Principles of Trauma Therapy,* 97–104.

The concept of intrinsic processing centres on the mind's inherent tendency to heal itself. A common traumatic symptom is to re-experience aspects of the traumatic event through either voluntary or involuntary recollection. Briere and Scott contend that through recollection the brain makes sense of, and integrates, the traumatic experience into one's self-concept and worldview. Processing the trauma serves to desensitise and 'internally resolve distressing thoughts, feelings, and memories'.[33] This perspective suggests that giving the client a structured, safe, and affirming way to engage with the traumatic memories may elevate and intensify the healing process. Intrinsic processing may lead to posttraumatic growth, witnessed through an increase in psychological resilience, new survival skills, and expanded self-awareness.[34]

The specific methods that comprise autoethnography and photovoice are compatible with the concept of intrinsic processing.[35] The focus of an autoethnographic photovoice project could be to revisit a traumatic event similar to the example I give at the beginning of this chapter. The first step would be to reflect on, and determine, the focus of the project.[36] Reflection encourages immersion into the traumatic experience.[37] Immersion may occur when looking through journals or writing down recollections of the event.[38] It may also happen when gathering outside information about the scope of the problem (see section three of this chapter) and similar stories to add to a broader understanding of the traumatic experience.[39] After gathering such information, writing a narrative that contains storytelling devices can help to create coherence of the distressing memories and emotions. The storytelling mechanisms give the author creative control over how each scene unfolds, the content and tone of the narrative, and the outcome of the story. The process of composing a photo requires formulating one's traumatic memories into symbolic or metaphorical images that represent an individual's experience with the trauma. Photovoice can also consist of sharing the photos with family, friends, or

---

33 Ibid, 98.

34 Ibid, 97–99.

35 M. Candace Christensen, 'Using Photovoice to Treat Trauma Resulting from Gender-Based Violence'. *Journal of Community Psychology* 46.6 (2018): 701–714; Genevieve Creighton, John L. Oliffe, Shauna Butterwick, and Elizabeth Saewyc, 'After the death of a friend: Young Men's Grief and Masculine Identities'. *Social Science & Medicine* 84 (2013): 35–43; Jan E. Sitvast, Tineke A. Abma, and Guy A.m. Widdershoven, 'Facades of Suffering: Clients Photo Stories About Mental Illness'. *Archives of Psychiatric Nursing* 24.5 (2010): 349–61.

36 Carolyn Ellis, Tony E. Adams, and Arthur P. Bochner. 'Autoethnography', 1/1.

37 John Briere, and Catherine Scott. *Principles of Trauma Therapy*, 97–99.

38 Carolyn Ellis, Tony E. Adams, and Arthur P. Bochner. 'Autoethnography', 1/1.

39 Ibid.

community members, which draws the community into helping the survivor process the trauma.[40] Through images, the survivor encourages viewers to identify and empathise with their experience of the trauma. As images also transcend language, culture, and learning levels, they make the story accessible for both the photographer and viewers.[41]

Hope is an essential component of effective treatment of trauma.[42] Intrusive distressing memories, flashbacks, and/or persistent fear can alter the worldview of a survivor so that they see anguish as part of their future. The challenge of trauma therapy is to help the survivor reframe their engagement with the trauma as an opportunity to develop self-awareness, resilience, and new coping skills. Reframing involves the careful cultivation of hope that the future holds opportunities for growth. As a tool for treating trauma, hope comprises both honouring the tremendous harm one has experienced and simultaneously recognising that just the act of engaging in treatment conveys strength, resilience, and optimism for future outcomes.

Autoethnographic photovoice provides a mechanism for a survivor to generate hope for the future.[43] The act of telling one's story empowers the author construct the story in a salient manner for the author. The effort helps the author to bear witness to challenges overcome and unearth coping mechanisms used in the past that may apply to the current situation. Having power over how the story unfolds also allows the author to create positive outcomes. Visualising positive outcomes can act as a strategy for achieving these results in real life, becoming a vehicle for envisioning hopefulness. By creating images for how we want the story to end, we generate possibilities for the present and future.[44]

5 Engaging Trauma Resulting from Sexual Violence through Autoethnography and Photovoice

In this section, I illustrate how an autoethnographic photovoice project promotes therapeutic engagement with trauma. I use the example presented above to document how the project fostered the intrinsic processing of trauma and nurtured a hopeful outlook. I use Briere and Scott's conceptualisation of

40 M. Candace Christensen, 'Using Photovoice,' 701–714.
41 Ibid.
42 John Briere and Catherine Scott, *Principles of Trauma Therapy,* 101–102.
43 M. Candace Christensen, 'Using Photovoice,' 701–714.
44 Ibid.

intrinsic processing and hope as a lens through which I analyse the results of this venture.[45]

Intrinsic processing helps the mind make sense of, and reconcile with, the traumatic experience(s). This tension functions as a natural mechanism to interact with the trauma symptoms, such as disturbing thoughts, emotions, and memories. Providing the survivor with a creative outlet for processing the trauma may enhance the inherent tendencies of the mind towards integrating the trauma into a new self-concept and worldview.[46]

My primary work on developing the story led me to immerse myself into sensory forms of self-reflection. To capture my memories, I closed my eyes and visited one scenario at a time. I visualised myself walking through each scene and tapped into my five senses: sight, smell, touch, sound, and hearing. For example, I tuned in to my touch-sense by asking myself what I feel in my body in a given scene. 'My solar plexus feels heavy; I constrict my throat; I contract my chest'. After sitting with these sensations for a few minutes, I recorded a free-flowing, stream-of-consciousness response to the sites of inquiry. As I wrote, I tried to stay inside the senses and emotions of the scene and captured the scene with as little researcher intrusion as possible. I wanted the story to remain raw to connect with the texture of the experience and the memories.

Connecting with the experience from an immersive, sensory, and physical standpoint enables the writer to interact with the trauma multi-dimensionally. At times, I inhabited my body during the memories. At other times, I hovered above each scene and watched myself participate as if I were a character on stage. My feelings changed with the shift in focus. I felt fear when I inhabited my body and anger when I observed myself from a distance. By immersing myself in the memories and then writing down my recollections, I bore witness to how my emotions, thoughts, and behaviours intersected at traumatic moments to shape my response to the trauma. Deconstructing and reconstructing the memories alleviated the self-blame and generated self-compassion. The deconstruction felt as though I was cleaning the emotional or psychological grime away from the memories. The reconstruction ebbed and flowed like an ocean tide. Like a brisk breeze prickling my skin, the purified retelling of the painful situation left me with goose bumps from the thrill of new growth.

Composing the photos helped me immerse myself in the painful emotions and distressing memories and transform them into symbols, colours, and

45 John Briere and Catherine Scott, *Principles of Trauma Therapy*, 97–104.

46 Ibid.

textures. The effort made the trauma corporeal and malleable, my anguish becoming like clay to reshape, reformulate, and transform into anything I wanted it to be. For example, with Figure 14.1, I converted the sister's ugly reaction to my dinner into a precisely curated still life of my junk food meal. I reclaimed and altered the sister's judgment by using the placement of food items, lighting, and colour filters to elevate the meal into a subject worthy of reflection.

The process of nurturing hope involves reframing the trauma as an opportunity to gain self-awareness, develop new coping mechanisms, and bolster resilience. The effort consists in being present with the anguish and embracing the role it plays in positive transformation. Crafting the story plunged me into my memories, which helped me to greet the trauma and build a relationship on my terms. I shaped how the trauma entered my mind, behaviour, and plans for the future. As the author, I took over creative control of how to unfold the story. Creating scenes for the story allowed me to see how choices I have made since the rape led me to a positive, fulfilling career and partnership. Writing the story helped me link seemingly disparate pieces into a coherent mosaic.

With respect to the story, Figure 14.4 provides a strong example of how the photovoice fostered a hopeful outlook. I was out walking with my dog, Luna, and she found the skeleton of a deer, a vertebral column, and she started rolling on the remains. The spine symbolises psychological and emotional strength or the lack thereof. Reaching for the bones, I saw arches, windows, and secret vaults, as if I was looking up at the ceiling of a gothic cathedral. Luna and I wanted to take the bones home, but we left them in the woods. Other creatures would appreciate the ossein wreckage too. As a memento, Luna caught the scent of a deer carcass on her fur, and I took a photo. I rolled up my sleeve to show my 'grandmothers' tattoo' – comprised of a flower I associate with each of my grandmothers – picked up the ribcage and snapped several photos. I settled on an image that illustrates the ribcage as the raw distress I experienced, and the tattooed arm as my social support system, representing the fierce women that made my existence possible. My scrunched hand in the middle functions like a heart pumping blood into the ribcage, transforming it with the soul force of my grandmothers.

6 Conclusion

This chapter has shown how autoethnography and photovoice allow the victim's involvement in a dramatic encounter with sexual violence to generate a hopeful perspective on learning to live with the trauma. The combination of an autoethnographic framework to situate the researcher – in this case myself – as the subject of the research and photovoice methods as the vehicle for engaging with the trauma has yielded resolutive significance. To do so, I created both a narrative that portrays my perception and experiences with past sexual violence and photos that provide symbolic and metaphorical images associated with the memories of the event. By writing the autoethnographic photovoice project, I have had the opportunity not only to consider how my story has unfolded between one experience with sexual violence at age 18 and my current work 28 years later, but also to build a transformative relationship with the trauma. Through creative engagement, I have managed to apply trauma treatment concepts advanced by Briere and Scott in such a way that I no longer need to maintain silence about what happened.[47] Rather, through composing the images and corresponding narratives I have emerged stronger, aware of the emotional strength gained since the assault. Now, I can hold the experience in a complex place encompassing distress and outrage alongside compassion and vitality. In the end, thanks to the intrinsic processing of debilitating sexual subjugation, I have even transformed the trauma into a dynamic force that fosters inspiration and creation.

Bibliography

Adams, Tony E., Carolyn Ellis, and Stacy Holman Jones. *Autoethnography*. Oxford: Oxford University Press, 2015.

American Psychiatric Association. *Diagnostic and Statistical Manual of Mental Disorders: DSM-5*. Washington, DC: American Psychiatric Publishing, 2014.

Bourke, Joanna. *Rape: A History from 1860 to the Present.* London: Virago, 2007.

Briere, John, and Catherine Scott. *Principles of Trauma Therapy: A Guide to Symptoms, Evaluation, and Treatment.* 2nd ed. Los Angeles: SAGE, 2015.

Brown, Laura S. *Cultural Competence in Trauma Therapy: Beyond the Flashback.* Washington, DC: American Psychological Association, 2009.

Buchwald, Emilie, Pamela R. Fletcher, and Martha Roth, eds. *Transforming a Rape Culture.* Rev. ed. Minneapolis, MN: Milkweed Editions, 2005.

Campbell, Rebecca, Emily Dworkin, and Giannina Cabral. 'An Ecological Model of the Impact of Sexual Assault on Women's Mental Health'. *Trauma, Violence, & Abuse* 10.3 (2009): 225–246.

Cantor, David, Bonnie Fisher, Susan Helen Chibnall, Reanne Townsend, Hyunshik Lee, Gail Thomas, and Carol Bruce. *Report on the AAU Campus Climate Survey on Sexual*

47 Briere and Scott, op. cit. 97–104.

Assault and Sexual Misconduct. Washington, DC: Association of American Universities, 2015.

Centers for Disease Control. 'Sexual Violence: Consequences'. Viewed 20 December 2017. https://www.cdc.gov/violenceprevention/sexualviolence/consequences.html.

Chonody, Jill, Barbara Ferman, Jill Amitrani-Welsh, and Travis Martin. 'Violence Through the Eyes of Youth: A Photovoice Exploration'. *Journal of Community Psychology* 41.1 (2012): 84–101.

Christensen, M. Candace. 'Using Photovoice to Treat Trauma Resulting from Gender-Based Violence'. *Journal of Community Psychology* 46.6 (2018): 701–714.

Collins, Peter, and Anselma Gallinat. *The Ethnographic Self as Resource: Writing Memory and Experience into Ethnography*. New York: Berghahn Books, 2013.

Creighton, Genevieve, John L. Oliffe, Shauna Butterwick, and Elizabeth Saewyc. 'After the Death of a Friend: Young Men's Grief and Masculine Identities'. *Social Science & Medicine* 84 (2013): 35–43.

Desyllas, Moshoula Capous. 'Using Photovoice with Sex Workers: The Power of Art, Agency and Resistance'. *Qualitative Social Work: Research and Practice* 13.4 (2013): 477–501.

Ellis, Carolyn, and Arthur P. Bochner. 'Autoethnography, Personal Narrative, Reflexivity: Researcher as Subject'. In *Handbook of Qualitative Research*, edited by Norman K. Denzin and Yvonna S. Lincoln, 733–768. Thousand Oaks, CA: SAGE, 2000.

Ellis, Carolyn, Tony E. Adams, and Arthur P. Bochner. 'Autoethnography: An Overview'. *Forum: Qualitative Sozialforschung/Forum: Qualitative Social Research* 12.1 (2011). Viewed January 03, 2018. http://www.qualitative-research.net/index.php/fqs/article/view/1589/3095.

Freire, Paulo. *Pedagogy of the Oppressed*. New York: Herder & Herder. 1970.

Gubrium, Aline, Krista Harper, and Marty Otañez. *Participatory Visual and Digital Research in Action*. Walnut Creek, CA: Left Coast Press, Inc. 2015.

Hoover, Stephanie M., Andrew F. Luchner, and Rachel F. Pickett. 'Nonpathologizing Trauma Interventions in Abnormal Psychology Courses'. *Journal of Trauma & Dissociation* 17.2 (2016): 151–164.

Lykes, M. Brinton. 'Silence(ing), Voice(s) and Gross Violations of Human Rights: Constituting and Performing Subjectivities through PhotoPAR'. *Visual Studies* 25.3 (2010): 238–254.

Mitchell, Claudia, and Susan Allnutt. 'Photographs and/as Social Documentary', In *Handbook of the Arts in Qualitative Research*, edited by J. Gary Knowles and A. Cole, 251–263.Thousand Oaks, CA: SAGE, 2008.

Schaub, Danielle. 'Reading Myself and Worlds: Coping Strategies in the Face of Cumulative Trauma'. *What Happened? Re-presenting Traumas, Uncovering Recoveries: Processing Individual and Collective Traumas*. Eds. Elspeth McInnes and Danielle Schaub. Leiden: Brill, 2018, 158–186.

Sitvast, Jan E., Tineke A. Abma, and Guy A.M. Widdershoven. 'Facades of Suffering: Clients Photo Stories About Mental Illness'. *Archives of Psychiatric Nursing* 24.5 (2010): 349–61.

Wang, Caroline C. 'Photovoice: A Participatory Action Research Strategy Applied to Women's Health'. *Journal of Women's Health* 8.2 (1999): 185–192.

Wang, Caroline, and Mary Ann Burris. 'Photovoice: Concept, Methodology, and Use for Participatory Needs Assessment'. *Health Education & Behavior* 24.3 (1997): 369–387.

World Health Organization. *Understanding and Addressing Violence Against Women.* Geneva: World Health Organization, 2012.

Yuan, Nicole P., Mary P. Koss, and Mirto Stone. 'Current Trends in Psychological Assessment and Treatment Approaches for Survivors of Sexual Trauma'. VAWnet, last modified April 2006. Viewed 26 December 2017. < https://vawnet.org/sites/default/files/materials/files/2016-09/AR_SVTreatment.pdf>.

CHAPTER 15

Creating and Contextualising Trauma-Related Contemporary Choreography

Marie France Forcier

Abstract

As a mid-career professional dance artist and emerging scholar, I engage in research focusing on the creation and analysis of choreography through the post-traumatic lens. Originally concerned with the aesthetic impact of psychological dissociation on movement, my creative focus has widened to incorporate recall narratives for abuse-related trauma survivors. In 2015, I completed the creative process and presentation of *Scars Are All the Rage*, a 30-minute trio commissioned by a major Canadian dance presenter. In accordance with my activist and artistic values, I directed the work for realistic performances, an approach met with much unease from Danceworks, the presenter, who suggested modifications to the piece and disseminated warning advisories about its content prior to its opening presentation. Was this reaction's foremost outcome the protection of audience members or the weakening of their viewing experiences? Detailing and analysing *Scars Are All the Rage*'s creative and presentational process, this chapter considers how trauma-related choreographic performances may be optimally contextualised for general audiences.

Keywords

trauma-related art – choreography – dance – creative process – performance – post-traumatic stress – state-based choreography – abuse-related trauma – presentation

1 Introduction

Is romanticising trauma in the performing arts a socially responsible approach to adopt, or is revealing its realism a better choice? How should abuse-portraying movement be responsibly and optimally contextualised for viewers? In March 2015, I presented *Scars Are All the Rage* (SAR) for the first time at Toronto's Harbourfront Centre Theatre. A then new 30-minute piece of contemporary choreography, *SAR* explored the somatic repercussions and cyclical nature of abuse-related trauma through horse-training imagery. Hard to watch according to a number of accounts, the work underlined the rise of trauma culture and western societies' growing desensitisation to sexual voyeurism. Following a detailed account of the foundational research preceding the creation of *SAR*, the chapter will define its creative process, providing information on its initial premise, early exploratory stages, symbols' development, and directional strategies. *SAR*'s presentation process is also described, mostly in regards to dissemination, performance, and media and audience response. An analysis will follow, considering creator-to-presenter interactions and presentational frameworks.

2 Background: 2002–2014

In the aftermath of a few months' time during which I survived a street assault, was coerced to an unwanted abortion by authority figures, and lived through a verbally and physically abusive relationship, I suffered complex post-traumatic stress disorder (PTSD). My symptoms manifested in the form of severe dissociation, which impacted the quality of my work as a professional dancer in concrete and significant ways. To use the words of trauma researcher Judith Herman, I felt 'unsafe in [my] bod[y]', like many other trauma survivors.[1] I lost awareness of my centre of gravity, my proprioceptive abilities decreased, my concentration and memory suffered, and my overt emotional responses to simple choreographers' directives became problematically disproportional. As an unfortunate result, my employment prospects disappeared. Having built a primary skillset in dance from a young age and developed my sense of identity around it, I nonetheless remained in the field and re-oriented my activities towards choreography. Thanks to cognitive-behavioural therapy, I was able to resume a thriving life within two years of receiving a PTSD diagnosis and enjoyed a healthy choreographic career in the years following.

Given the sustained high-functionality I had been exhibiting, I was puzzled when, ten years after my recovery, repeating images conjuring psychological dissociation – most significantly characterised by dancers' vacant visual focus – began emerging unpremeditatedly in my choreographic work. Attracted on a visceral level to the aesthetics produced by this change, I dedicated

1 Judith Herman, *Trauma and Recovery* (New York: Basic Books, 1992), 160.

research to the creation and analysis of contemporary choreography through the post-traumatic lens. The academic investigation unfolded between 2012 and 2014 led me to create a number of short choreographic studies. I also devised and refined a methodology exploring embodied memory as a source for movement. In essence, what I have been referring to as the *somatic-to-motor recall amplification method* relies on somatic sensations triggered by recalling one's own life events: I would lay in a comfortable supine position and perform body-scanning imagery-based exercises until I reached a deep state of somatic attuning. From that state I would then recall and concentrate on varying events from my past and identify corresponding places of somatosensory change; in other words, I checked areas of my body reacting to the recall, and the specific qualities of that reaction: tensing, crushing, tingling, etc. Still immobile and attuned, I would then work on amplifying that physical sensation through visualisation, to the point where I felt the urge to move through discomfort. The ensuing movement sequence was retained, and used as ground for choreographic expansion.

Although requiring profound somatic attuning, this methodology appears to produce honest movement easily triggering a viewer's kinaesthetic empathy. I have used it in processes when I was the sole creator/performer of a work, and in non-academic, professional contexts involving mature artists. Movement creation in this setting requires increased engagement on the performer's part: the more precise the personal memory and the more somatically attuned the dancer, the more evocative the movement. Contrary to most situations in which movement instigators benefit from maintaining an audience's perspective while creating, 'choreography and performance may be inseparable when developing state-based movement related to trauma and/or embodied memories'.[2] The

> movement instigator, whether he/she is the choreographer or the creatively contributing performer, [may] need to be in a performance mode in order to generate genuine state-based vocabulary in process. If the movement instigator does not approach the task with full emotional investment, the movement might lack specificity or "feel" wrong and need to be discarded sooner or later.[3]

2 Marie France Forcier, 'Creating Contemporary Choreography Through the Post-Traumatic Lens' (MFA thesis, York University, 2014).

3 Ibid., 35.

Beyond the initial production of movement, my findings have also applied to staging and composition. Noteworthy in this chapter's context, I found that

> day-to-day objects incorporated as props or set pieces help to contextualise the work in reality. Because contemporary dance is abstract, state-based work is somatic, and psychological trauma, private and internal, trauma-based choreographic work [when exclusively consisting of physical motion executed on a bare stage] could easily look as though it portrays an alternate reality.[4]

Adding commonly recognisable elements (i.e. like food items, furniture, etc.) to trauma-related choreography helps to circumvent this pitfall. I also 'discovered that, as a general rule, emotionally distressing elements bear more resonance when balanced with neutrally or positively perceived ones',[5] as for example, mundane costuming, a beautifully executed movement or the use of humour. Indeed, experiencing laughter's pleasure in rapid succession with witnessing a performer's emotional distress creates dissonance, converting passive audience members into active, accountable ones, who might question their reactions' appropriateness.

By the time I completed my research and re-integrated the dance profession on a full-time basis in April 2014, I sensed that I was at a pivotal point of my development as an artist, and that I should ride on the momentum I had been generating by further deepening my investigation of trauma and choreography's intersection.

3 Creative Process: Initial Premise – Late Spring 2014

Although academic research had enabled me to make fundamental discoveries in terms of my practice, the time and human resources at my disposal while a graduate student had restricted the artistic depth I could access. Having worked primarily as a soloist or with undergraduate student dancers during that period, the next logical step for me was to find fellow professional dancers to collaborate with, dancers who had developed the capacity to let go of form and proper technical execution in order to follow genuine somato-emotional impulses in movement development and performance. Thus, in May 2014, I approached Louis Laberge-Côté, Molly Johnson and Justine Comfort, three

4 Ibid., 37.
5 Ibid., 37.

experienced performers with whom I shared various histories of collaboration, to discuss their possible participation in the creative process and performance of an eventual choreographic work questioning the commodification of trauma as a source of entertainment in mainstream media, *SAR*. All three artists agreed to take part in the project.

A few months prior to this, DanceWorks, a respected dance presenting organisation, had contractually retained my services to present a new 30-minute choreographic work the following year. Having

> beg[u]n as a collective of independent dance artists in 1977 [, DanceWorks] [... has grown] to become Toronto's leading presenter of independent dance. Strong in the belief that dance has the power to illuminate, engage and transform all who participate, DanceWorks [claims to] offer seasons of eclectic, exhilarating choreography programmed to intrigue, challenge and enthral.[6]

Because of the platform's significance, given that the presenter had given me full artistic license during each of our four prior collaborations, and to honour my concurrent creative interests, I decided to choreograph *SAR* for the venue.

As its title loosely indicates, *Scars Are All the Rage* reflects my original intention to create a choreographic piece simultaneously inspired by two premises: the dancers' and my own scarring memories and trauma culture's exponential growth. I envisioned that the work would be based in dark humour, expanding on my pre-established research integrating positively perceived features in trauma-related art.

To accommodate the artistic team members' common availabilities and to allow for periods of perspective, the creative process was initially scheduled to unfold in Toronto over three separate one-month-long residencies.

4 Creative Process: July 2014 – Early Exploration

As a choreographer, I am not one to arrive with a pre-constructed series of steps to teach the dancers. I prefer to create on the bodies present in the room, in accordance with dynamics at play on a given day (figure 15.1). Given the humorously inclined collaborators, the early creation days for *SAR* were rather playful, despite our common awareness of the subject matter. During those

6 Danceworks, *About DanceWorks*, Viewed on 8 December 2016, http://www.danceworks.ca/about/index.html.

FIGURE 15.1 Johnson and Laberge-Côté in rehearsal.
PHOTO BY CRAIG CHAMBERS. ©2015.

weeks, I created a series of short 2- to 5-minute long sections, each exploring different ideas. Produced among other excerpts were a superhero-themed duet, a manipulation-heavy trio in which Comfort was being pushed around, and a series of slowly transitioning pornographic still images.

Although not initially at the material's obvious forefront, the notion of trauma was identifiable in the choreographic material from the beginning. Invited to periodically attend and respond to my creative process, Canadian freelance Arts reviewer Mark Mann wrote:

> I watched the first part of your rehearsal [...] in a sort of pleasurable delirium, absorbing your process and basically just enjoying myself, sensing the risk you were taking and appreciating it. But then you ran through the sequence in which Molly is manipulated sexually by Louis, and suddenly the experience was very different. [...] The way Molly's hands are at first frozen at her side, that affected me. It directly expressed the way abuse accesses desire.[7]

Mann's observation intrigued me: I decided to further explore tensed stillness and sexually suggestive manipulation side-by-side as images. Ultimately performed downstage centre, in silence, over an uncomfortable amount of time, the sequence first noticed by Mann ended up becoming a defining part of the final piece. To my creative eye, the image conjured up the freeze response – a last resort in surviving a traumatic experience when neither fight nor flight is available, potentially leading to dissociative disorders – as outlined by Stephanie Dinklebach in her description of the implicit nature of trauma memory.[8]

At the end of the first creative residency period, we had accumulated over 20 minutes of potentially usable material. My intention for the work moving forward had become more precise: I was going to give *SAR* the structure of a stereotypical Japanese-style game show built around bizarre challenges, in which the participants were prompted to re-enact their traumatic memories in exchange for points. I was enthusiastic about this premise, because it allowed for the incorporation of props and dissonant humour, while exposing the commodification of trauma in mainstream entertainment through means of enlargement.

---

7 Mark Mann, 'Seeing and Wanting', *ForcierNorman* (blog), *WordPress*, November 24, 2014, Viewed on 1 February 2016, https://forciernorman.wordpress.com/2014/11/24/seeing-and-wanting/.

8 Stephanie Dinklebach, 'Art thou troubled ...': 'The Therapeutic Effect of Music-Experiencing in the Context of Trauma Reprocessing', unpublished paper presented at the Sixth Global Conference on 'Trauma: Theory and Practice' in Budapest, Hungary, 11–13 March 2016.

5 Creative Process: December 2014 – Tonal Shift

When we returned to the studio, my goal was to further develop our existing material towards choreographic completion, within the parameters of a perverse game show. Although the plan was clear and my intention firm, it soon became obvious that my directorial tendencies were steering us away from that concept. My motive seemed to have shifted unconsciously: instead of capitalising on our existing material's sense of play, I felt compelled to hone in on its most sinister elements. The more uncomfortable my reaction to the resulting choreographic images, the more validated I felt. Intuitively, each of my attempts to re-insert humour into the score felt wrong.

Mid-way through the December creation residency, I finally gave in and abandoned the game show idea, along with any conscious attempts to balance darkness with humour or positivity. I was well aware that I was not only delaying the work's completion by doing so, but that I was also exposing myself to the risk of creating a one-dimensional piece. Both of those prospects were anxiety arising on financial, creative and personal levels.

By the end of the second creation period, we had discarded over half of the material built in July 2014, and replaced it with 25 minutes of continuous choreography. Defining elements had emerged: hierarchy as a social order among the characters, abuse as a recycled behaviour, hair grabbing as a repeated motif (Figure 15.3), a moveable black riser as a podium (Figure 15.2), and horse training imagery as an overarching theme. The space on stage was now conceptualised both as a barn and a rounded training ring; the dancers' travelling movement paths were often times circular, systematised by this circuit.

In reaction to viewing our December residency's final rehearsal, Mark Mann wrote:

> my body was wincing at your rehearsal on Monday, and making little sounds of shock and denial, and I think I even put my hand in my mouth. I don't think it's too strong to say that this piece is terrifying.[9]

I was beginning to grasp that by having shifted creative gears, I was now overtly tackling abuse-related ideas with realism in my work and that, while this realistic approach created much greater potential for making a social impact, it also demanded substantially more consideration on my part. Feeling

9 Mark Mann, 'Above the Fire', *ForcierNorman* (blog), *WordPress*, January 24, 2015, Viewed on 1 February 2016, https://forciernorman.wordpress.com/2015/01/24/above-the-fire/.

FIGURE 15.2 The Podium: Rehearsal.
PHOTO BY CRAIG CHAMBERS © 2015.

FIGURE 15.3 Pony Training: Rehearsal.
PHOTO BY CRAIG CHAMBERS © 2015.

a responsibility to treat the subject matter with the specificity and respect it deserved, I added a full month to our work schedule, in spite of the related additional costs.

6 Creative Process: Symbolism – January 2015

Over the holiday break, I spotted deer eating frozen carrots in Northern Québec while having SAR on my mind. From simultaneous exposure to both ideas, I realised that carrots could be perceived as phallic symbols and rewards in horse training if used as props in the context of my developing piece. As I mentioned in the Background section of this paper, I consider food items common utility props helping to ground trauma-related choreography in reality. Upon our first rehearsal back together after the holidays, I began experimenting with adding large carrots to the dancers' scores. Immediately interested in the new options provided and additional layers of meaning uncovered by the addition, I decided to re-organise the choreography's material and staging in function of the new prop. Contained in six antique wooden buckets (Figure 15.4), the carrots were distributed on a semi-circle marking the performers' horse-training ring.

Gradually over the course of our January rehearsals, the carrots developed meaning as torture instruments, beginning to serve abuse-related capacities. In convergence, the movement tendencies were becoming increasingly more violent and realistic: Laberge-Côté was stretching Comfort's mouth with his fingers emulating a bit mouthpiece (Figure 15.5); Johnson was throwing buckets-full of carrots on Comfort's body, etc. By the end of January 2015, *SAR*'s main movement and structure were essentially completed. The performers' visual focus, emotional interpretation and movement intentionality, however, remained to be defined.

7 Creative Process: February 2015 – Direction

During the final creation period, the dancers and I participated in at-length discussions to check-in on one-another's mental state. I was particularly weary of pushing them too far physically and emotionally with my directorial requests. I was also apprehensive choreographically speaking, inexperienced in presenting work devoid of levity with what could be perceived as significant shock value. Trauma in entertainment's moral correctitude was what I was aiming to question, not conform to. How could I gauge if I was making my premise choreographically clear enough for the general public to grasp? Having extensive

FIGURE 15.4 Carrots in Antique Bucket.
PHOTO BY CRAIG CHAMBERS. © 2015.

FIGURE 15.5 The Bit Mouthpiece.
PHOTO BY CRAIG CHAMBERS. © 2015.

personal and academic experience in the workings of trauma, I was confronted with perspective issues. From having seen *SAR* over and over again in rehearsal, I was developing growing desensitisation to my own work and, in an attempt to re-experience the empathy originally felt when first developing the material, I reacted by directing dancers to push their movement's brutality to higher and higher extremes. The strategy was failing, the violence becoming dangerously close to gratuitous. Of the experience in an email exchange, Johnson, the dancer with whom I had been collaborating the longest among the three, wrote:

> from our discussions and from the inside, it feels like the second half [of the piece] is struggling [...] because we become too cognizant of our actions, and [...] because it relies heavily on physical oppression. [...] [I] think it's really hard to maintain that kind of violence and to convince an audience of it. [I]t's important that the way we physicalize things is realistic, but I think it's less effective when the violence becomes too real, or too recognizable. [A]audiences are both highly susceptible to and easily desensitized by that kind of image – either way, we risk them putting up a wall.[10]

10 Johnson, Molly, email to author, 24 February 2015.

Acutely aware of the issue, I still felt conflicted about scaling back – I felt a responsibility to reflect the magnitude of a trauma victim's experience. From an activist standpoint, I thought that it was high time that we as a society acknowledged the full malevolence of abuse and the lingering anguish of trauma. Horrid and graphic images hunt the abused and PTSD afflicted on an on-going and uncontrollable basis, how could I justify camouflaging, or worse, romanticising this reality in my art? Fortunately, additional conversations with Laberge-Côté, Johnson and my long-time collaborator composer James Bunton helped me understand and organise my creative drives integrally. Among other commonly developed useful insight, we rationalised that the perpetrator's vulnerability needed to be incorporated to our abuse-narrating choreographic landscape, for two main reasons: to give the characters tri-dimensionality, and to remain truthful to the fact that, cyclical by nature, abuse often results from trauma-induced behaviour, a consideration alluding to Compulsive Trauma Re-Enactment, which Dinklebach speculatively attributes to an addiction to hormonal release and short-term amnesia brought forth by the experience of trauma.[11] On the topic, Johnson shared that

> what [she] understood about abuse is that it is a cycle – in many cases a learned behaviour that is passed on, and even if the abuse itself does not carry on, there is an imprint left in the victim.[12]

Following the realisation, Laberge-Côté's interpretation as the main perpetrator in the piece became far less malicious in body language and movement power, and far more pain-motivated. In its final incarnation, his choreographic score included core contractions, indirect movement paths, laughter distorting into muffled screams, etc.

The recognisability and exactitude of the post-traumatic reality I was aiming to integrate in *SAR* was also examined during this final creation residency. Hearing Johnson repeat my early creative process words to me was helpful.

> I remember you saying that what you were interested in showing was not so much the act of abuse, but the repercussions of the act, this imprint of what has happened. […] I think the scenes that work and that you are (I think) happiest with, [sic] are the ones that show these physical traces in our bodies (circular patterns, destabilised movements) and where the

11 Stephanie Dinklebach, 'Art thou troubled …', op. cit.

12 Molly Johnson, email to author, 24 February 2015.

> violence/abuse is abstracted and maintained as a training device, a way of enforcing the cycle of trauma.[13]

It helped me understand and articulate in concrete ways that I had been creating a distorted recall narrative characterising the post-traumatic mental landscape, as opposed to a fictionalised enactment of abusive acts. Laurie Vickroy states at the opening of her work *Trauma and Contemporary Fiction* that

> trauma narratives [...] have taken an important place among diverse artistic, scholarly, and testimonial representations in illuminating the personal and public aspects of trauma and in elucidating our relationship to memory and forgetting within the complex interweavings of social and psychological relationships.[14]

In the greater context of contributing to the collective trauma narrative with a choreographic representation, SAR finally made sense to me. I embraced the prospect as my guiding principle to move forward. With the newfound clarity provided, making coherent directorial decisions came with greater ease.

I removed most of the brutality in the material and made room for the *implied* idea of violence: a character hovering menacingly over another, a destabilised walking pattern around the training ring, a shaky and indirect arm pathway leading to manipulation, etc. Within the post-traumatic landscape narrative paradigm, the transformation conserved the realism I was intent on keeping, while circumventing the need to apply overt audience-alienating brutality.

8 Presentation Process: Interaction with the Presenter – March 2015

Given the sensitivity of its topic, SAR's proper contextualisation in the media and program guide was an anticipated issue, which my artistic collaborators and I dissected with great care during the later half of our creative process. The strategy we agreed upon was to provide the public with necessary information regarding the work's subject matter, while steering clear from putting any emphasis on the contents' audacity. We recognised that language specificity was greatly significant in avoiding to shape expectations: we were

---

13 Ibid.

14 Laurie Vickroy, *Trauma and Survival in Contemporary Fiction* (Charlottesville: University of Virginia Press, 2002), 1.

equally susceptible to fall short for the cutting-edge art enthusiast, and to deter the more conservative folk from attending if we mentioned that the work was pushing boundaries. Also of consequence, we wanted to be careful not to adopt an apologetic tone inadvertently when contextualising *SAR*, which would automatically discredit our stance in presenting the work.

We devised a two-fold dissemination plan. Firstly, I was going to remain transparent yet succinct about the research topic with the media. Following an interview with me, *The Toronto Star*'s dance reviewer Michael Crabb reported:

> 'My work is not pretty', says Toronto choreographer Marie France Forcier. [...] Forcier's bold admission is hardly the most seductive way to market a dance performance but hers is an audience that looks for more than the sensory pleasure of beautiful bodies moving to lyrical music. They want real meat – and Forcier has plenty to throw their way. Her new work, which she says does not fit in any tidy performance category, explores with uncompromising directness a subject of personal interest and academic research [... ,] the lingering trauma of human abuse – physical and psychological.[15]

Secondly, I was going to provide our audience with carefully worded background information on the research in my choreographer's notes for the performance's program guide. A standard and concise, '*Mature Content*' disclaimer would also be included. My drafted notes read as follows:

> Scars Are All the Rage* (World Premiere)
>
> **Mature Content: Nudity.*
>
> A few years ago, I started developing an appreciation for the aesthetics of discomfort in dance and other art forms. This led me to research Post-Traumatic Expression in choreography – first academically, then professionally. *Scars Are All the Rage* is part of this exploration. Through composing with animal training-like imagery, I aimed at drawing parallels with certain realities of abuse while remaining sensitive to psychological trauma's complexities.
>
> Cyclical by nature, abuse regularly results from learnt behaviour: a perpetrator was often a victim in the first place. While we grow culturally desensitised to violence in two-dimensional media, for real-life

15 Michael Crabb, 'Marie France Forcier Delves into Trauma with Dance', *Toronto Star*, 11 March 2015, Viewed on 6 December 2016, https://www.thestar.com/entertainment/stage/2015/03/11/marie-france-forcier-delves-into-trauma-with-dance.html.

> victims, unshakable traces linger. Somatic experiences are re-lived uncontrollably and unwelcome images appear at intervals: graphic, distorted. Nightmare-like.[16]

In the weeks preceding the show, I articulately shared our preferred dissemination strategy with DanceWorks, our presenter, explaining the reasoning behind our choices both in person and over a thorough email exchange. I emphasised that "[we] want[ed] to ensure that our audience underst[oo]d that[,] from an artistic point of view, we [were] not apologetic about the content of the work",[17] and expressed that it was our wish to refrain from framing our work with references to audacity.

My interactions with DanceWorks' representatives increased in frequency in early March 2015, as *SAR*'s theatrical premiere approached. As previously mentioned, when working with the presenter in the past, I had experienced unchallenged artistic freedom. As such, I was destabilised when upon their viewing of the finished work in rehearsal on 4 March 2015, the organisation's agents began expressing implied criticism and overt doubt about my creative choices. They assumed that the work was going to offend audiences, that it may re-traumatise susceptible individuals, that patrons would judge the presentation not to be 'Art', and that a number of them, scandalised, would walk out during the performance. DanceWorks' agents additionally requested that I modify a sexually suggestive, yet fully clothed image from a preview excerpt they had arranged for me to present at the Canadian Opera Company the very next day, in promotion for the show (Figure 15.6).

Invalidating DanceWorks' reservations, the choreographic excerpt in question was performed well and received enthusiastically by a traditionally conservative opera crowd on 5 March 2015. The presentation generated a lengthy post-show discussion addressing the power of kinaesthetic empathy and issues surrounding human abuse. None of the audience members left the venue; on the contrary, several viewers stayed behind after the event to thank me personally for addressing a matter of social importance.

Regardless of this positive outcome, which the presenter witnessed in person, Danceworks took additional measures contextualising *SAR* for its patrons in the week preceding its premiere performance: The presenter cancelled *SAR's* performance as part of a scheduled senior high school matinee, a decision that disappointed me given my strong belief that young adults are a

16 DanceWorks Harbourfront Centre NextSteps 14/15 Mainstage Series DW210 *Forcier/Norman*, March 11 2015.

17 Forcier, Marie France, email to DanceWorks' agents, 6 March 2015.

FIGURE 15.6 Image removed from excerpt.
PHOTO BY CRAIG CHAMBERS. © 2015.

critical demographic to include in discussions regarding abusive behaviour and its effects.

Secondly, neglecting my creative team's clearly communicated dissemination requests, DanceWorks and Harbourfont Centre – the venue – sent the following advisory to all ticket holders:

> Thank you for purchasing tickets for DW210 featuring *Scars Are All the Rage* [...] Please be aware that the company [...] wants you to know the following advisory: *Scars Are All the Rage* explores the somatic repercussions of abuse-related trauma. Highly suggestive, the work highlights the rise of trauma culture and our growing desensitisation to sexual voyeurism for its entertainment value. Please be aware that this performance contains mature content with sexual overtones and may be disturbing to some patrons. Please confirm receipt of this message, to avoid also receiving a phone call![18]

Lastly, the printed program guide advisory expended on the *Mature Content-Nudity* disclaimer I had originally submitted. Indeed, the following addition

18 Harbourfront Centre, email forwarded to author, 10 March 2015.

was made to DanceWorks' curatorial statement: "PLEASE NOTE: *Scars Are All the Rage* depicts mature content and may be disturbing to some patrons."[19]

9 Presentation Process: Performance and Response – March 2015

SAR's initial run was performed between 12 and 14 March 2015, and was mostly positively received. In her review of the performance, writer Christina Strynatka expressed:

> Scars Are All the Rage [is] a dance that came with a 'depicts mature content and may be disturbing to some patrons' warning in the program guide. Yes, there was a bit of upper body nudity and yes, there was a bit of lower body fondling, but to diminish it to such common terms detracts from the dance's overall aesthetic. This is a dance that's bold, daring and forces you to confront the uncomfortable, with a nod to the – shall we say? – *perceived rigor* of horse training. "Scars Are All the Rage" is a bit hard to watch sometimes, but good art should be because it reaches at the depths of those places we like to hide away, and shakes the truth in front of our faces until we acknowledge its existence.[20]

Several audience members communicated with me in the weeks following the performances. Among the letters came the following lines:

> I wanted to let you know how truthful and affirming it felt for me. [...] So much of what was portrayed echoed real events in my own childhood and I have not had that kind of validation of my lived experience in such a publically shared way. It is totally different than reading a narrative about domestic violence because reading is still a solidary re-experience, not a shared one, and not a physical one either. And a wordless dance portrayal, unlike a play, allows for the truth of one's physical memories [...] to resonate and feel finally acknowledged.[21]

---

19 DanceWorks Harbourfront Centre NextSteps 14/15 Mainstage Series DW210 *Forcier/Norman*, March 11 2015.

20 Christina Strynatka, 'DanceWorks Double Bill "Forcier/Norman" Varied in Presentation', *Examiner*, 13 March, 2015, Viewed on 31 January, 2016, http://www.examiner.com/review/danceworks-double-bill-forcier-norman-varied-presentation.

21 Anonymous, email to author, 24 March 2015.

In Serenati's view art provides communication and understanding to others; as an extension, I would like to propose that art – in my case, trauma-narrating choreography – can serve as a common frame of reference for trauma survivors to objectively discuss aspects of their own trauma with others, decreasing the vulnerability brought forth by disclosure. [22]

10 Analysis

In the days leading to, and over the course of, the performance run, I felt robbed, disrespected and vastly discouraged. *SAR* had been framed with questionable language, and our audience members were primed to receive it within an alarmist context over which I had no power. The discussions I had been hoping to generate about abuse and trauma might never unfold, the audiences' capacity for developing empathy when seeing the work having likely been compromised by their manufactured guardedness and/or unmet stylistic expectations. The work's purpose was being overshadowed by the unintended promise for subversion implied in the released advisory, a promise that the piece, by nature, was doomed to fail at keeping. I was aggravated that the advisory had been sent under my name (i.e. the company) without my knowledge or consent. At the time, I judged DanceWorks' contextualisation of the work misinformed, conservative, damaging, and out of proportion.

On the other side of the experience, benefitting from a few years of detachment, I better appreciate that the presenter might have been operating from what Linder describes as the non-survivors' 'lack of readiness to accept humanity's infinite capacity for darkness',[23] even when portrayed on stage. As Linder describes it when comparing survivors and non-survivors' existential perception, the presenter was perhaps fearful that their patrons would resist allowing a reality they did not possess a framework for to exist.[24] I suspect that had I initiated regular communication with the presenter, from an earlier point in the process and in direct regards to the work's topical and stylistic development, it would have prevented dissention.

22 Nick Qinn Serenati, 'Illness Is a Window: Reframing Leukemia Through Dharma Art', in this volume.

23 Jacqueline Linder, 'Through the Looking-Glass: Child Sexual Abuse from the Inside-Out', in this volume.

24 Ibid.

As evidenced by Strynatka's comments in relationship to warnings in the program guide having had a diminishing effect on the work, the contextualisation did have a negative impact on the members of the audience. However, one can only speculate on the outcome of the presentations would the audience not have been warned of its potential for disturbance, as was the nature of my original request. Years of discussions with contemporary dance artists, audiences, and trauma researchers on the matter have led to the consensus that language specificity functions as the primary consideration when contextualising trauma-related choreography. I now realise that my original strategy to remain honest but succinct might not have sufficed to protect whoever in attendance might have been vulnerable to images suggestive of abuse. Using a *trigger warning* terminology while steering clear of allusions to *disturbance* or *audacity* might be the most efficient formula when contextualising trauma-descriptive choreographic work.

11 Conclusion

Creating *SAR* and presenting it through a third party keep informing me to this day, as a creator, arts educator and trauma survivor. I am convinced that glorifying abuse-related trauma survival in the performing arts serves as a pernicious deterrent to taking much needed action towards creating victim support and re-evaluating punitive measures for perpetrators. Confronting audiences with realistic physical representations of the post-traumatic landscape appears to function as a far more effective incentive in the matter, as long as relevant information pertaining to artistic intent, process and content is shared articulately and transparently. As neuroscientist Antonio Damasio demonstrated through his study of the insula, 'consciousness is fundamentally a product of how we interpret the physical sensations that we experience'.[25] Perhaps the choreographic physicalising of this consciousness, by virtue of bypassing the symbolic intermediates of language in trauma narration, is the clearest way to explain post-traumatic realities for all to understand.

25 David Emerson and Elizabeth Hopper, 'Introduction to *Overcoming Yoga Through Yoga: Reclaiming Your Body*', edited by Bessel A. Van Der Kolk (Berkeley: North Atlantic Books, 2011), xxiii.

Bibliography

Crabb, Michael Crabb., 'Marie France Forcier Delves into Trauma with Dance', *Toronto Star*, 11 March 2015. Viewed on 6 December 2016, https://www.thestar.com/entertainment/stage/2015/03/11/marie-france-forcier-delves-into-trauma-with-dance.html.

Dinklebach, Stephanie. '"Art Thou Troubled ...": The Therapeutic Effect of Music-Experiencing in the Context of Trauma Reprocessing'. Unpublished paper read at the Sixth Global Conference on 'Trauma: Theory and Practice' in Budapest, Hungary, 11–13 March 2016.

Emmerson, David, and Elizabeth Hopper. Introduction to *Overcoming Yoga Through Yoga: Reclaiming Your Body*. Ed. Bessel A. Van Der Kolk, xxiii. Berkeley: North Atlantic Books, 2011.

Herman, Judith. *Trauma and Recovery.* New yorkYork: Basic Books, 1992.

Forcier, Marie France. Creating Contemporary Choreography Through the Post-Traumatic Lens. MFA Thesis, York University, 2014.

Mann, Mark. 'Above the Fire', *ForcierNorman* (blog). *WordPress*, 24 January 2015. Viewed on 1 February 2016, https://forciernorman.wordpress.com/2015/01/24/above-the-fire/.

Mann, Mark. 'Seeing and Wanting' *ForcierNorman* (blog). *WordPress*, 24 November 2014. Viewed on 1 February 2016. https://forciernorman.wordpress.com/2014/11/24/seeing-and-wanting/.

Strynaka, Christina. 'DanceWorks Double Bill "Forcier/Norman" Varied in Presentation'. *Examiner.com*, 13 March 2015. Viewed on 31 January 2016. http://www.examiner.com/review/danceworks-double-bill-forcier-norman-varied-presentation.

Vickroy, Laurie. *Trauma and Survival in Contemporary Fiction.* Charlottesville: University of Virginia Press, 2002.

CHAPTER 16

Eating Disorders: Traumatic Context and Interventions

Diedra L. Clay

Abstract

Historically, women's eating disorders have been denominated with such terms as 'chlorosis', 'neurasthenia' and 'hysteria'. Since the 1970s an increase in eating disorders have been noticed, possibly correlated with the general phenomenon of cultural gender role change, posited as attributable to the confusion between the terms 'sex' and 'gender'. The biological term 'sex' works for both female and male, while the socially given term 'gender' is either masculine or feminine. This traumatic bifurcation implicitly involves a cultural dualism. The theoretical consideration of eating disorders has been likened to the crystallisation of culture, with three cultural axes: the dualist axis, control axis, and gender/power axis. Dualism can be thought of as a denied dependency on a subordinated or traumatised other. Within this frame, human existence bifurcates into two territories or substances: that of the body and materiality, as contrasting that of the mental and spiritual. The body must be escaped from a prison and an enemy with which to struggle. In this battle, thinness represents a triumph of the will over the body. The control axis is informed by the experience of one's hungers as being out of control. One's ability to ignore hunger and pain evidences one's control over one's own body, often the only control one experiences. The gender/power axis is informed by the experience of one's 'female' portions of one's body, usually at menarche, as a disgusting appropriation of one's body by fat. These symptoms emerge as an unconscious protest at the limitations of the traditional female role. Successful interventions with eating disorders take these intersecting factors into account. This chapter will expose the range of current treatment interventions in consideration of the traumatic context.

Keywords

traumatic cultural context – interventions – gender role – dualism – female – eating disorders

 | DOI:10.1163/9789004407947_018

1 Introduction

> Historians long ago began to write the history of the body. They have studied the body in the field of historical demography or pathology; they have considered it as the seat of needs and appetites, as the locus of physiological processes and metabolisms, as a target for the attacks of germs or viruses; they have shown to what extent historical processes were involved in what might seem to be the purely biological 'events' such as the circulation of bacilli, or the extension of the lifespan. But the body is also directly involved in a political field; power relations have an immediate hold upon it; they invest it, mark it, train it, torture it, force it to carry out tasks, to perform ceremonies, to emit signs.[1]

The death of the singer Karen Carpenter in 1983 served to focus mass media attention, and therefore mass population attention, on the phenomenon of clinical eating disorders in general and anorexia nervosa in particular.[2] Ms. Carpenter's highly popular success in her singing career, combined with her extreme preoccupation with her weight, struck a profound and dramatic cultural chord. The extreme dissonance between her rapid stardom and her equally rapid and abrupt death from anorexia nervosa helped to convince people of the extreme seriousness of clinical eating disorders. For some, her death was the very first instance of an eating disorder entering into the popular cultural awareness. Many theories emerged regarding the circumstances behind the development of her clinical eating disorder. Soon after, medical and health care professionals began to recognise, regularly diagnose and treat clinical eating disorders in both in- and out-patient treatment centres. Eating disorders became recognisable in popular press and general cultural knowledge.

As a viewable cultural phenomenon, a close examination of clinical eating disorders must necessarily connect with a careful and thorough exploration of the categories of gender and embodiment. Most people diagnosed with, and hospitalised for, anorexia nervosa are female.[3] An important descriptive criterion for the diagnosis of anorexia nervosa is the presence of significant

1 Michel Foucault, *Discipline and Punish: The Birth of the Prison* (New York: Vintage/Random House, 1979), 25.

2 Joel Samberg, 'Remembering Karen Carpenter, 30 Years Later', *NPR Music* (website), 4 February 2013, Viewed on 9 April 2015, http://www.npr.org/2013/02/04/171080334/remembering-karen-carpenter-30-years-later.

3 Susan Faludi, *Backlash: The Undeclared War Against American Women* (New York: Doubleday, 1991), 202.

negative disturbances in an individual's body perception.[4] Thus in light of the current incidence of clinical eating disorder cases a consideration of the interconnecting aspects of gender and embodiment proves essential.

In this chapter, the term gender is used broadly to outline an analytic category for an examination that traditionally refers to the study of sex, sex roles, gender, gender roles, gender bias, gender role identity, gender expectations, gender role attitudes, sexism, femininity, masculinity, androcentrism and language use.[5] Similarly, the term embodiment is used as an analytic category for examination to refer to body image, body image expectations, biological sex, one's experience of being in one's body, and one's relationship to one's body.[6]

The literature in the respective areas of gender, embodiment and clinical eating disorders includes hundreds of psychological analyses, experimental studies, meta-studies, single case studies, treatment recommendations and theoretical formulations. Much of the clinical literature on eating disorders attempts to link eating disorders with one or another specific pathogenic condition, such as depressive, perceptual, hypothalamic or affective geneses. Psychologists, analysts, therapists, physicians and medical providers historically have provided a plethora of rationales for the origin, development, and treatment of clinical eating disorders.[7] Nevertheless, both anorexia nervosa and bulimia nervosa appear in ever-increasingly diverse populations of women, in diverse cultures, which drastically reduces the possibility of describing a single distinctive clinical profile for either.[8] A polyvocal search must therefore be embraced, in order to study the phenomena. Our examination will review the historical, cultural, and religious underpinnings of this disorder.

2 History

Traditionally, women's health disorders have been denominated in a wide variety of ways. Terms used have included such descriptions as 'young women's disease', 'chlorosis', 'neurasthenia', and 'hysteria.' For example, the Hippocratic texts

4 Attia, Evelyn; Becker, Anne E.; Bryant-Waugh, Rachel; Hoek, Hans W.; Kreipe, Richard E.; Marcus, Marsha D.; Mitchell, James E.; Striegel, Ruth H.; Walsh, B. Timothy; Wilson, G. Terence; Wolfe, Barbara E.; Wonderlich, Stephen./Feeding and Eating Disorders in DSM-5. In: *American Journal of Psychiatry*, 170.11 (2013) 1237–1239.

5 Mary Gergen and Sara Davis, *Towards a New Psychology of Gender* (New York: Routledge, 1997), 39.

6 Ibid., 40.

7 Ibid., 42.

8 Susan Bordo, *Unbearable Weight* (Berkeley, CA: University of California Press, 1993), 139–164.

of fourth century Greece described a 'young women's disease' that began just at menarche and was graphically characterised by amenorrhea, wasting away, great hunger, vomiting, depression, suicidal ideation, anxiety, aches and pains and breathing difficulties.[9] Other historical authors described a disorder known as 'chlorosis', wherein young girls exhibited symptoms of amenorrhea, appetite disturbance, bingeing and vomiting, depression, anxiety, headache, slenderness, breathing difficulties and insomnia, as well as a disturbed body image.[10]

Savage portrayed a typical case of 'neurasthenia' as one in which

> a woman, generally single … becomes bed-ridden, often refuses her food, or is capricious about it, taking strange things at odd times, or pretending to starve. … The body wastes, and the face has the thin, anxious look not unlike that represented by Rossetti in many of his pictures of women.[11]

Breuer and Freud described a malady that they called 'hysteria', so named because it was believed to originate in the patient's uterus.[12] It served as 'a dramatic medical metaphor for everything that men found mysterious or unmanageable in the opposite sex'.[13] Chronic vomiting, depression, anxiety, headache, difficulty breathing, insomnia, menstrual irregularity and anorexia characterised this disorder. As can be seen historically, the above descriptions of the disorders have many similar qualities to the common contemporary understanding of clinical eating disorders.

In current psychological permutations, the descriptive criteria for anorexia nervosa consist of the following characteristics: the patient (a) manifests a refusal to maintain a minimally normal body weight, (b) becomes intensely afraid of gaining weight, and (c) exhibits significant disturbance in the perception of the shape or size of the body. Anorectics are also amenorrheic, primarily due to abnormally low oestrogen levels on account of the diminished pituitary secretion of follicle-stimulating hormones and luteinising hormones.[14]

---

9 Ibid., 1–44.

10 Mary R. Lefkowitz and Maureen B. Fant, *Women's Life in Greece and Rome,* 1–294 (Baltimore: Johns Hopkins University Press, 1982).

11 George H. Savage, *Insanity and Allied Neurosis* (Philadelphia: Henry C. Lea, 1884), 90.

12 Joseph Breuer and Sigmund Freud, *Studies on Hysteria* (New York: Penguin Press, 1982), 1–170.

13 Mark S. Micale, 'Hysteria and Historiography: A Review of Past and Present Writings', *History of Science* 27 (1989): 319.

14 Attia, Evelyn; Becker, Anne E.; Bryant-Waugh, Rachel; Hoek, Hans W.; Kreipe, Richard E.; Marcus, Marsha D.; Mitchell, James E.; Striegel, Ruth H.; Walsh, B. Timothy; Wilson, G. Terence; Wolfe, Barbara E.; Wonderlich, Stephen./Feeding and Eating Disorders in DSM-5. In: *American Journal of Psychiatry*, 170.11 (2013) 1237–1239.

Anorectics can be described as either the restricting type or the binge-eating/purging type. The restricting type or anorectic typically restricts food intake through fasting or dieting, or by excessive exercise. The binge-eating/purging type most often indulges in regular binge eating and then purges through self-induced vomiting or through the misuse of laxatives, diuretics or enemas.[15]

Bulimics, on the other hand, have:

1. Recurrent episodes of binge eating. An episode of binge eating requires both: (a) eating, in a discreet period such as within any two-hour period, an amount of food definitely larger than most people would eat during a similar period and under similar circumstances; and (b) experiencing the sense of a lack of control over the eating during the episode, such as feeling the inability to stop eating or to control what or how much is eaten.
2. Recurrent inappropriate compensatory behaviour in order to prevent weight gain, such as (a) self-induced vomiting; (b) misuse of laxatives, diuretics, enemas or other medications; (c) fasting or (d) excessive exercise.
3. Both binge eating and inappropriate compensatory behaviours, on average, at least twice every week for at least three months.
4. Self-evaluation unduly influenced by body shape or weight.
5. The disturbance not occurring exclusively during episodes of anorexia nervosa.

One may specify the bulimia type as either purging or non-purging. For purging types, during the current episode of bulimia nervosa, the person has regularly engaged in self-induced vomiting or the misuse of laxatives, diuretics or enemas. For non-purging types, during the current episode of bulimia nervosa, the person has used other inappropriate compensatory behaviours such as fasting or excessive exercise. The non-purging type person does not regularly engage in self-induced vomiting or misuse of laxatives, diuretics or enemas.[16]

3 Triggers

The meaning of gender and embodiment in the experience of a woman with a clinical eating disorder is characterised by a number of events that cause the patient to spiral downward into hopelessness, depression and

15 American Psychiatric Association, *op. cit.*
16 American Psychiatric Association, *op. cit.*

negative self-esteem. The literature consistently addresses the importance of others' perceptions, specifically a negative comment from an important and significant person in authority provoking and continuing to reinforce anorexic-type behaviour.[17] The provocation results, in part, from the authoritative significant persons' critical attitudes toward the age, gender, and body of the person addressed, as well as their own perceptions of the ideal feminine body and their own age and gender.[18] The clinical eating disordered individual, in many cases, develops the disorder as an attempt to 'gain control' over their body to counter the significant authority figure's critical and negative evaluation of her body. In turn, after triggering the disordered eating behaviour, negative self-esteem related to body image can directly influence the development, persistence, and perpetuation of the clinical eating disorder.[19]

Apart from a significant person's pejorative appraisal, the media – such as television, advertising, social networking, and fashion magazines – can directly and negatively influence perceptions of the ideal feminine body.[20] The media often present the ideal woman as physically flawless.[21] Television and media in print often drastically modify women's bodies to show an idealised version rather than the actual picture with accurate proportions of the women photographed. Women exposed to such excessive, idealised and often impossible to achieve societal demands of physical perfection may succumb to these ideals and measure their own success, self-worth, and self-esteem by externally comparing their own bodies with unrealistic internalised images. In adopting cultural expectations – in taking a critical perspective and treating the feminine body as an object – women with a clinical eating disorder can be 'caught up in a power situation of which they are themselves the bearers'[22] and actively produce the feminine body as an object to herself.[23] The anorexic woman's perceptions of the feminine body may then intertwine with her perceptions of the feminine role as negative, limiting and devalued in society.

---

17 Hilde Bruch, *Eating Disorders: Obesity, Anorexia Nervosa, and the Person Within* (New York: Basic Books 1973), 90.

18 Ibid, 102.

19 Rita Snyder and Lynn Hasbrouck, 'Feminist Identity, Gender Traits, and Symptoms of Disturbed Eating among College Women', *Psychology of Women Quarterly* 20.4 (1996): 593–598.

20 Ibid., 593–598.

21 Faludi, *Backlash*, 203.

22 Foucault, *Discipline and Punish*, 25.

23 Faludi, *Backlash*, 203.

4 Traumatic Context

Changes in the incidences of clinical eating disorders over the few last decades have increased astonishingly. In the 1970s, when Bruch published her pioneering works on eating disorders, she could still state that anorexia was very 'rare indeed'.[24] Subsequently, however, the statistics for clinical eating disorder indicators grew by leaps and bounds. For example, almost half of the women in the United States are on a diet on any given day and 80 percent of women state their dissatisfaction with their appearance.[25] Epidemiological statistics show that eating disorders affect five to ten million adolescent girls and women as opposed to one million for boys and men.[26] Far from rare, eating disorders are now indeed epidemic.

Contemporarily, clinical eating disorders have acquired a cultural legitimacy as a significant set of psychological disorders in their own right. As Perlick and Silverstein hinted, the historical syndromes called young women's disorder, chlorosis, neurasthenia and hysteria (outlined in the History section above) correlate with a general phenomenon of cultural gender role change.[27] Currently, a cultural shift has occurred in the expectations of women's behaviour. According to Perlick and Silverstein, larger populations of women graduate from college than in previous generations, and this newer population may be highly influenced by their perceptions of their mothers' limited lives and restricted opportunities.[28]

Feminist scholars such as Plumwood hold that central to the exploration of clinical eating disorders is the confusion over the categories of 'sex' and 'gender'.[29] Much of the Western cultural tradition has variously blurred

24 Hilde Bruch, *The Golden Cage: The Enigma of Anorexia Nervosa* (New York: Vintage, 1979), 1–171.

25 Linda Smolak, Michael P. Levine, and Ruth Striegel-Moore, *The Developmental Psychopathology of Eating Disorders: Implications for Research, Prevention, and Treatment*, 1–464 (Mahway, NJ: Lawrence Erlbaum Associates, 1996).

26 Janis H. Crowther, Eve M. Wolf and Nancy E. Sherwood, 'Epidemiology of Bulimia Nervosa', *The Etiology of Bulimia Nervosa: The Individual and Familial Context*, Eds. Janis H. Crowther and Daniel L Tenenbaum, 4–16 (Washington, DC: Hemisphere Publishing Corporation, 1992).

27 Deborah Perlick and Brett Silverstein, 'Faces of Female Discontent: Depression, Disordered Eating, and Changing Gender Roles', in *Feminist Perspectives on Eating Disorders*, Eds. Patricia Fallon, Melanie A. Katzman and Susan C. Wooley, 77–93 (New York: Guilford Press, 1994).

28 Ibid., 77–93.

29 Val Plumwood, 'Do We Need a Sex Gender Distinction?' *Radical Philosophy* 51 (1989): 2–11.

and emphasised the difference between sex and gender. Stoller defined the distinction:

> With a few exceptions, there are two sexes, male and female. To determine sex one must assay the following conditions – chromosomes, external genitalia, internal genitalia, gonads, hormonal states and secondary sex characteristics. One's sex, then, is determined by an algebraic sum of all these qualities, and as is obvious, most people fall under one of the two separate bell curves, the one of which is called 'male', the other 'female'.
>
> Gender is a term that has psychological and cultural rather than biological connotations, if the proper terms for sex are 'male' and 'female', the corresponding terms for gender are 'masculine' and 'feminine', these latter being quite independent of (biological) sex. Gender is the amount of masculinity and femininity found in a person, and obviously, while there are mixtures of both in many humans, the normal male has a preponderance of masculinity and the normal female a preponderance of femininity.[30]

From this perspective, sex, or that which is biological, is seen to be normally male or female, while gender, or that which is socially given, is masculine or feminine. This distinction is usually blurred into uniform terms such as 'sexual differences', meaning that which has to do with a particular person inclusive of sex and gender. Consider the use of the word *mother* to indicate one who both bears and nurtures a child, yet giving birth (biological) and raising a child (sociological) are decidedly different functions.

Plumwood held that if the relationship between the two is viewed as one between a culture and its physical environment, in that a culture can shape the way a physical environment is classified and indeed the physical features of it and vice versa, then each remains distinguishable aspects of the world so as to require considering and focusing on them separately.[31] Though intertwined and interdependent, each is a separate and distinct phenomenon.

The sex versus gender distinction outlined above implicitly involves a dualism. Western culture has packed considerations of this dualist polarisation with implications of *the female* (nature, body and passivity) and *the male* (culture, reason and freedom) pointing to the male as separate and controlling.

30 Robert J. Stoller, *Sex and Gender* (New York: Science House, 1968), 158.

31 Plumwood, ibid., 10.

Western primary cultural thinking rests on this dualist thinking. With conception, for example, the sperm is commonly thought to compete to travel, surround and fight to win the right to implant the egg in the moment of conception. The average acculturated person would be surprised to know that the egg travels through the womb to the sperm, languishing for days waiting for the egg's arrival. The same holds for the egg emitting enzymes which either allow or disallow the penetration of the membrane by the sperm, effectively choosing which individual sperm will fertilise the egg. Dualist thinking has clearly shaped the very perception of conception.

Dualism, in this sense, amounts to denied dependency on a subordinated other; this determines a structure in which the denial and domination-subordination relation shapes the identity of both. Simone de Beauvoir stated the dualism in this way:

> The terms masculine and feminine are used symmetrically only as a matter of form, as on legal papers. In actuality, the relation of the two sexes is not quite like that of two electrical poles, for man represents both the positive and the neutral, as is indicated by the common use of man to designate human beings in general; whereas woman represents only the negative, defined by limiting criteria, without reciprocity. In the midst of an abstract discussion it is vexing to hear a man say: 'You think thus and so because you are a woman;' but I know that my only defence is to reply: 'I think thus and so because it is true,' thereby removing my subjective self from the argument. It would be out of the question to reply: 'And you think the contrary because you are a man', for it is understood that the fact of being a man is no peculiarity.
>
> … [T]here is an absolute human type, the masculine. Woman has ovaries, a uterus; these peculiarities imprison her in her subjectivity, circumscribe her within the limits of her own nature. It is often said that she thinks with her glands. Man superbly ignores the fact that his anatomy also includes glands, such as the testicles, and that they secrete hormones. He thinks of his body as a direct and normal connection with the world, which he believes he apprehends objectively, whereas he regards the body of woman as a hindrance, a prison, weighed down by everything peculiar to it.[32]

From de Beauvoir's perspective, the very definition of woman and the bias that associates woman with characteristics considered negative allow and prepare

32 Simone de Beauvoir, *The Second Sex*, xvii-xviii (New York: Vintage, 1974).

for objectification and domination. In psychological language, the distinction between the class of females and the set of characteristics associated with them essentially explains why psychology has been called 'phallocentric' and has produced a false androcentrism.

False androcentrism, in this sense, has been described as an implicit 'natural' orientation towards an erroneous cultural ideal of a 'neutral' sex, one that holds itself as the standard against which to measure all humans, male and female. As this androcentric subject is implicitly male, the standard turns out to be phallocentric. Irigaray went so far as to state that Western culture in general is 'phallogocentric',[33] suggesting that our cultural orientation is towards values and ideals governed by a social ideal of androcentrism. The application of the androcentric model to women, Irigaray held, objectifies, delimits, devalues and ignores the unique difference of perspective and experience that women bring to the world.[34]

Conversely, the sex-gender distinction has been critiqued as one that assumes the arbitrariness of the connection between the body and gender.[35] This perspective assumes that gender, a matter of consciousness, is constructed on the body and that the body is passive and neutral regarding the formation of consciousness. Masculine and feminine behaviours are taken to be arbitrary, socially inscribed on an indifferent consciousness joined to an indifferent body. Hence, the sex-gender distinction implicitly involves a body-consciousness distinction of a rationalist or Cartesian type, with the body assumed neutral and passive. The consciousness assumed, however, remains neutral or implicitly male, whereas the object of discussion is the feminine equated with the body. This perspective removes the very possibility of speaking from a woman's unique subjectivity and promotes an objectification of the feminine. Irigaray commented on the objectification of the feminine:

> Once imagine that woman imagines and the object loses its fixed, obsessional character. ... If there is no more 'earth' to press down/repress, to work, to represent, but also and always to desire (for one's own), no opaque matter which in theory does not know herself, then what pedestal remains for the ex-sistence of the 'subject'? If the earth turned and more especially turned upon herself, the erection of the subject might thereby be disconcerted and risk losing its elevation and penetration. For what would there be to rise up from and exercise his power over? And in?[36]

33 Luce Irigaray, *Speculum of the Other Woman* (New York: Cornell University Press, 1985).
34 Luce Irigaray, *This Sex Which is Not One* (New York: Cornell University Press, 1985).
35 Judith Butler, *Bodies That Matter: On the Discursive Limits of Sex* (New York: Routledge, 1993).
36 Irigaray, *This Sex Which is Not One*, 1–219.

Irigaray posited that the subject, always masculine, needs the objectification of the feminine and the body upon which to base his theories. In making the feminine into a property of his language, the masculine subject appropriates her, dominates her, and defines her according to his own needs and definitions, not to her own. As a cultural phenomenon, one could call this set of assumptions masculinism, one that assumes the subject as male or androcentric at best. This perspective excludes woman and the body, radically defined as other and ultimately dominated. Yet, the subject is always a sexed subject and the body is always a situated body, hence no neutral or passive body underlies gender.

Trying to treat gender as something inherently neutral is therefore mistaken, a mistake situated in the radical separation of particular gender characteristics, as well as the removal of the body from consideration. In this sense, the body has been objectified, transformed into that which must be dominated, controlled, manipulated and ordered.

As Elwin Susan John has posited, '… the human body is a space and a canvass for the expression of human sufferings,'[37] highlighting the idea that the body has been formulated to carry cultural inscriptions. As receivers and participants of this cultural baggage, women with eating disorders can be seen as internalising and perpetuating this self-objectification. This self-objectification can be viewed as actual struggle for definition:

> The struggle for definition is veritably the struggle for life itself. In the typical Western, two men fight for the possession of a gun that has been thrown to the ground; whoever reaches the weapon first, shoots and lives; his adversary is shot and dies. In ordinary life, the struggle is not for guns but for words; whoever first defines the situation is the victor; his adversary, the victim. For example, in the family, husband and wife, mother and child do not get along; who first defines whom as troublesome or mentally sick? Or in the apocryphal story about Emerson visiting Thoreau in jail; Emerson asks : 'Henry, what are you doing over there?' Thoreau replies: 'Ralph, what are you doing over there?' In short, he who first seizes the word thus dominates and lives; and he who is defined is subjugated and may be killed.[38]

In this view, the development of a clinical eating disorder can be seen as an attempt to define self in response to a cultural definition and subsequent

37 Elwin, Susan John, 'I Used To Be Human Once: Trauma and Reconfigurations of the Body in Chemical Disasters', in this volume.

38 Rosa P. Eschholz and V. Clark, *Language Awareness* (London: St. Martin's Press, 1986), 337.

domination of the woman's self-perception. The eating disordered woman seeks to define herself first, by controlling her eating and therefore her body, consciously or unconsciously. Elwin Susan John calls this phenomenon '... the 'body' holds a unique status of being what is affected and also being a tool for protest.'[39]

As clinical eating disorders have gained cultural validity and general recognition since Karen Carpenter's death, many empirical studies have been performed that directly and causally link the clinical eating disorder phenomenon with various gender role aspects.[40] Some studies held that eating disorders may be affiliated, but are not directly connected to a more traditional gender role identity.[41] Other alternate studies posited an actual direct connection between the preponderance of femininity and clinically disordered eating patterns.[42] After review, vast disagreements exist in the clinical eating disorder literature regarding the phenomenon of gender roles.[43]

What is even more unclear is the intertwining meaning of gender and embodiment in those women with clinically diagnosed eating disorders. Butler pulled apart the classic sex versus gender distinction as a meaningless question, not relevant for examination, as she held that gender and the body already circumscribe existence.[44] Within this framework, the analysis of distinct characteristics such as gender role is irrelevant.[45] Separation of a particular characteristic to examine in detail is impossible, as each quality is inextricably informed by other qualities.

Honouring this inextricability, Bordo directly connected the theoretical consideration of clinical eating disorders with gender and the body in her analysis of the psychopathology of anorexia as the very crystallisation or embodiment of culture. This conceptualisation of clinical eating disorders is the most encompassing of the theoretical constructs in the current clinical and

39 Elwin Susan John, ibid.

40 Mark E. Johnson, Christiane Brems and Pamela Fischer, 'Sex Role Conflict, Social Desirability, and Eating-Disorder Attitudes and Behaviors', *Journal of General Psychology* 123.1 (1996): 75–87.

41 Ellen C. Flannery-Schroeder and Joan C. Chrisler, 'Body Esteem, Eating Attitudes, and Gender-Role Orientation in Three Age Groups of Children', *Current Psychology: Developmental, Learning, Personality, Social* 15.3 (1996): 235–248.

42 Snyder and Hasbrouck, 'Feminist Identity, Gender Traits, and Symptoms of Disturbed Eating among College Women', *Psychology of Women Quarterly,* 20.4, 593–598.

43 Helen Malson, 'Women under Erasure: Anorectic Bodies in Postmodern Context', *Journal of Community and Applied Social Psychology* 9.2 (1999): 137–153.

44 Butler, *Bodies that Matter*, 1–256.

45 Judith Butler, *Gender Trouble: Feminism and the Subversion of Identity* (New York: Routledge, 1990), 1–272.

theoretical literature. Bordo held that the phenomenon of clinical eating disorders is synchronous with three cultural axes, which therefore encompass the clinical eating-disordered persons' worldview: the dualist axis, the control axis and the gender-power axis.[46]

The dualist axis is characterised by the view that human existence is bifurcated into two territories or substances: that of the body and materiality, and alternatively, that of the mental and spiritual. The thinking of our cultural philosophical ancestors, such as Plato, Augustine and Descartes, fully promoted, and in fact, demanded the dualist perspective as priority. For each of these philosophers, the body was considered alien, something to escape from, a confinement or an enemy, and that which threatens and thwarts our every attempt at control. Far from philosophical, however, those with eating disorders similarly embrace this perspective concerning their very own bodies. For these people, the body is something from which they must escape – a prison or an enemy against which to struggle. The body is not seen as self, but as other, that which must be conquered and dominated. In this battle, thinness represents an eventual desired triumph of the spirit or the will over the body, an essentially dualist stance.

The control axis is informed by this person's experience of her body, life and hungers as being out of control. The bulimic may shamefully feel that once she starts eating, she cannot control herself, and may also actively dissociate during eating. The anorectic is usually a perfectionist, wanting to shine in all aspects of her life. The anorectic syndrome may occur as a result of her initiating a diet rather casually, after which she becomes hooked on the intoxicating feelings of control and accomplishment – often the only control she may experience in her life.

The gender-power axis reflects the fact that women, by far, are more obsessed and less satisfied with their bodies than men and are permitted less physical latitude with their bodies by themselves, men and culture.[47] Current statistics claim that four out of five women feel dissatisfied with their appearance. The average American woman is five feet four inches tall and weighs 140 pounds, whereas fashion models are on average five feet eleven inches tall and 117 pounds, making models thinner than 98 percent of women.[48] This comparison worsens after the manipulation of models' pictures, often showing body proportions of an impossible ratio. Many clinical eating-disordered persons experience

46 Bordo, *Unbearable Weight*, 1–44.

47 Ibid., 1–44.

48 Smolak, Levine and Striegel-Moore, *The Developmental Psychopathology of Eating Disorders*, 1–464.

the female portions of their bodies as a disgusting appropriation of their body by fat. They experience amenorrhea as a profound relief from the burden of menstruation and procreation. These symptoms can be seen as conscious or unconscious feminist protest at the restricting limitations of the traditional female role, representing a striving for a cultural shift in gender role considerations.

5 Treatment Implications

Successful interventions with clinical eating disorders take the multiplicity of intersecting factors discussed above into account. Clinical eating disorders are most often successfully treated when diagnosed very early, before the problematic behaviours solidify and become inextricably entrenched in the anorectic's psyche and routine behaviour patterns. The anorectic's very sense of self crystallise to encompass restricting eating and excessive exercise, so an earlier intervention can lead to more favourable outcomes. Unfortunately, due to the social approval that girls with bodies that conform towards a feminine ideal, individuals with clinical eating disorders may often deny their problem for years and thus may not receive necessary medical or psychological attention until they have already become seriously entrenched in their behaviour patterns and are dangerously thin and malnourished.[49] People with bulimia are often normal weight and may unfortunately often be able to hide their illness from family members, friends, and medical personnel for years. Clinical eating disorders in males may be overlooked because they have been historically rare in boys and men.[50]

Consequently, getting – and keeping – people with these disorders into early treatment, while essential, can be extremely challenging and difficult to accomplish. The longer abnormal eating behaviours persist, the more the behaviours become deep-seated and it is increasingly difficult to overcome the disorder and its negative effects on the body, which may, over time, become permanent. In some cases, long-term wrap-around medical hospitalisation treatment may be required, in order to entirely disrupt the negative behaviour pattern. Families and friends offering support and encouragement can play an essential, critical, and important role in the success of the treatment program, and aftercare regimen.[51]

---

49 Ibid, 1–464.

50 American Psychiatric Association, *Diagnostic and Statistical Manual of Mental Disorders*.

51 Snyder and Hasbrouck, 'Feminist Identity, Gender Traits, and Symptoms of Disturbed Eating among College Women', *Psychology of Women Quarterly*, 20.4, 593–598.

Once a clinical eating disorder is diagnosed, the clinician must determine whether the patient is in immediate medical danger and requires hospitalisation. Although some patients can be successfully treated as outpatients, many more need extensive hospital care, given the extreme risks associated with clinical eating disorders. Conditions that may warrant hospitalisation include excessive and rapid weight loss, serious metabolic or endocrine disturbances, clinical depression or risk of suicide, risk of heart attack or stroke, severe binge eating and purging, and psychosis.

The complex interaction of cultural, emotional, psychological and physiological problems in clinical eating disorders calls for a comprehensive physical examination and treatment plan involving, ideally, an internist, a nutritionist, a psychologist and a prescriber. The use of long-term individual psychotherapy, family therapy and cognitive-behavioural therapy contribute to the common successful long-term interventions. Group therapy, in which patients share their experiences with other patients with similar problems, proves especially effective for individuals with bulimia.[52] The patients benefit through sharing their experiences with like-minded others who do not judge them, often the first time the patient may have experienced such unbiased witnessing. Cognitive-behaviour therapists focus on changing eating behaviours usually by rewarding and/or modelling wanted behaviour, in order to interrupt problematic eating behaviour and shape healthier eating behaviour. Token economies are one example of this strategy. Family-focused therapists intervene with patients and their family systems to change problematic dynamics into more healthful support for the patient. Key in any therapeutic approach is to help patients work to change the distorted and rigid thinking patterns associated with clinical eating disorders, as well as to change the actual disordered eating patterns.

Some form of extensive longer-term psychotherapy is usually necessary to help those with clinical eating disorders deal with their illnesses and possible concomitant underlying emotional issues. The psychotherapy should be provided by an appropriately credentialed mental health professional who meets with the patient individually to provide extended and ongoing emotional support while the patient begins and continues to understand and cope with the illness. Behaviour change should be expected to be an extremely slow process and contiguous long-term care for family members is also highly recommended.

Scientists supported by the National Institute for Mental Health have examined the effectiveness of combining psychotherapy and medications.

52 Crowther, Wolf and Sherwood, op.cit., 4–16.

Researchers found that both intensive group therapy and antidepressant medications, combined or alone, benefited patients.[53] In another study of bulimia, the combined use of cognitive-behavioural therapy and antidepressant medications was most beneficial.[54] The combination treatment was particularly effective in preventing relapse once medications were discontinued. For patients with binge-eating disorder, cognitive-behavioural therapy and antidepressant medications may also prove useful.[55] Antidepressant medications commonly used to treat bulimia include desipramine, imipramine and fluoxetine. For anorexia, some antidepressant medications may be effective when combined with other forms of treatment. Fluoxetine has also been useful in treating some patients with binge-eating disorder. These antidepressants may also treat any co-occurring depression.[56]

The efforts of mental health professionals need to be combined with those of other health care professionals in order to obtain the most effective treatments for persons with clinical eating disorders. In addition to psychotherapists, physicians may treat any medical complications the patient experiences and nutritionists may advise the patient on diet and eating regimens. The challenge of treating clinical eating disorders increases with the metabolic changes associated with them. Just to maintain a stable weight, individuals with anorexia may actually have to consume more calories than would individuals without an eating disorder of similar weight and age. This information is important for the patients and the clinicians who treat them. Consuming calories is exactly what the person with anorexia wishes to avoid, yet must do to regain the weight necessary for recovery. In contrast, some normal-weight people with bulimia may gain excess weight if they consume the number of calories required to maintain normal weight in others of similar size and age.

6 Conclusion

A thorough understanding of the relevant cultural history, triggers, traumatic context, and evidence-based effective treatments for anorexia must be assessed in order to effectively treat an anorexic patient. It will be essential to address the prevalent negative cultural perceptions of bodies in order to increase women's

53 Ibid., 4–16.
54 Ibid., 4–16.
55 American Psychiatric Association, *Diagnostic and Statistical Manual of Mental Disorders.*
56 Ibid.

self-esteem. The increase in self-esteem and the decrease of negative perceptions of their own bodies will in turn assist the woman to change her internalised dialogue regarding her body, and change previously pejorative evaluations to more positive self-talk. It will be essential that the future efforts of mental health professionals will need to be combined with those of other health professionals to obtain the best wrap-around treatment for those with clinical eating disorders.

Bibliography

American Psychiatric Association. *Diagnostic and Statistical Manual of Mental Disorders,* 5th ed. Washington, DC: American Psychiatric Association, 2013.

Bordo, Susan. *Unbearable Weight.* Berkeley, CA: University of California Press, 1993.

Breuer, Joseph, and Sigmund Freud. *Studies on Hysteria.* New York: Penguin Press, 1982.

Bruch, Hilde. *Eating Disorders: Obesity, Anorexia Nervosa, and the Person Within.* New York: Basic Books, 1973.

Bruch, Hilde. *The Golden Cage: The Enigma of Anorexia Nervosa.* New York: Vintage, 1979.

Butler, Judith. *Bodies that Matter: On the Discursive Limits of Sex.* New York: Routledge, 1993.

Butler, Judith. *Gender Trouble: Feminism and the Subversion of Identity.* New York: Routledge, 1990.

Crowther, Janis H., Eve M. Wolf, and Nancy E. Sherwood. 'Epidemiology of Bulimia Nervosa.' *The Etiology of Bulimia Nervosa: The Individual and Familial Context,* edited by Janis H. Crowther and Daniel L. Tenenbaum, 4–16. Washington, DC: Hemisphere Publishing Corporation, 1992.

Eschholz, Rosa P., and V. Clark. *Language Awareness.* London: St. Martin's Press, 1986.

de Beauvoir, Simone. *The Second Sex.* New York: Vintage, 1974.

Faludi, Susan. *Backlash: The Undeclared War against American Women.* New York: Doubleday, 1991.

Flannery-Schroeder, Ellen C., and Joan C. Chrisler. 'Body Esteem, Eating Attitudes, and Gender-Role Orientation in Three Age Groups of Children.' *Current Psychology: Developmental, Learning, Personality, Social* 15.3 (1996): 235–248.

Foucault, Michel. *Discipline and Punish: The Birth of the Prison.* New York: Vintage/Random House, 1979.

Gergen, Mary and Sara Davis. *Towards a New Psychology of Gender.* New York: Routledge, 1997.

Irigaray, Luce. *Speculum of the Other Woman.* New York: Cornell University Press, 1985.

Irigaray, Luce. *This Sex Which Is Not One.* New York: Cornell University Press, 1985.

Johnson, Mark E., Christiane Brems, and Pamela Fischer. 'Sex Role Conflict, Social Desirability, and Eating-Disorder Attitudes and Behaviors.' *Journal of General Psychology* 123.1 (1996): 75–87.

Lefkowitz, Mary R. and Maureen B. Fant. *Women's Life in Greece and Rome.* Baltimore: Johns Hopkins University Press, 1982.

Malson, Helen. 'Women under Erasure: Anorectic Bodies in Postmodern Context.' *Journal of Community and Applied Social Psychology* 9.2 (1999): 137–153.

Micale, Mark S. 'Hysteria and Historiography: A Review of Past and Present Writings.' *History of Science* 27.78 (1989): 319–351.

Perlick, Deborah, and Brett Silverstein. 'Faces of Female Discontent: Depression, Disordered Eating, and Changing Gender Roles.' *Feminist Perspectives on Eating Disorders*, edited by Patricia Fallon, Melanie A. Katzman and Susan C. Wooley, 77–93. New York: Guilford Press, 1994.

Plumwood, Val. 'Do We Need a Sex Gender Distinction?' *Radical Philosophy* 51 (1989): 2–11.

Samberg, Joel. 'Remembering Karen Carpenter, 30 Years Later.' *NPR Music* (website), 4 February 2013. Viewed on 9 April 2015. http://www.npr.org/2013/02/04/171080334/remembering-karen-carpenter-30-years-later.

Savage, George H. *Insanity and Allied Neurosis.* Philadelphia: Henry C. Lea, 1884.

Smolak, Linda, Michael P. Levine, and Ruth Striegel-Moore. *The Developmental Psychopathology of Eating Disorders: Implications for Research, Prevention, and Treatment.* Mahway, NJ: Lawrence Erlbaum Associates, 1996.

Snyder, Rita, and Lynn Hasbrouck. 'Feminist Identity, Gender Traits, and Symptoms of Disturbed Eating among College Women.' *Psychology of Women Quarterly* 20.4 (1996): 593–598.

Stoller, Robert J. *Sex and Gender.* New York: Science House, 1968.

Index of Names

Index of Terms

www.ingramcontent.com/pod-product-compliance
Lightning Source LLC
LaVergne TN
LVHW011109300926
849160LV00008B/323
* 9 7 8 9 0 0 4 4 0 5 4 3 1 *